Tell us what you think about Shojo Beat Manga!

Our survey is now available online. Go to:

shojobeat.com/mangasurvey

Help us make our product offerings better!

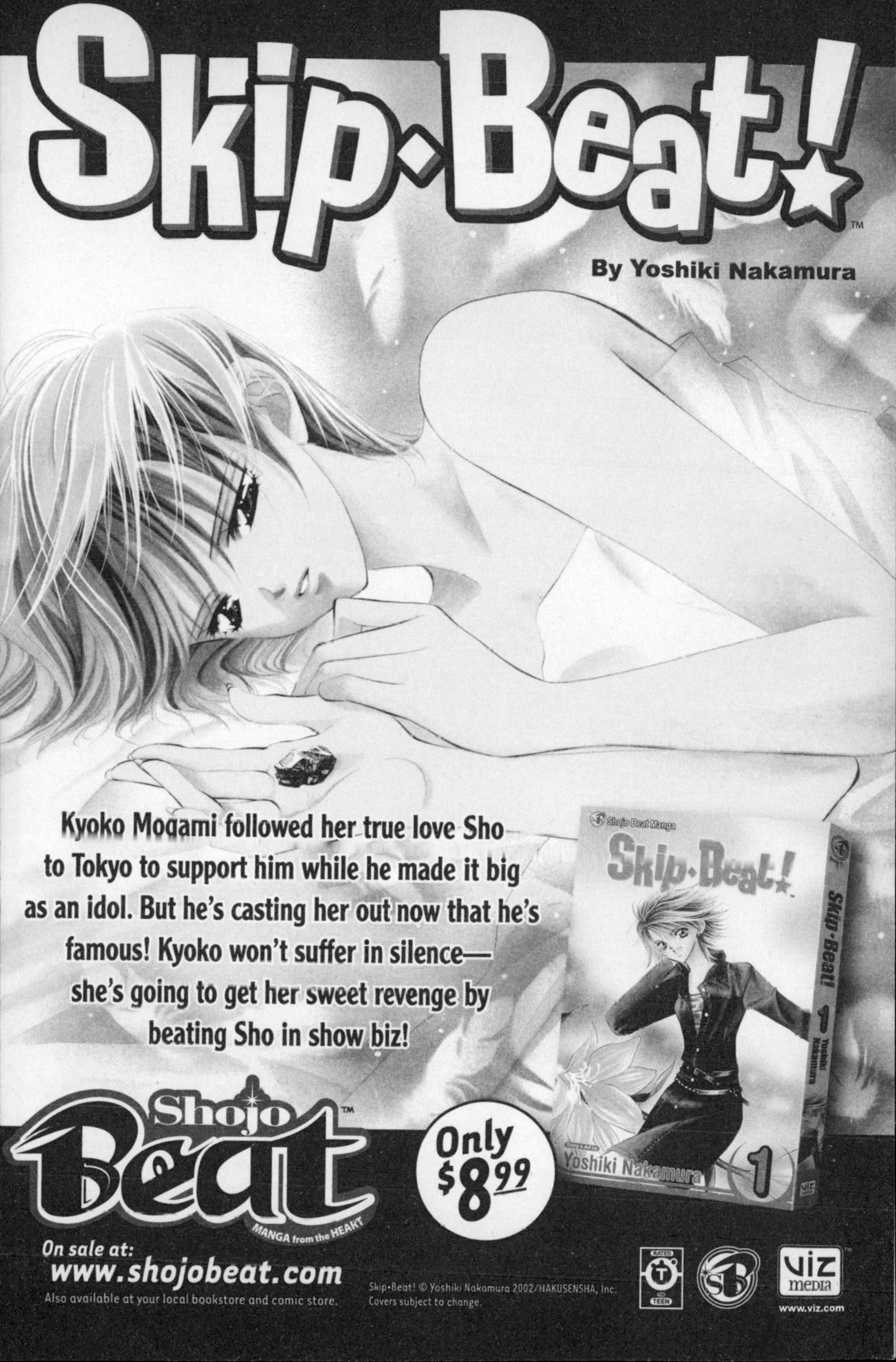

Skip·Beat!
By Yoshiki Nakamura
Kyoko Mogami followed her true love Sho to Tokyo to support him while he made it big as an idol. But he's casting her out now that he's famous! Kyoko won't suffer in silence—she's going to get her sweet revenge by beating Sho in show biz!
Shojo Beat Manga
Skip·Beat!
Yoshiki Nakamura
1
Shojo Beat
MANGA from the HEART
Only $8.99
On sale at:
www.shojobeat.com
Also available at your local bookstore and comic store.
Skip•Beat! © Yoshiki Nakamura 2002/HAKUSENSHA, Inc.
Covers subject to change.
RATED T TEEN
VIZ media
www.viz.com

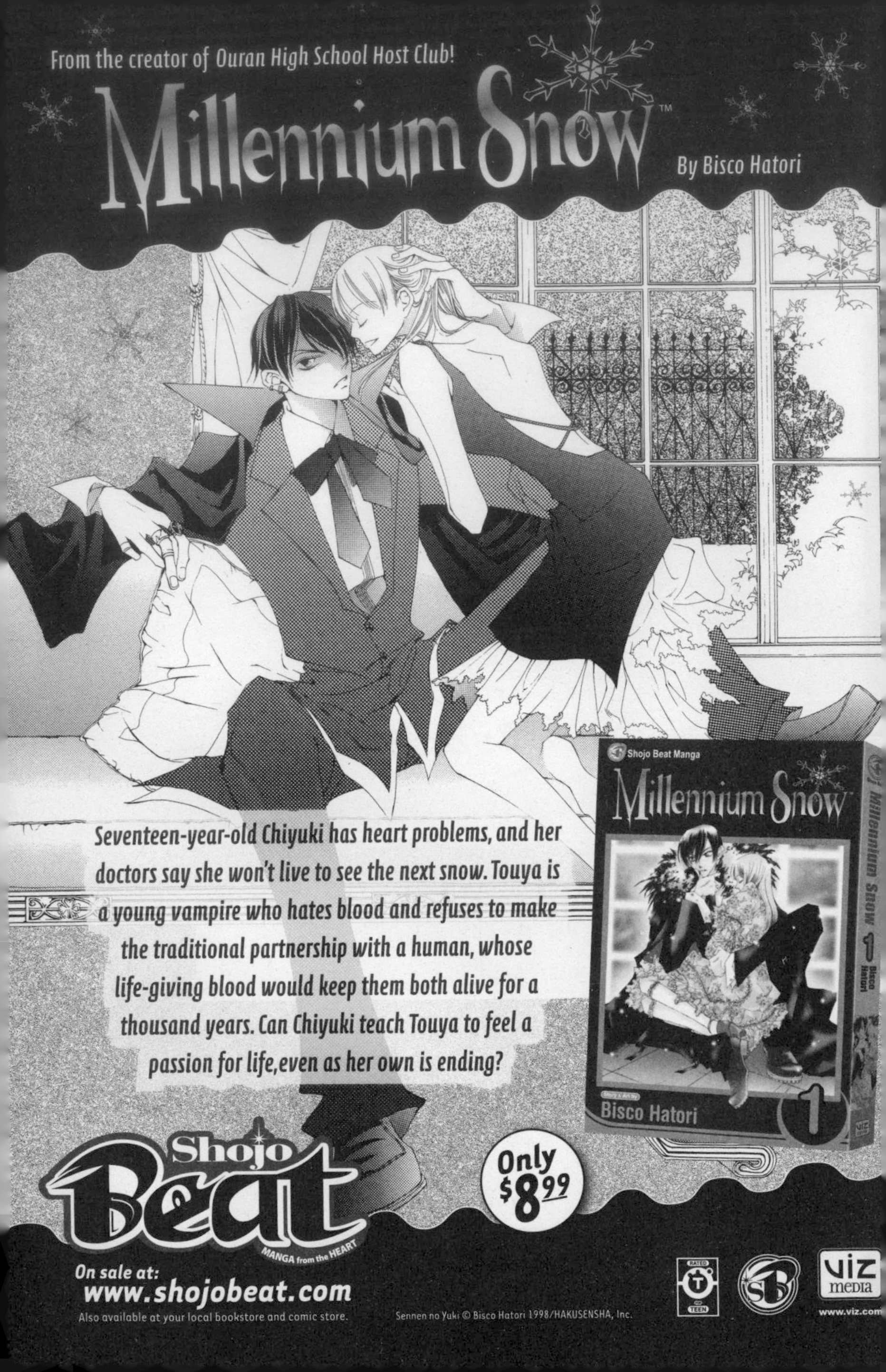
From the creator of Ouran High School Host Club!
Millennium Snow™
By Bisco Hatori
Seventeen-year-old Chiyuki has heart problems, and her doctors say she won't live to see the next snow. Touya is a young vampire who hates blood and refuses to make the traditional partnership with a human, whose life-giving blood would keep them both alive for a thousand years. Can Chiyuki teach Touya to feel a passion for life,even as her own is ending?
Shojo Beat Manga
Millennium Snow
Bisco Hatori
1
Only $8.99
Shojo Beat
MANGA from the HEART
On sale at:
www.shojobeat.com
Also available at your local bookstore and comic store.
Sennen no Yuki © Bisco Hatori 1998/HAKUSENSHA, Inc.
RATED T TEEN
viz media
www.viz.com

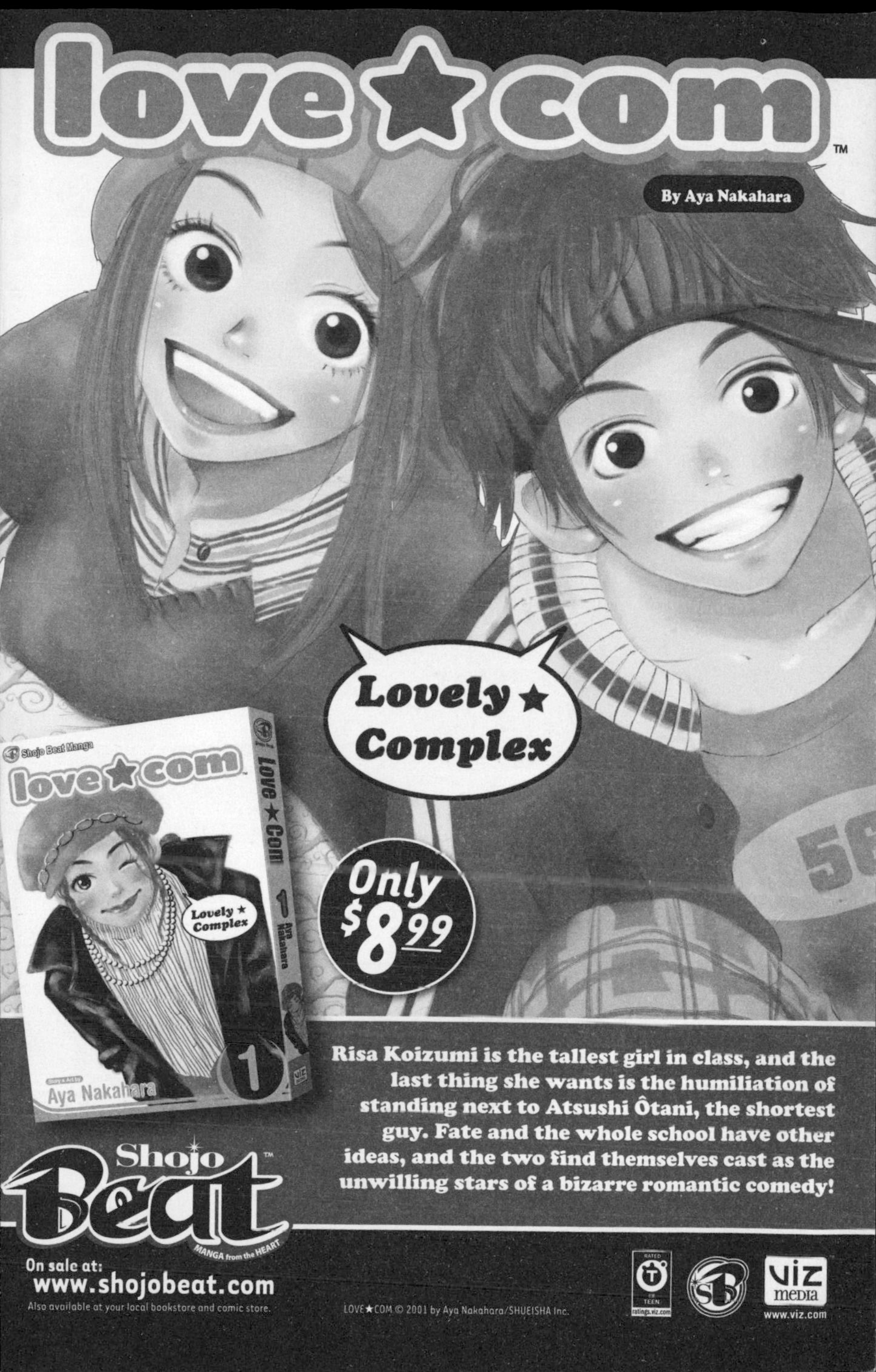
love★com™
By Aya Nakahara
Lovely★ Complex
Shojo Beat Manga
love★com
Love★Com
1
Aya Nakahara
Lovely★ Complex
Story & Art by
Aya Nakahara
Only $8.99
Risa Koizumi is the tallest girl in class, and the last thing she wants is the humiliation of standing next to Atsushi Ôtani, the shortest guy. Fate and the whole school have other ideas, and the two find themselves cast as the unwilling stars of a bizarre romantic comedy!
Shojo Beat™
MANGA from the HEART
On sale at:
www.shojobeat.com
Also available at your local bookstore and comic store.
LOVE★COM © 2001 by Aya Nakahara/SHUEISHA Inc.
RATED T TEEN
ratings.viz.com
viz media
www.viz.com

OURAN HIGH SCHOOL HOST CLUB
Vol. 9
The Shojo Beat Manga Edition

STORY AND ART BY BISCO HATORI

Translation & English Adaptation/RyoRca & John Werry, HC Language Solutions
Touch-up Art & Lettering/George Caltsoudas
Graphic Design/Izumi Evers
Editor/Nancy Thistlethwaite

Editor in Chief, Books/Alvin Lu
Editor in Chief, Magazines/Marc Weidenbaum
VP of Publishing Licensing/Rika Inouye
VP of Sales/Gonzalo Ferreyra
Sr. VP of Marketing/Liza Coppola
Publisher/Hyoe Narita

Printed in Canada

Published by VIZ Media, LLC
P.O. Box 77010
San Francisco, CA 94107

Shojo Beat Manga Edition
10 9 8 7 6 5 4 3 2
First printing, July 2007
Second printing, August 2007

store.viz.com

PARENTAL ADVISORY
OURAN HIGH SCHOOL HOST CLUB is rated T for Teen and is recommended for ages 13 and up. This volume contains some sexual themes.

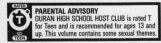

Ouran High School

Host Club™

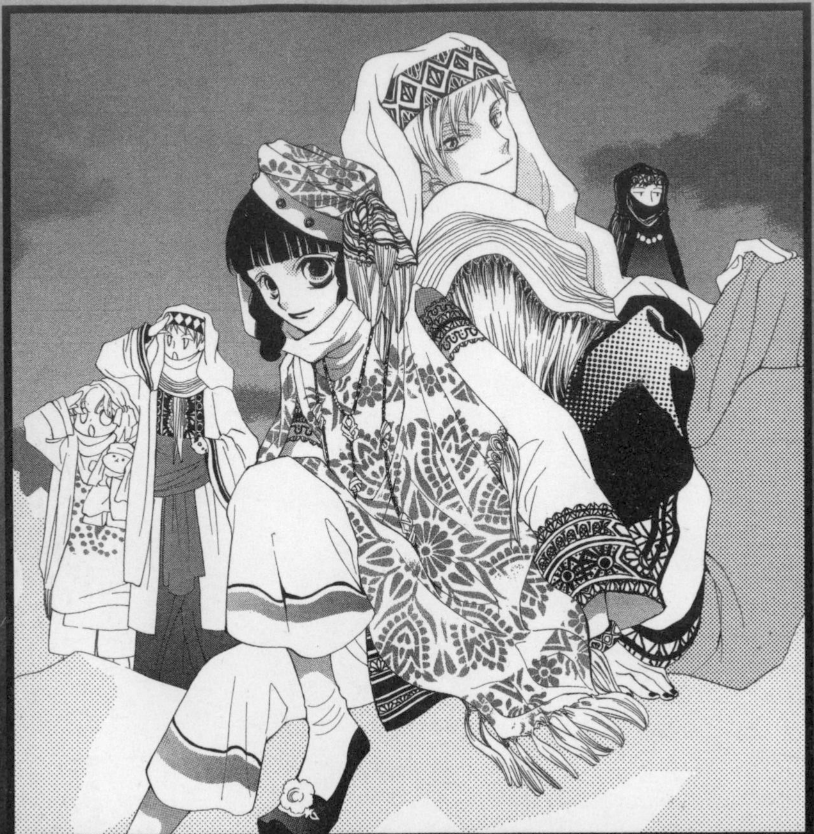

Vol. 9

Bisco Hatori

Ouran High School

Host Club™

Vol. 9

CONTENTS

THE ONE NOT ME IS HIKARU, AND THE ONE NOT HIKARU IS ME.

WE ARE SEPARATE INDIVIDUALS.

THIS IS ABSOLUTE.

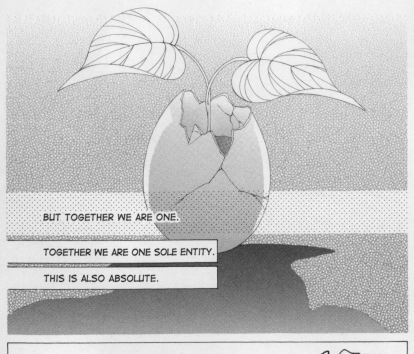

BUT TOGETHER WE ARE ONE.

TOGETHER WE ARE ONE SOLE ENTITY.

THIS IS ALSO ABSOLUTE.

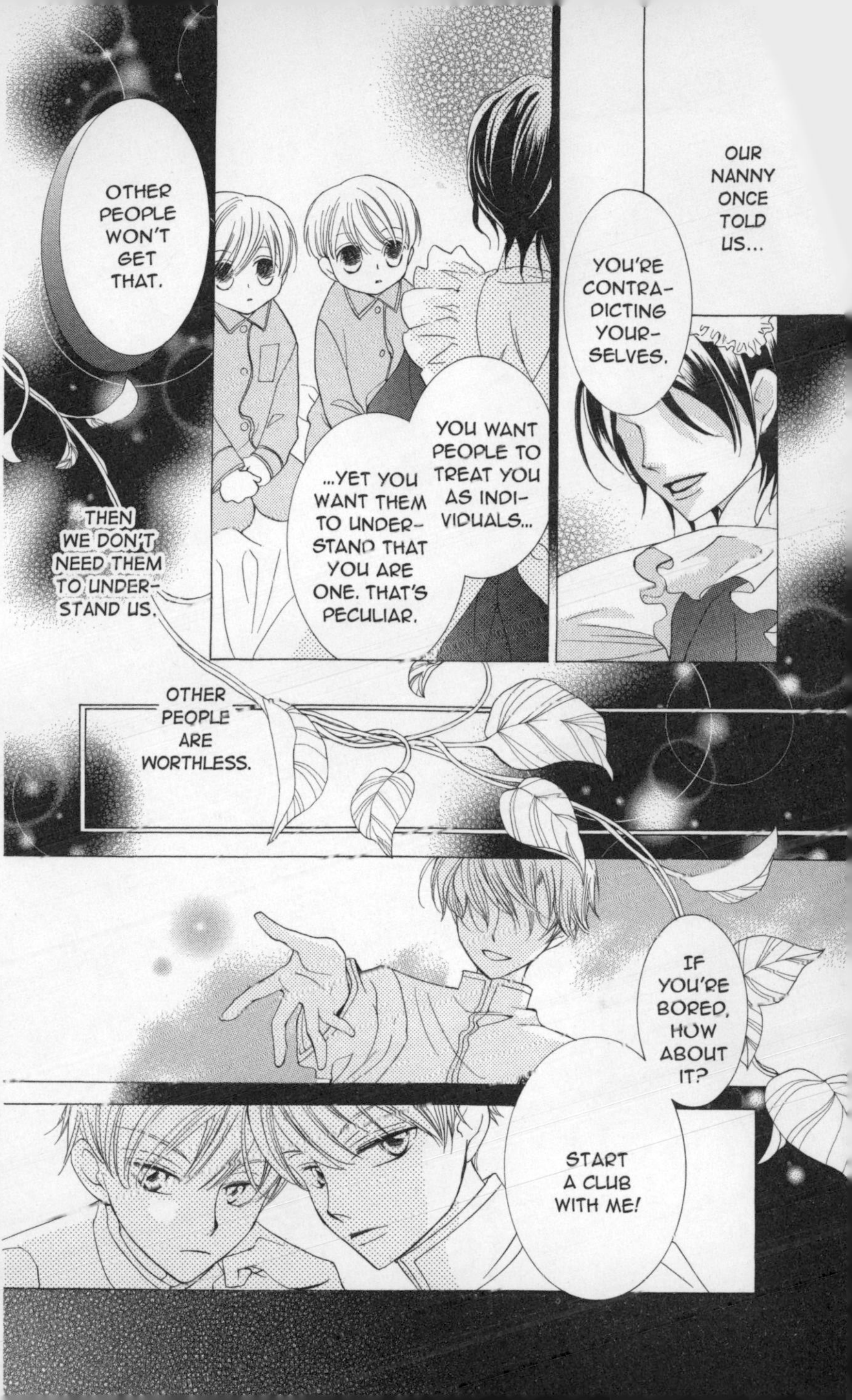
OUR NANNY ONCE TOLD US...
YOU'RE CONTRA-DICTING YOUR-SELVES.
YOU WANT PEOPLE TO TREAT YOU AS INDI-VIDUALS...
...YET YOU WANT THEM TO UNDER-STAND THAT YOU ARE ONE. THAT'S PECULIAR.
OTHER PEOPLE WON'T GET THAT.
THEN WE DON'T NEED THEM TO UNDER-STAND US.
OTHER PEOPLE ARE WORTHLESS.
IF YOU'RE BORED, HOW ABOUT IT?
START A CLUB WITH ME!

EPISODE 37
OTHER PEOPLE CAN'T UNDERSTAND THE SIMPLEST THING.
WE ALWAYS THOUGHT EVERYONE ELSE WAS STUPID.
OURAN HIGH SCHOOL HOST CLUB

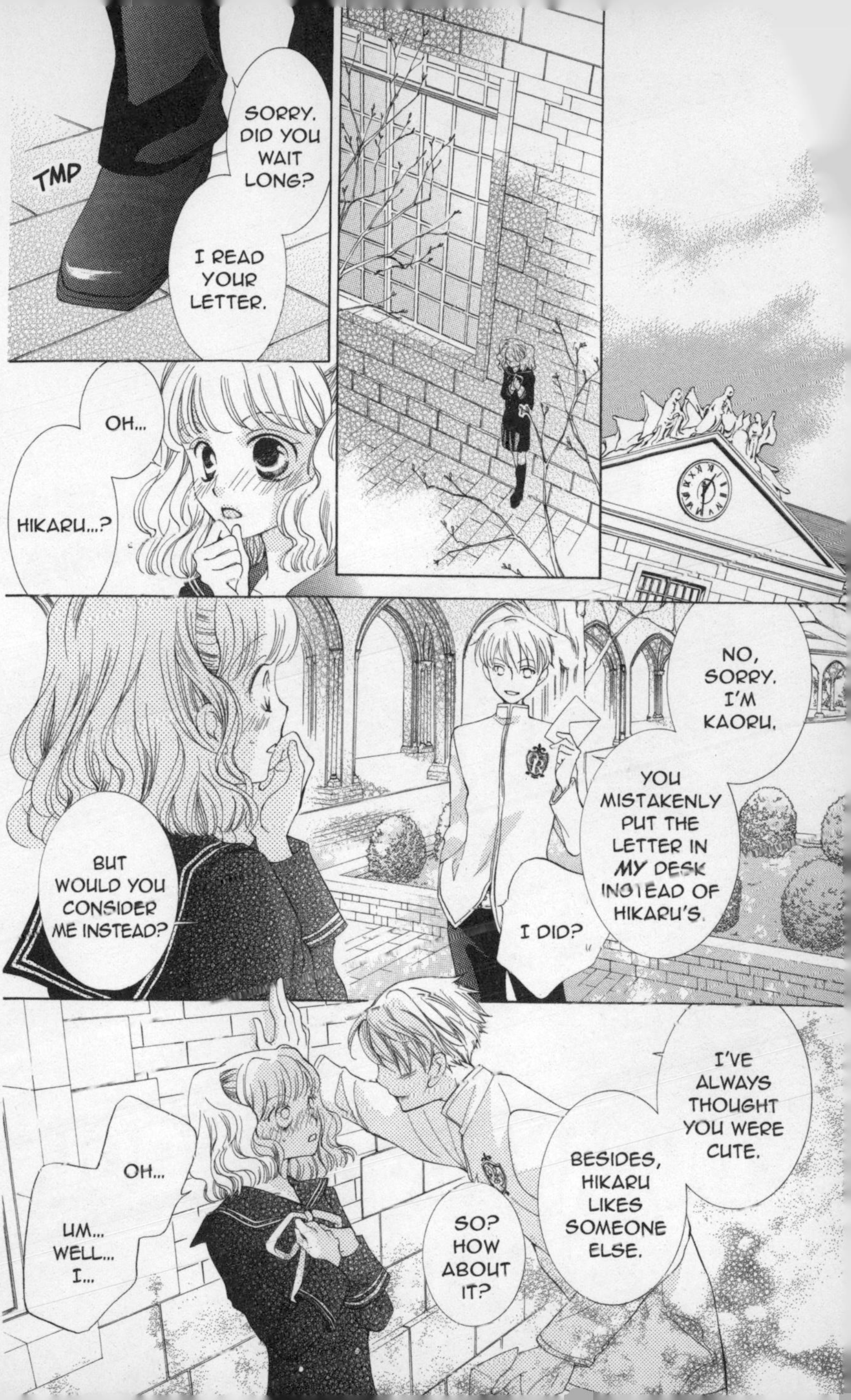
SORRY. DID YOU WAIT LONG?
TMP
I READ YOUR LETTER.
OH...
HIKARU...?
NO, SORRY. I'M KAORU.
YOU MISTAKENLY PUT THE LETTER IN MY DESK INSTEAD OF HIKARU'S.
I DID?
BUT WOULD YOU CONSIDER ME INSTEAD?
I'VE ALWAYS THOUGHT YOU WERE CUTE.
BESIDES, HIKARU LIKES SOMEONE ELSE.
SO? HOW ABOUT IT?
OH...
UM... WELL... I...

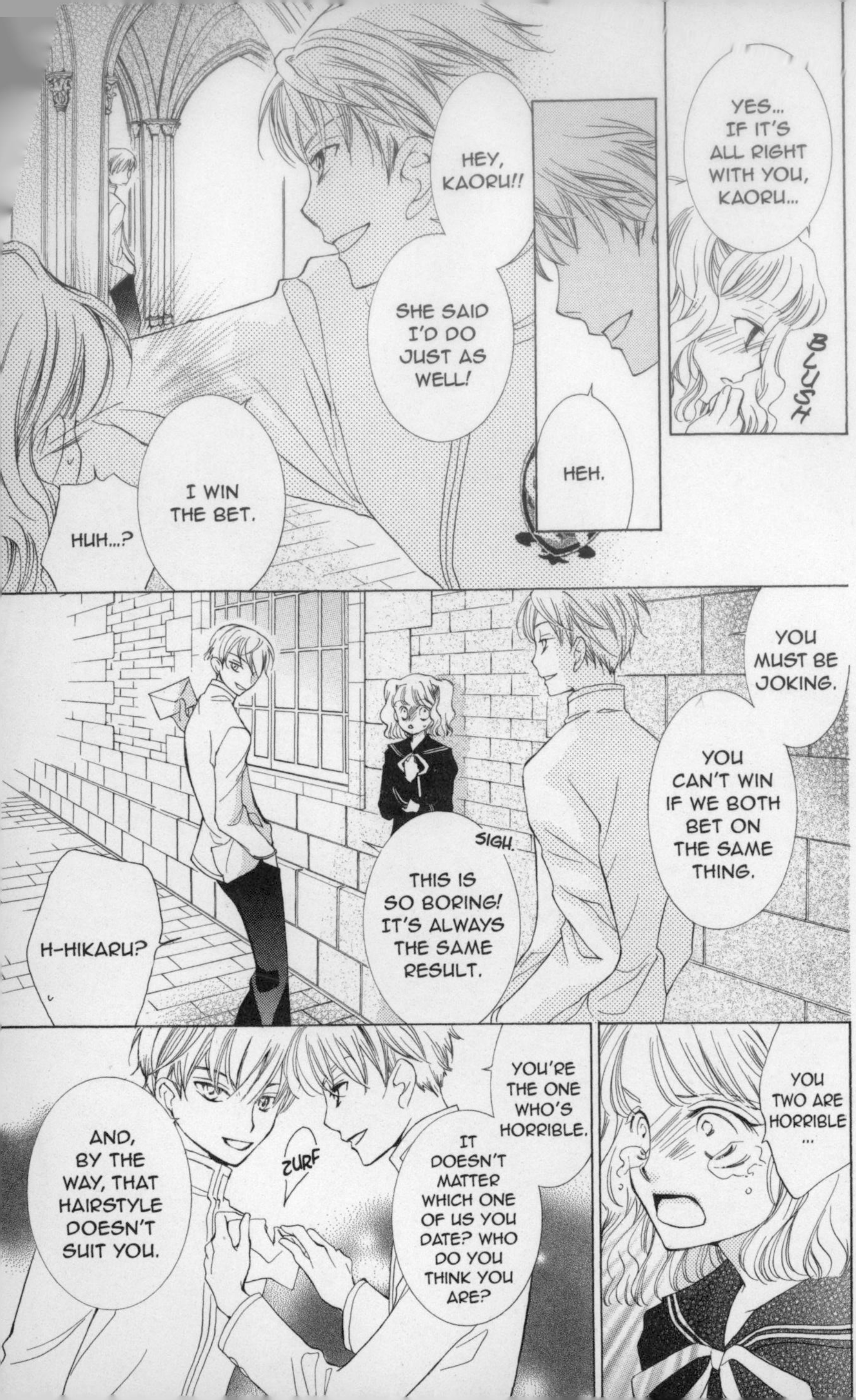
YES... IF IT'S ALL RIGHT WITH YOU, KAORU...
BLUSH
HEH.
HEY, KAORU!!
SHE SAID I'D DO JUST AS WELL!
I WIN THE BET.
HUH...?
YOU MUST BE JOKING.
YOU CAN'T WIN IF WE BOTH BET ON THE SAME THING.
SIGH.
THIS IS SO BORING! IT'S ALWAYS THE SAME RESULT.
H-HIKARU?
YOU TWO ARE HORRIBLE ...
YOU'RE THE ONE WHO'S HORRIBLE.
IT DOESN'T MATTER WHICH ONE OF US YOU DATE? WHO DO YOU THINK YOU ARE?
ZURF
AND, BY THE WAY, THAT HAIRSTYLE DOESN'T SUIT YOU.

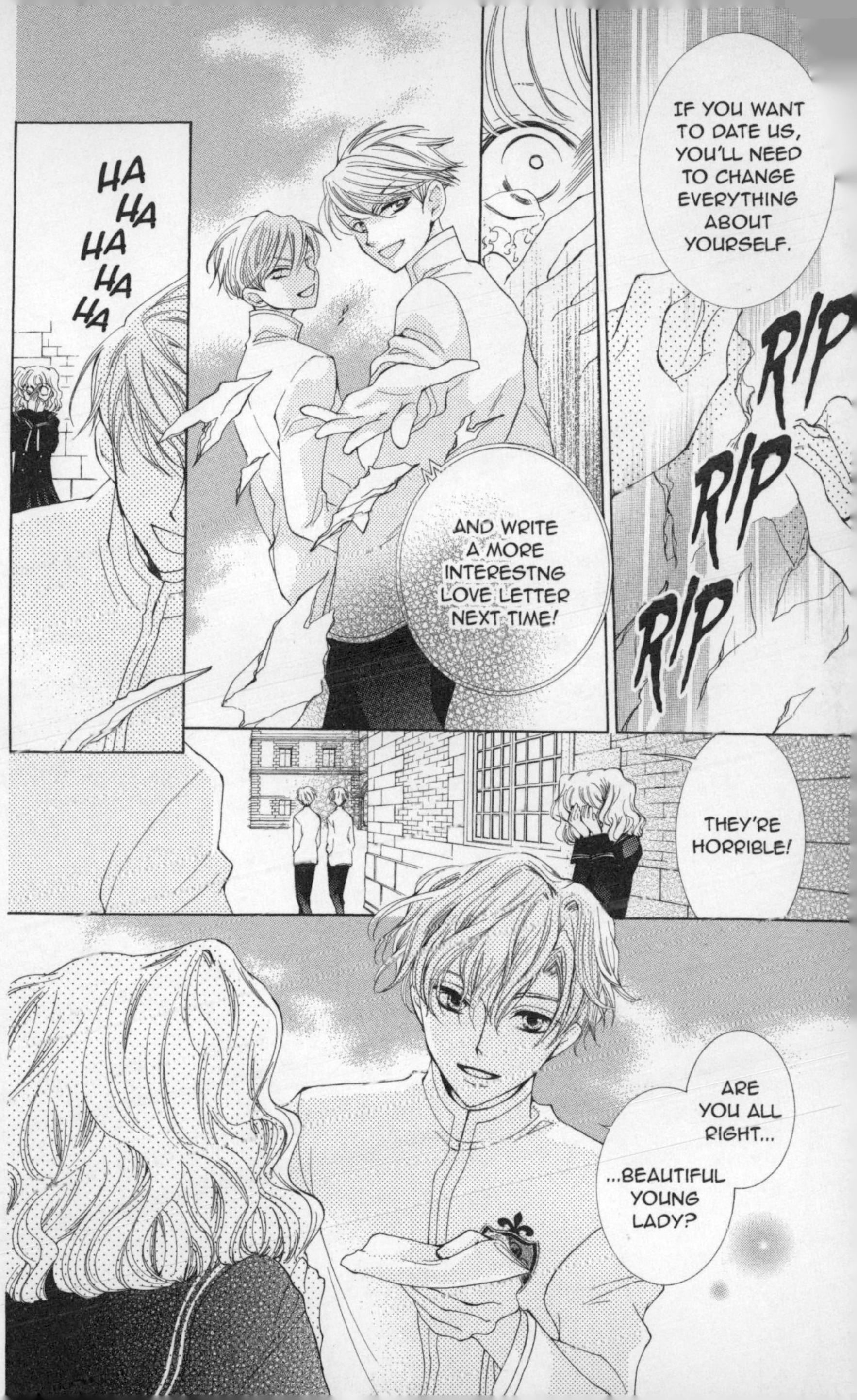
IF YOU WANT TO DATE US, YOU'LL NEED TO CHANGE EVERYTHING ABOUT YOURSELF.
RIP RIP RIP
AND WRITE A MORE INTERESTNG LOVE LETTER NEXT TIME!
HA HA HA HA HA
THEY'RE HORRIBLE!
ARE YOU ALL RIGHT...
...BEAUTIFUL YOUNG LADY?

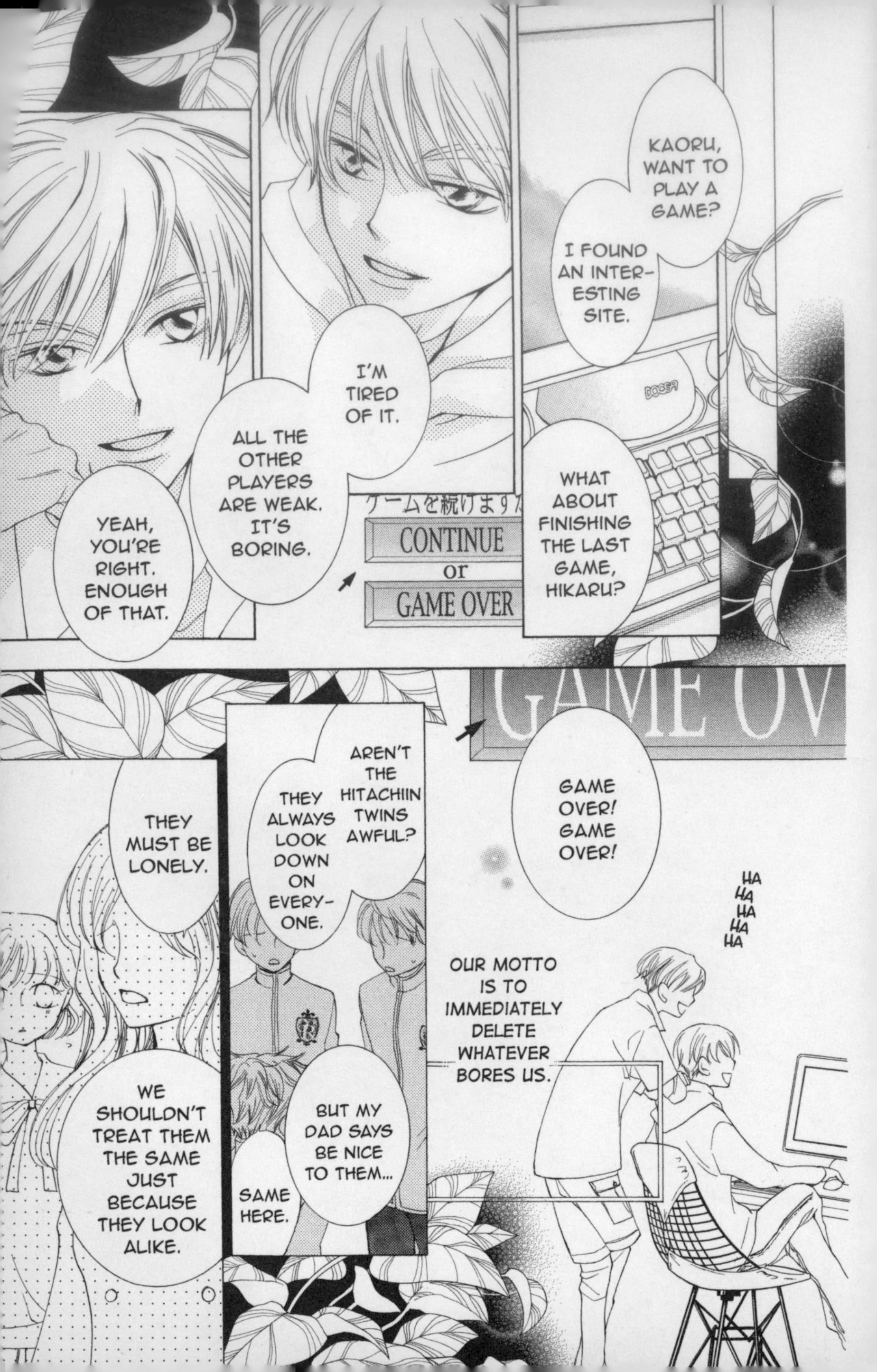
KAORU, WANT TO PLAY A GAME?
I FOUND AN INTERESTING SITE.
WHAT ABOUT FINISHING THE LAST GAME, HIKARU?
ゲームを続けます
CONTINUE
or
GAME OVER
I'M TIRED OF IT.
ALL THE OTHER PLAYERS ARE WEAK. IT'S BORING.
YEAH, YOU'RE RIGHT. ENOUGH OF THAT.
GAME OV
GAME OVER! GAME OVER!
HA HA HA HA HA
OUR MOTTO IS TO IMMEDIATELY DELETE WHATEVER BORES US.
AREN'T THE HITACHIIN TWINS AWFUL?
THEY ALWAYS LOOK DOWN ON EVERYONE.
BUT MY DAD SAYS BE NICE TO THEM...
SAME HERE.
THEY MUST BE LONELY.
WE SHOULDN'T TREAT THEM THE SAME JUST BECAUSE THEY LOOK ALIKE.

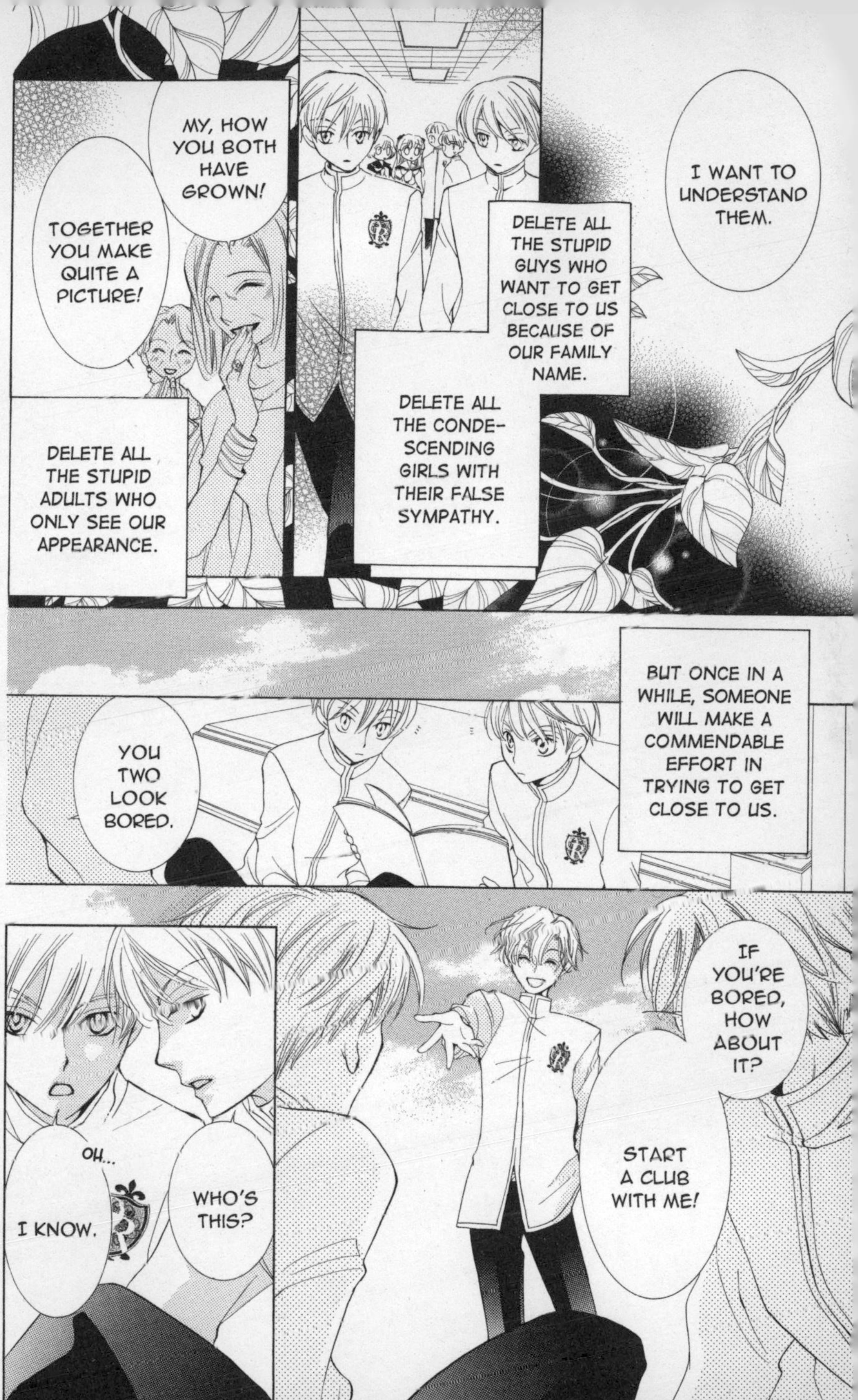
I WANT TO UNDERSTAND THEM.
DELETE ALL THE STUPID GUYS WHO WANT TO GET CLOSE TO US BECAUSE OF OUR FAMILY NAME.
DELETE ALL THE CONDE-SCENDING GIRLS WITH THEIR FALSE SYMPATHY.
MY, HOW YOU BOTH HAVE GROWN!
TOGETHER YOU MAKE QUITE A PICTURE!
DELETE ALL THE STUPID ADULTS WHO ONLY SEE OUR APPEARANCE.
BUT ONCE IN A WHILE, SOMEONE WILL MAKE A COMMENDABLE EFFORT IN TRYING TO GET CLOSE TO US.
YOU TWO LOOK BORED.
IF YOU'RE BORED, HOW ABOUT IT?
START A CLUB WITH ME!
WHO'S THIS?
OH... I KNOW.

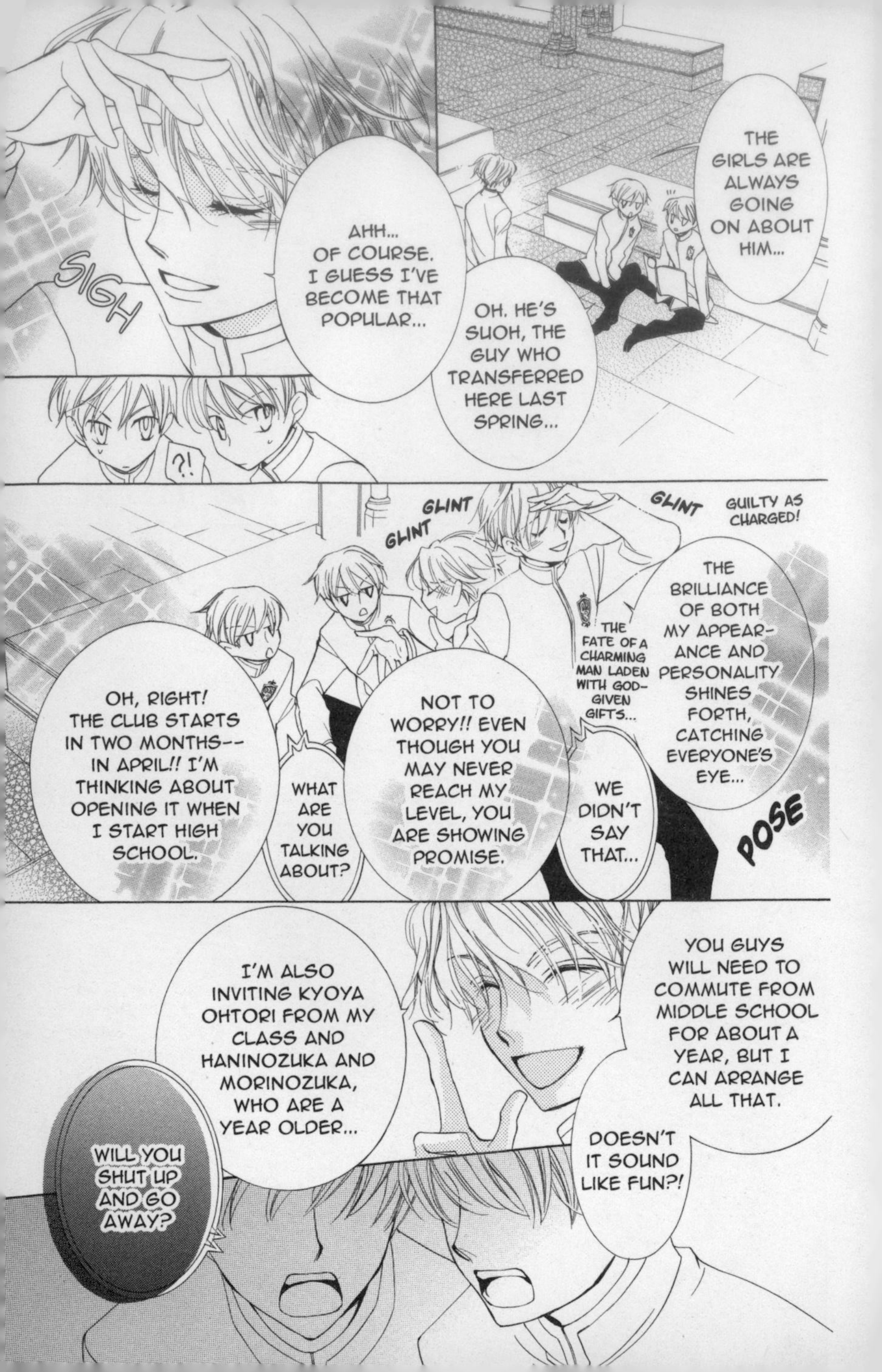
THE GIRLS ARE ALWAYS GOING ON ABOUT HIM...
OH. HE'S SUOH, THE GUY WHO TRANSFERRED HERE LAST SPRING...
AHH... OF COURSE. I GUESS I'VE BECOME THAT POPULAR...
SIGH
?!
GLINT
GLINT
GLINT
GUILTY AS CHARGED!
THE BRILLIANCE OF BOTH MY APPEAR-ANCE AND PERSONALITY SHINES FORTH, CATCHING EVERYONE'S EYE...
THE FATE OF A CHARMING MAN LADEN WITH GOD-GIVEN GIFTS...
POSE
WE DIDN'T SAY THAT...
NOT TO WORRY!! EVEN THOUGH YOU MAY NEVER REACH MY LEVEL, YOU ARE SHOWING PROMISE.
WHAT ARE YOU TALKING ABOUT?
OH, RIGHT! THE CLUB STARTS IN TWO MONTHS-- IN APRIL!! I'M THINKING ABOUT OPENING IT WHEN I START HIGH SCHOOL.
YOU GUYS WILL NEED TO COMMUTE FROM MIDDLE SCHOOL FOR ABOUT A YEAR, BUT I CAN ARRANGE ALL THAT.
DOESN'T IT SOUND LIKE FUN?!
I'M ALSO INVITING KYOYA OHTORI FROM MY CLASS AND HANINOZUKA AND MORINOZUKA, WHO ARE A YEAR OLDER...
WILL YOU SHUT UP AND GO AWAY?

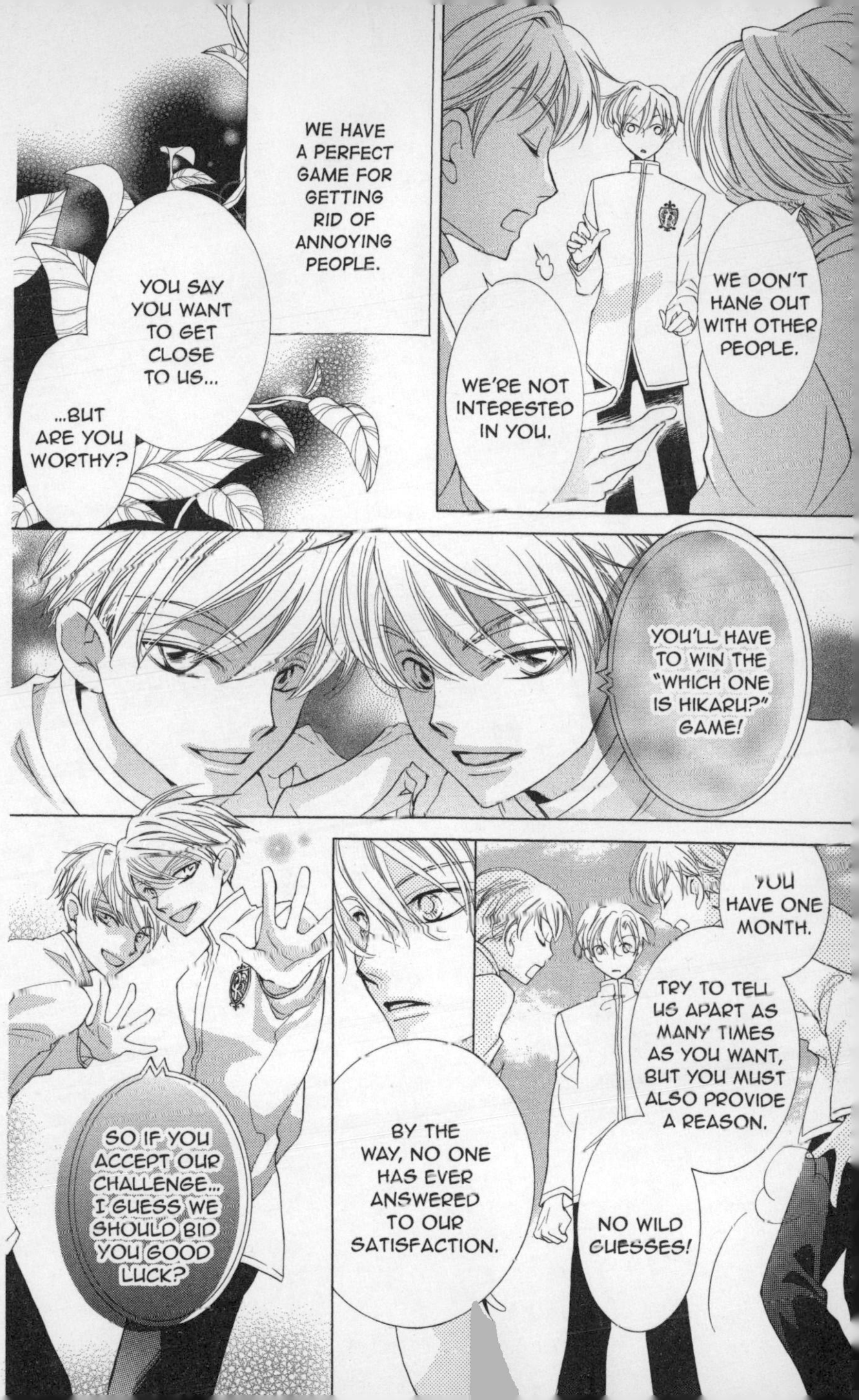
WE DON'T HANG OUT WITH OTHER PEOPLE.
WE'RE NOT INTERESTED IN YOU.
WE HAVE A PERFECT GAME FOR GETTING RID OF ANNOYING PEOPLE.
YOU SAY YOU WANT TO GET CLOSE TO US...
...BUT ARE YOU WORTHY?
YOU'LL HAVE TO WIN THE "WHICH ONE IS HIKARU?" GAME!
YOU HAVE ONE MONTH.
TRY TO TELL US APART AS MANY TIMES AS YOU WANT, BUT YOU MUST ALSO PROVIDE A REASON.
NO WILD GUESSES!
BY THE WAY, NO ONE HAS EVER ANSWERED TO OUR SATISFACTION.
SO IF YOU ACCEPT OUR CHALLENGE... I GUESS WE SHOULD BID YOU GOOD LUCK?

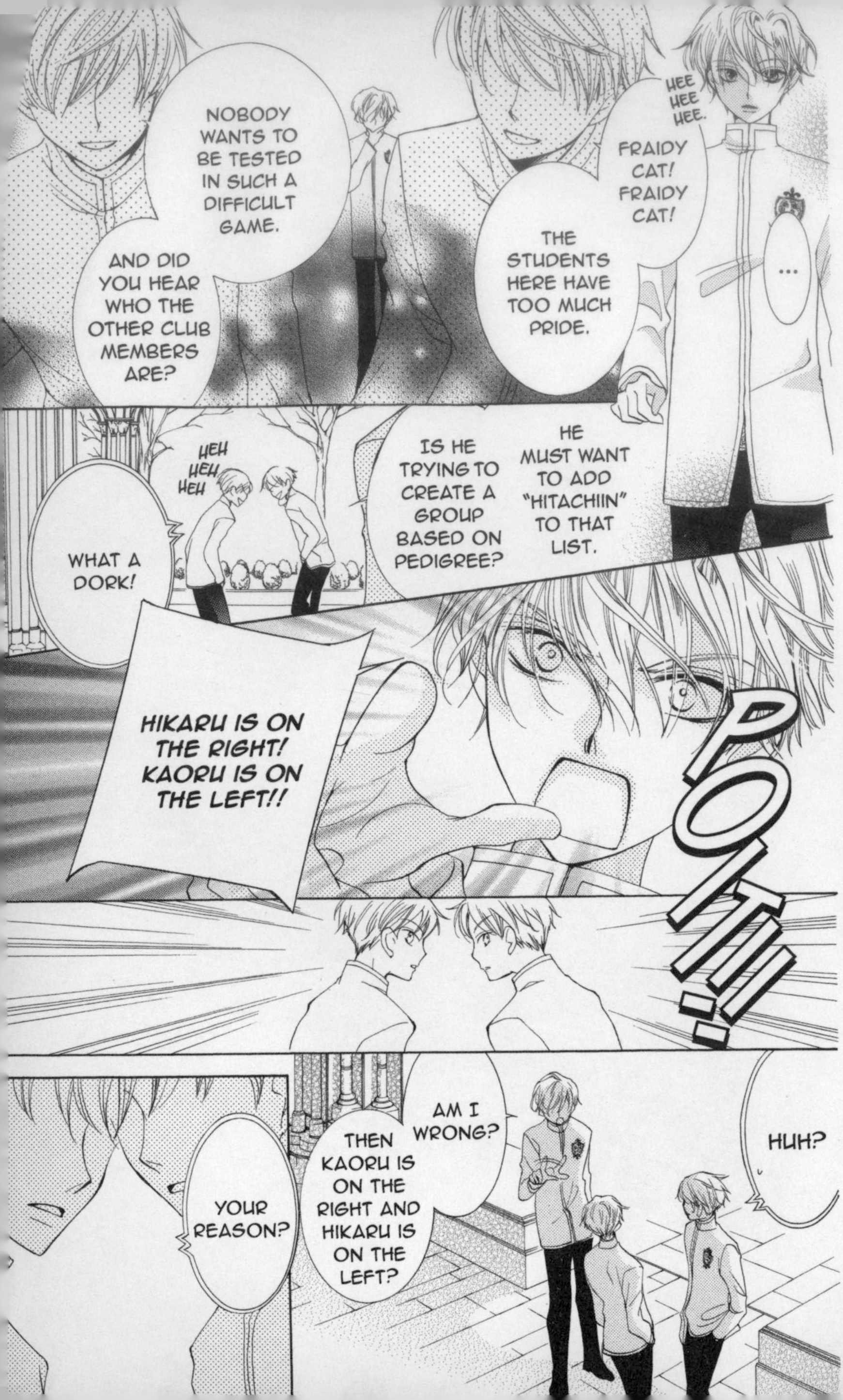
HEE HEE HEE.
FRAIDY CAT! FRAIDY CAT!
...
THE STUDENTS HERE HAVE TOO MUCH PRIDE.
NOBODY WANTS TO BE TESTED IN SUCH A DIFFICULT GAME.
AND DID YOU HEAR WHO THE OTHER CLUB MEMBERS ARE?
HE MUST WANT TO ADD "HITACHIIN" TO THAT LIST.
IS HE TRYING TO CREATE A GROUP BASED ON PEDIGREE?
HEH HEH HEH
WHAT A DORK!
POIT!!
HIKARU IS ON THE RIGHT! KAORU IS ON THE LEFT!!
HUH?
AM I WRONG?
THEN KAORU IS ON THE RIGHT AND HIKARU IS ON THE LEFT?
YOUR REASON?

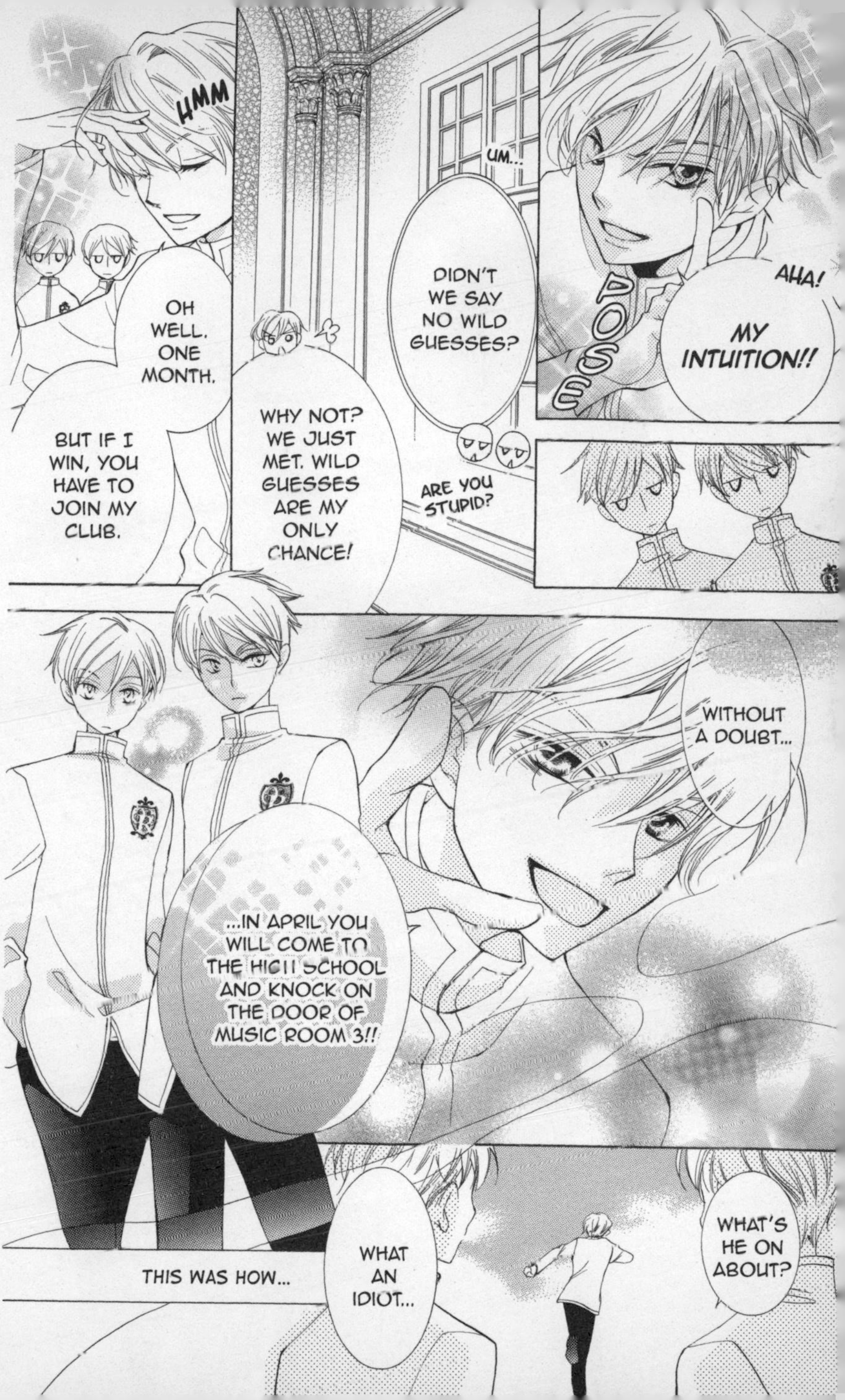
AHA!
MY INTUITION!!
POSE
UM...
DIDN'T WE SAY NO WILD GUESSES?
ARE YOU STUPID?
WHY NOT? WE JUST MET. WILD GUESSES ARE MY ONLY CHANCE!
HMM
OH WELL. ONE MONTH.
BUT IF I WIN, YOU HAVE TO JOIN MY CLUB.
WITHOUT A DOUBT...
...IN APRIL YOU WILL COME TO THE HIGH SCHOOL AND KNOCK ON THE DOOR OF MUSIC ROOM 3!!
WHAT'S HE ON ABOUT?
WHAT AN IDIOT...
THIS WAS HOW...

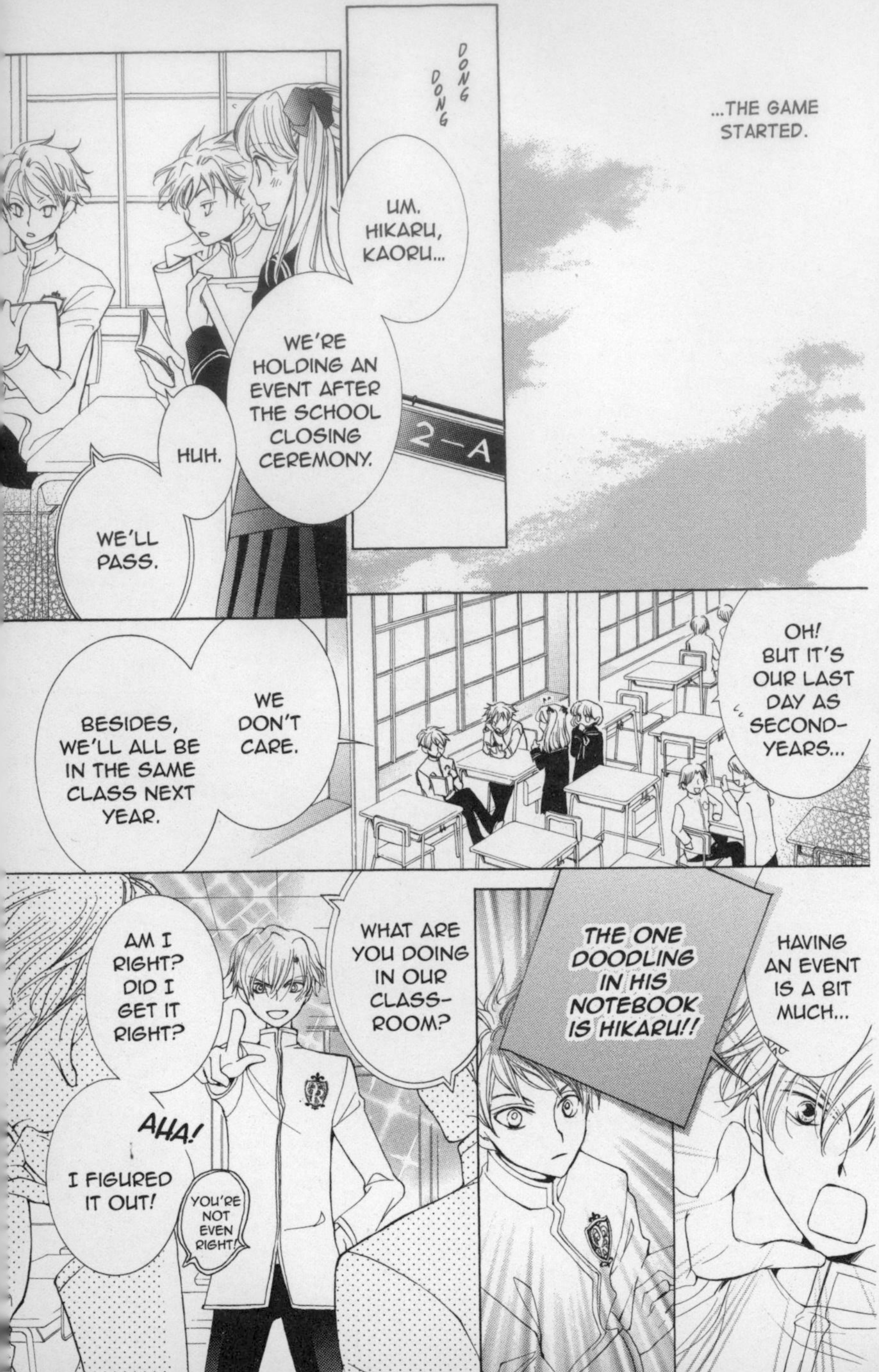
...THE GAME STARTED.
DONG DONG
UM. HIKARU, KAORU...
WE'RE HOLDING AN EVENT AFTER THE SCHOOL CLOSING CEREMONY.
2-A
HUH.
WE'LL PASS.
OH! BUT IT'S OUR LAST DAY AS SECOND-YEARS...
WE DON'T CARE.
BESIDES, WE'LL ALL BE IN THE SAME CLASS NEXT YEAR.
HAVING AN EVENT IS A BIT MUCH...
THE ONE DOODLING IN HIS NOTEBOOK IS HIKARU!!
WHAT ARE YOU DOING IN OUR CLASS-ROOM?
AM I RIGHT? DID I GET IT RIGHT?
AHA!
I FIGURED IT OUT!
YOU'RE NOT EVEN RIGHT!

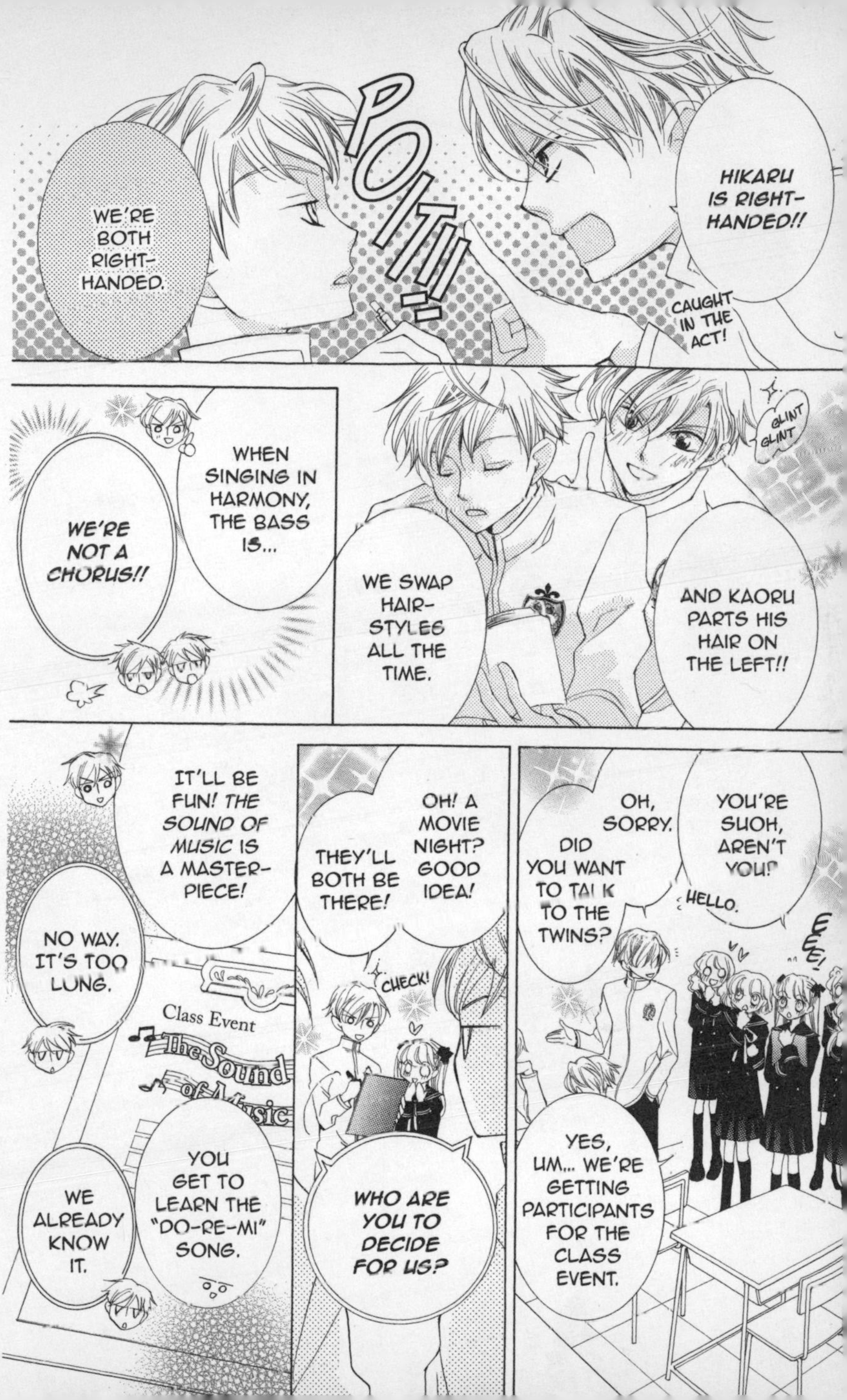
HIKARU IS RIGHT-HANDED!!
POIT!!
WE'RE BOTH RIGHT-HANDED.
CAUGHT IN THE ACT!
GLINT GLINT
AND KAORU PARTS HIS HAIR ON THE LEFT!!
WE SWAP HAIR-STYLES ALL THE TIME.
WHEN SINGING IN HARMONY, THE BASS IS...
WE'RE NOT A CHORUS!!
YOU'RE SUOH, AREN'T YOU?
HELLO.
EEE!
OH, SORRY.
DID YOU WANT TO TALK TO THE TWINS?
YES, UM... WE'RE GETTING PARTICIPANTS FOR THE CLASS EVENT.
OH! A MOVIE NIGHT? GOOD IDEA!
THEY'LL BOTH BE THERE!
CHECK!
WHO ARE YOU TO DECIDE FOR US?
IT'LL BE FUN! *THE SOUND OF MUSIC* IS A MASTER-PIECE!
NO WAY. IT'S TOO LONG.
Class Event
The Sound of Music
YOU GET TO LEARN THE "DO-RE-MI" SONG.
WE ALREADY KNOW IT.

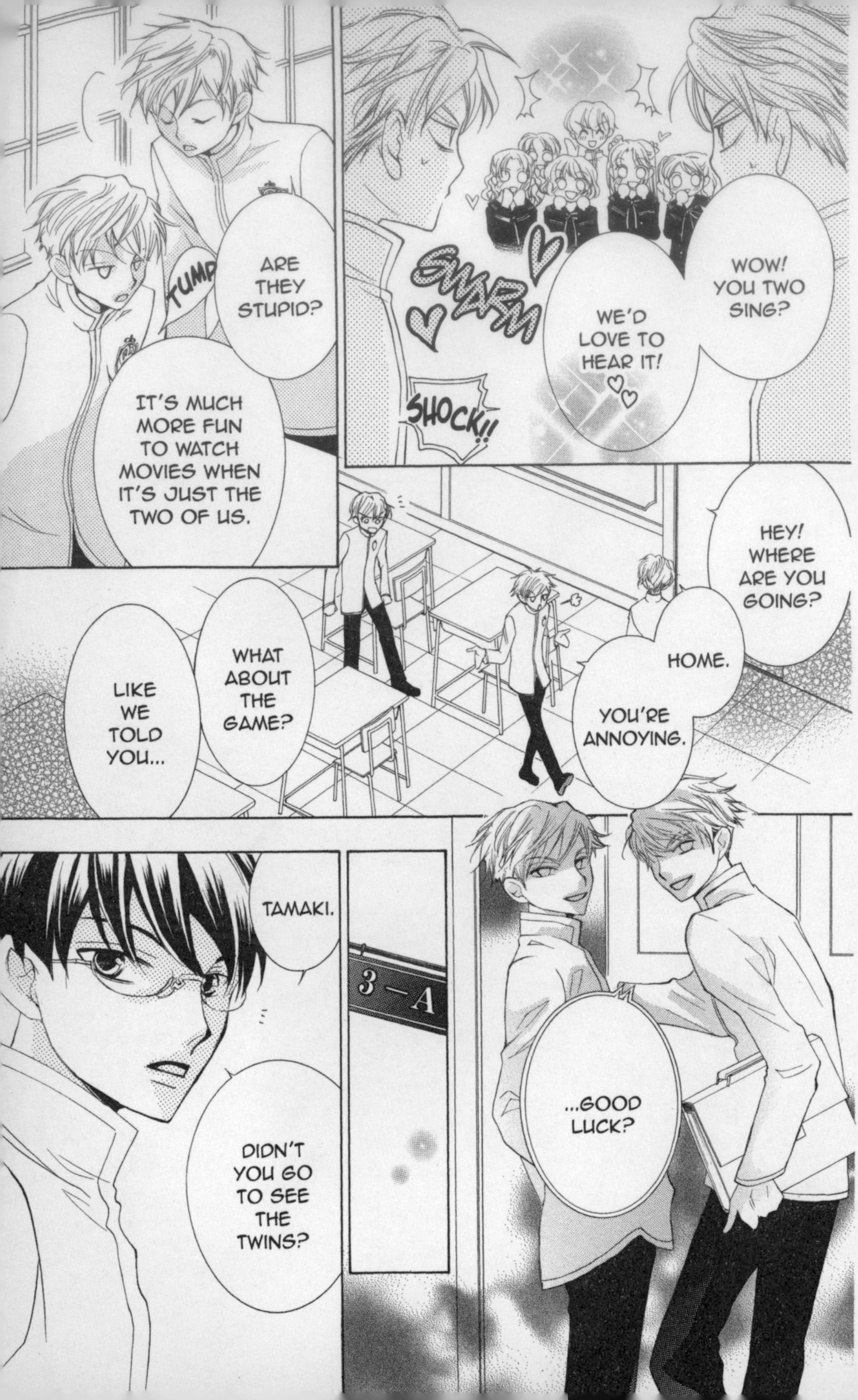
WOW! YOU TWO SING?
WE'D LOVE TO HEAR IT!
SWARM
SHOCK!!
ARE THEY STUPID?
TUMP
IT'S MUCH MORE FUN TO WATCH MOVIES WHEN IT'S JUST THE TWO OF US.
HEY! WHERE ARE YOU GOING?
HOME.
YOU'RE ANNOYING.
WHAT ABOUT THE GAME?
LIKE WE TOLD YOU...
...GOOD LUCK?
3-A
TAMAKI.
DIDN'T YOU GO TO SEE THE TWINS?

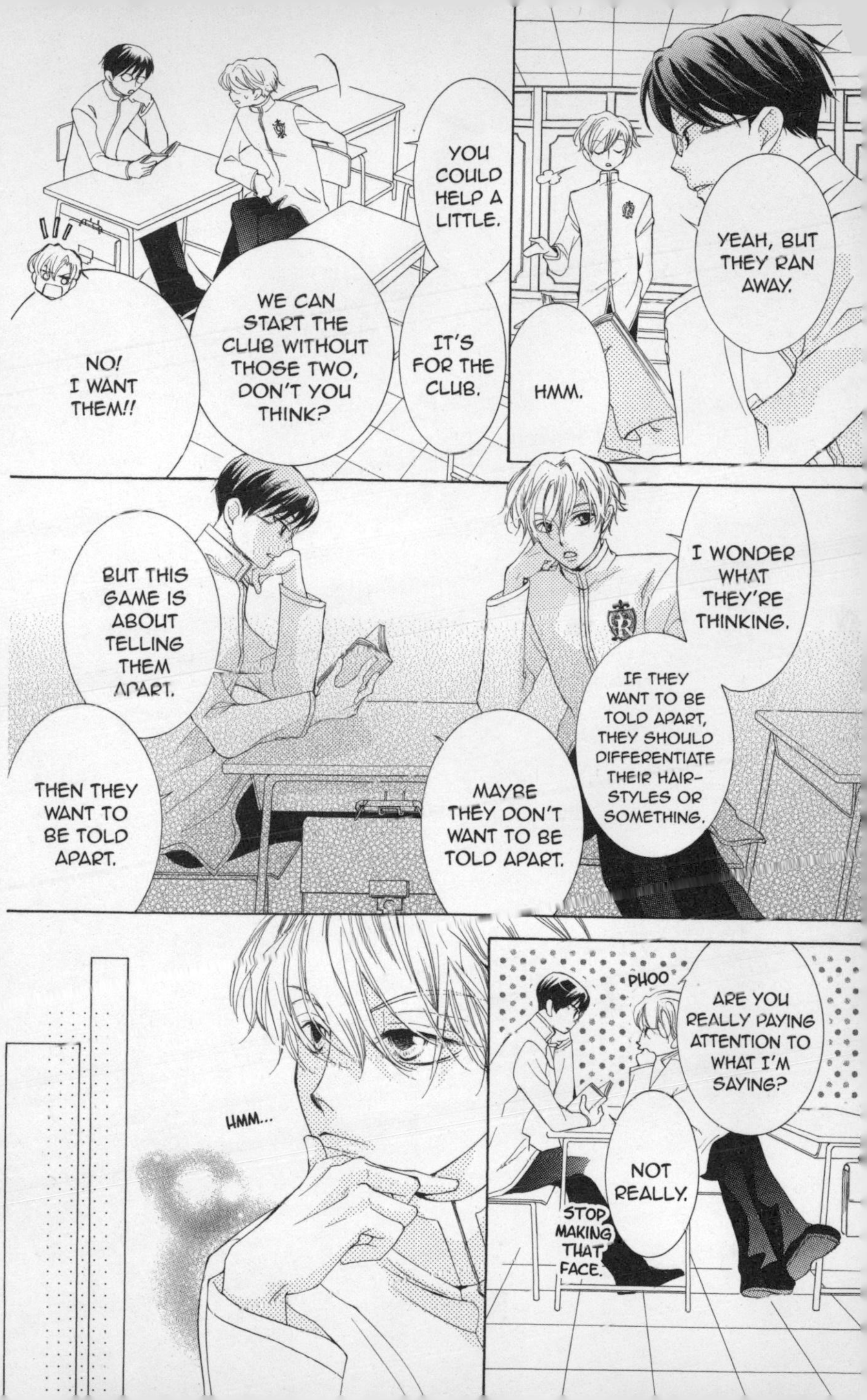
YEAH, BUT THEY RAN AWAY.
HMM.
YOU COULD HELP A LITTLE.
IT'S FOR THE CLUB.
WE CAN START THE CLUB WITHOUT THOSE TWO, DON'T YOU THINK?
NO! I WANT THEM!!
I WONDER WHAT THEY'RE THINKING.
BUT THIS GAME IS ABOUT TELLING THEM APART.
IF THEY WANT TO BE TOLD APART, THEY SHOULD DIFFERENTIATE THEIR HAIR-STYLES OR SOMETHING.
MAYBE THEY DON'T WANT TO BE TOLD APART.
THEN THEY WANT TO BE TOLD APART.
PHOO
ARE YOU REALLY PAYING ATTENTION TO WHAT I'M SAYING?
NOT REALLY.
STOP MAKING THAT FACE.
HMM...

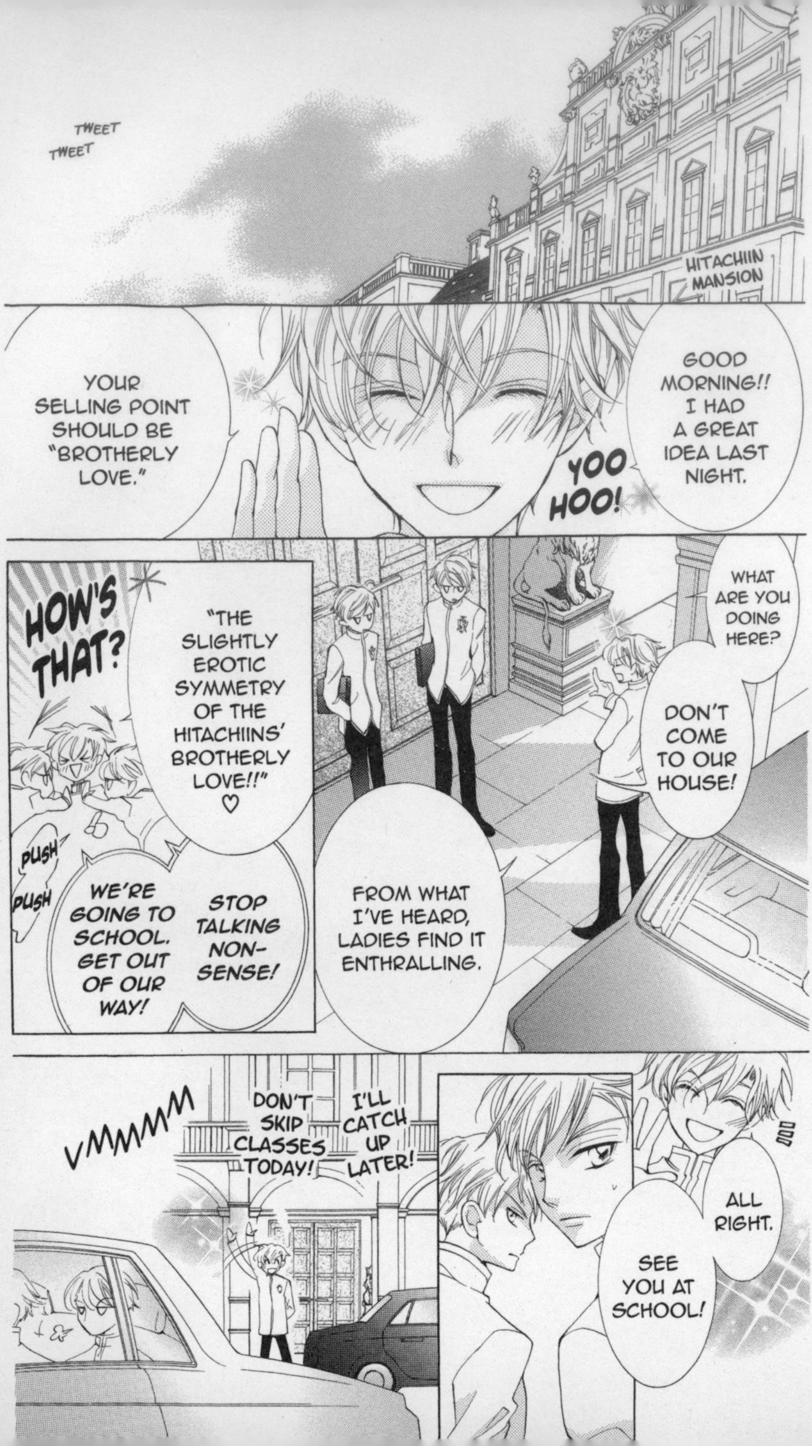
TWEET
TWEET
HITACHIIN MANSION
GOOD MORNING!! I HAD A GREAT IDEA LAST NIGHT.
YOO HOO!
YOUR SELLING POINT SHOULD BE "BROTHERLY LOVE."
WHAT ARE YOU DOING HERE?
DON'T COME TO OUR HOUSE!
FROM WHAT I'VE HEARD, LADIES FIND IT ENTHRALLING.
"THE SLIGHTLY EROTIC SYMMETRY OF THE HITACHIINS' BROTHERLY LOVE!!" ♡
HOW'S THAT?
STOP TALKING NON-SENSE!
WE'RE GOING TO SCHOOL. GET OUT OF OUR WAY!
PUSH
PUSH
ALL RIGHT.
SEE YOU AT SCHOOL!
I'LL CATCH UP LATER!
DON'T SKIP CLASSES TODAY!
VMMMM

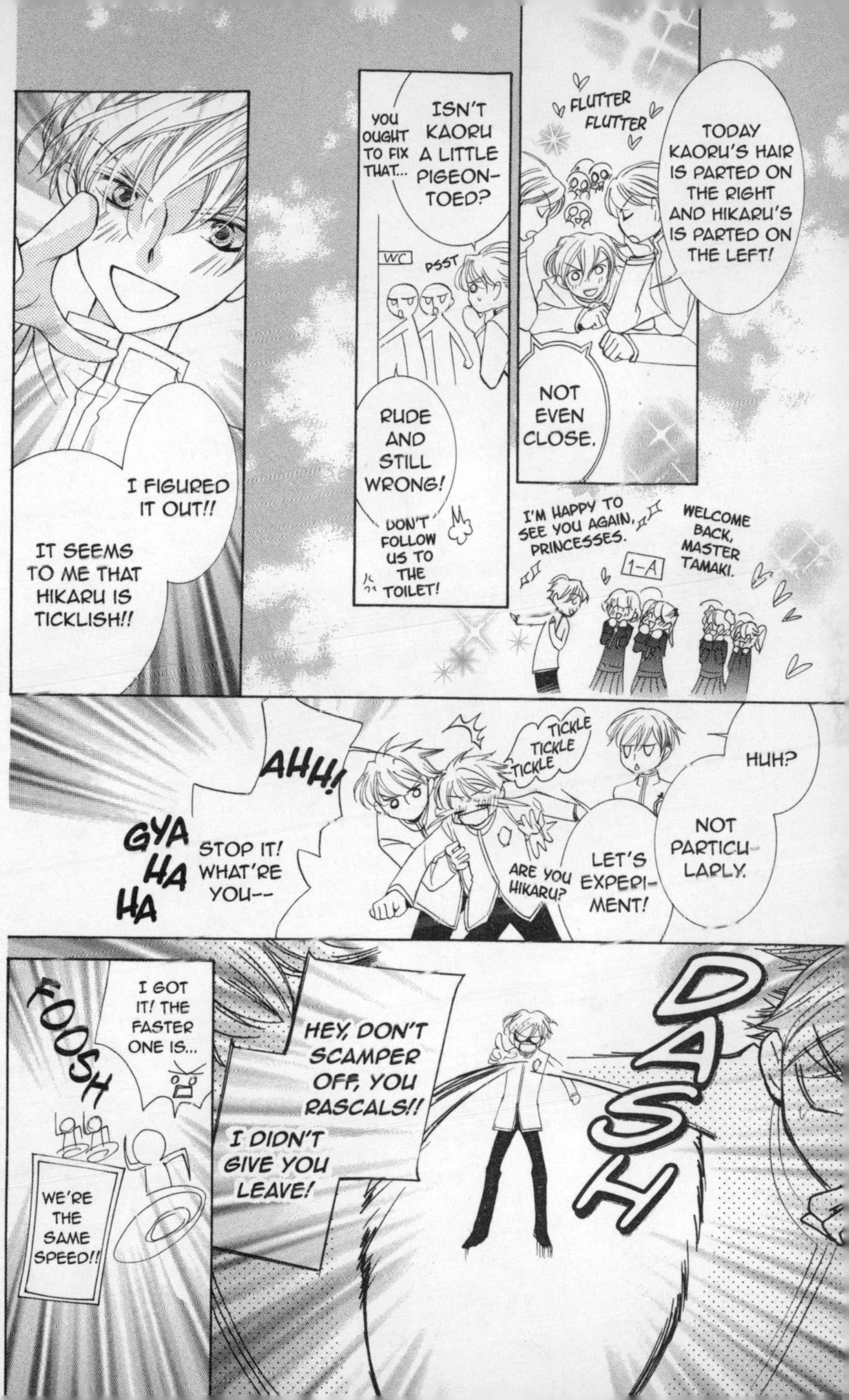
TODAY KAORU'S HAIR IS PARTED ON THE RIGHT AND HIKARU'S IS PARTED ON THE LEFT!
FLUTTER FLUTTER
NOT EVEN CLOSE.
ISN'T KAORU A LITTLE PIGEON-TOED?
YOU OUGHT TO FIX THAT...
WC
PSST
RUDE AND STILL WRONG!
DON'T FOLLOW US TO THE TOILET!
WELCOME BACK, MASTER TAMAKI.
I'M HAPPY TO SEE YOU AGAIN, PRINCESSES.
1-A
I FIGURED IT OUT!!
IT SEEMS TO ME THAT HIKARU IS TICKLISH!!
HUH?
NOT PARTICULAPLY.
LET'S EXPERIMENT!
ARE YOU HIKARU?
TICKLE TICKLE TICKLE
AHH!
STOP IT! WHAT'RE YOU--
GYA HA HA
DASH
HEY, DON'T SCAMPER OFF, YOU RASCALS!!
I DIDN'T GIVE YOU LEAVE!
I GOT IT! THE FASTER ONE IS...
FOOSH
WE'RE THE SAME SPEED!!

HEY!
HALT!
AHH!
SWIP
PISH! WHERE DID THEY GO?
HUFF HUFF
DID WE LOSE HIM?
HEY! WHERE ARE YOU?
I THINK SO.
WHAT IS WITH THAT GUY?
HE CHASED US LIKE SOME SORT OF DEMON!
I DIDN'T GIVE YOU LEAVE!
NO... NOT A DEMON BUT...
YEAH... I WAS THINKING THE SAME THING.
HE USES LORDLY SPEECH, DOESN'T HE?
BAHA!!

1

✿HOW DO YOU DO? THIS IS HATORI, SHE WHO HAS BEEN MAKING A FUSS ABOUT GETTING A FURBY? BUT NOW I WANT A DOG. WHAT'S WITH ME? AM I LONELY OR SOMETHING...? BUT A CAT SOUNDS NICE TOO. HMM... (FANTASIZING)♡♡

✿WELL, *HOST CLUB* HAS REACHED VOLUME 9. THIS STORY MARKS THE END OF THE EPISODES ABOUT THE FORMATION OF THE CLUB.

I ALWAYS THOUGHT THE STORY OF THE TWINS WOULD BE THE DARKEST ONE EVER IN *HOST CLUB* (BECAUSE OF THEIR HORRIBLE PERSONALITY), BUT WHEN I SAT DOWN TO DO IT, THANKS TO TAMAKI, IT TURNED OUT TO BE LIGHTER THAN I EXPECTED... YEAH, IT WAS ALL RIGHT!! BUT IT DOESN'T HAVE ANY "KRAKKA-BOOM" LIGHTNING IN THE BACKGROUND OR ANY SEA-URCHIN FLASHES... FOR THE FIRST TIME EVER!!! I NOTICED THIS WHILE I WAS DRAWING AND WAS SHOCKED.

(...BY THE FACT THAT I ALWAYS DREW THEM BEFORE...).

SEA-URCHIN FLASH

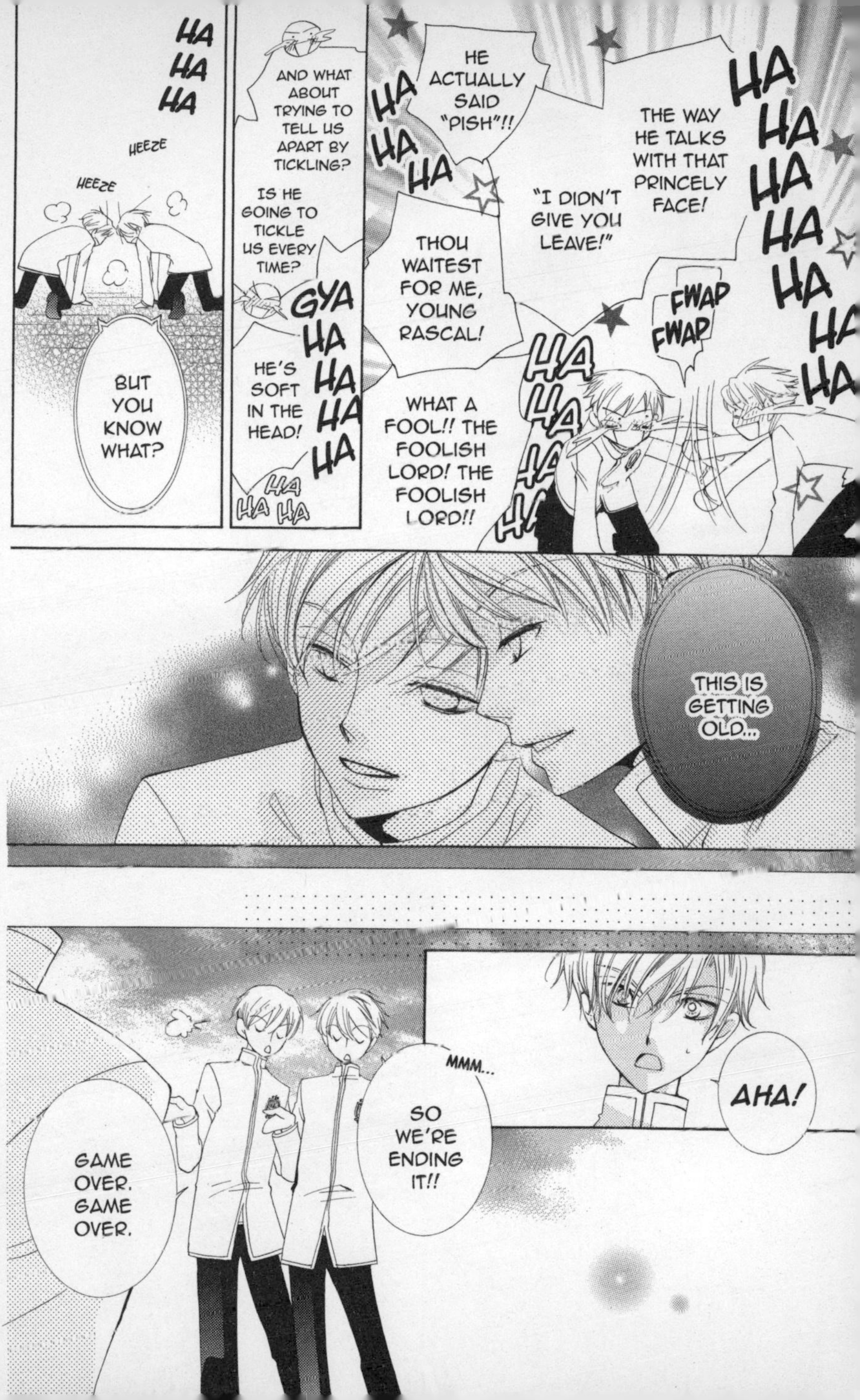
HA HA HA HA HA HA HA HA
THE WAY HE TALKS WITH THAT PRINCELY FACE!
"I DIDN'T GIVE YOU LEAVE!"
HE ACTUALLY SAID "PISH"!!
HA HA HA
FWAP FWAP
THOU WAITEST FOR ME, YOUNG RASCAL!
HA HA HA HA
WHAT A FOOL!! THE FOOLISH LORD! THE FOOLISH LORD!!
AND WHAT ABOUT TRYING TO TELL US APART BY TICKLING?
IS HE GOING TO TICKLE US EVERY TIME?
GYA HA HA HA HA
HE'S SOFT IN THE HEAD!
HA HA HA
HA HA HA
HEEZE
HEEZE
BUT YOU KNOW WHAT?
THIS IS GETTING OLD...
AHA!
MMM...
SO WE'RE ENDING IT!!
GAME OVER. GAME OVER.

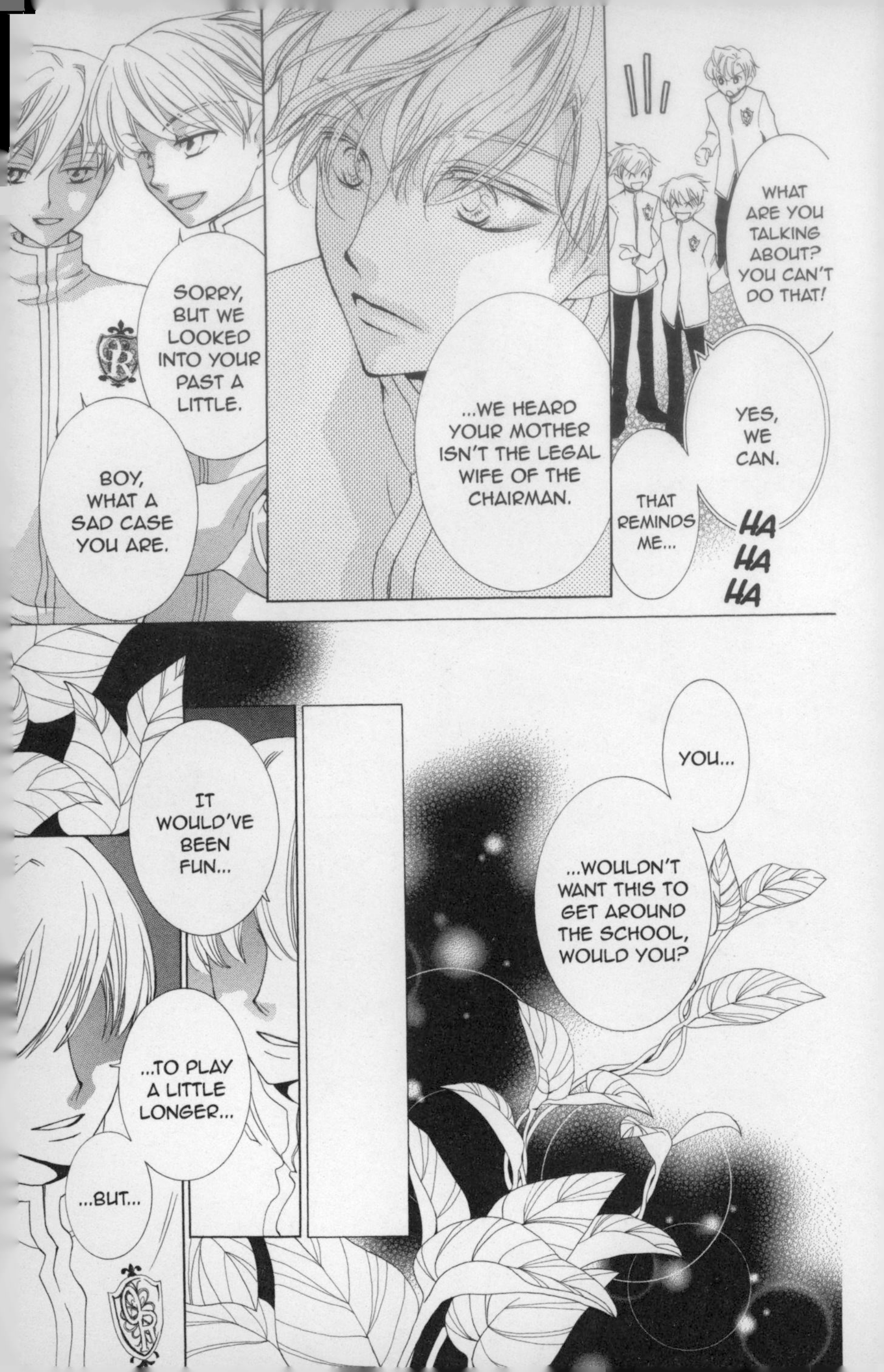
WHAT ARE YOU TALKING ABOUT? YOU CAN'T DO THAT!
YES, WE CAN.
HA HA HA
THAT REMINDS ME...
...WE HEARD YOUR MOTHER ISN'T THE LEGAL WIFE OF THE CHAIRMAN.
SORRY, BUT WE LOOKED INTO YOUR PAST A LITTLE.
BOY, WHAT A SAD CASE YOU ARE.
YOU...
...WOULDN'T WANT THIS TO GET AROUND THE SCHOOL, WOULD YOU?
IT WOULD'VE BEEN FUN...
...TO PLAY A LITTLE LONGER...
...BUT...

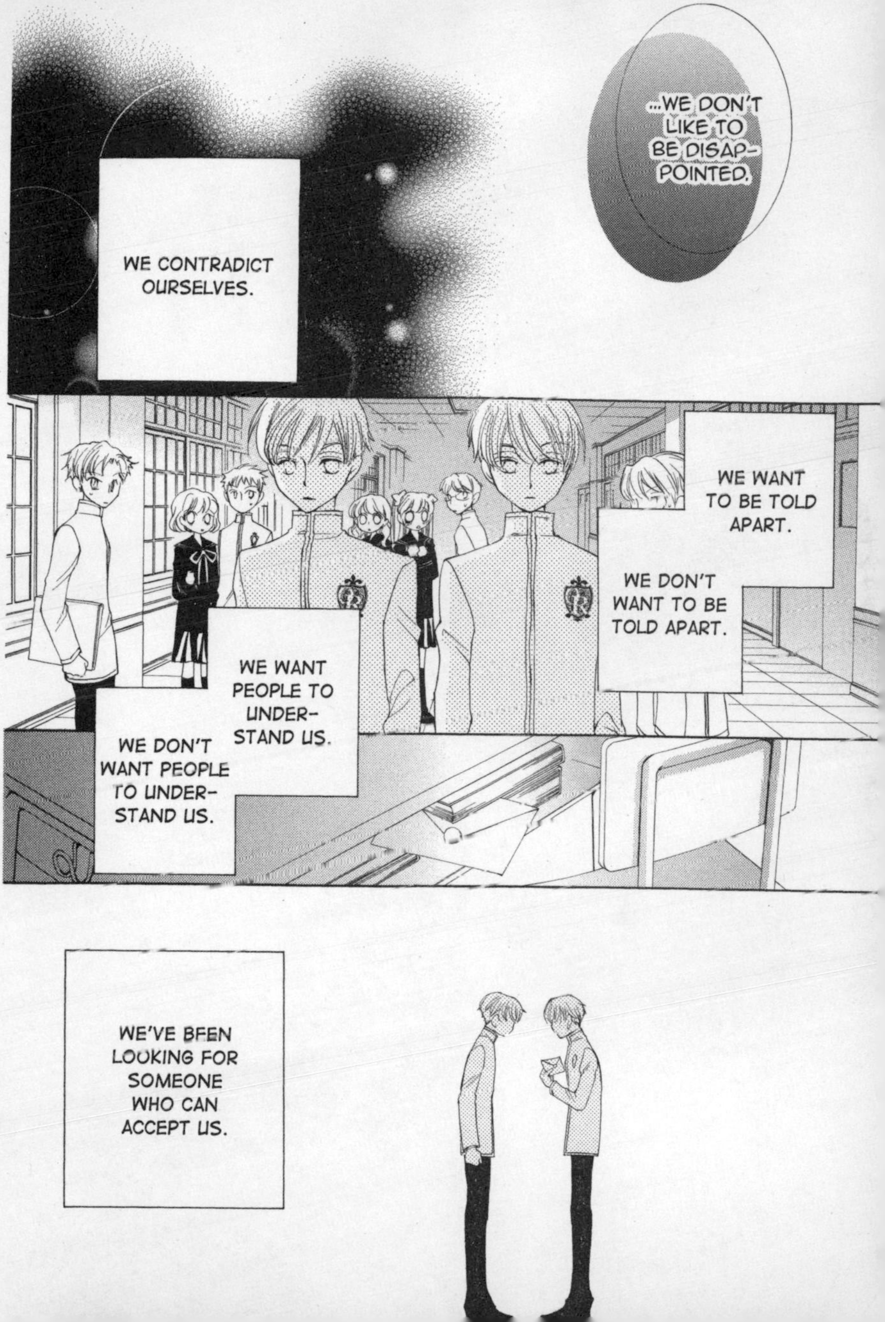
...WE DON'T LIKE TO BE DISAPPOINTED.
WE CONTRADICT OURSELVES.
WE WANT TO BE TOLD APART.
WE DON'T WANT TO BE TOLD APART.
WE WANT PEOPLE TO UNDERSTAND US.
WE DON'T WANT PEOPLE TO UNDERSTAND US.
WE'VE BEEN LOOKING FOR SOMEONE WHO CAN ACCEPT US.

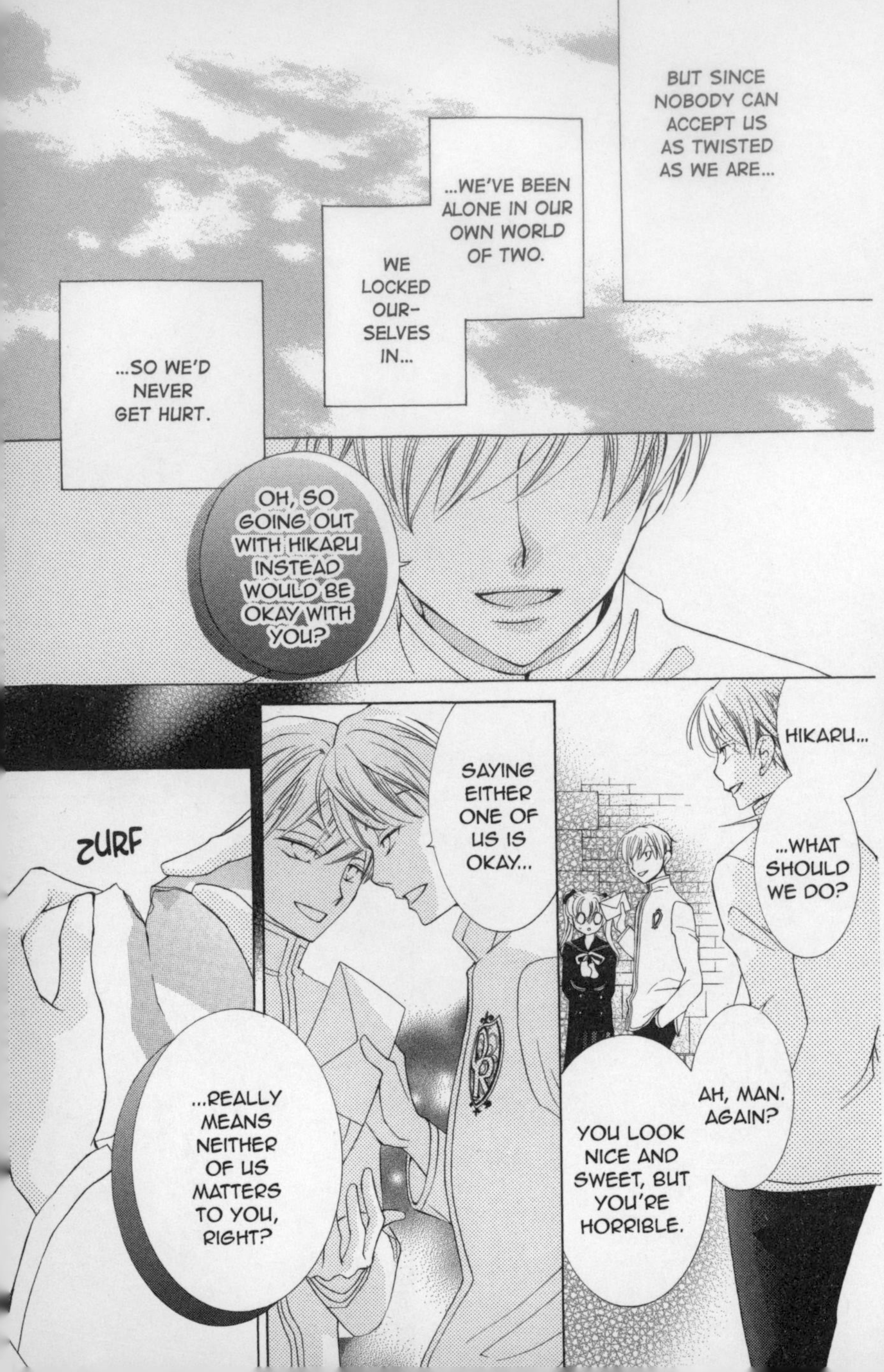
BUT SINCE NOBODY CAN ACCEPT US AS TWISTED AS WE ARE...
...WE'VE BEEN ALONE IN OUR OWN WORLD OF TWO.
WE LOCKED OUR-SELVES IN...
...SO WE'D NEVER GET HURT.
OH, SO GOING OUT WITH HIKARU INSTEAD WOULD BE OKAY WITH YOU?
HIKARU...
...WHAT SHOULD WE DO?
AH, MAN. AGAIN?
YOU LOOK NICE AND SWEET, BUT YOU'RE HORRIBLE.
SAYING EITHER ONE OF US IS OKAY...
...REALLY MEANS NEITHER OF US MATTERS TO YOU, RIGHT?
ZURF

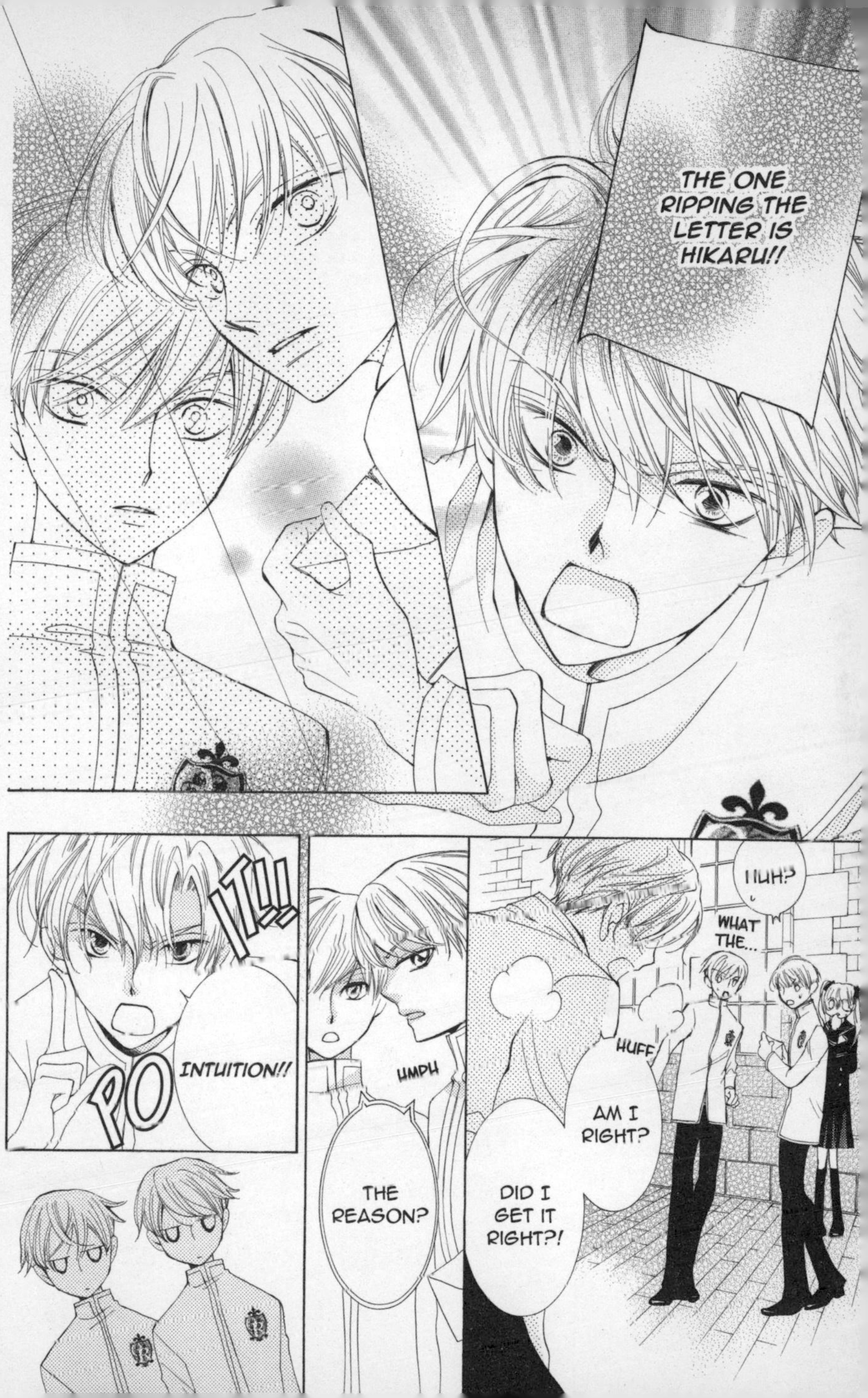
THE ONE RIPPING THE LETTER IS HIKARU!!
HUH?
WHAT THE...
HUFF
AM I RIGHT?
DID I GET IT RIGHT?!
UMPH
THE REASON?
IT!!
PO
INTUITION!!

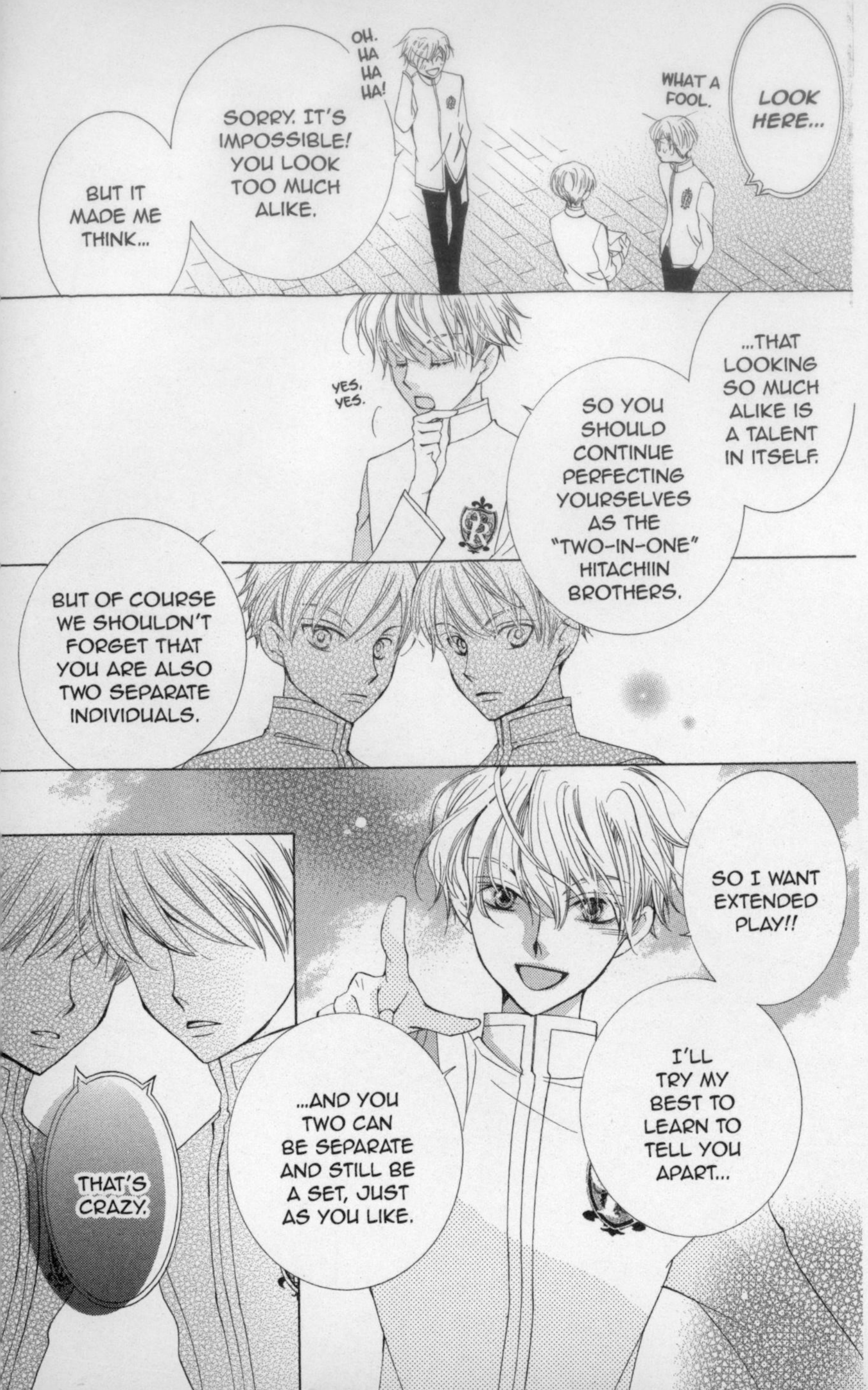
LOOK HERE...
WHAT A FOOL.
OH. HA HA HA!
SORRY. IT'S IMPOSSIBLE! YOU LOOK TOO MUCH ALIKE.
BUT IT MADE ME THINK...
...THAT LOOKING SO MUCH ALIKE IS A TALENT IN ITSELF.
YES, YES.
SO YOU SHOULD CONTINUE PERFECTING YOURSELVES AS THE "TWO-IN-ONE" HITACHIIN BROTHERS.
BUT OF COURSE WE SHOULDN'T FORGET THAT YOU ARE ALSO TWO SEPARATE INDIVIDUALS.
SO I WANT EXTENDED PLAY!!
I'LL TRY MY BEST TO LEARN TO TELL YOU APART...
...AND YOU TWO CAN BE SEPARATE AND STILL BE A SET, JUST AS YOU LIKE.
THAT'S CRAZY.

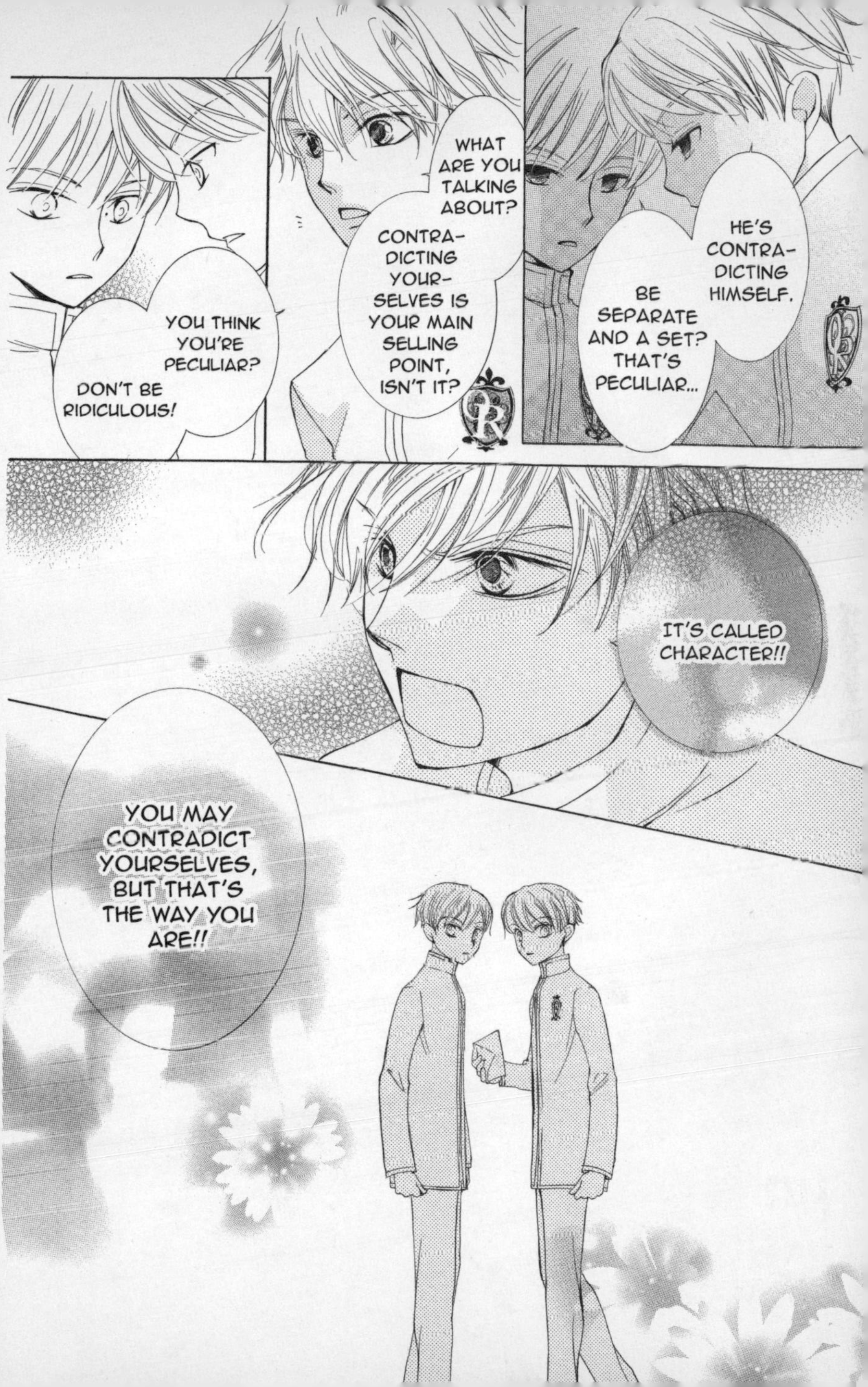
HE'S CONTRA-DICTING HIMSELF.
BE SEPARATE AND A SET? THAT'S PECULIAR...
WHAT ARE YOU TALKING ABOUT?
CONTRA-DICTING YOUR-SELVES IS YOUR MAIN SELLING POINT, ISN'T IT?
YOU THINK YOU'RE PECULIAR?
DON'T BE RIDICULOUS!
IT'S CALLED CHARACTER!!
YOU MAY CONTRADICT YOURSELVES, BUT THAT'S THE WAY YOU ARE!!

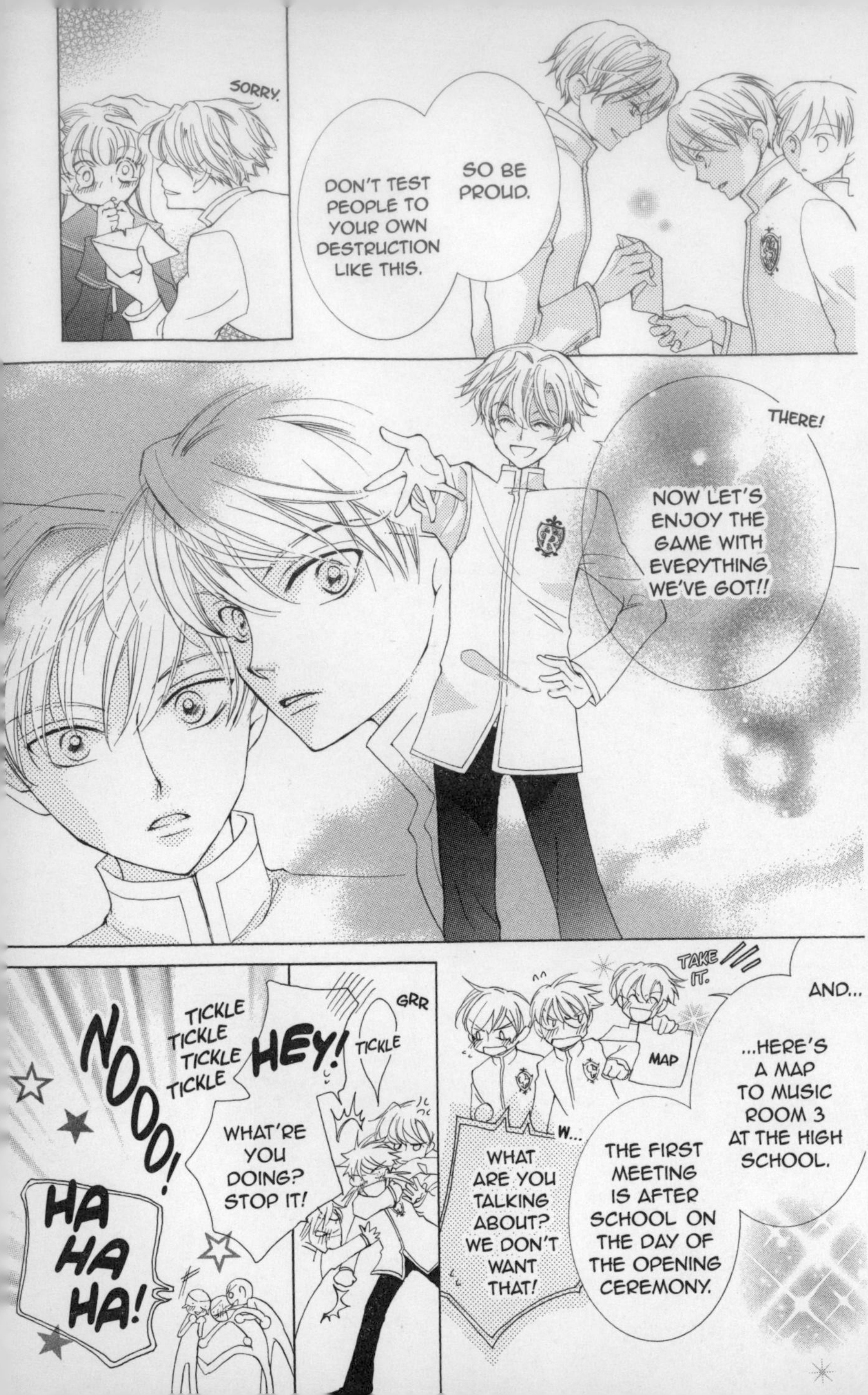
SO BE PROUD.
DON'T TEST PEOPLE TO YOUR OWN DESTRUCTION LIKE THIS.
SORRY.
THERE!
NOW LET'S ENJOY THE GAME WITH EVERYTHING WE'VE GOT!!
AND...
...HERE'S A MAP TO MUSIC ROOM 3 AT THE HIGH SCHOOL.
TAKE IT.
MAP
THE FIRST MEETING IS AFTER SCHOOL ON THE DAY OF THE OPENING CEREMONY.
W...
WHAT ARE YOU TALKING ABOUT? WE DON'T WANT THAT!
GRR
TICKLE
HEY!
TICKLE TICKLE TICKLE TICKLE
WHAT'RE YOU DOING? STOP IT!
NOOOO!
HA HA HA HA!

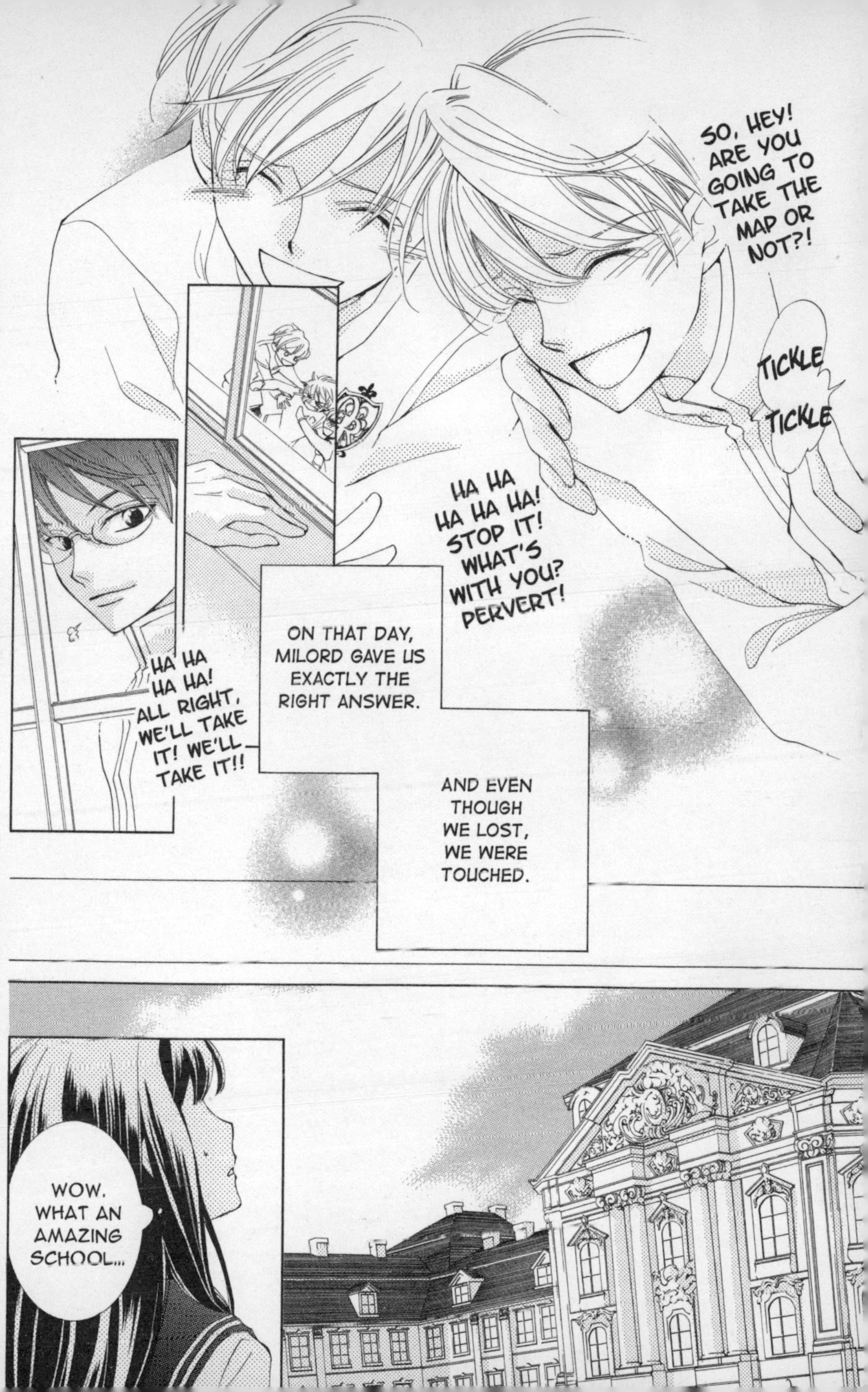
SO, HEY! ARE YOU GOING TO TAKE THE MAP OR NOT?!
TICKLE
TICKLE
HA HA HA HA HA! STOP IT! WHAT'S WITH YOU? PERVERT!
HA HA HA HA! ALL RIGHT, WE'LL TAKE IT! WE'LL TAKE IT!!
ON THAT DAY, MILORD GAVE US EXACTLY THE RIGHT ANSWER.
AND EVEN THOUGH WE LOST, WE WERE TOUCHED.
WOW. WHAT AN AMAZING SCHOOL...

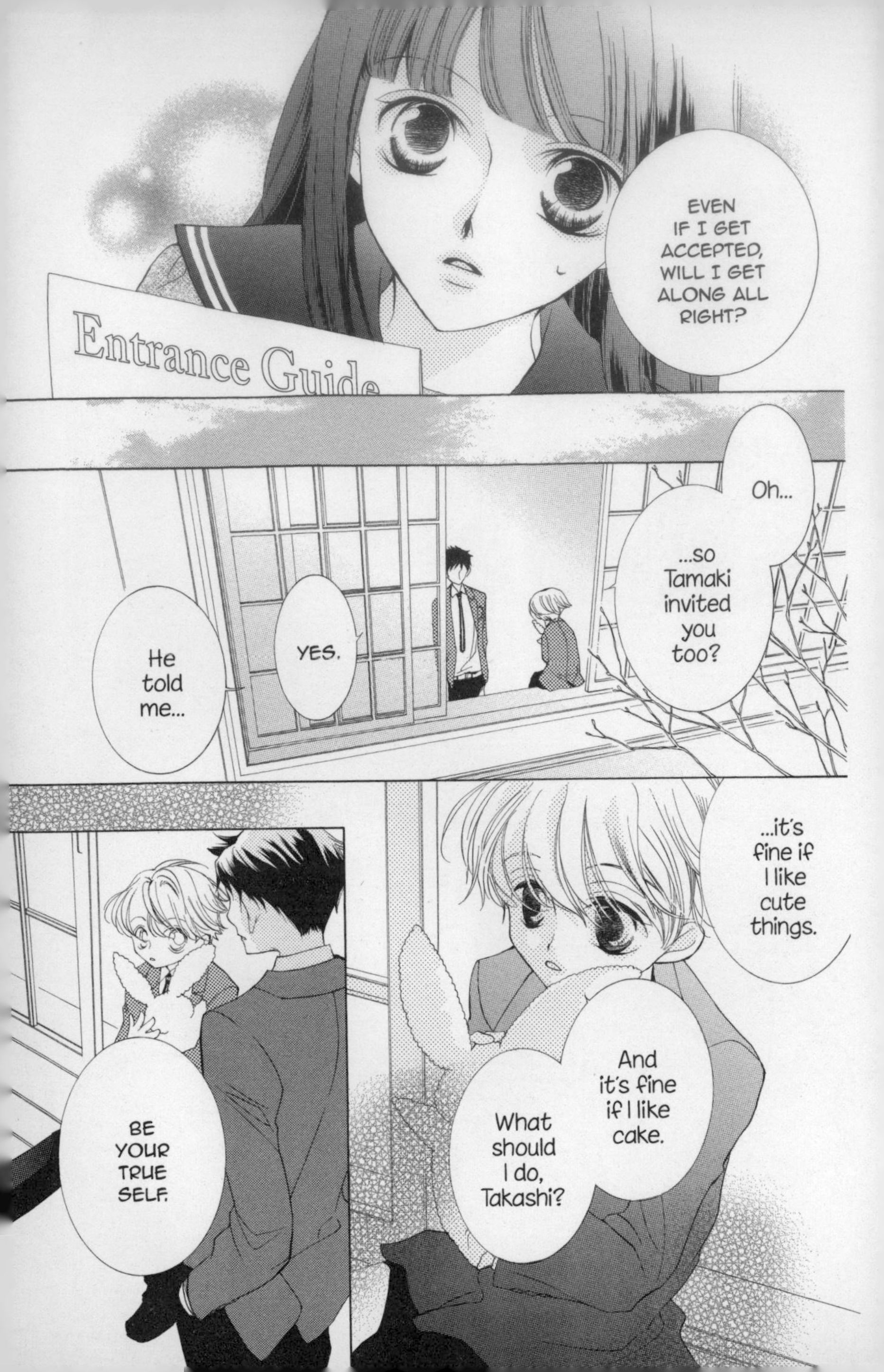
EVEN IF I GET ACCEPTED, WILL I GET ALONG ALL RIGHT?
Entrance Guide
Oh...
...so Tamaki invited you too?
YES.
He told me...
...it's fine if I like cute things.
And it's fine if I like cake.
What should I do, Takashi?
BE YOUR TRUE SELF.

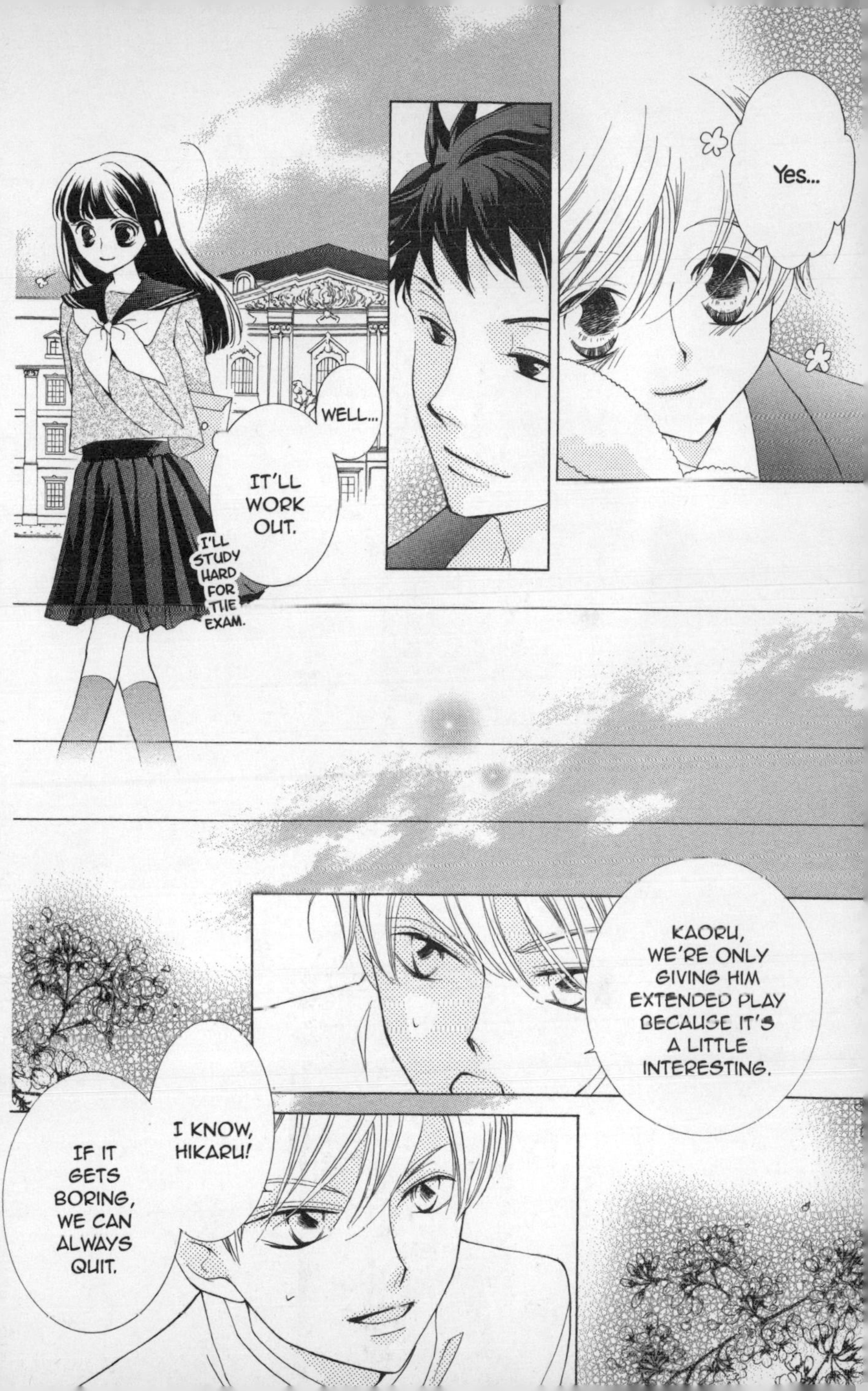
Yes...
WELL...
IT'LL WORK OUT.
I'LL STUDY HARD FOR THE EXAM.
KAORU, WE'RE ONLY GIVING HIM EXTENDED PLAY BECAUSE IT'S A LITTLE INTERESTING.
I KNOW, HIKARU!
IF IT GETS BORING, WE CAN ALWAYS QUIT.

Music Room 3

SHOULD WE OPEN IT TOGETHER?

HERE WE GO...

LET'S OPEN THE DOOR.

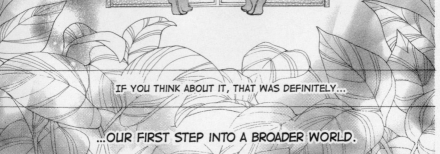

IF YOU THINK ABOUT IT, THAT WAS DEFINITELY...

...OUR FIRST STEP INTO A BROADER WORLD.

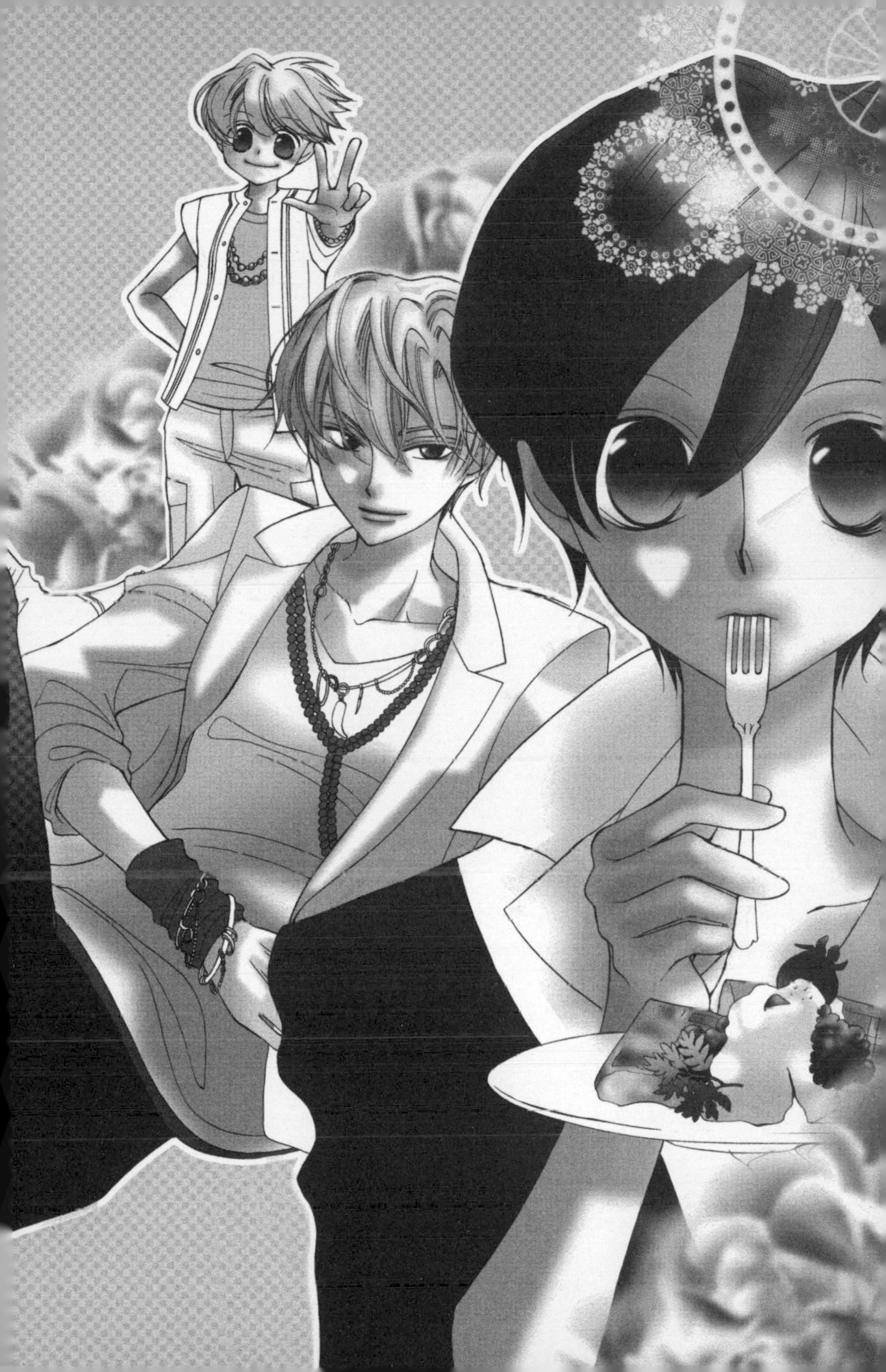

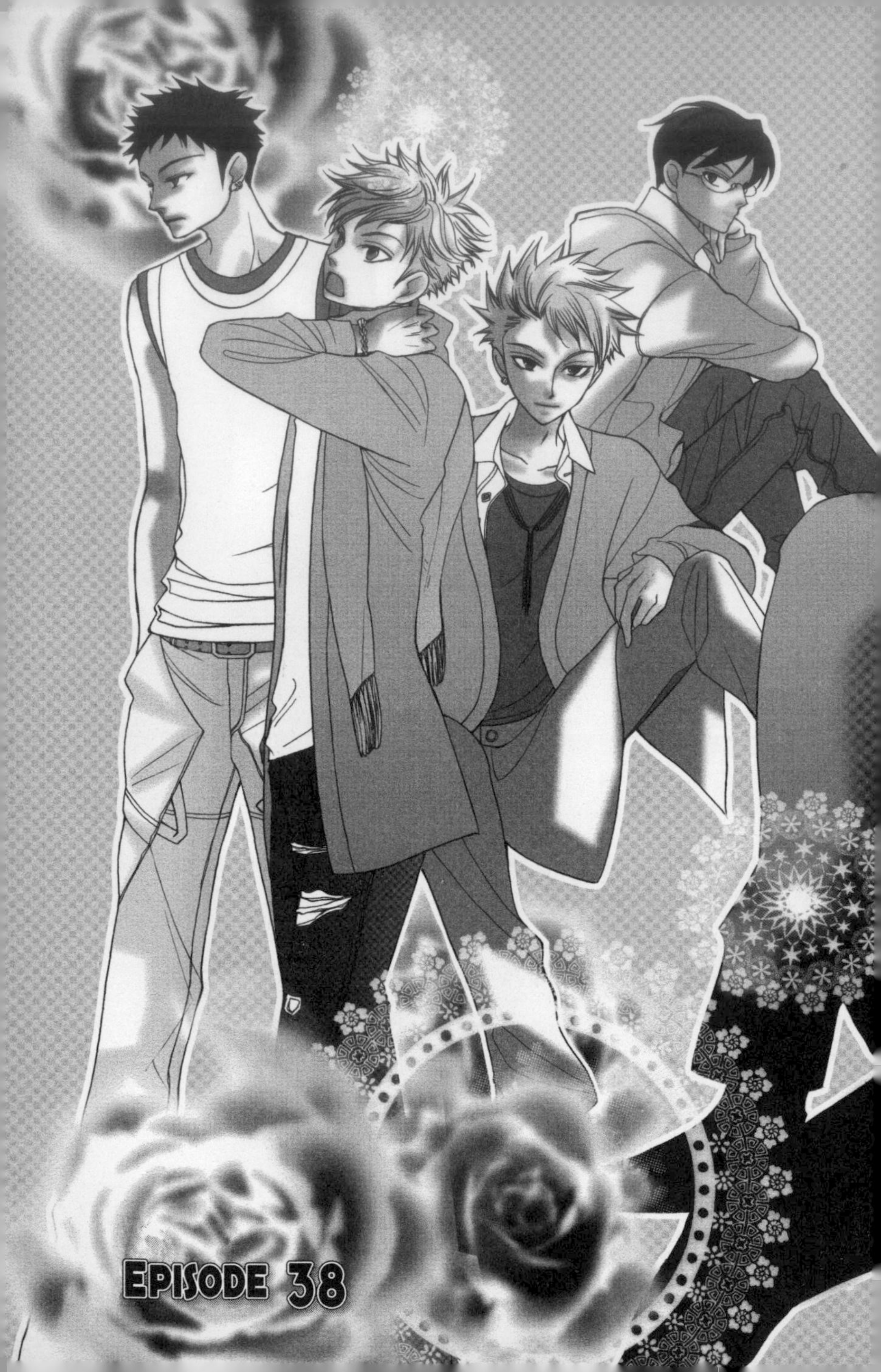
Episode 38

GUEST ROOM: FAXES ①

SPECIAL THANKS TO
KUMIKO TAKAHASHI!!

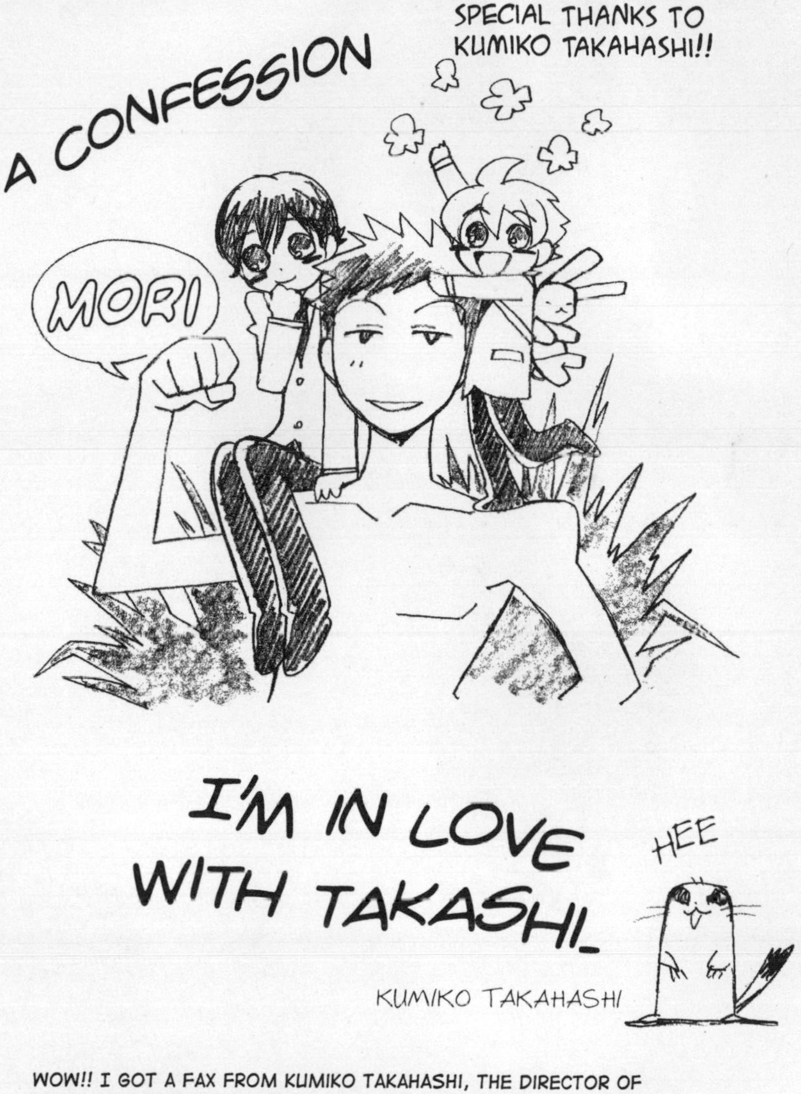
A CONFESSION
MORI
I'M IN LOVE WITH TAKASHI_
HEE
KUMIKO TAKAHASHI

WOW!! I GOT A FAX FROM KUMIKO TAKAHASHI, THE DIRECTOR OF CHARACTER DESIGN FOR THE *HOST CLUB* ANIME!! (JOYOUS TEARS) WELL, ACTUALLY I PESTERED HER FOR IT!! EVERYONE COMPLIMENT ME FOR BEING BRAVE AND REPEATEDLY BUGGING HER!!♡♡ CUTE!!♡♡

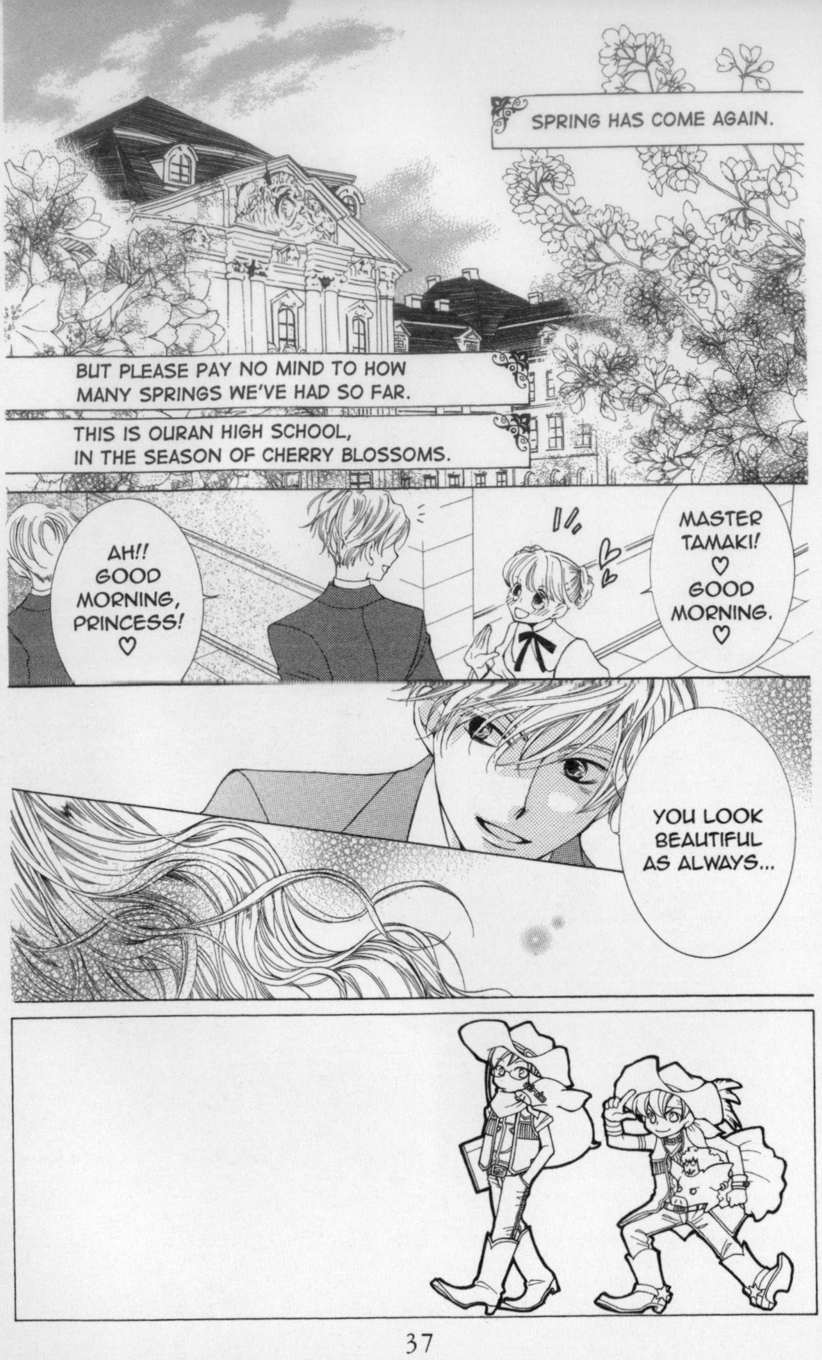
SPRING HAS COME AGAIN.
BUT PLEASE PAY NO MIND TO HOW MANY SPRINGS WE'VE HAD SO FAR.
THIS IS OURAN HIGH SCHOOL, IN THE SEASON OF CHERRY BLOSSOMS.
MASTER TAMAKI! ♡ GOOD MORNING. ♡
AH!! GOOD MORNING, PRINCESS! ♡
YOU LOOK BEAUTIFUL AS ALWAYS...

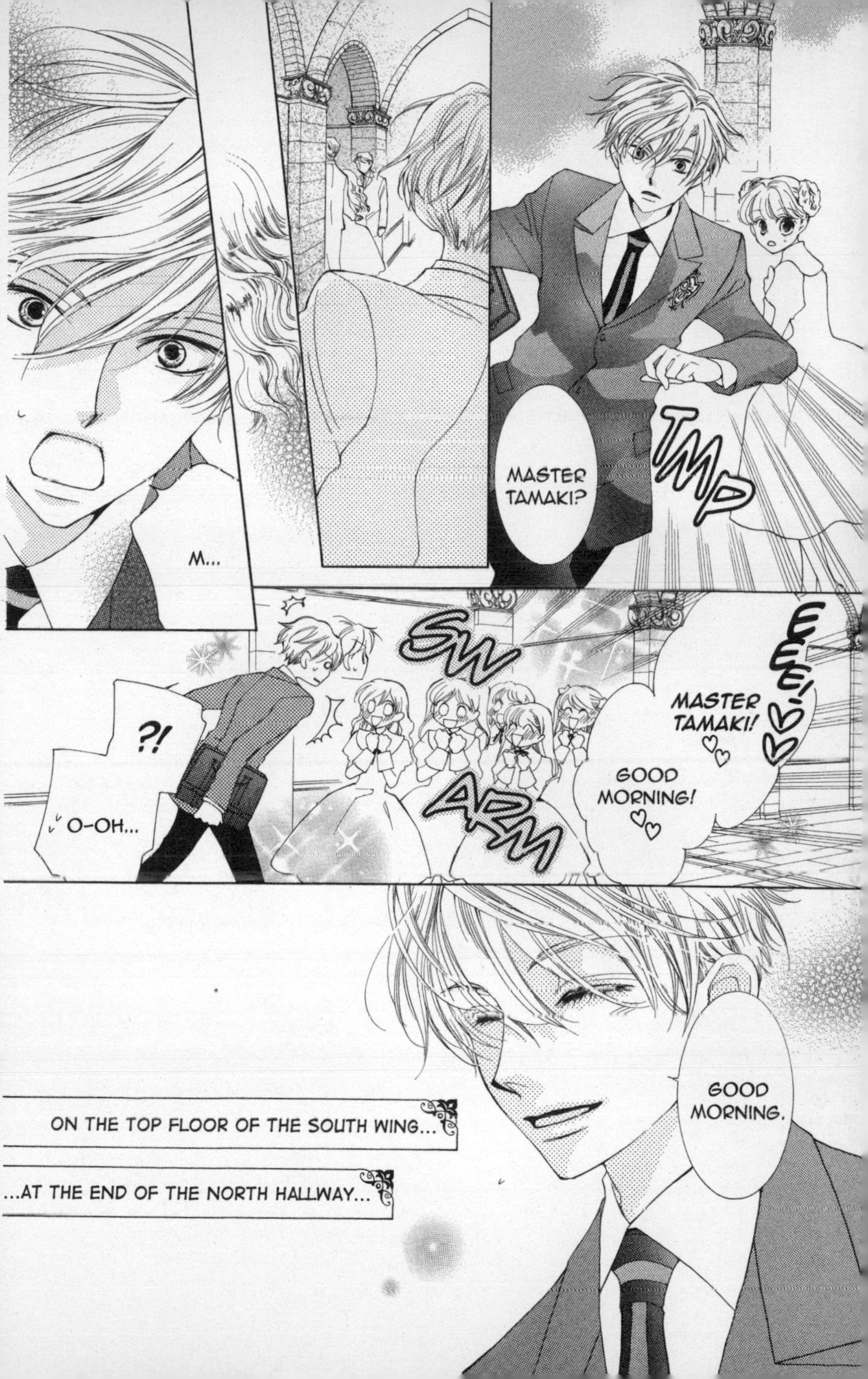
MASTER TAMAKI?
TMP
M...
EEE!
MASTER TAMAKI!
GOOD MORNING!
SW
ARM
?!
O-OH...
GOOD MORNING.
ON THE TOP FLOOR OF THE SOUTH WING...
...AT THE END OF THE NORTH HALLWAY...

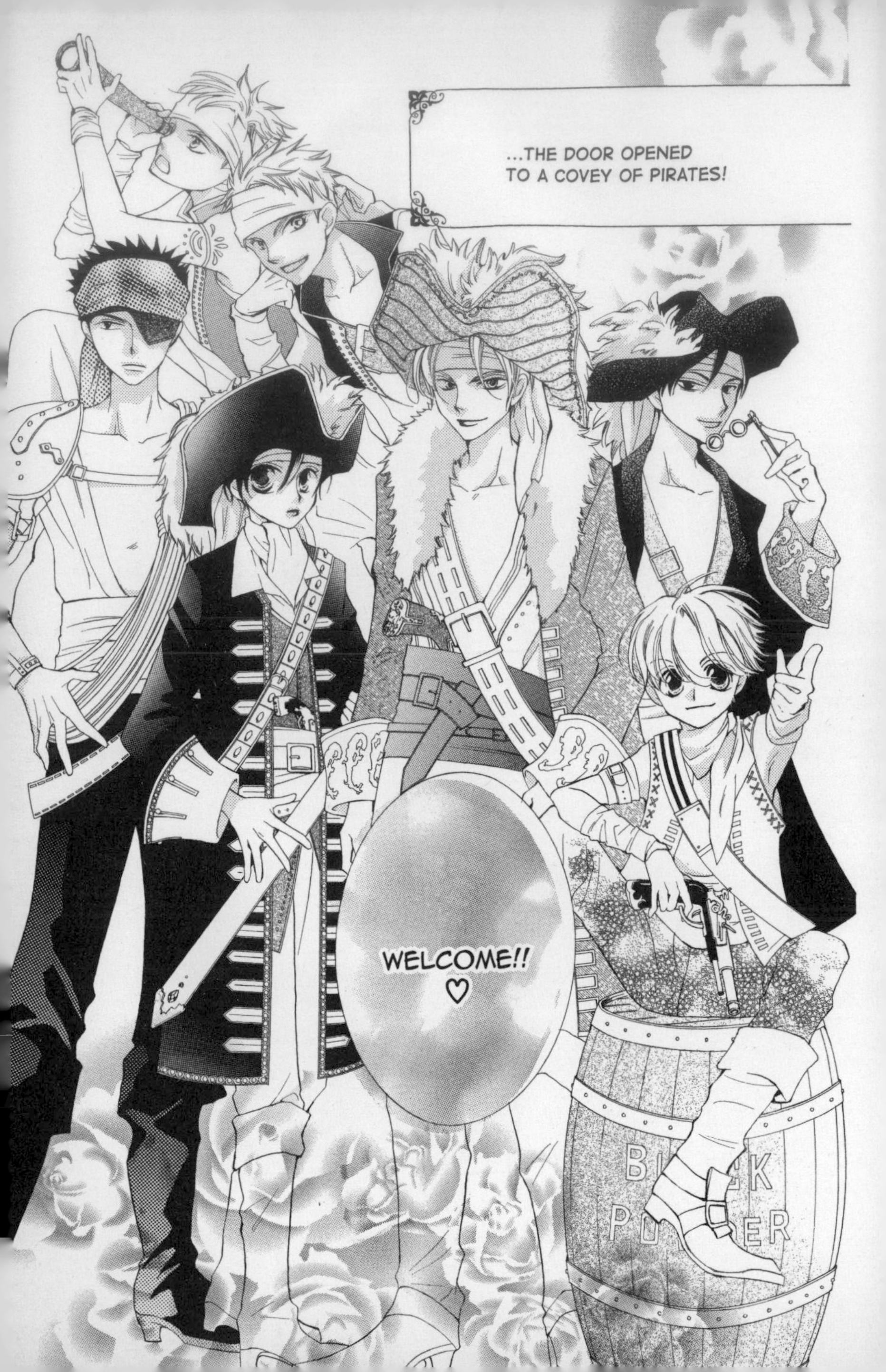
...THE DOOR OPENED TO A COVEY OF PIRATES!
WELCOME!! ♡

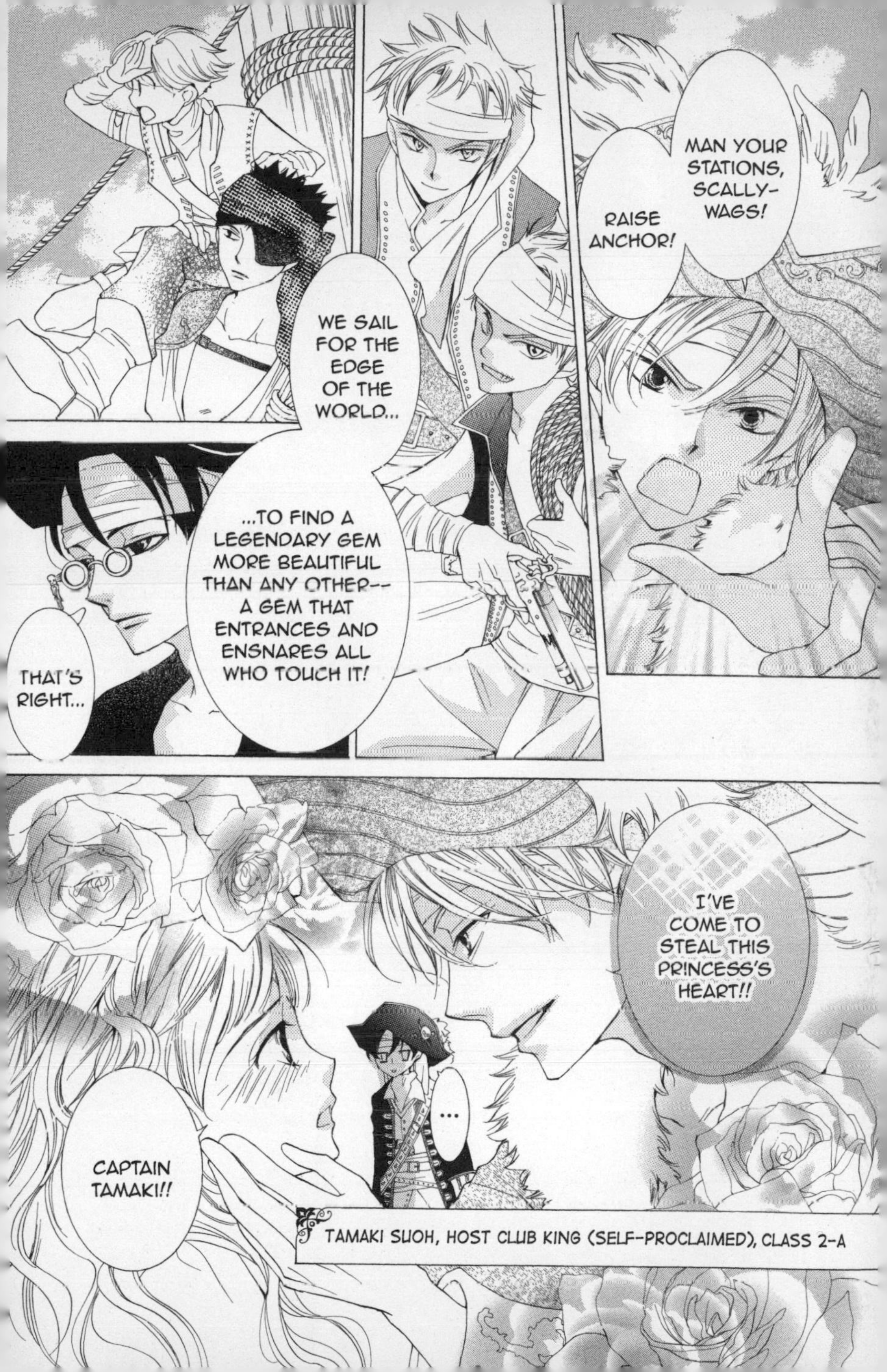
MAN YOUR STATIONS, SCALLY-WAGS!
RAISE ANCHOR!
WE SAIL FOR THE EDGE OF THE WORLD...
...TO FIND A LEGENDARY GEM MORE BEAUTIFUL THAN ANY OTHER-- A GEM THAT ENTRANCES AND ENSNARES ALL WHO TOUCH IT!
THAT'S RIGHT...
I'VE COME TO STEAL THIS PRINCESS'S HEART!!
...
CAPTAIN TAMAKI!!
TAMAKI SUOH, HOST CLUB KING (SELF-PROCLAIMED), CLASS 2-A

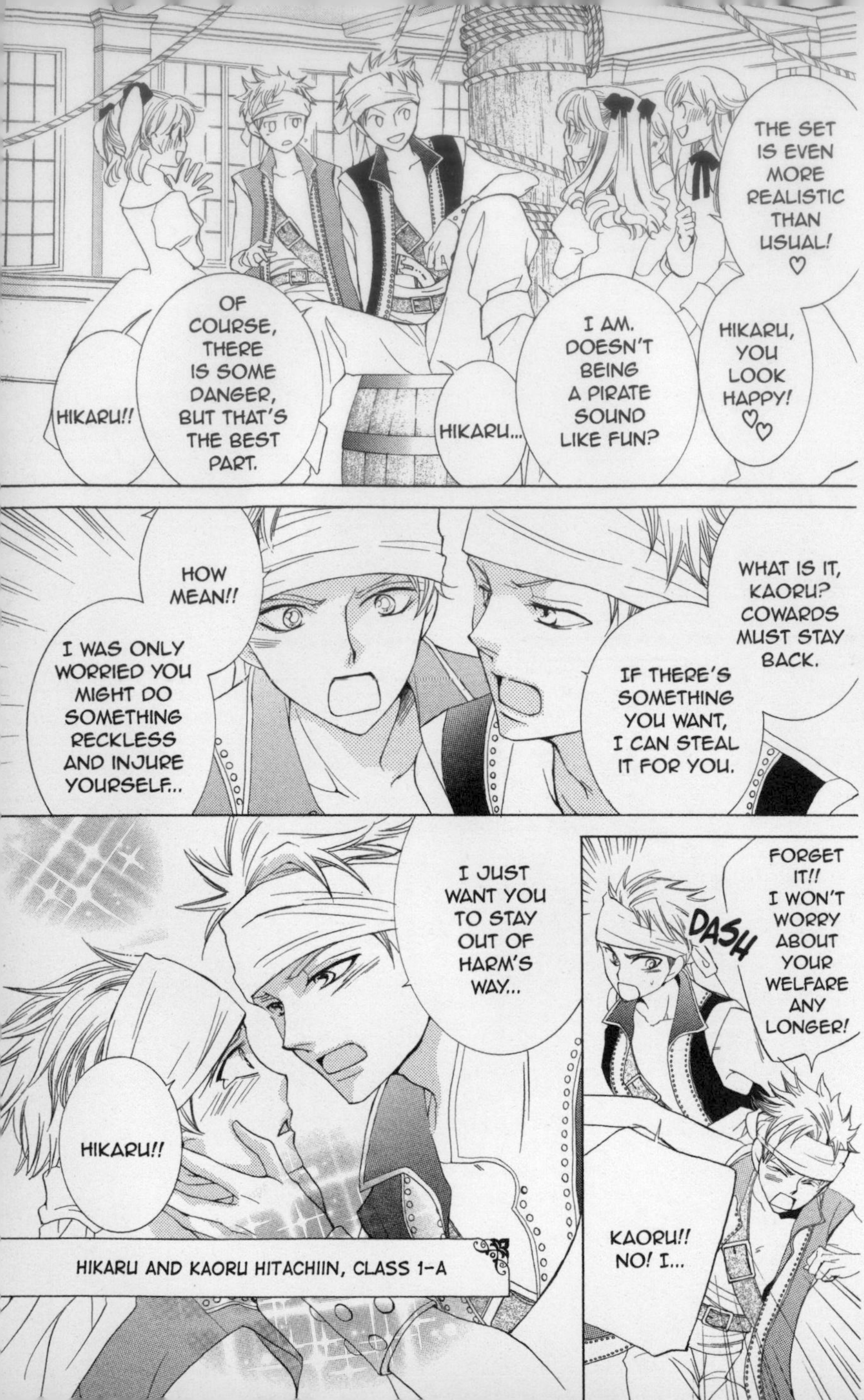
THE SET IS EVEN MORE REALISTIC THAN USUAL! ♡
HIKARU, YOU LOOK HAPPY! ♡♡
I AM. DOESN'T BEING A PIRATE SOUND LIKE FUN?
HIKARU...
OF COURSE, THERE IS SOME DANGER, BUT THAT'S THE BEST PART.
HIKARU!!
WHAT IS IT, KAORU? COWARDS MUST STAY BACK.
IF THERE'S SOMETHING YOU WANT, I CAN STEAL IT FOR YOU.
HOW MEAN!!
I WAS ONLY WORRIED YOU MIGHT DO SOMETHING RECKLESS AND INJURE YOURSELF...
FORGET IT!! I WON'T WORRY ABOUT YOUR WELFARE ANY LONGER!
DASH
KAORU!! NO! I...
I JUST WANT YOU TO STAY OUT OF HARM'S WAY...
HIKARU!!
HIKARU AND KAORU HITACHIIN, CLASS 1-A

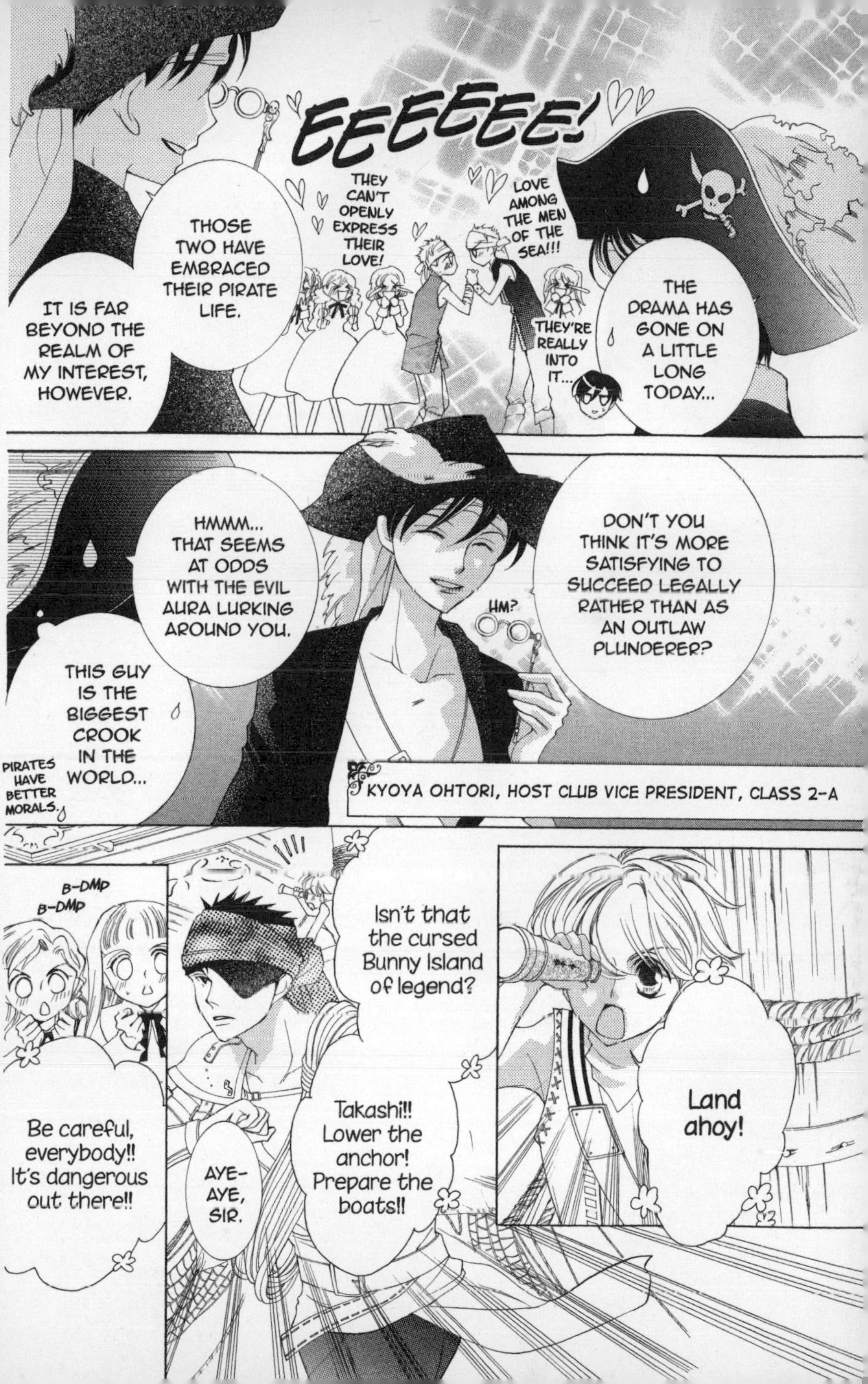
EEEEEEE!
THE DRAMA HAS GONE ON A LITTLE LONG TODAY...
LOVE AMONG THE MEN OF THE SEA!!!
THEY'RE REALLY INTO IT...
THEY CAN'T OPENLY EXPRESS THEIR LOVE!
THOSE TWO HAVE EMBRACED THEIR PIRATE LIFE.
IT IS FAR BEYOND THE REALM OF MY INTEREST, HOWEVER.
DON'T YOU THINK IT'S MORE SATISFYING TO SUCCEED LEGALLY RATHER THAN AS AN OUTLAW PLUNDERER?
HM?
HMMM... THAT SEEMS AT ODDS WITH THE EVIL AURA LURKING AROUND YOU.
THIS GUY IS THE BIGGEST CROOK IN THE WORLD...
PIRATES HAVE BETTER MORALS.
KYOYA OHTORI, HOST CLUB VICE PRESIDENT, CLASS 2-A
Land ahoy!
Isn't that the cursed Bunny Island of legend?
Takashi!! Lower the anchor! Prepare the boats!!
AYE-AYE, SIR.
B-DMP
B-DMP
Be careful, everybody!! It's dangerous out there!!

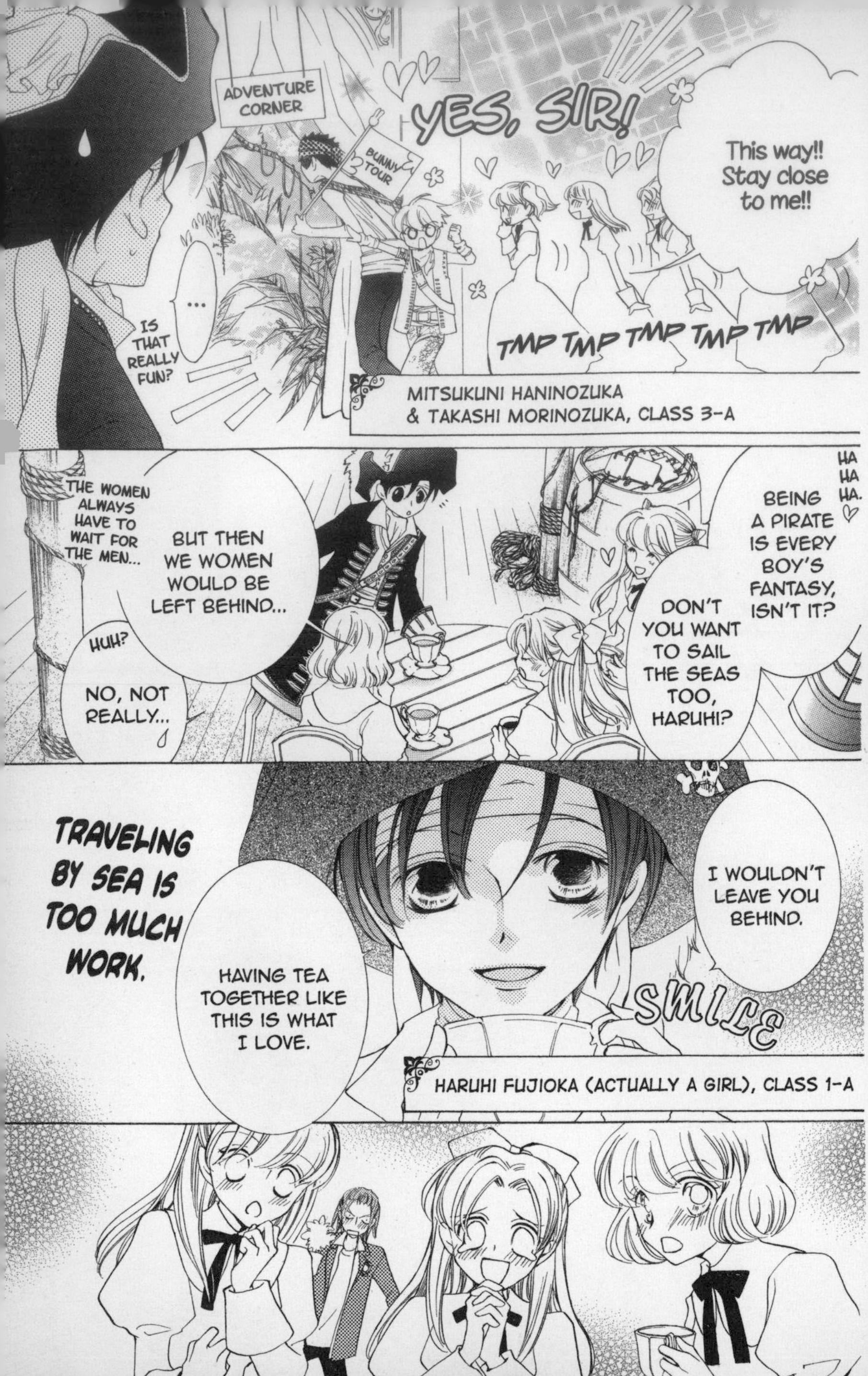
This way!! Stay close to me!!
YES, SIR!
BUNNY TOUR
ADVENTURE CORNER
TMP TMP TMP TMP TMP
...
IS THAT REALLY FUN?
MITSUKUNI HANINOZUKA & TAKASHI MORINOZUKA, CLASS 3-A
HA HA HA.
BEING A PIRATE IS EVERY BOY'S FANTASY, ISN'T IT?
DON'T YOU WANT TO SAIL THE SEAS TOO, HARUHI?
THE WOMEN ALWAYS HAVE TO WAIT FOR THE MEN...
BUT THEN WE WOMEN WOULD BE LEFT BEHIND...
HUH?
NO, NOT REALLY...
I WOULDN'T LEAVE YOU BEHIND.
SMILE
HAVING TEA TOGETHER LIKE THIS IS WHAT I LOVE.
TRAVELING BY SEA IS TOO MUCH WORK.
HARUHI FUJIOKA (ACTUALLY A GIRL), CLASS 1-A

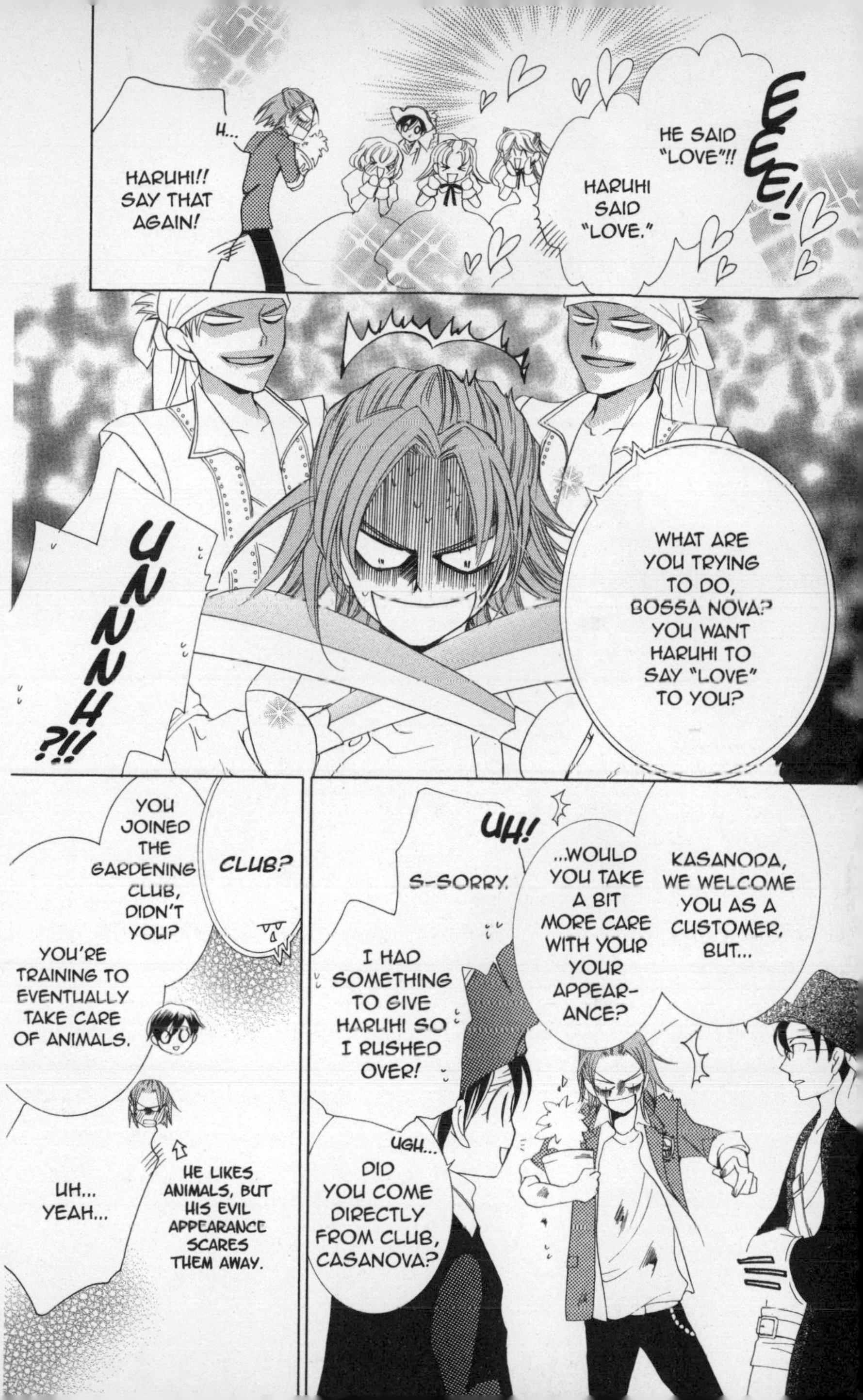

EEEE!
HE SAID "LOVE"!!
HARUHI SAID "LOVE."
H...
HARUHI!! SAY THAT AGAIN!
WHAT ARE YOU TRYING TO DO, BOSSA NOVA? YOU WANT HARUHI TO SAY "LOVE" TO YOU?
UNNNH?!!
KASANODA, WE WELCOME YOU AS A CUSTOMER, BUT...
...WOULD YOU TAKE A BIT MORE CARE WITH YOUR YOUR APPEARANCE?
UH!
S-SORRY.
I HAD SOMETHING TO GIVE HARUHI SO I RUSHED OVER!
UGH...
DID YOU COME DIRECTLY FROM CLUB, CASANOVA?
CLUB?
YOU JOINED THE GARDENING CLUB, DIDN'T YOU?
YOU'RE TRAINING TO EVENTUALLY TAKE CARE OF ANIMALS.
UH... YEAH...
HE LIKES ANIMALS, BUT HIS EVIL APPEARANCE SCARES THEM AWAY.

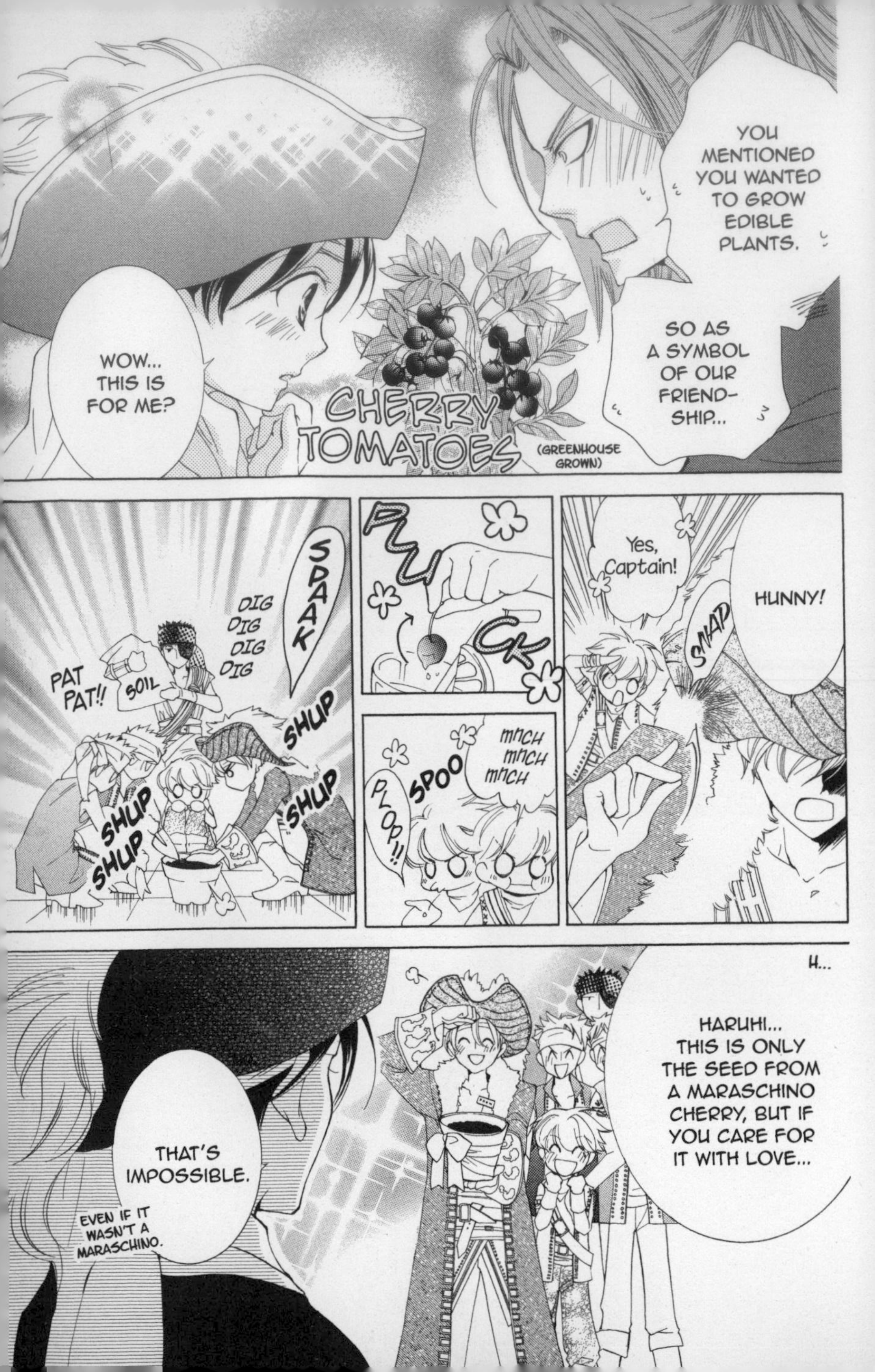
YOU MENTIONED YOU WANTED TO GROW EDIBLE PLANTS.
SO AS A SYMBOL OF OUR FRIEND-SHIP...
CHERRY TOMATOES
(GREENHOUSE GROWN)
WOW... THIS IS FOR ME?
HUNNY!
SNAP
Yes, Captain!
PLUUCK
mnch mnch mnch
SPOO
PLOP!!
SPAAK
DIG DIG DIG DIG
SOIL
PAT PAT!!
SHUP
SHUP
SHUP SHUP
H...
HARUHI... THIS IS ONLY THE SEED FROM A MARASCHINO CHERRY, BUT IF YOU CARE FOR IT WITH LOVE...
THAT'S IMPOSSIBLE.
EVEN IF IT WASN'T A MARASCHINO.

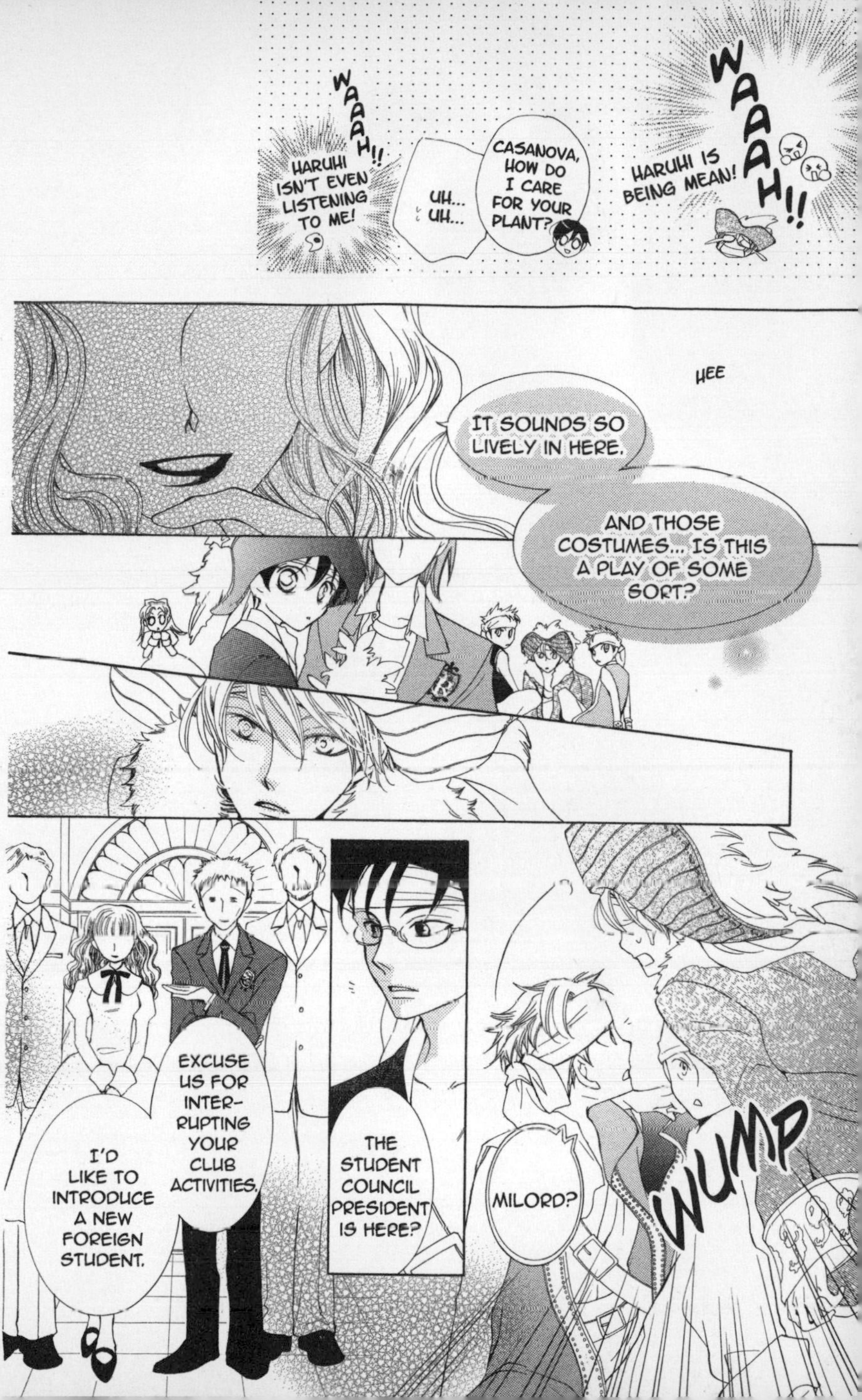
HARUHI IS BEING MEAN!
WAAAH!!
CASANOVA, HOW DO I CARE FOR YOUR PLANT?
UH... UH...
HARUHI ISN'T EVEN LISTENING TO ME!
WAAAH!!
HEE
IT SOUNDS SO LIVELY IN HERE.
AND THOSE COSTUMES... IS THIS A PLAY OF SOME SORT?
WUMP
MILORD?
THE STUDENT COUNCIL PRESIDENT IS HERE?
EXCUSE US FOR INTER-RUPTING YOUR CLUB ACTIVITIES.
I'D LIKE TO INTRODUCE A NEW FOREIGN STUDENT.

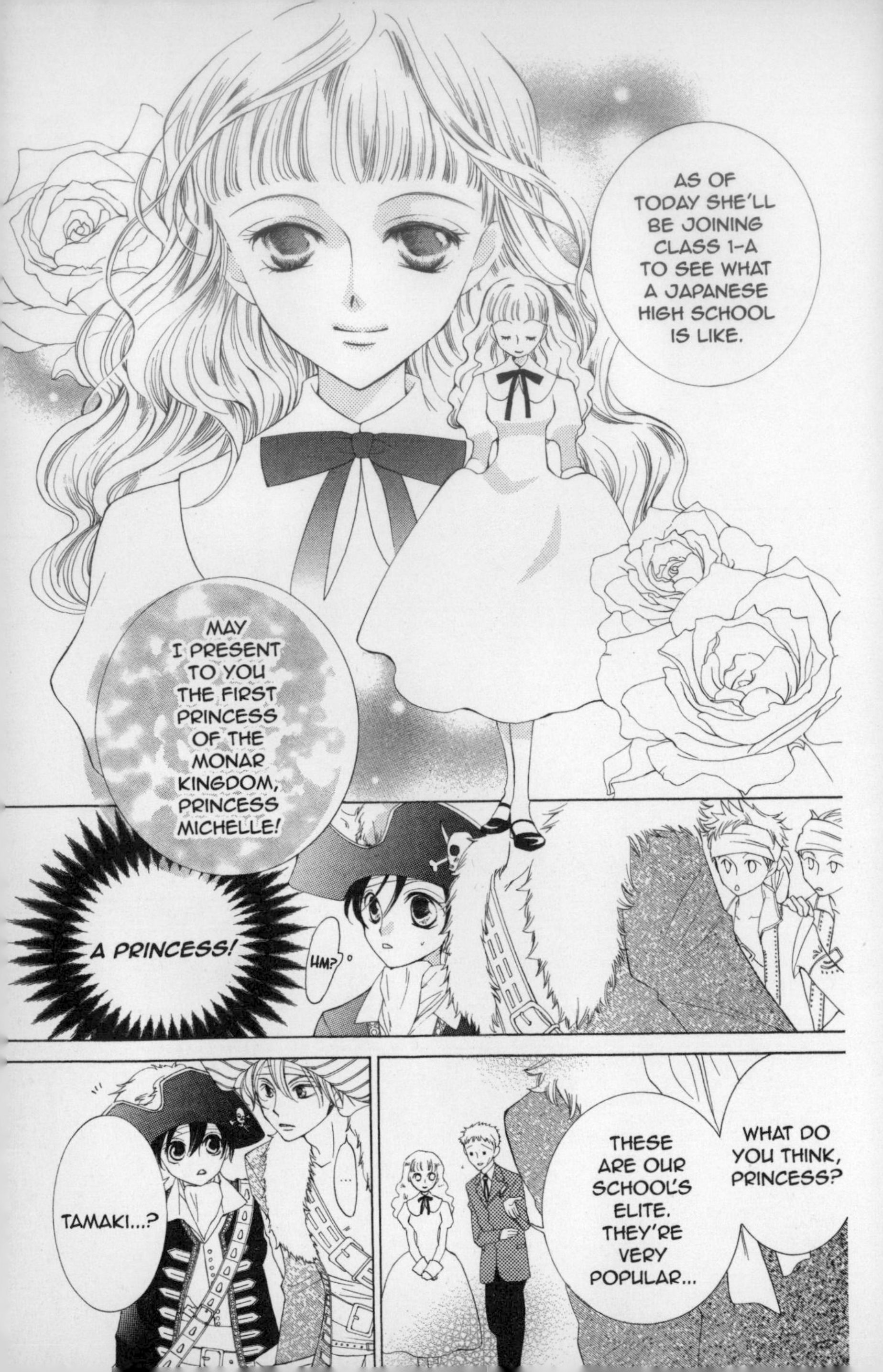
AS OF TODAY SHE'LL BE JOINING CLASS 1-A TO SEE WHAT A JAPANESE HIGH SCHOOL IS LIKE.
MAY I PRESENT TO YOU THE FIRST PRINCESS OF THE MONAR KINGDOM, PRINCESS MICHELLE!
HM?
A PRINCESS!
WHAT DO YOU THINK, PRINCESS?
THESE ARE OUR SCHOOL'S ELITE. THEY'RE VERY POPULAR...
...
TAMAKI...?

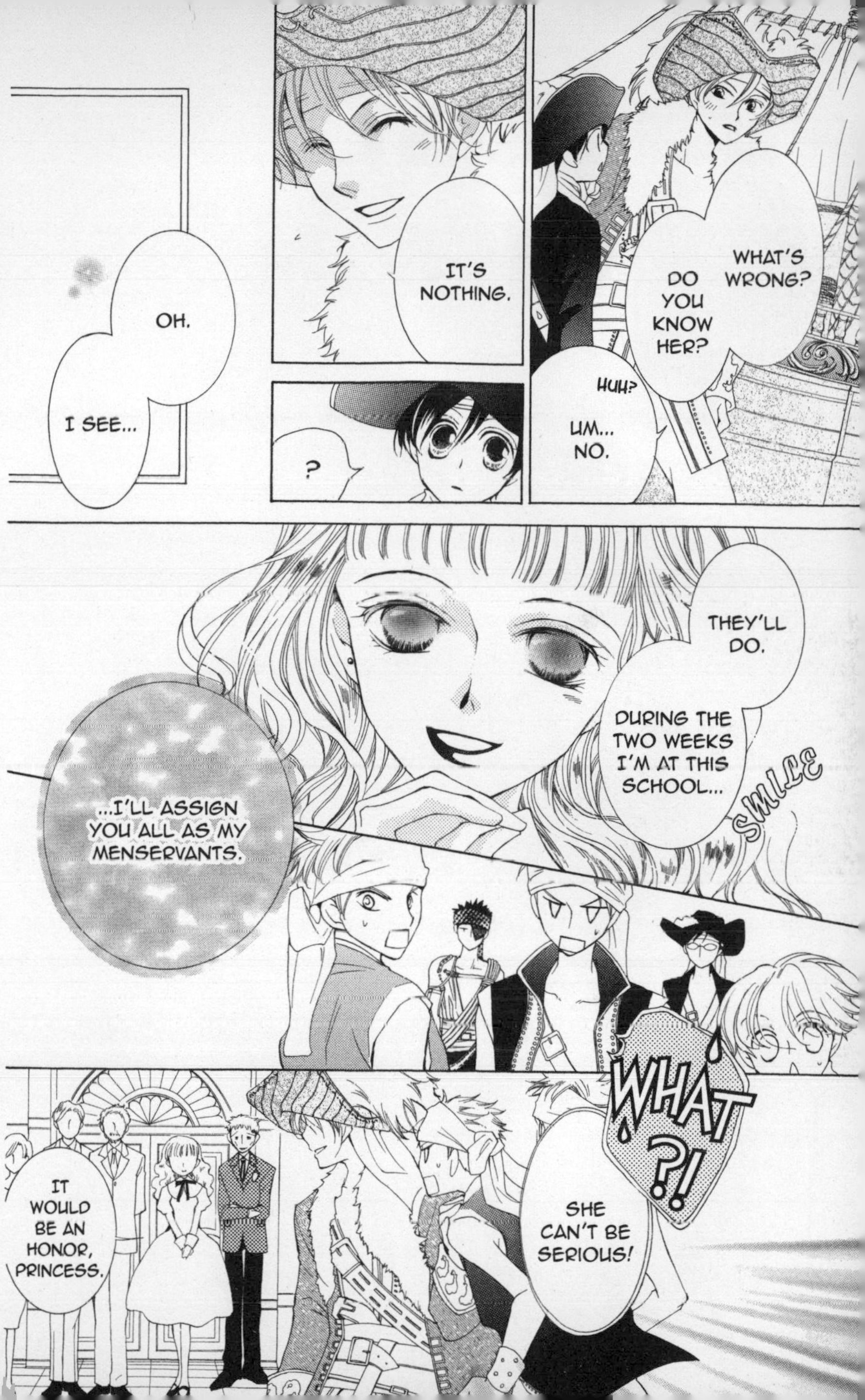
WHAT'S WRONG?
DO YOU KNOW HER?
HUH?
UM... NO.
IT'S NOTHING.
?
OH.
I SEE...
THEY'LL DO.
DURING THE TWO WEEKS I'M AT THIS SCHOOL...
SMILE
...I'LL ASSIGN YOU ALL AS MY MENSERVANTS.
WHAT?!
SHE CAN'T BE SERIOUS!
IT WOULD BE AN HONOR, PRINCESS.

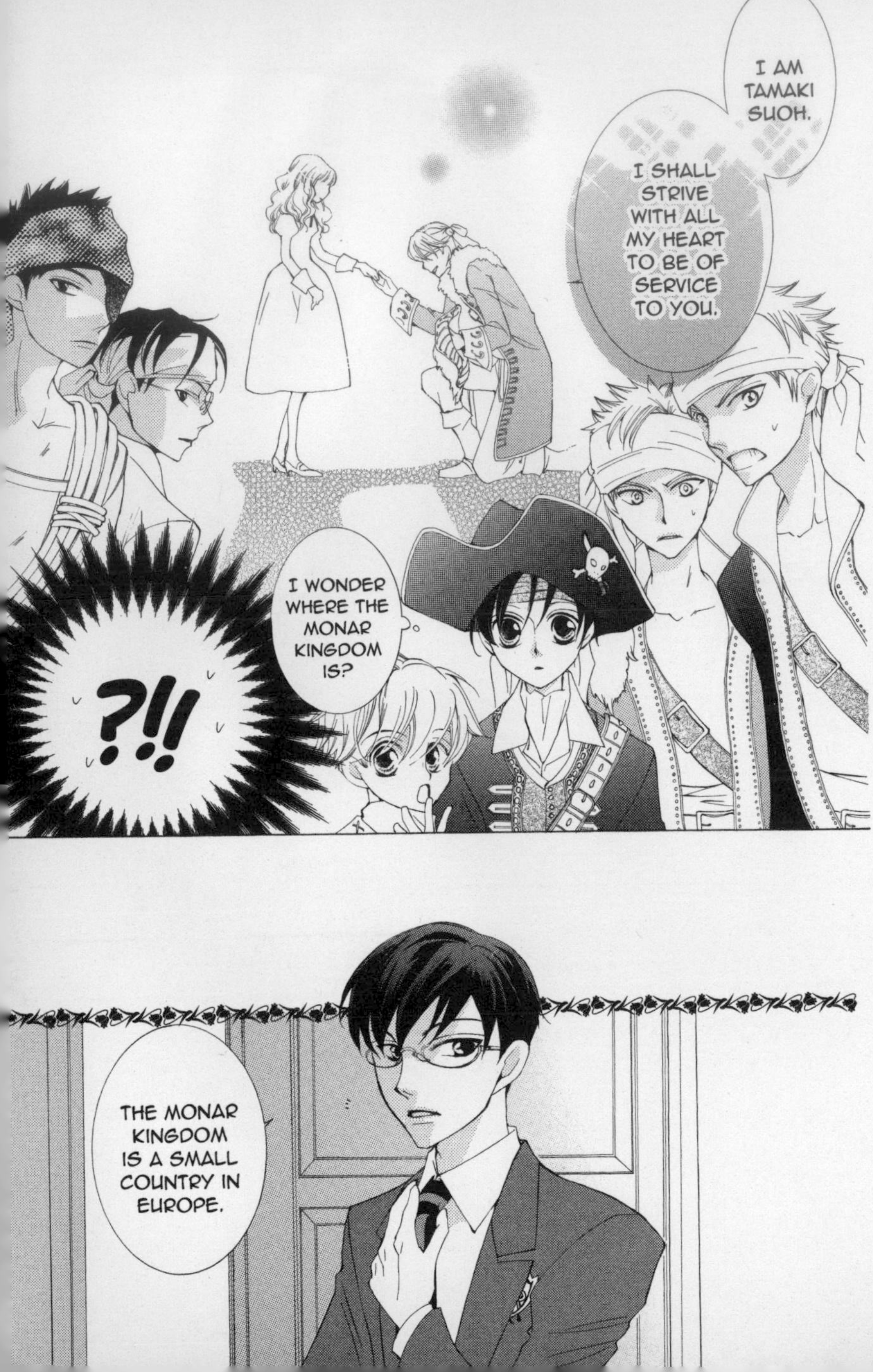
I AM TAMAKI SUOH.
I SHALL STRIVE WITH ALL MY HEART TO BE OF SERVICE TO YOU.
I WONDER WHERE THE MONAR KINGDOM IS?
?!!
THE MONAR KINGDOM IS A SMALL COUNTRY IN EUROPE.

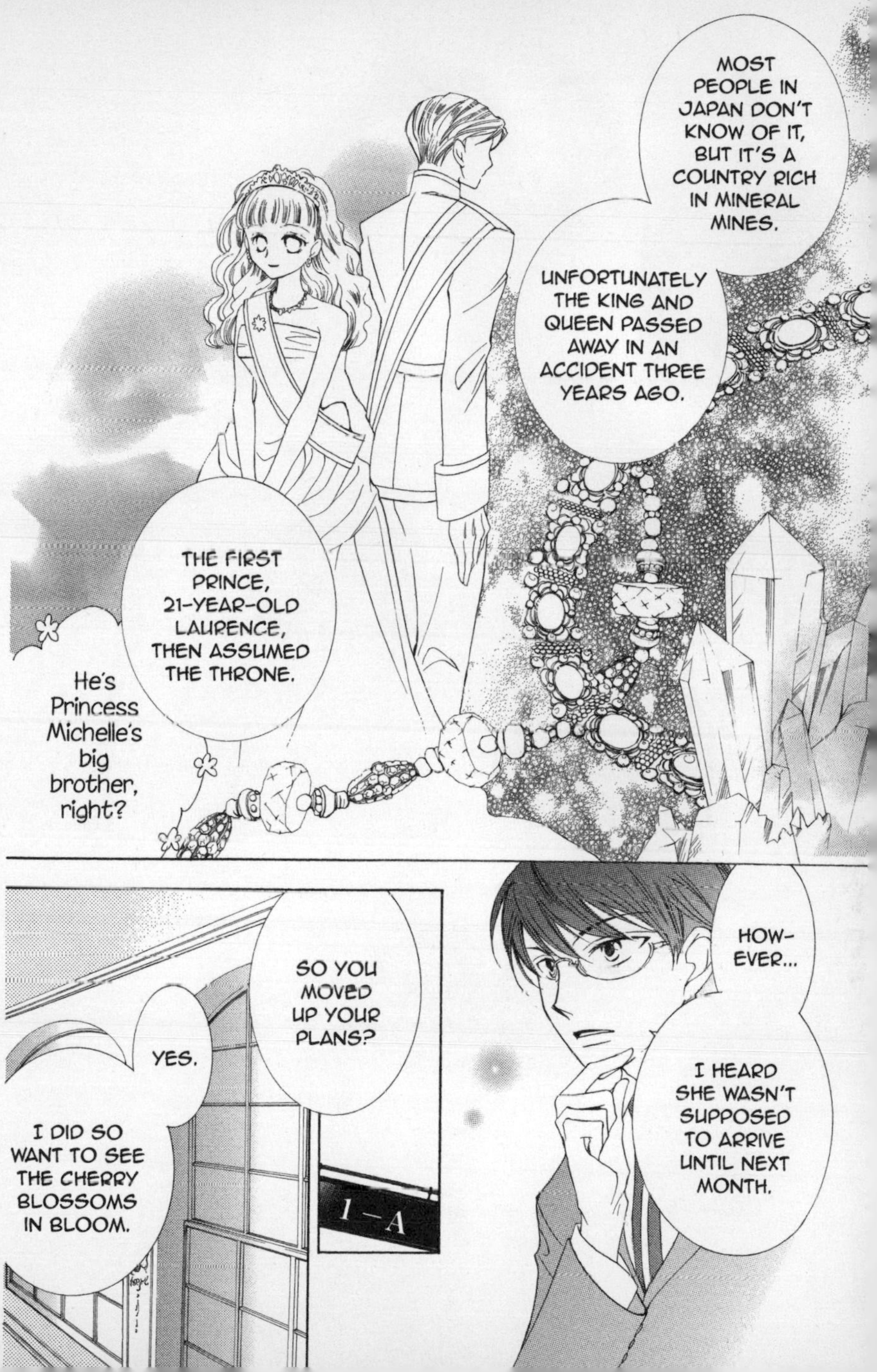
MOST PEOPLE IN JAPAN DON'T KNOW OF IT, BUT IT'S A COUNTRY RICH IN MINERAL MINES.
UNFORTUNATELY THE KING AND QUEEN PASSED AWAY IN AN ACCIDENT THREE YEARS AGO.
THE FIRST PRINCE, 21-YEAR-OLD LAURENCE, THEN ASSUMED THE THRONE.
He's Princess Michelle's big brother, right?
HOW-EVER...
I HEARD SHE WASN'T SUPPOSED TO ARRIVE UNTIL NEXT MONTH.
SO YOU MOVED UP YOUR PLANS?
YES.
I DID SO WANT TO SEE THE CHERRY BLOSSOMS IN BLOOM.
1-A

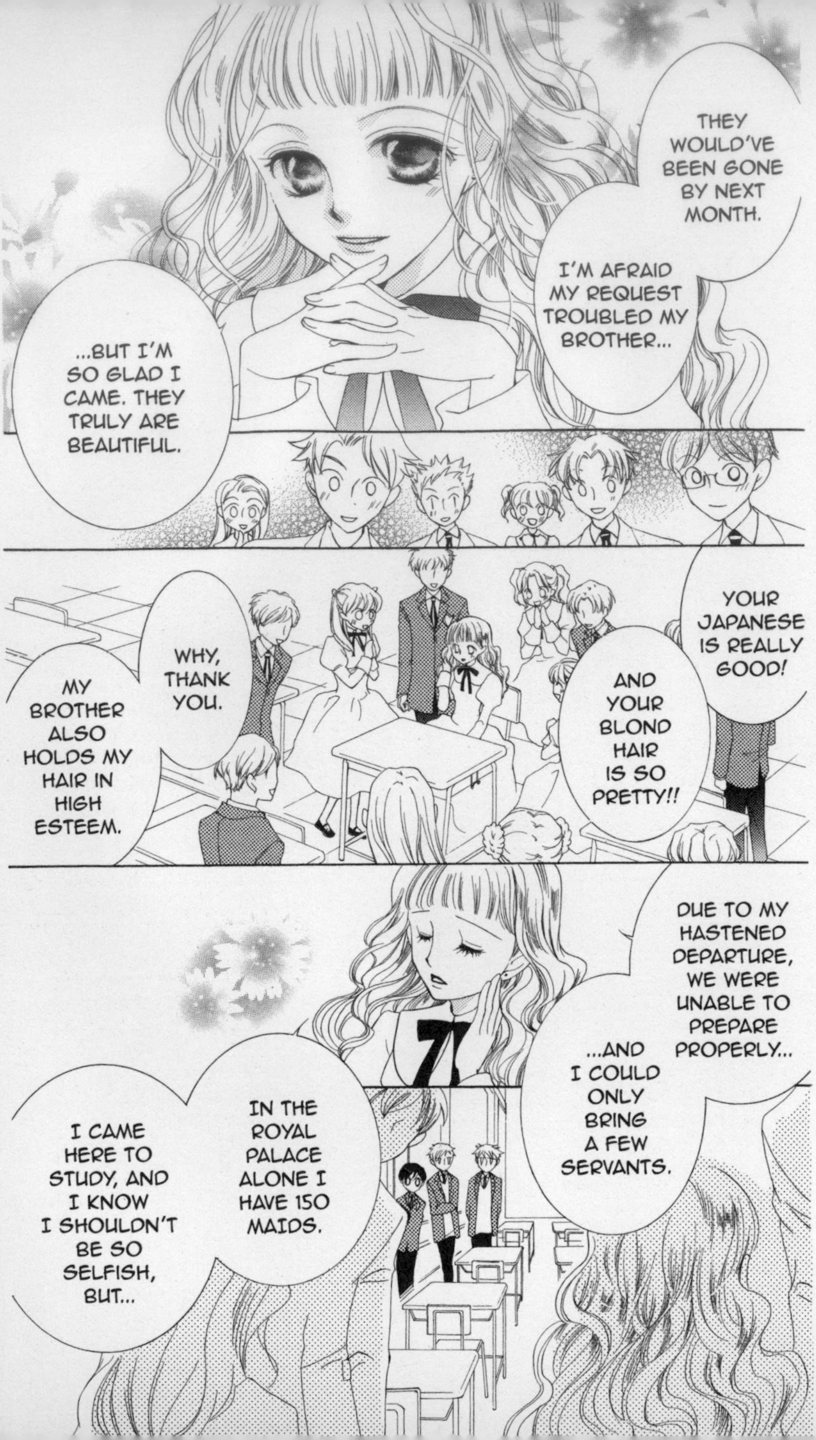
THEY WOULD'VE BEEN GONE BY NEXT MONTH.
I'M AFRAID MY REQUEST TROUBLED MY BROTHER...
...BUT I'M SO GLAD I CAME. THEY TRULY ARE BEAUTIFUL.
YOUR JAPANESE IS REALLY GOOD!
AND YOUR BLOND HAIR IS SO PRETTY!!
WHY, THANK YOU.
MY BROTHER ALSO HOLDS MY HAIR IN HIGH ESTEEM.
DUE TO MY HASTENED DEPARTURE, WE WERE UNABLE TO PREPARE PROPERLY...
...AND I COULD ONLY BRING A FEW SERVANTS.
IN THE ROYAL PALACE ALONE I HAVE 150 MAIDS.
I CAME HERE TO STUDY, AND I KNOW I SHOULDN'T BE SO SELFISH, BUT...

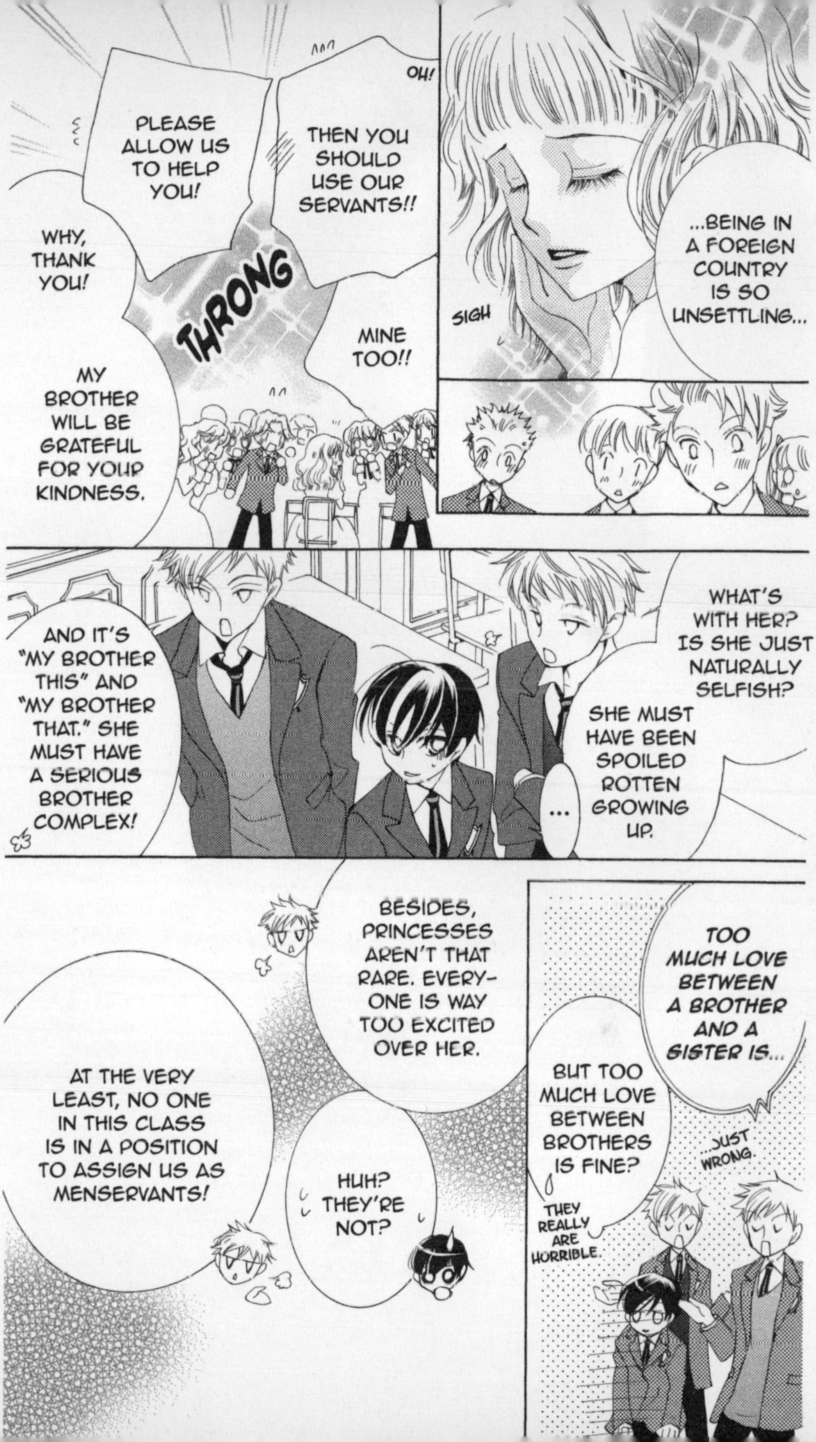
...BEING IN A FOREIGN COUNTRY IS SO UNSETTLING...
SIGH
OH!
THEN YOU SHOULD USE OUR SERVANTS!!
PLEASE ALLOW US TO HELP YOU!
WHY, THANK YOU!
THRONG
MINE TOO!!
MY BROTHER WILL BE GRATEFUL FOR YOUR KINDNESS.
WHAT'S WITH HER? IS SHE JUST NATURALLY SELFISH?
SHE MUST HAVE BEEN SPOILED ROTTEN GROWING UP.
...
AND IT'S "MY BROTHER THIS" AND "MY BROTHER THAT." SHE MUST HAVE A SERIOUS BROTHER COMPLEX!
TOO MUCH LOVE BETWEEN A BROTHER AND A SISTER IS...
...JUST WRONG.
BUT TOO MUCH LOVE BETWEEN BROTHERS IS FINE?
THEY REALLY ARE HORRIBLE.
BESIDES, PRINCESSES AREN'T THAT RARE. EVERY-ONE IS WAY TOO EXCITED OVER HER.
AT THE VERY LEAST, NO ONE IN THIS CLASS IS IN A POSITION TO ASSIGN US AS MENSERVANTS!
HUH? THEY'RE NOT?

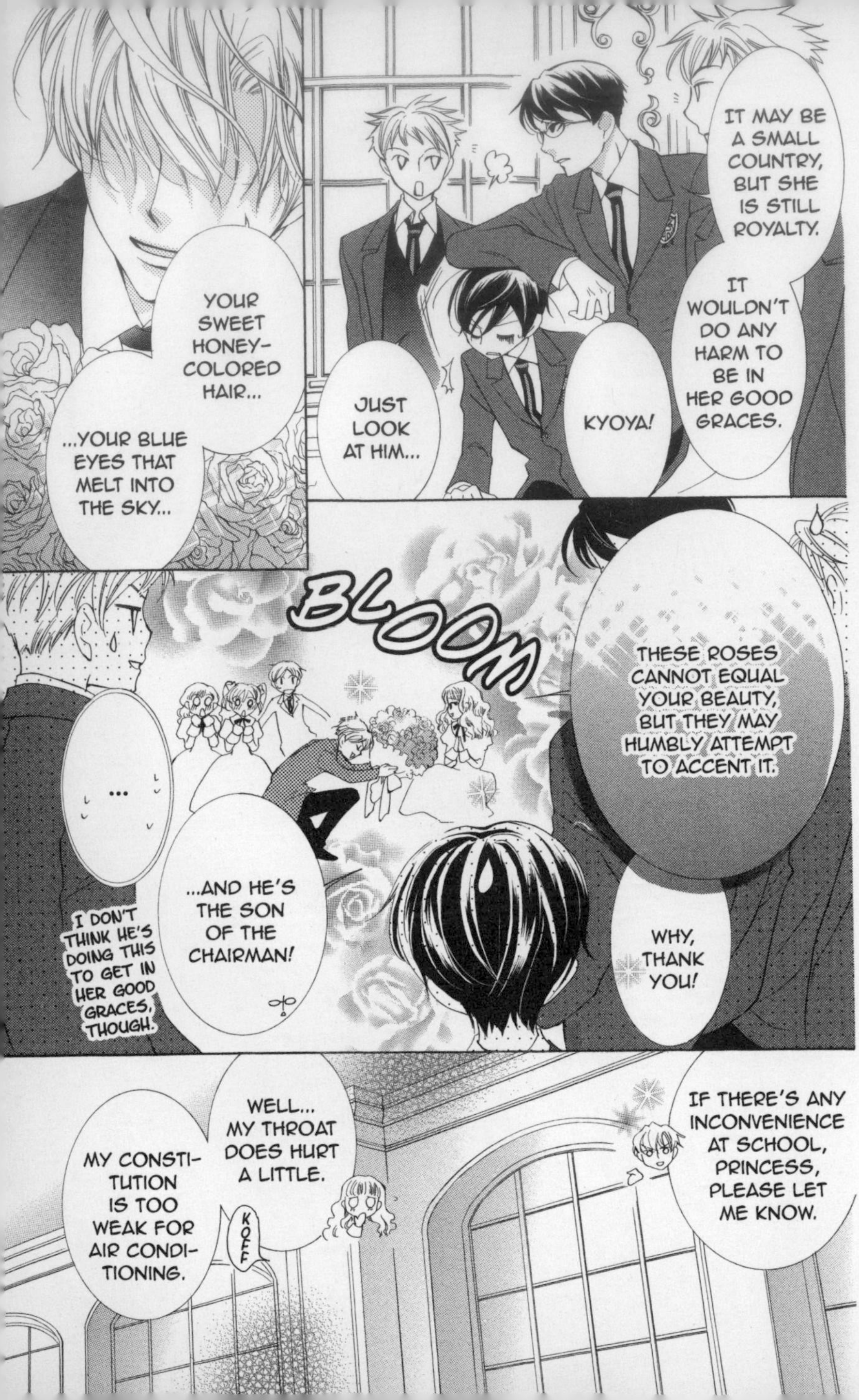
IT MAY BE A SMALL COUNTRY, BUT SHE IS STILL ROYALTY.
IT WOULDN'T DO ANY HARM TO BE IN HER GOOD GRACES.
KYOYA!
JUST LOOK AT HIM...
YOUR SWEET HONEY-COLORED HAIR...
...YOUR BLUE EYES THAT MELT INTO THE SKY...
BLOOM
THESE ROSES CANNOT EQUAL YOUR BEAUTY, BUT THEY MAY HUMBLY ATTEMPT TO ACCENT IT.
WHY, THANK YOU!
...AND HE'S THE SON OF THE CHAIRMAN!
...
I DON'T THINK HE'S DOING THIS TO GET IN HER GOOD GRACES, THOUGH.
IF THERE'S ANY INCONVENIENCE AT SCHOOL, PRINCESS, PLEASE LET ME KNOW.
WELL... MY THROAT DOES HURT A LITTLE.
KOFF
MY CONSTITUTION IS TOO WEAK FOR AIR CONDITIONING.

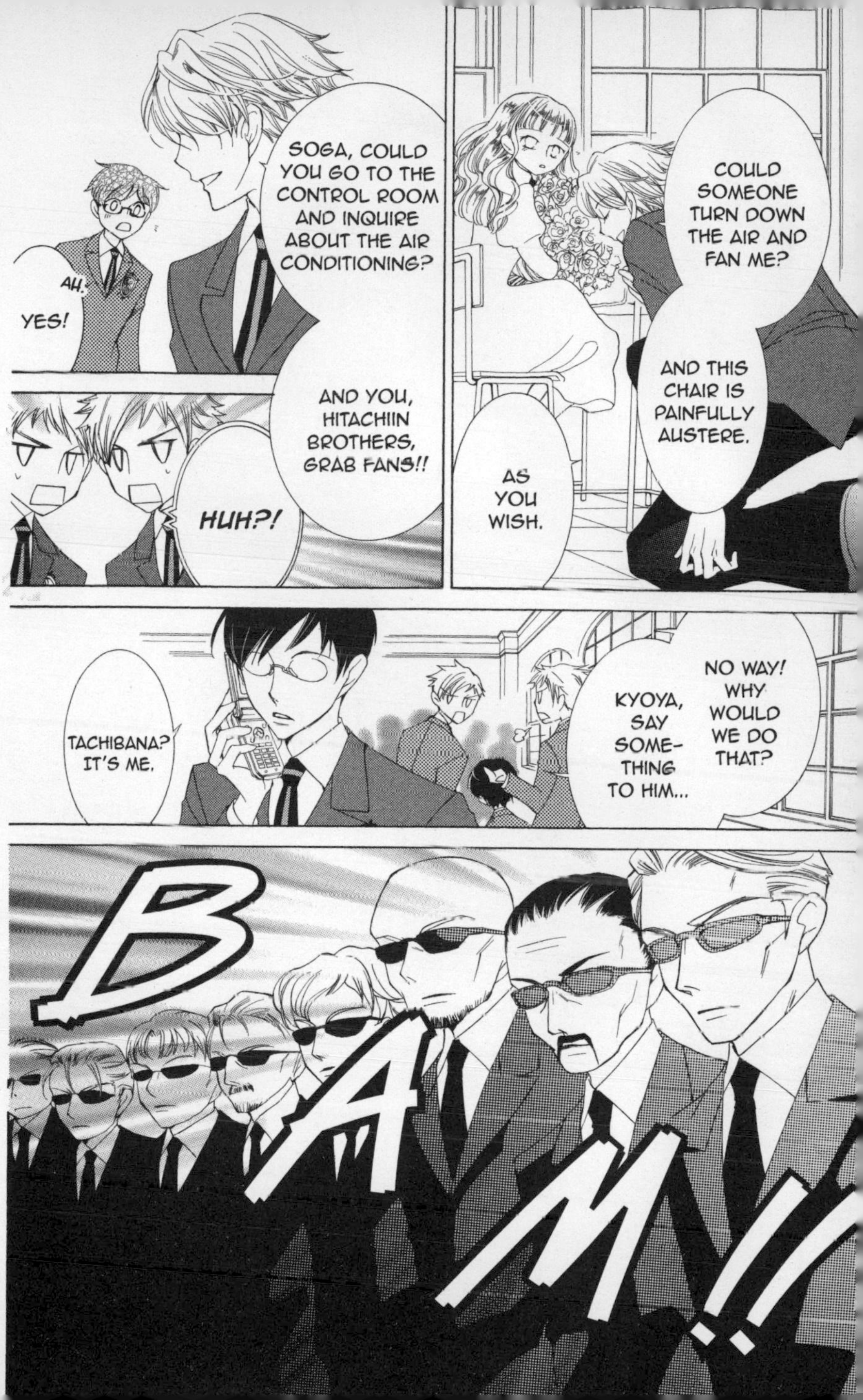
COULD SOMEONE TURN DOWN THE AIR AND FAN ME?
AND THIS CHAIR IS PAINFULLY AUSTERE.
AS YOU WISH.
SOGA, COULD YOU GO TO THE CONTROL ROOM AND INQUIRE ABOUT THE AIR CONDITIONING?
AH.
YES!
AND YOU, HITACHIIN BROTHERS, GRAB FANS!!
HUH?!
NO WAY! WHY WOULD WE DO THAT?
KYOYA, SAY SOME-THING TO HIM...
TACHIBANA? IT'S ME.
BAM!!

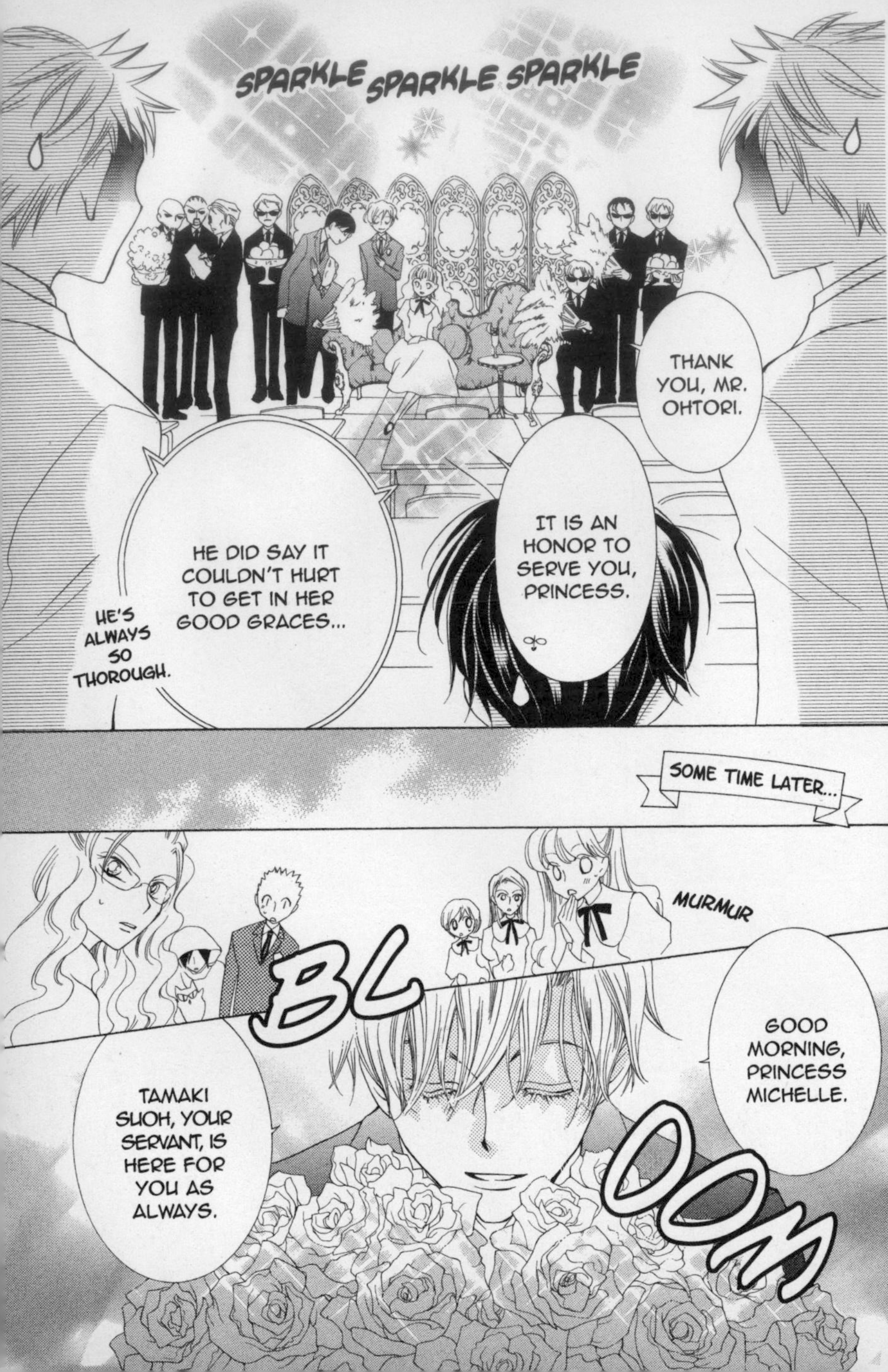
SPARKLE SPARKLE SPARKLE
THANK YOU, MR. OHTORI.
IT IS AN HONOR TO SERVE YOU, PRINCESS.
HE DID SAY IT COULDN'T HURT TO GET IN HER GOOD GRACES...
HE'S ALWAYS SO THOROUGH.
SOME TIME LATER...
MURMUR
GOOD MORNING, PRINCESS MICHELLE.
BL
TAMAKI SUOH, YOUR SERVANT, IS HERE FOR YOU AS ALWAYS.
OOM

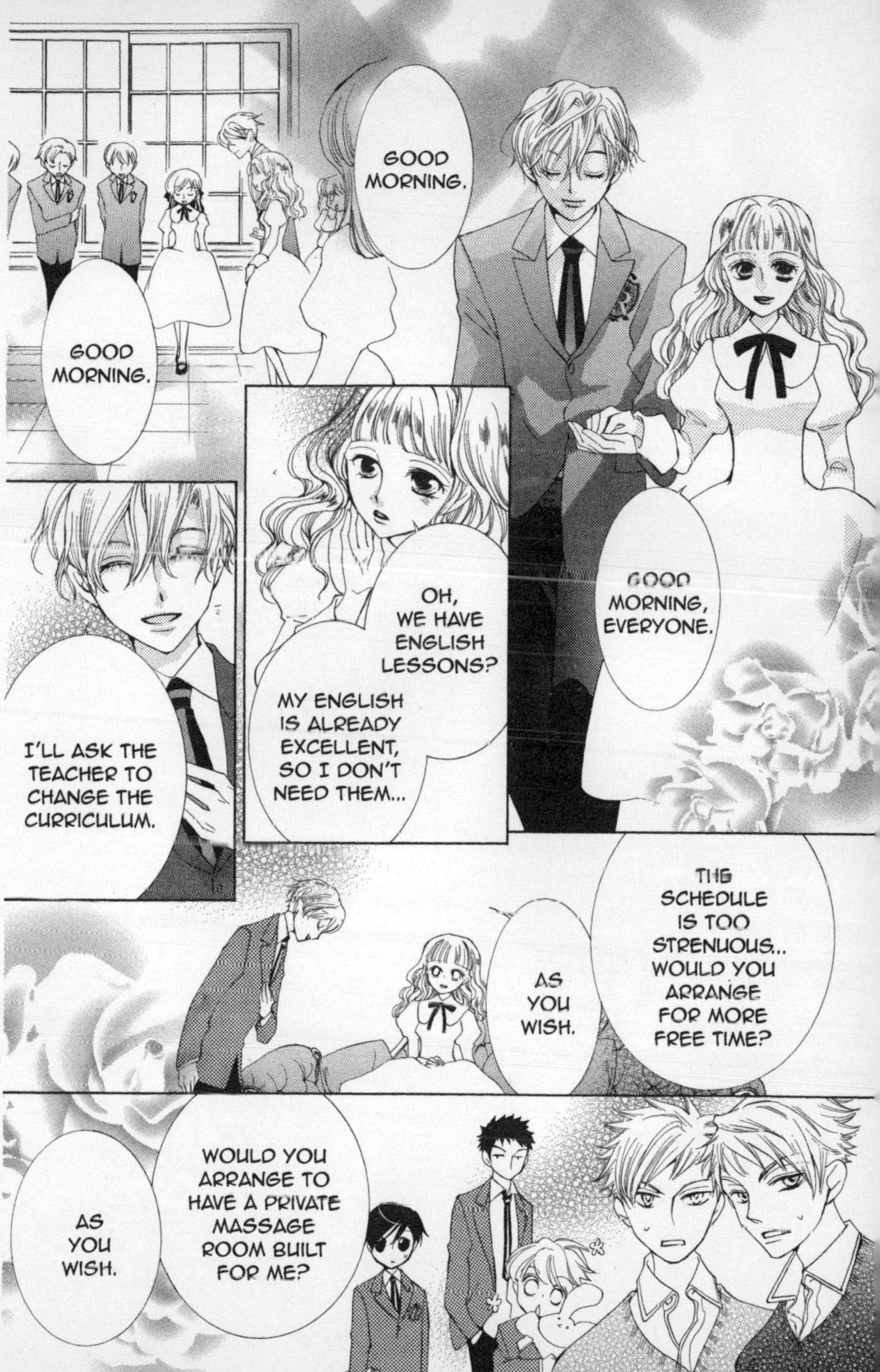
GOOD MORNING.
GOOD MORNING.
GOOD MORNING, EVERYONE.
OH, WE HAVE ENGLISH LESSONS?
MY ENGLISH IS ALREADY EXCELLENT, SO I DON'T NEED THEM...
I'LL ASK THE TEACHER TO CHANGE THE CURRICULUM.
THE SCHEDULE IS TOO STRENUOUS... WOULD YOU ARRANGE FOR MORE FREE TIME?
AS YOU WISH.
WOULD YOU ARRANGE TO HAVE A PRIVATE MASSAGE ROOM BUILT FOR ME?
AS YOU WISH.

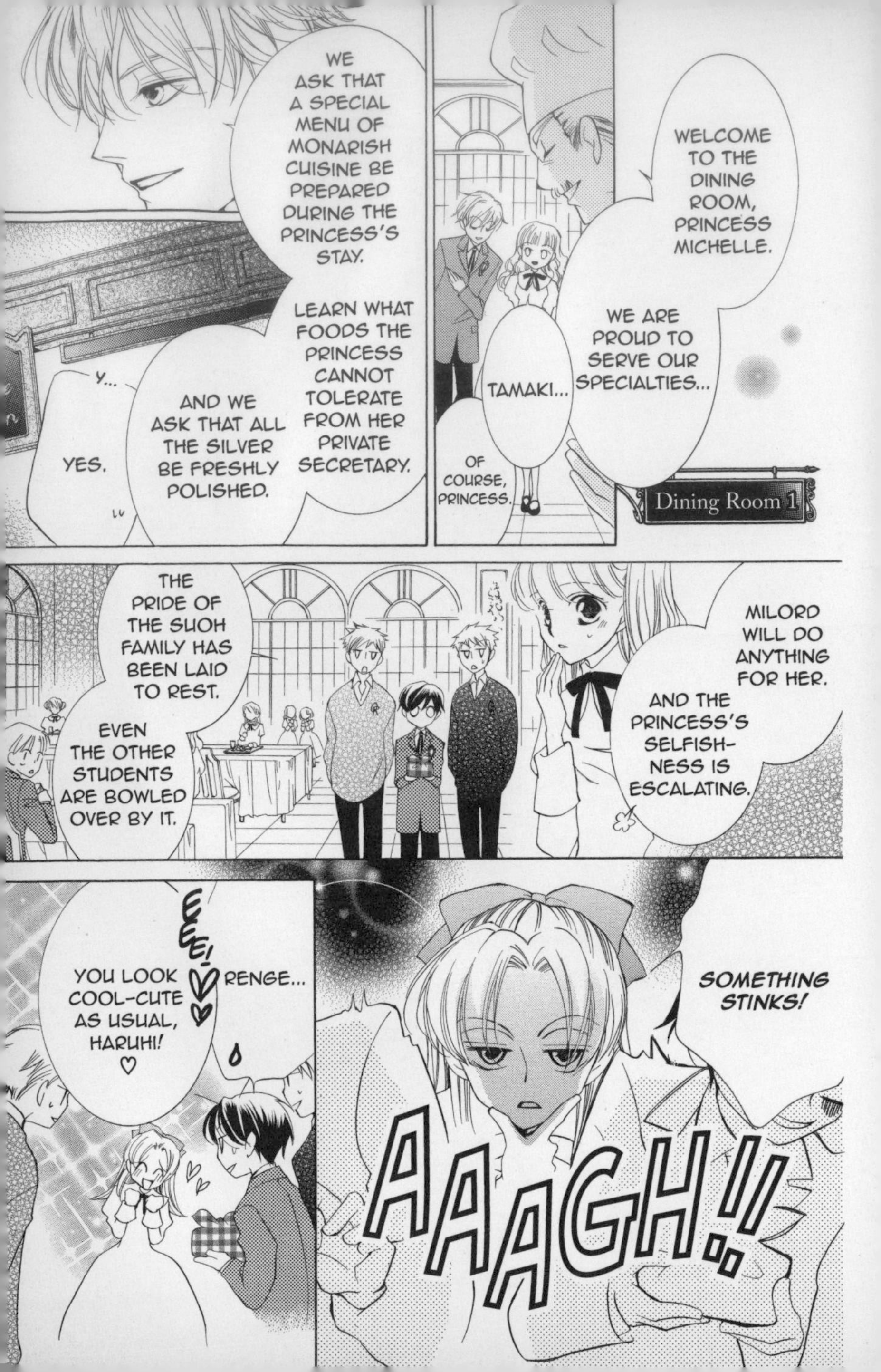
WELCOME TO THE DINING ROOM, PRINCESS MICHELLE.
WE ARE PROUD TO SERVE OUR SPECIALTIES...
TAMAKI...
OF COURSE, PRINCESS.
Dining Room 1
WE ASK THAT A SPECIAL MENU OF MONARISH CUISINE BE PREPARED DURING THE PRINCESS'S STAY.
LEARN WHAT FOODS THE PRINCESS CANNOT TOLERATE FROM HER PRIVATE SECRETARY.
AND WE ASK THAT ALL THE SILVER BE FRESHLY POLISHED.
Y...
YES.
MILORD WILL DO ANYTHING FOR HER.
AND THE PRINCESS'S SELFISH-NESS IS ESCALATING.
THE PRIDE OF THE SUOH FAMILY HAS BEEN LAID TO REST.
EVEN THE OTHER STUDENTS ARE BOWLED OVER BY IT.
SOMETHING STINKS!
AAAGH!!
EEE!
RENGE...
YOU LOOK COOL-CUTE AS USUAL, HARUHI! ♡

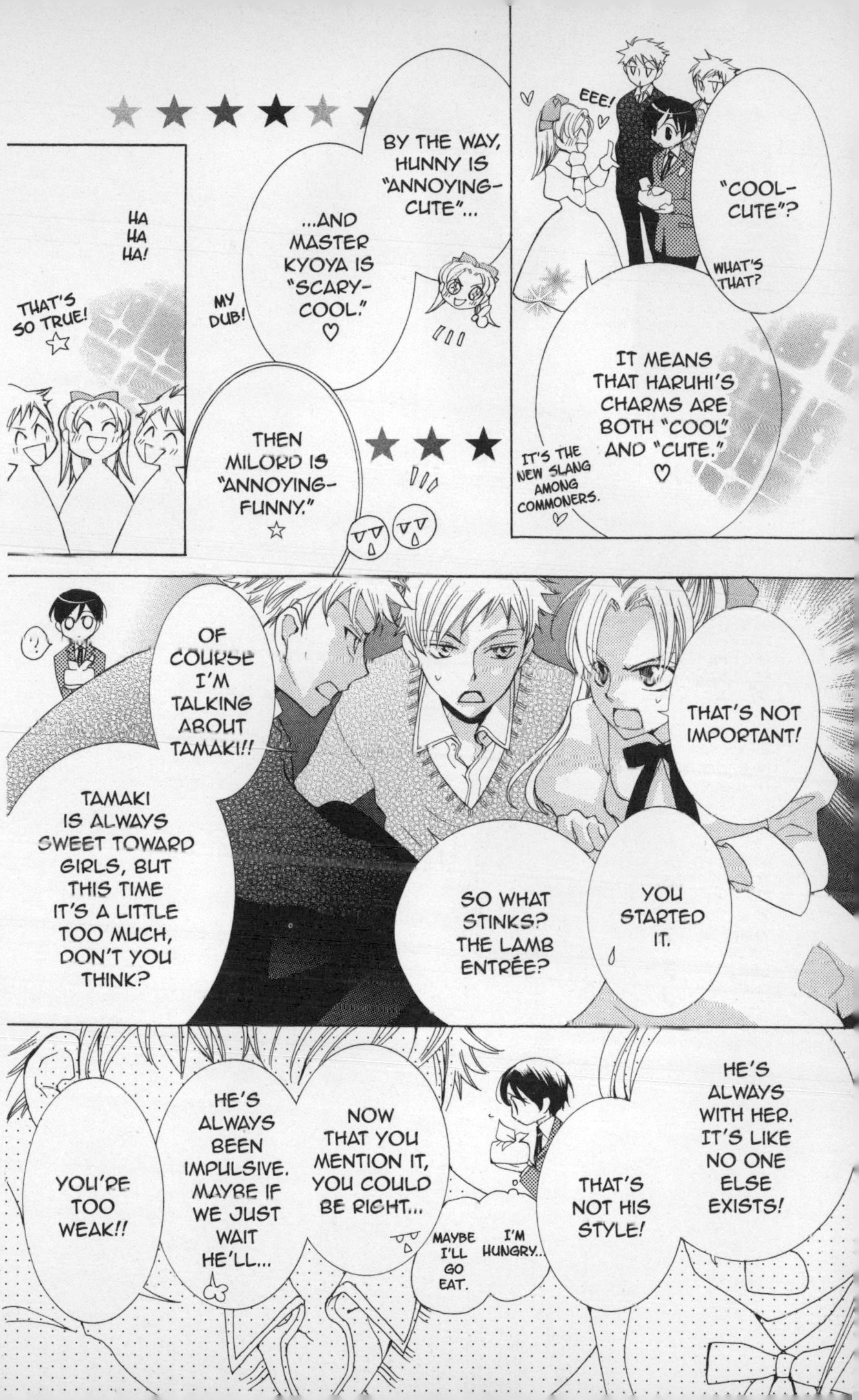
EEE!
"COOL-CUTE"?
WHAT'S THAT?
IT MEANS THAT HARUHI'S CHARMS ARE BOTH "COOL" AND "CUTE." ♡
IT'S THE NEW SLANG AMONG COMMONERS. ♡
BY THE WAY, HUNNY IS "ANNOYING-CUTE"...
...AND MASTER KYOYA IS "SCARY-COOL." ♡
MY DUB!
THEN MILORD IS "ANNOYING-FUNNY." ☆
HA HA HA!
THAT'S SO TRUE! ☆
THAT'S NOT IMPORTANT!
OF COURSE I'M TALKING ABOUT TAMAKI!!
YOU STARTED IT.
SO WHAT STINKS? THE LAMB ENTRÉE?
TAMAKI IS ALWAYS SWEET TOWARD GIRLS, BUT THIS TIME IT'S A LITTLE TOO MUCH, DON'T YOU THINK?
HE'S ALWAYS WITH HER. IT'S LIKE NO ONE ELSE EXISTS!
THAT'S NOT HIS STYLE!
I'M HUNGRY...
MAYBE I'LL GO EAT.
NOW THAT YOU MENTION IT, YOU COULD BE RIGHT...
HE'S ALWAYS BEEN IMPULSIVE. MAYBE IF WE JUST WAIT HE'LL...
YOU'RE TOO WEAK!!

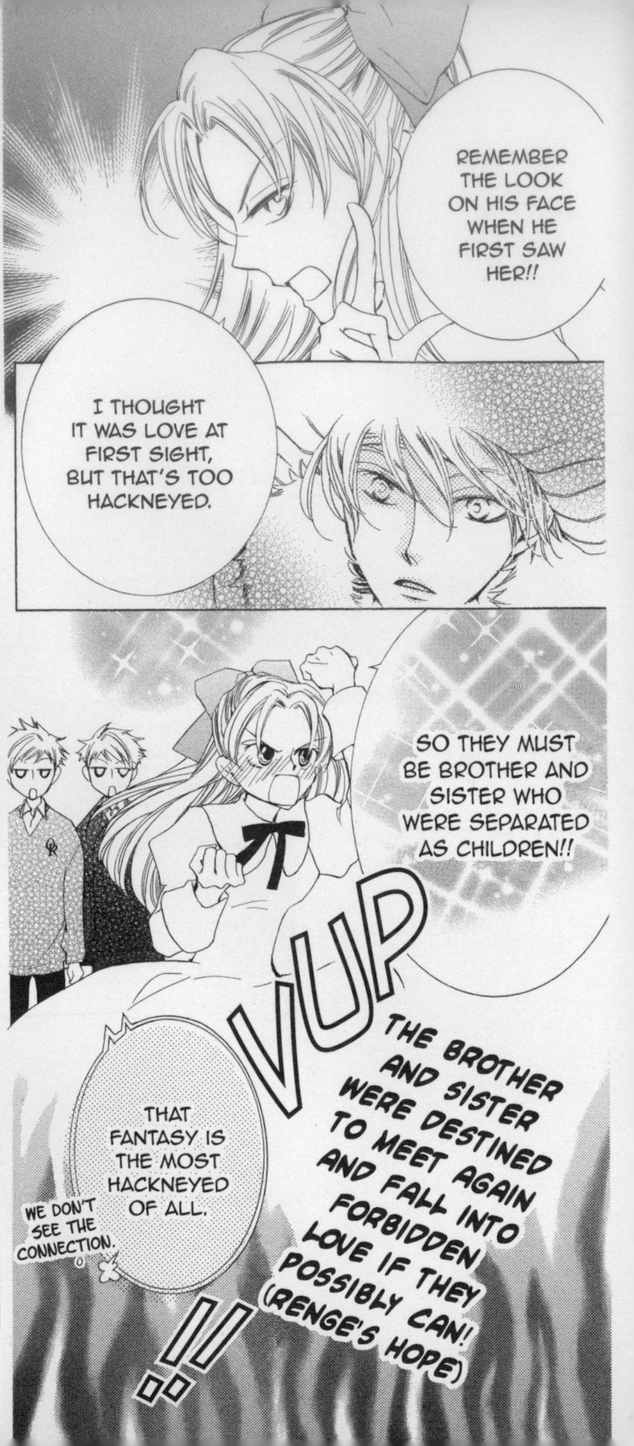
REMEMBER THE LOOK ON HIS FACE WHEN HE FIRST SAW HER!!
I THOUGHT IT WAS LOVE AT FIRST SIGHT, BUT THAT'S TOO HACKNEYED.
SO THEY MUST BE BROTHER AND SISTER WHO WERE SEPARATED AS CHILDREN!!
VUP
THE BROTHER AND SISTER WERE DESTINED TO MEET AGAIN AND FALL INTO FORBIDDEN LOVE IF THEY POSSIBLY CAN! (RENGE'S HOPE)
!!
THAT FANTASY IS THE MOST HACKNEYED OF ALL.
WE DON'T SEE THE CONNECTION.

2

I'M ALWAYS DRAWING *HOST CLUB* WITH GREAT SIGHS AND MOANS, BUT THIS VOLUME WAS A REAL KILLER... THERE HAVE BEEN SO MANY TIMES IN THE PAST WHEN I THOUGHT, "I'M GOING TO MISS THE DEADLINE!!" BUT THIS TIME I REALLY, REALLY THOUGHT I WAS LEARNING WHAT IT MEANS TO BE HOPELESSLY BEHIND. I WAS GOING CRAZY WITH TERROR. AND IT HAPPENS EVERY MONTH!

BUT A MIRACLE HAPPENED. I BEGGED MY MANAGER IN TEARS, SAYING, "THERE'S NO WAY I CAN FINISH ON TIME!" AND ONE POWERFUL HELPER AFTER ANOTHER APPEARED BEFORE ME...

THANK YOU SO MUCH TO ALL MY FRIENDS AT *LALA* WHO TOOK TIME OUT OF THEIR BUSY SCHEDULES TO COME TO MY RESCUE. (THEIR NAMES ARE AT THE END OF THE BOOK!!) AND OF COURSE, THANKS TO ALL THE STAFF WHO SUPPORT ME ALL THE TIME!! AND TO MY DEAR YAMASHII, WHO EXTENDS THE DEADLINE TO THE VERY LIMIT FOR ME EVERY SINGLE TIME... I'M SORRY!

YOUR SUPPORT HELPS ME GET BY! *HOST CLUB* EXISTS BECAUSE OF YOU!!!

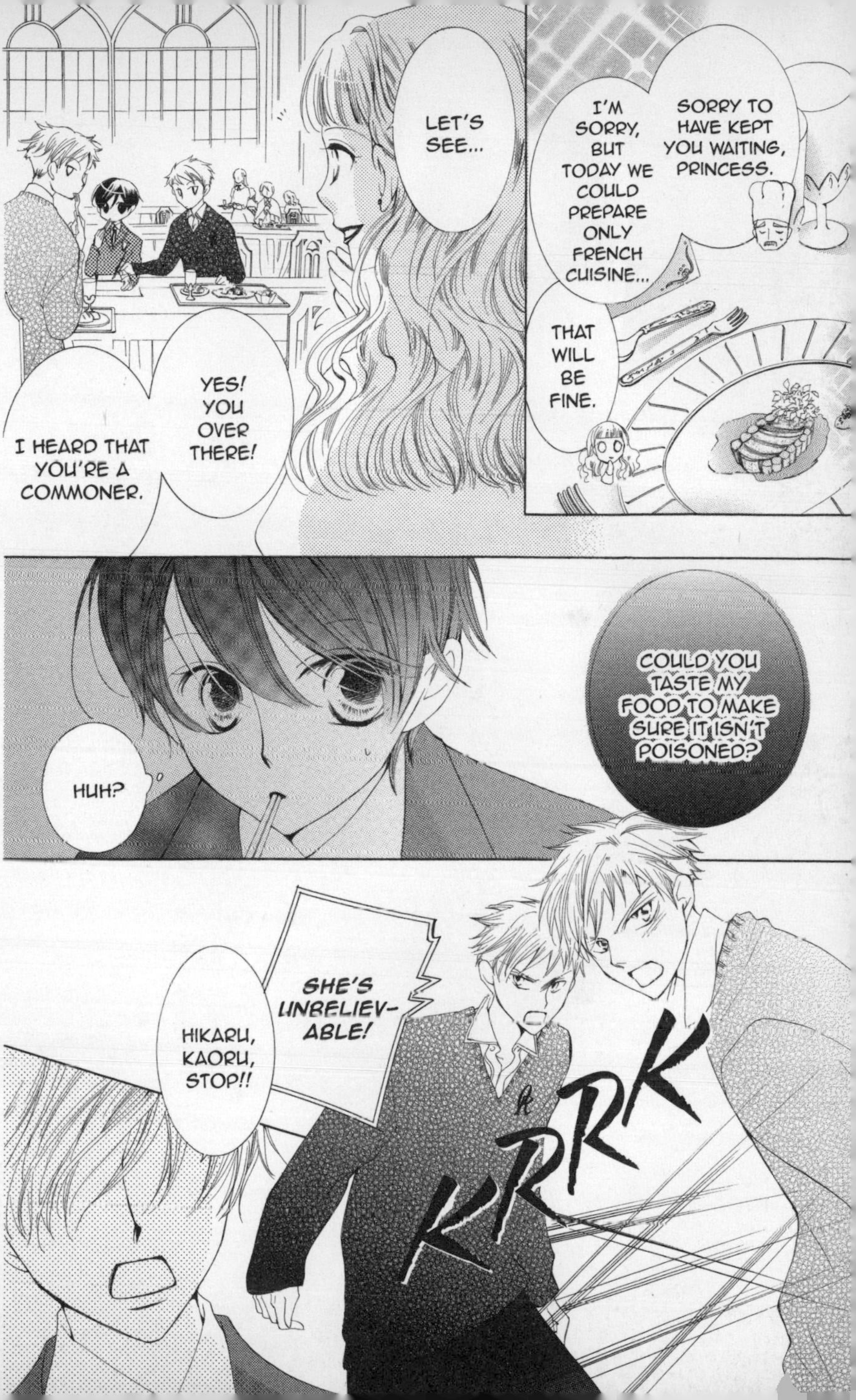
SORRY TO HAVE KEPT YOU WAITING, PRINCESS.
I'M SORRY, BUT TODAY WE COULD PREPARE ONLY FRENCH CUISINE...
THAT WILL BE FINE.
LET'S SEE...
YES! YOU OVER THERE!
I HEARD THAT YOU'RE A COMMONER.
COULD YOU TASTE MY FOOD TO MAKE SURE IT ISN'T POISONED?
HUH?
KRRK
SHE'S UNBELIEV-ABLE!
HIKARU, KAORU, STOP!!

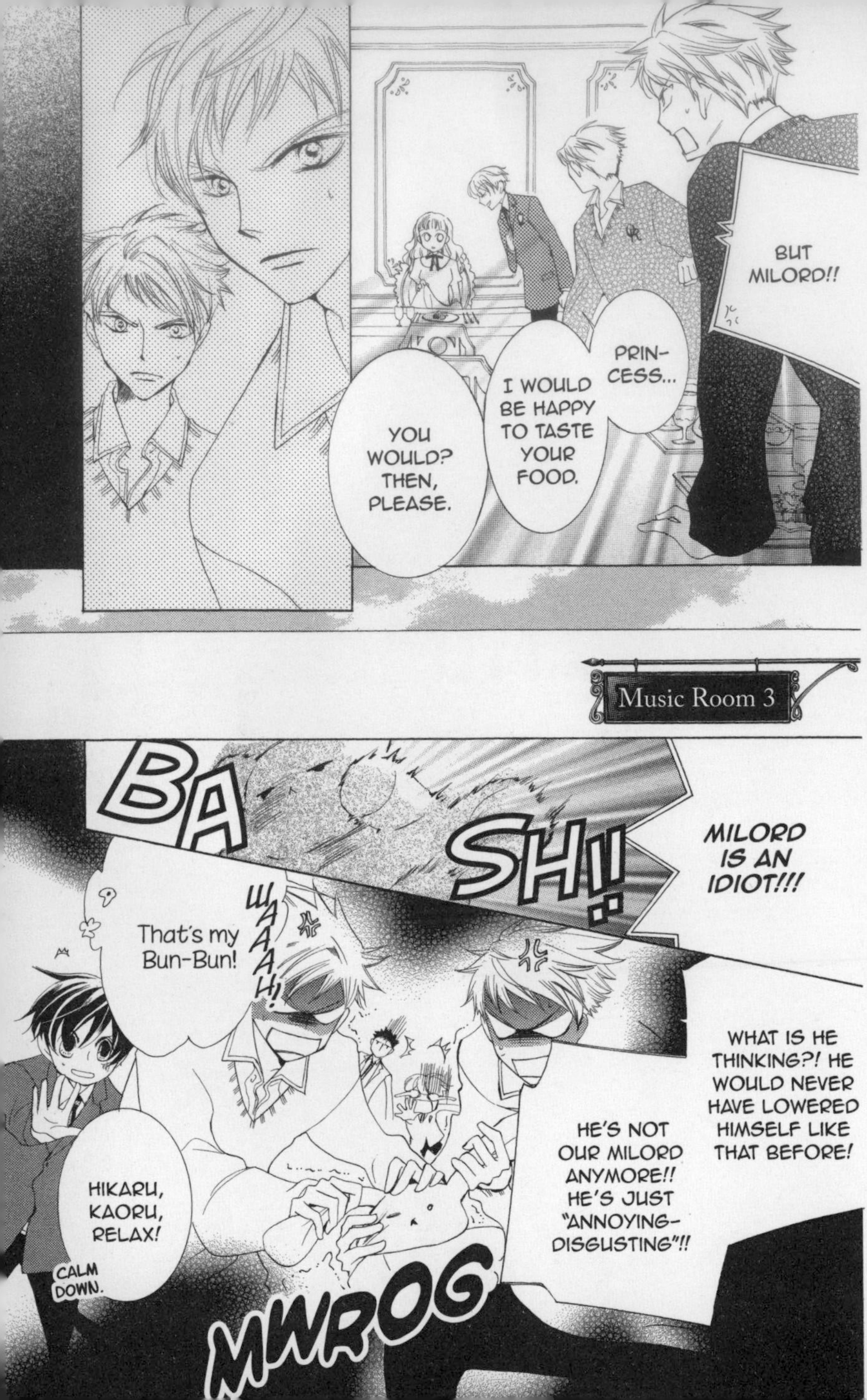
BUT MILORD!!
PRINCESS... I WOULD BE HAPPY TO TASTE YOUR FOOD.
YOU WOULD? THEN, PLEASE.
Music Room 3
BASH!!
MILORD IS AN IDIOT!!!
WHAT IS HE THINKING?! HE WOULD NEVER HAVE LOWERED HIMSELF LIKE THAT BEFORE!
HE'S NOT OUR MILORD ANYMORE!! HE'S JUST "ANNOYING-DISGUSTING"!!
WAAAAH!
That's my Bun-Bun!
HIKARU, KAORU, RELAX!
CALM DOWN.
MWROG

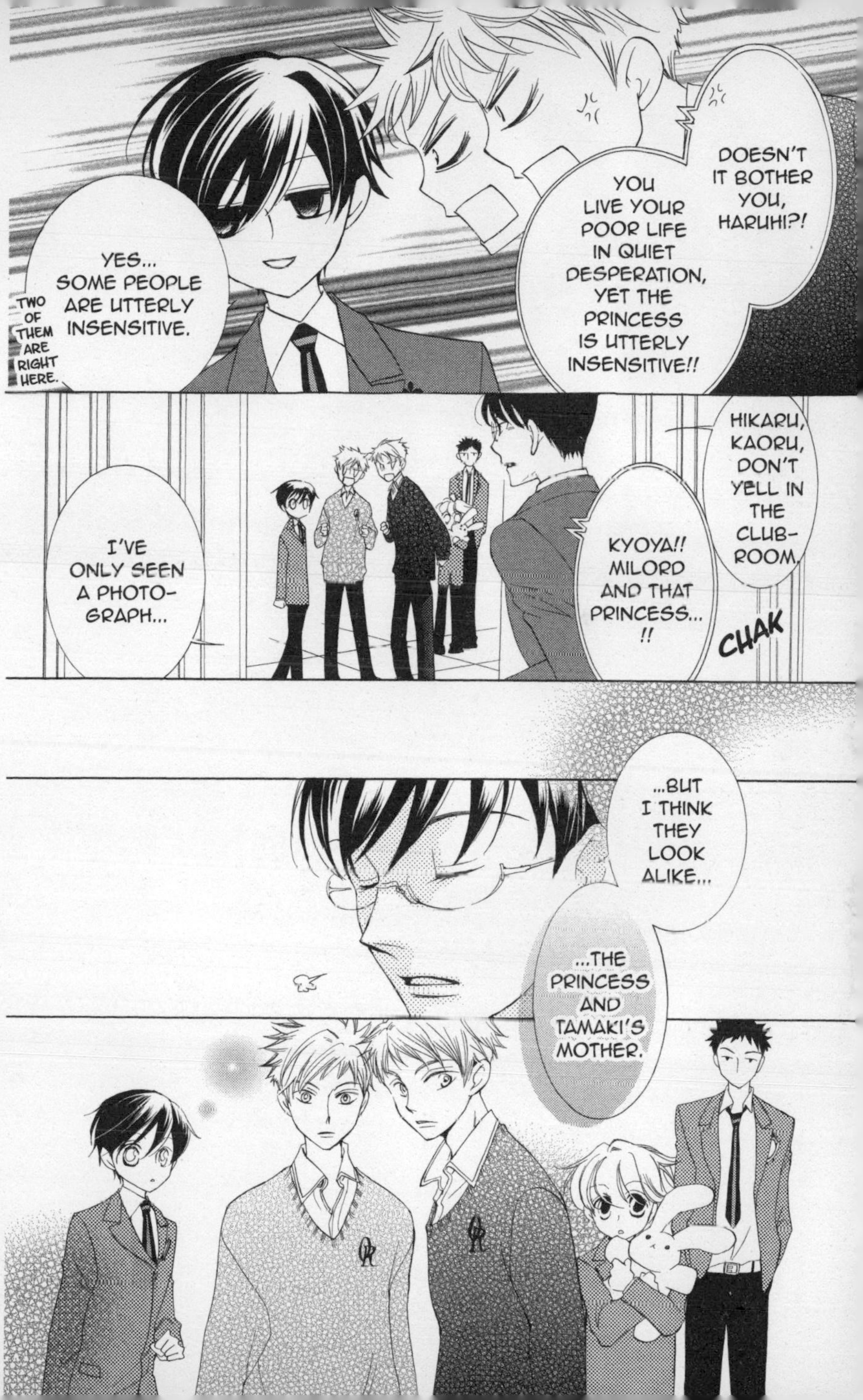

DOESN'T IT BOTHER YOU, HARUHI?!
YOU LIVE YOUR POOR LIFE IN QUIET DESPERATION, YET THE PRINCESS IS UTTERLY INSENSITIVE!!
YES... SOME PEOPLE ARE UTTERLY INSENSITIVE.
TWO OF THEM ARE RIGHT HERE.
HIKARU, KAORU, DON'T YELL IN THE CLUB-ROOM.
CHAK
KYOYA!! MILORD AND THAT PRINCESS... !!
I'VE ONLY SEEN A PHOTO-GRAPH...
...BUT I THINK THEY LOOK ALIKE...
...THE PRINCESS AND TAMAKI'S MOTHER.

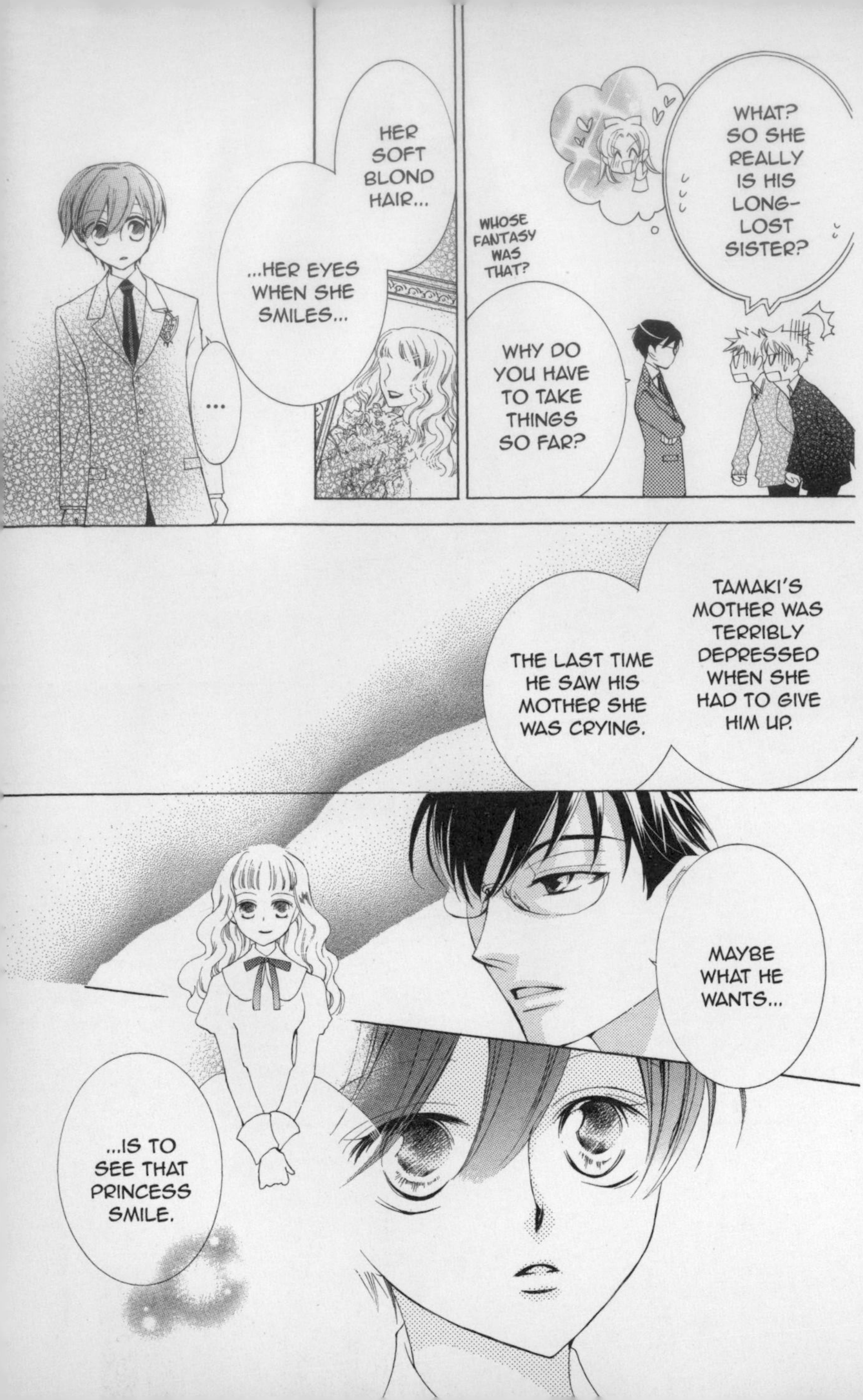
WHAT? SO SHE REALLY IS HIS LONG-LOST SISTER?
WHOSE FANTASY WAS THAT?
WHY DO YOU HAVE TO TAKE THINGS SO FAR?
HER SOFT BLOND HAIR...
...HER EYES WHEN SHE SMILES...
...
TAMAKI'S MOTHER WAS TERRIBLY DEPRESSED WHEN SHE HAD TO GIVE HIM UP.
THE LAST TIME HE SAW HIS MOTHER SHE WAS CRYING.
MAYBE WHAT HE WANTS...
...IS TO SEE THAT PRINCESS SMILE.

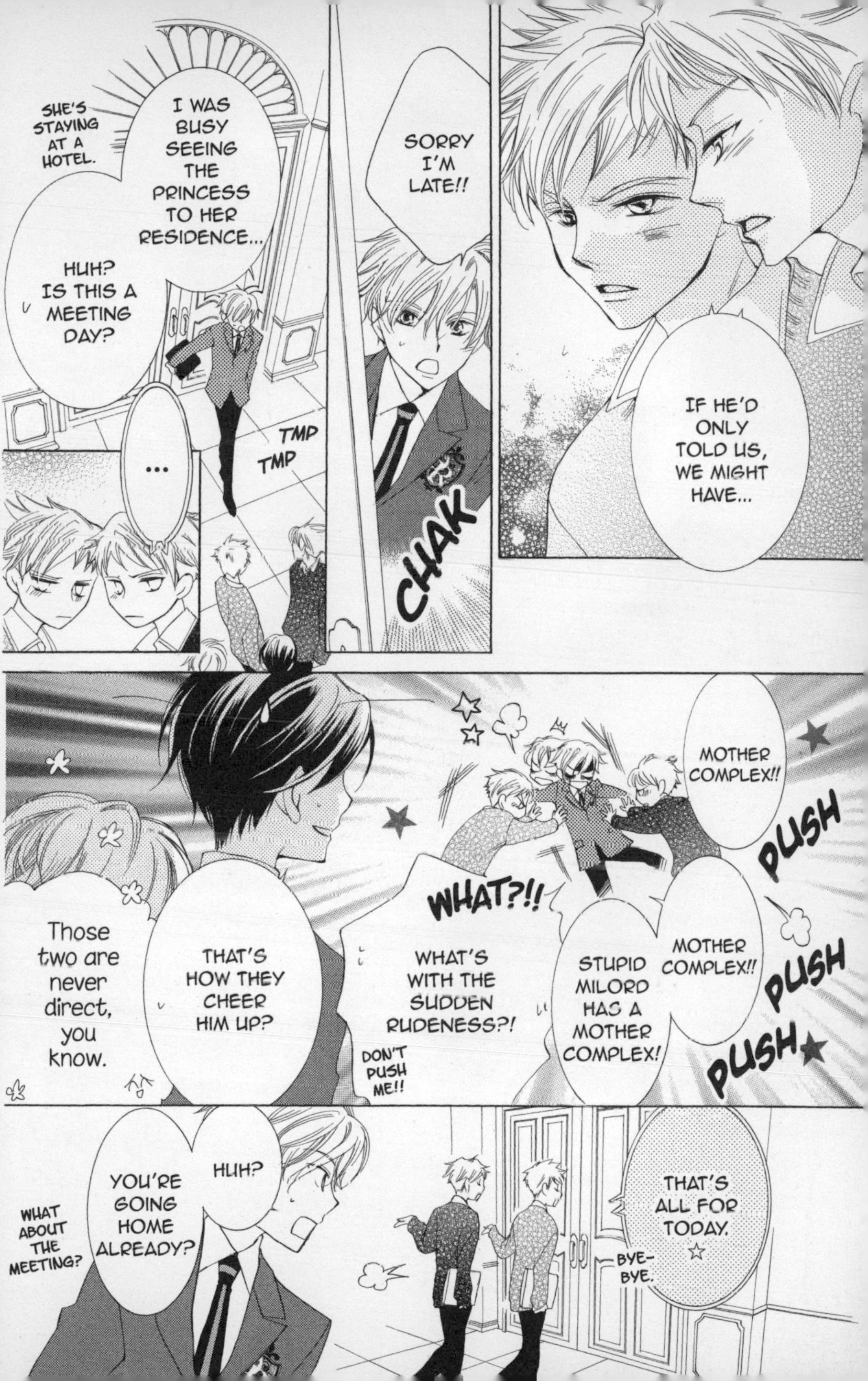
IF HE'D ONLY TOLD US, WE MIGHT HAVE...
SORRY I'M LATE!!
CHAK
I WAS BUSY SEEING THE PRINCESS TO HER RESIDENCE...
SHE'S STAYING AT A HOTEL.
HUH? IS THIS A MEETING DAY?
TMP
TMP
...
MOTHER COMPLEX!!
PUSH
MOTHER COMPLEX!!
STUPID MILORD HAS A MOTHER COMPLEX!
PUSH
PUSH
WHAT?!!
WHAT'S WITH THE SUDDEN RUDENESS?!
DON'T PUSH ME!!
THAT'S HOW THEY CHEER HIM UP?
Those two are never direct, you know.
THAT'S ALL FOR TODAY.
BYE-BYE.
HUH?
YOU'RE GOING HOME ALREADY?
WHAT ABOUT THE MEETING?

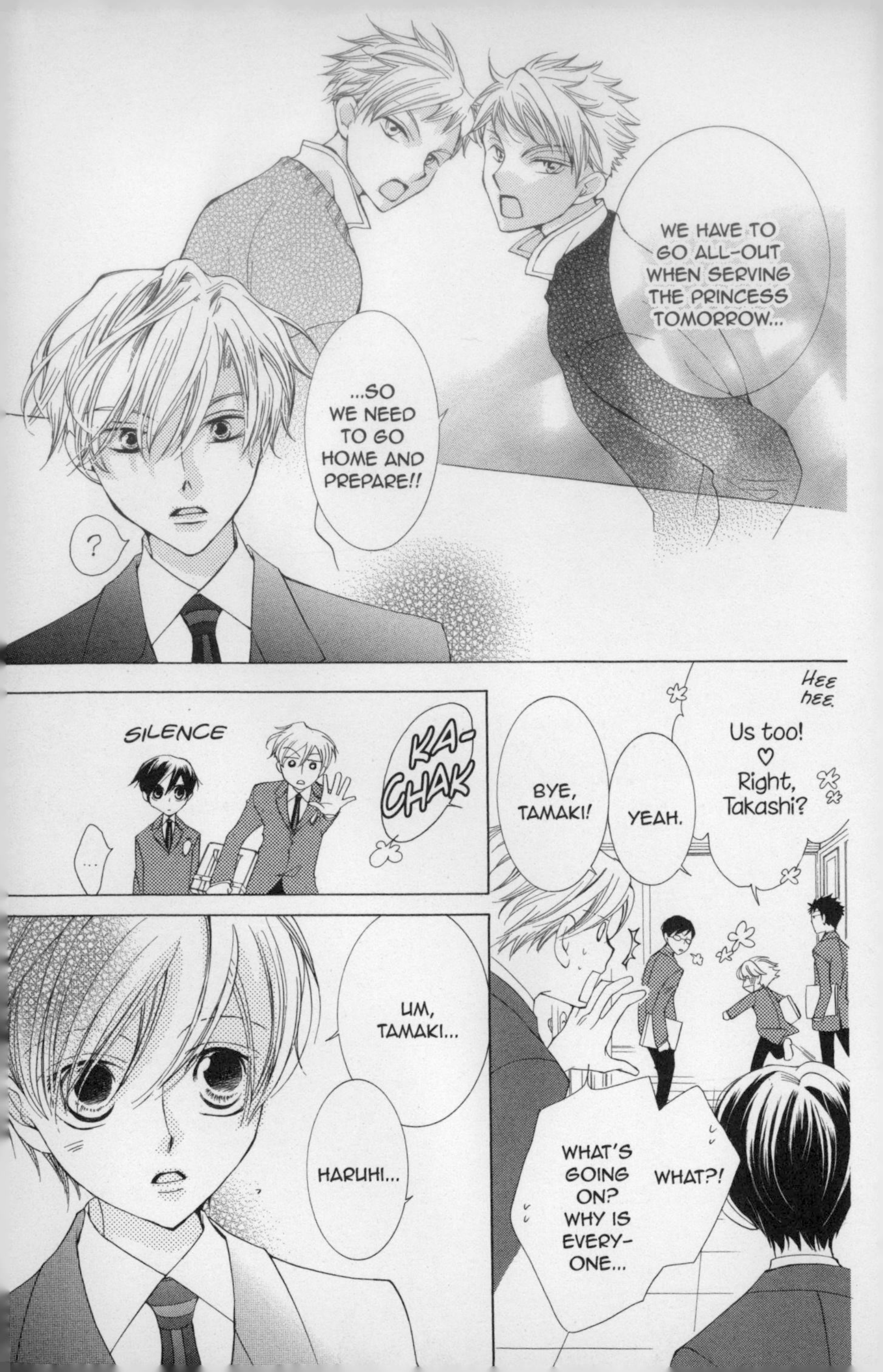
WE HAVE TO GO ALL-OUT WHEN SERVING THE PRINCESS TOMORROW...
...SO WE NEED TO GO HOME AND PREPARE!!
?
HEE HEE.
Us too! ♡ Right, Takashi?
YEAH.
BYE, TAMAKI!
WHAT?!
WHAT'S GOING ON? WHY IS EVERY-ONE...
KA-CHAK
SILENCE
...
UM, TAMAKI...
HARUHI...

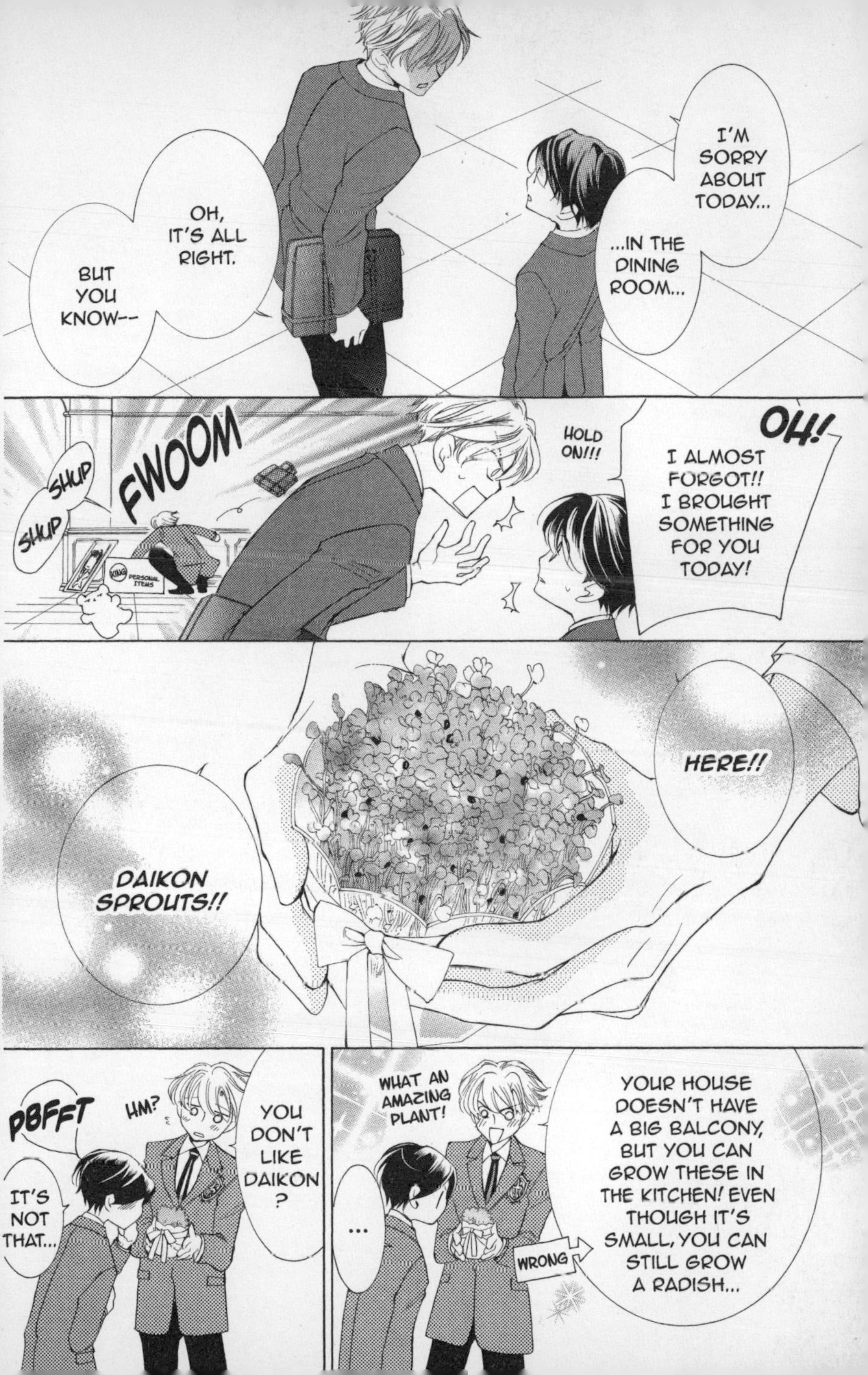
I'M SORRY ABOUT TODAY...
...IN THE DINING ROOM...
OH, IT'S ALL RIGHT.
BUT YOU KNOW--
OH! I ALMOST FORGOT!! I BROUGHT SOMETHING FOR YOU TODAY!
HOLD ON!!!
FWOOM
KING
PERSONAL ITEMS
SHUP
SHUP
HERE!!
DAIKON SPROUTS!!
YOUR HOUSE DOESN'T HAVE A BIG BALCONY, BUT YOU CAN GROW THESE IN THE KITCHEN! EVEN THOUGH IT'S SMALL, YOU CAN STILL GROW A RADISH...
WHAT AN AMAZING PLANT!
WRONG
...
YOU DON'T LIKE DAIKON?
HM?
PBFFT
IT'S NOT THAT...

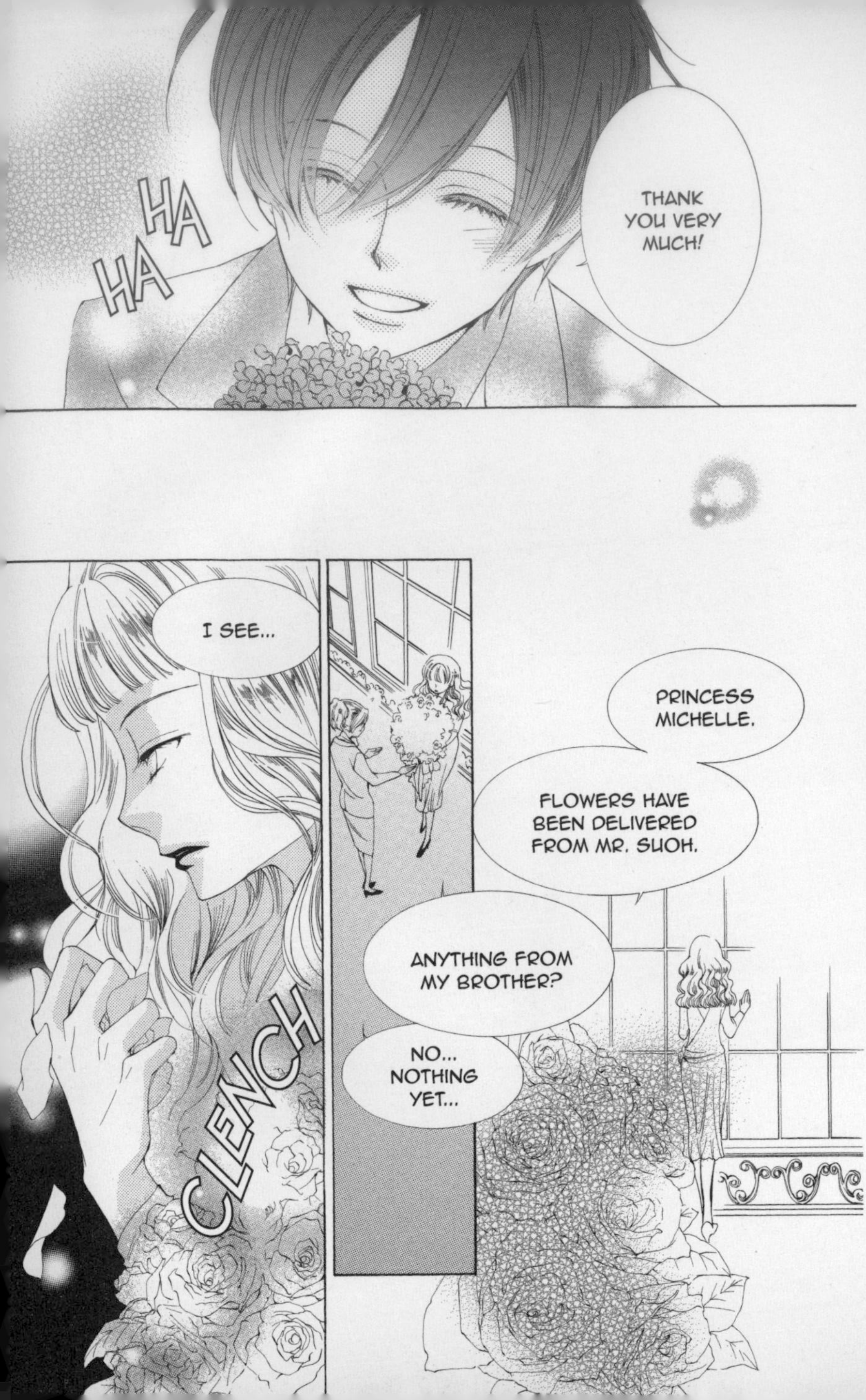
THANK YOU VERY MUCH!
HA HA
PRINCESS MICHELLE.
FLOWERS HAVE BEEN DELIVERED FROM MR. SUOH.
ANYTHING FROM MY BROTHER?
NO... NOTHING YET...
I SEE...
CLENCH

TAMAKI SUOH'S ROAD TO BECOMING A MODEL

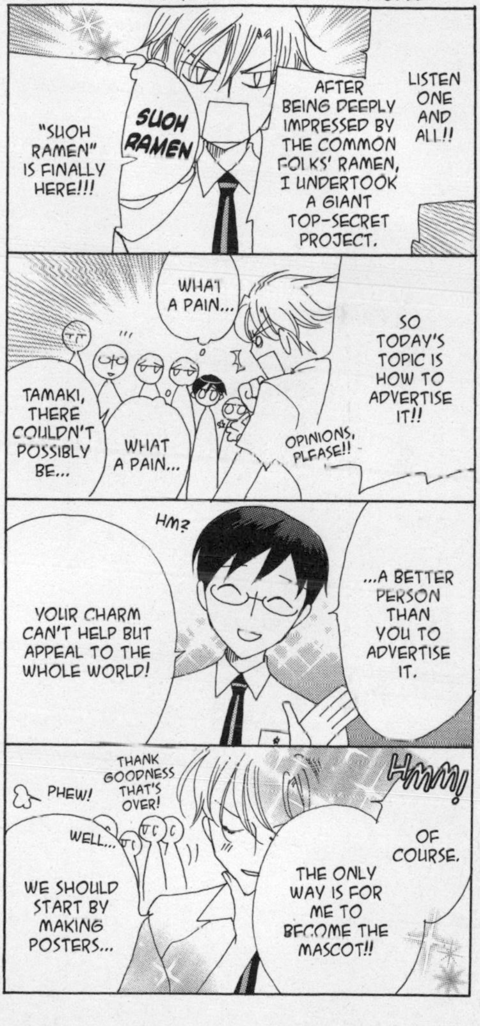
LISTEN ONE AND ALL!!
AFTER BEING DEEPLY IMPRESSED BY THE COMMON FOLKS' RAMEN, I UNDERTOOK A GIANT TOP-SECRET PROJECT.
SUOH RAMEN
"SUOH RAMEN" IS FINALLY HERE!!!
WHAT A PAIN...
SO TODAY'S TOPIC IS HOW TO ADVERTISE IT!!
OPINIONS, PLEASE!!
WHAT A PAIN...
TAMAKI, THERE COULDN'T POSSIBLY BE...
...A BETTER PERSON THAN YOU TO ADVERTISE IT.
HM?
YOUR CHARM CAN'T HELP BUT APPEAL TO THE WHOLE WORLD!
HMM!
OF COURSE.
THE ONLY WAY IS FOR ME TO BECOME THE MASCOT!!
THANK GOODNESS THAT'S OVER!
PHEW!
WELL...
WE SHOULD START BY MAKING POSTERS...

SO WE HAVE A POSTER.

Episode 39

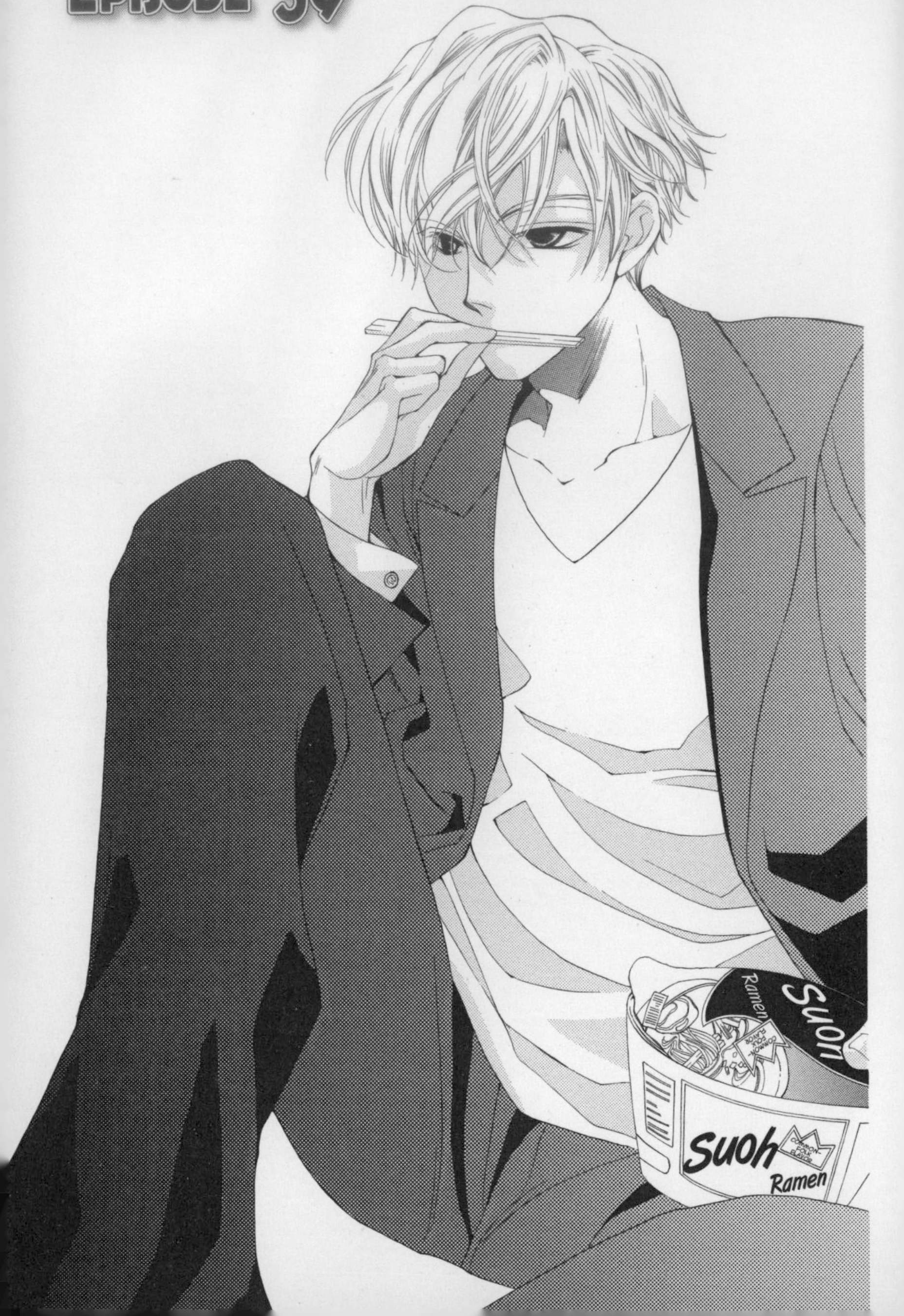
Suoh
Ramen
COMMON-FOLK FLAVOR
Suoh
COMMON-FOLK FLAVOR
Ramen

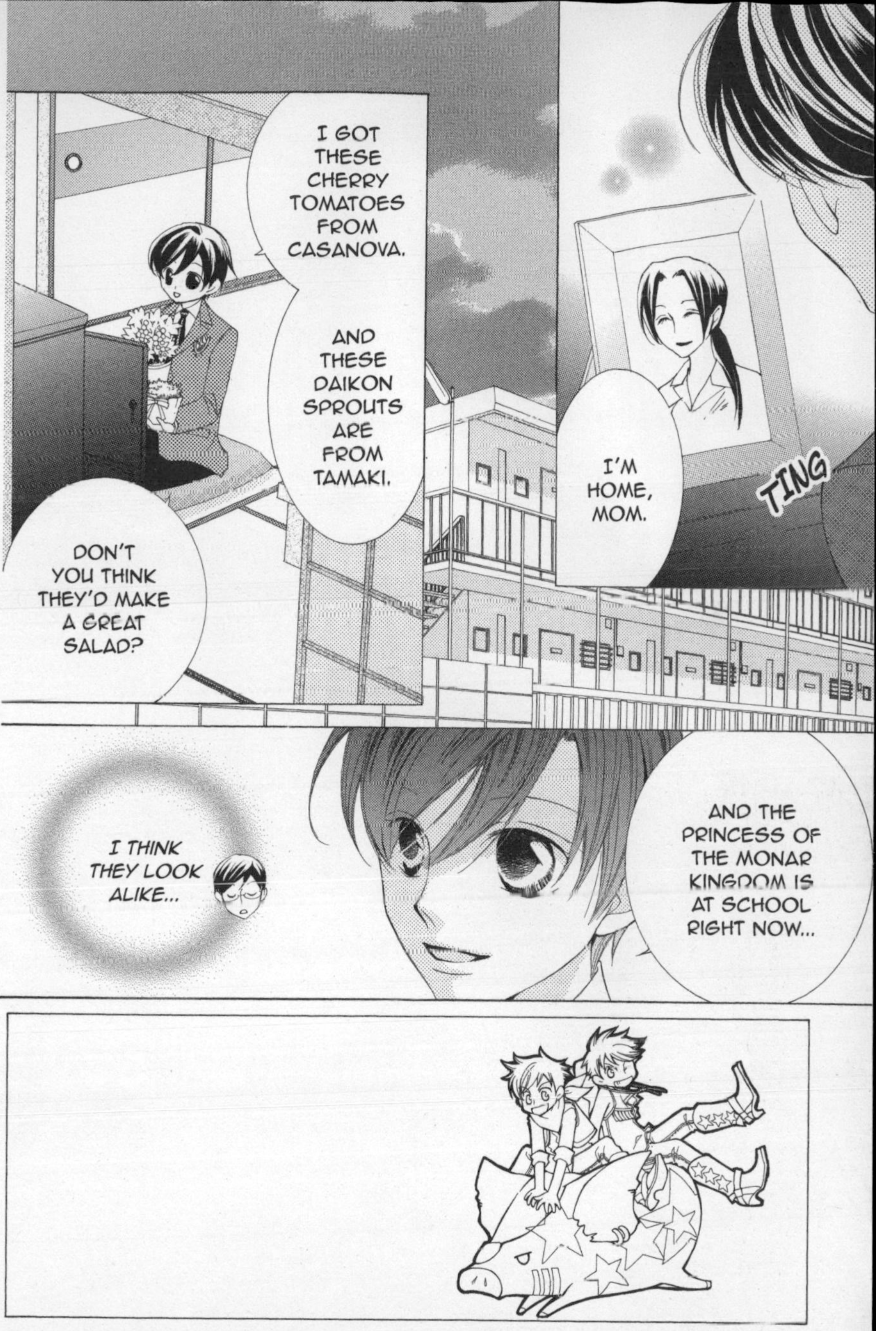
TING
I'M HOME, MOM.
I GOT THESE CHERRY TOMATOES FROM CASANOVA.
AND THESE DAIKON SPROUTS ARE FROM TAMAKI.
DON'T YOU THINK THEY'D MAKE A GREAT SALAD?
AND THE PRINCESS OF THE MONAR KINGDOM IS AT SCHOOL RIGHT NOW...
I THINK THEY LOOK ALIKE...

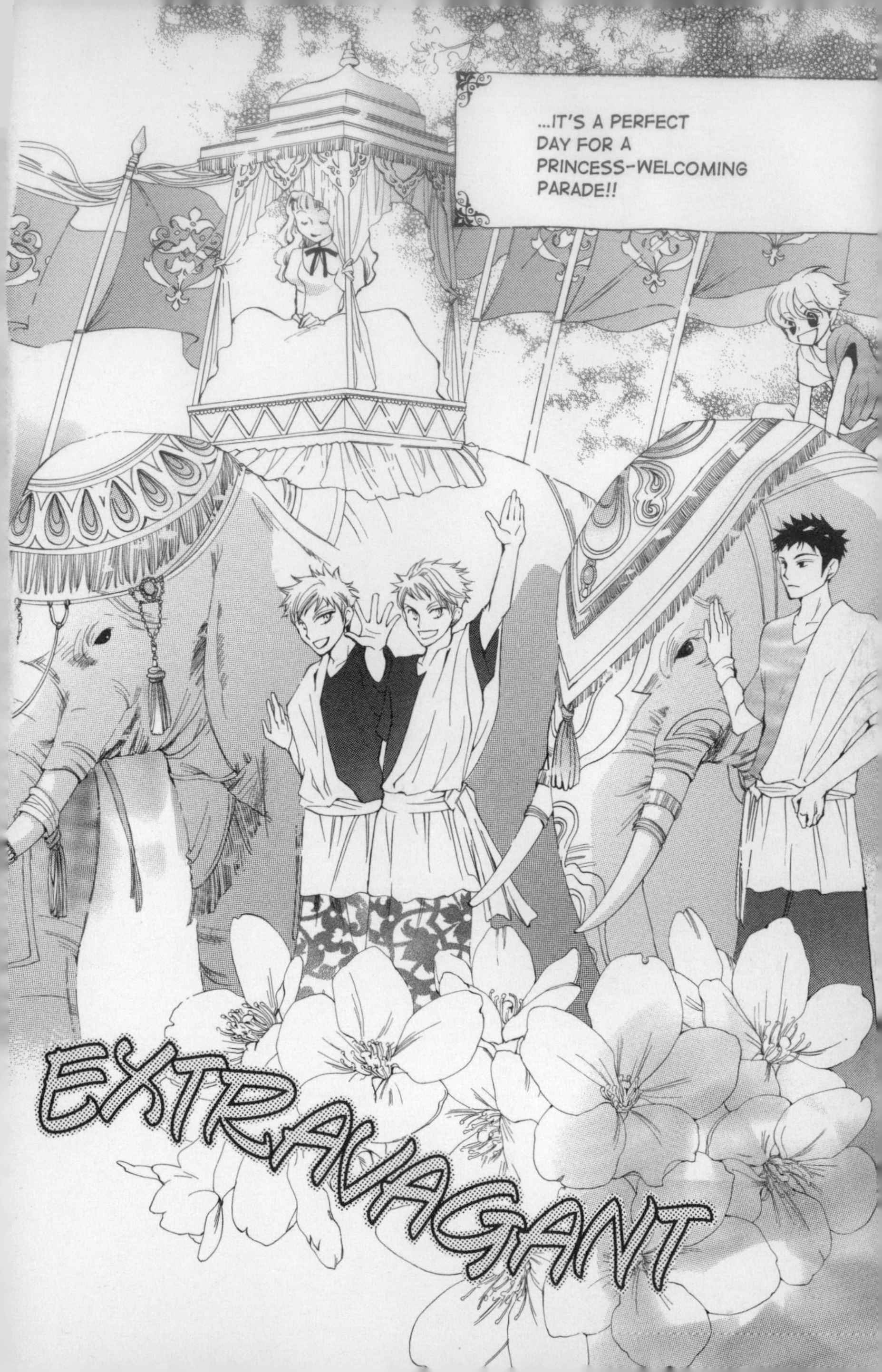
...IT'S A PERFECT DAY FOR A PRINCESS-WELCOMING PARADE!!
EXTRAVAGANT

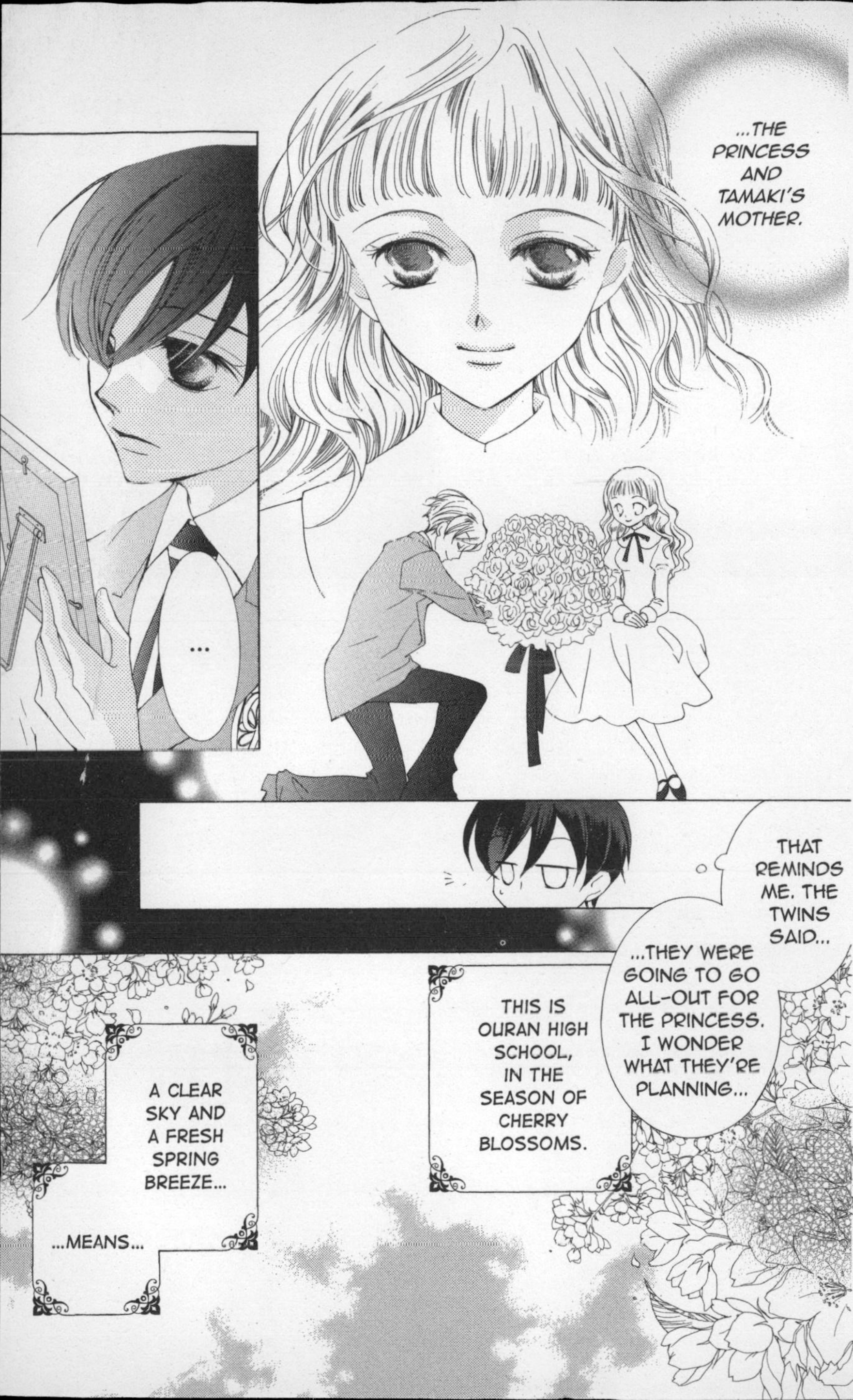
...THE PRINCESS AND TAMAKI'S MOTHER.
...
THAT REMINDS ME. THE TWINS SAID...
...THEY WERE GOING TO GO ALL-OUT FOR THE PRINCESS. I WONDER WHAT THEY'RE PLANNING...
THIS IS OURAN HIGH SCHOOL, IN THE SEASON OF CHERRY BLOSSOMS.
A CLEAR SKY AND A FRESH SPRING BREEZE...
...MEANS...

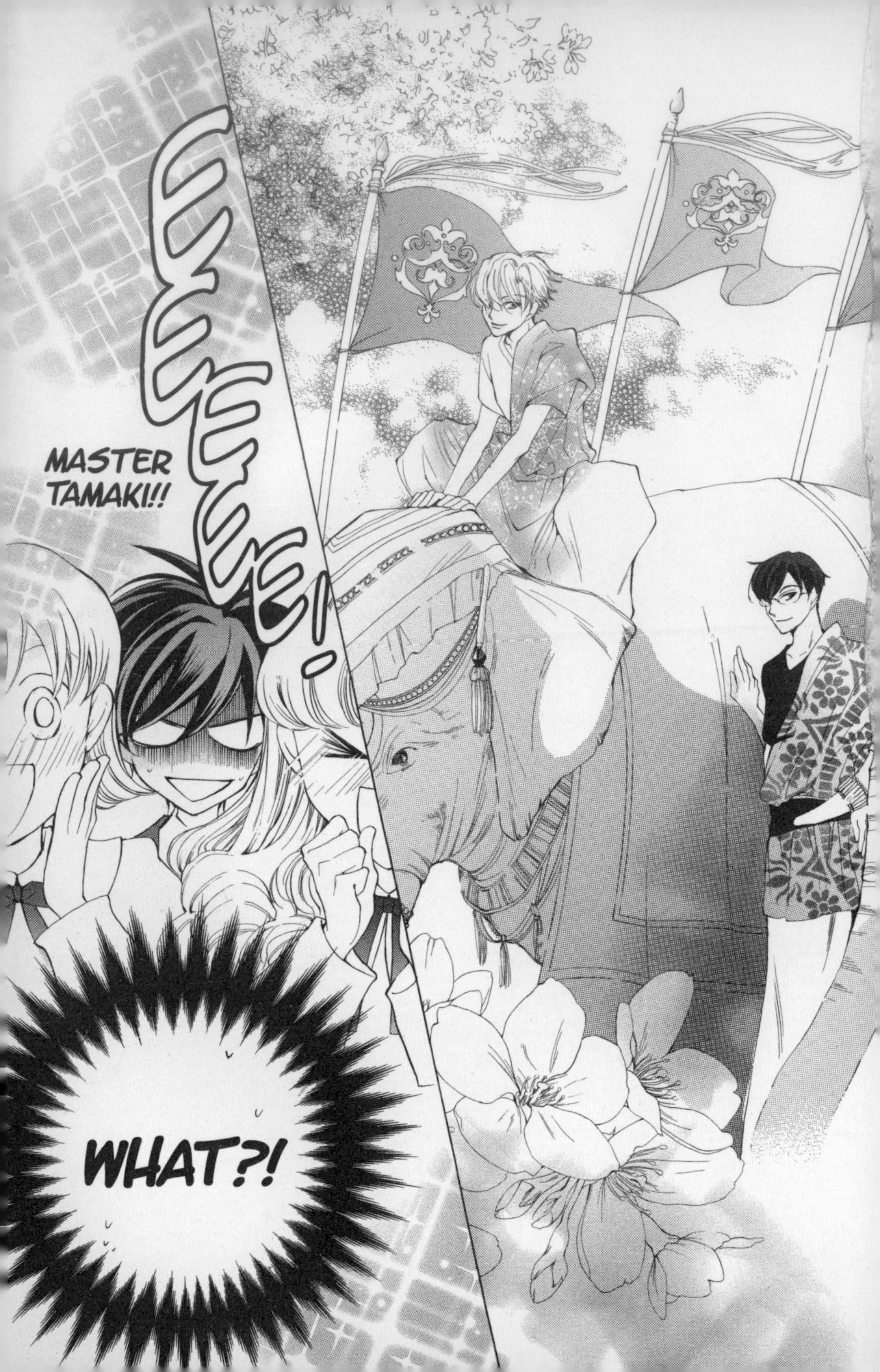
EEEEE!
MASTER TAMAKI!!
WHAT?!

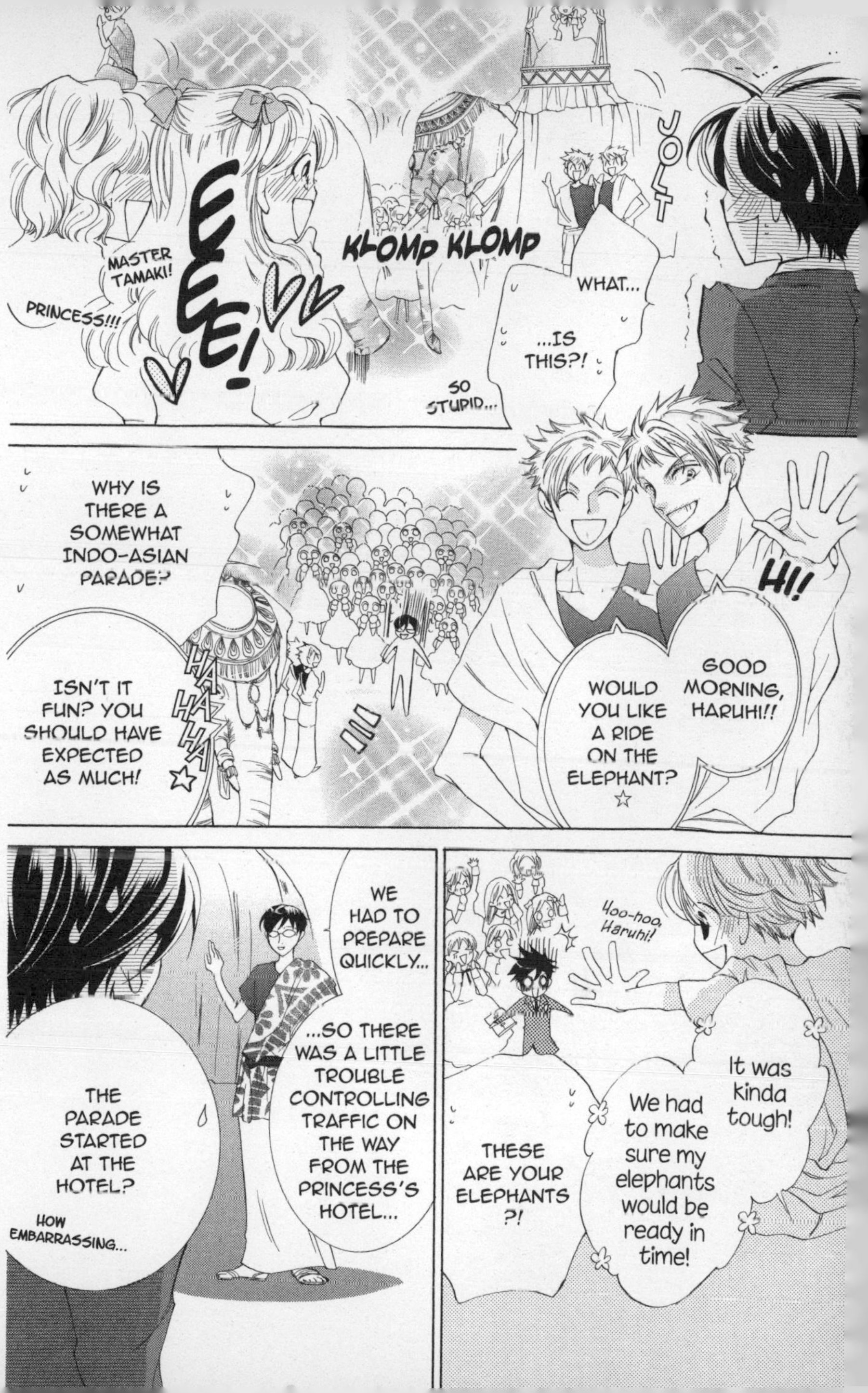
...
JOLT
WHAT...
...IS THIS?!
SO STUPID...
KLOMP KLOMP
EEEE!
MASTER TAMAKI!
PRINCESS!!!
HI!
GOOD MORNING, HARUHI!!
WOULD YOU LIKE A RIDE ON THE ELEPHANT? ☆
WHY IS THERE A SOMEWHAT INDO-ASIAN PARADE?
HA HA HA ☆
ISN'T IT FUN? YOU SHOULD HAVE EXPECTED AS MUCH!
Yoo-hoo, Haruhi!
It was kinda tough!
We had to make sure my elephants would be ready in time!
THESE ARE YOUR ELEPHANTS?!
WE HAD TO PREPARE QUICKLY...
...SO THERE WAS A LITTLE TROUBLE CONTROLLING TRAFFIC ON THE WAY FROM THE PRINCESS'S HOTEL...
THE PARADE STARTED AT THE HOTEL?
HOW EMBARRASSING...

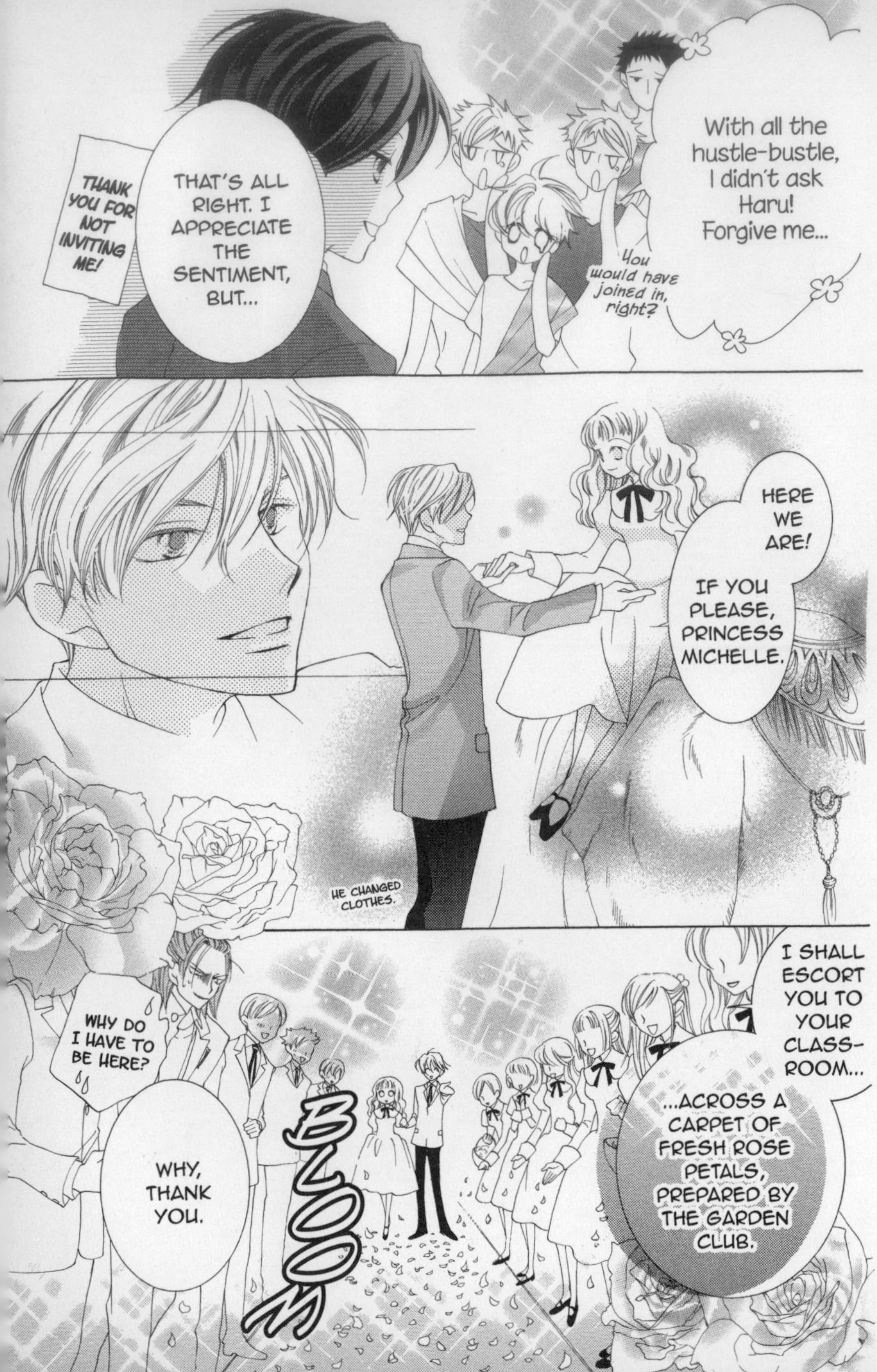
With all the hustle-bustle, I didn't ask Haru! Forgive me...
You would have joined in, right?
THAT'S ALL RIGHT. I APPRECIATE THE SENTIMENT, BUT...
THANK YOU FOR NOT INVITING ME!
HERE WE ARE!
IF YOU PLEASE, PRINCESS MICHELLE.
HE CHANGED CLOTHES.
I SHALL ESCORT YOU TO YOUR CLASS-ROOM...
...ACROSS A CARPET OF FRESH ROSE PETALS, PREPARED BY THE GARDEN CLUB.
BLOOM
WHY, THANK YOU.
WHY DO I HAVE TO BE HERE?

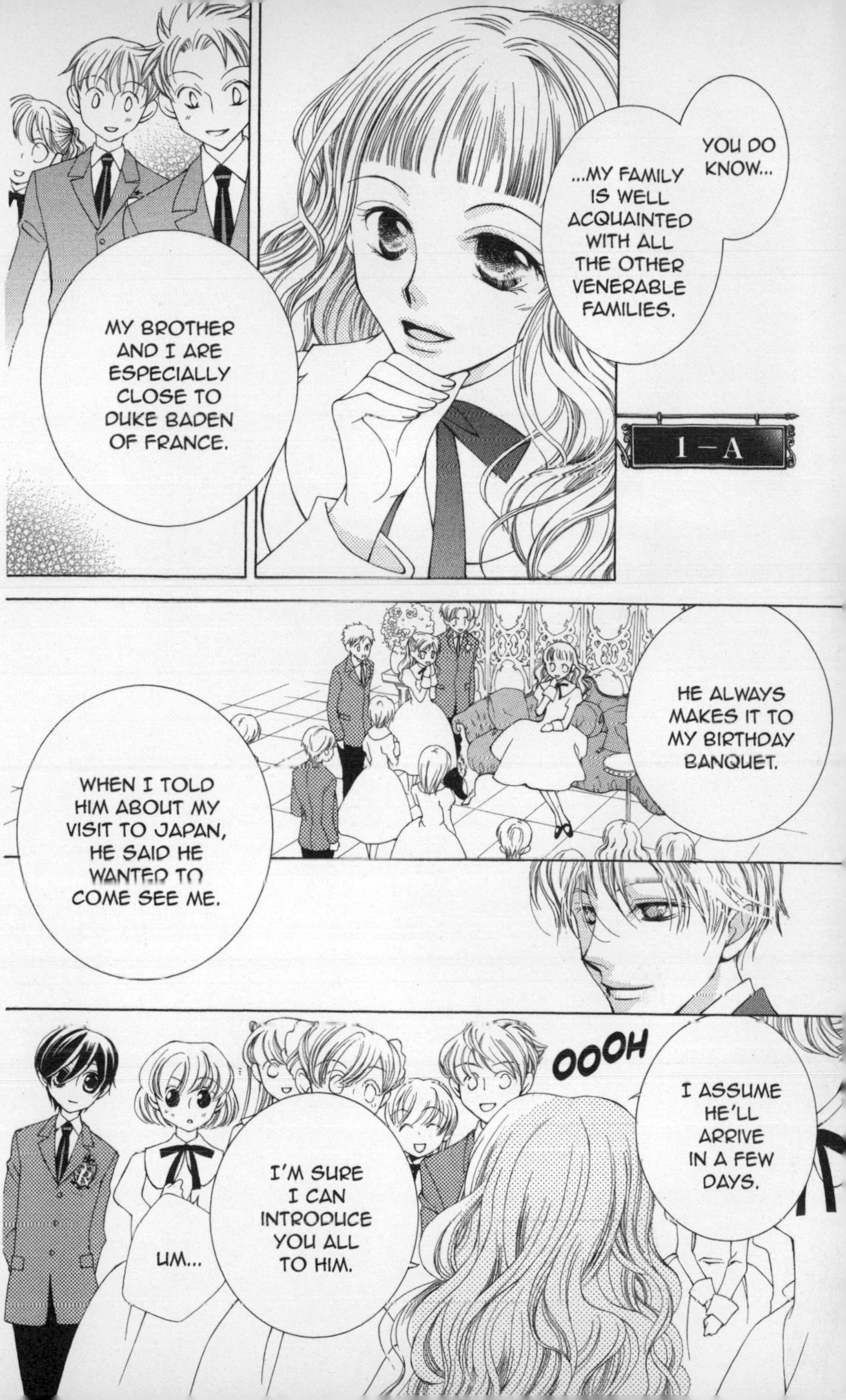
YOU DO KNOW...
...MY FAMILY IS WELL ACQUAINTED WITH ALL THE OTHER VENERABLE FAMILIES.
1-A
MY BROTHER AND I ARE ESPECIALLY CLOSE TO DUKE BADEN OF FRANCE.
HE ALWAYS MAKES IT TO MY BIRTHDAY BANQUET.
WHEN I TOLD HIM ABOUT MY VISIT TO JAPAN, HE SAID HE WANTED TO COME SEE ME.
OOOH
I ASSUME HE'LL ARRIVE IN A FEW DAYS.
I'M SURE I CAN INTRODUCE YOU ALL TO HIM.
UM...

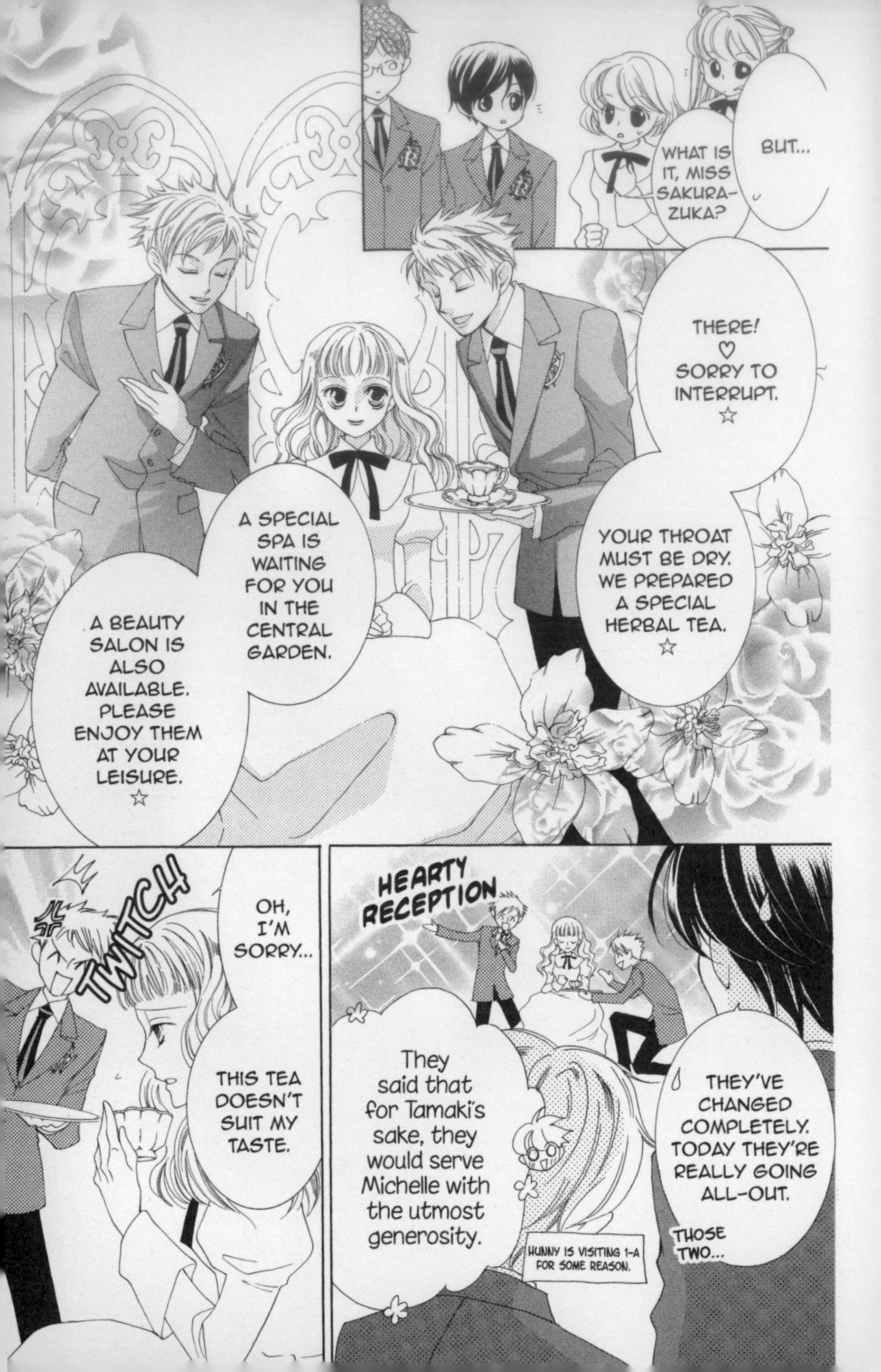
BUT...
WHAT IS IT, MISS SAKURAZUKA?
THERE! ♡ SORRY TO INTERRUPT. ☆
YOUR THROAT MUST BE DRY. WE PREPARED A SPECIAL HERBAL TEA. ☆
A SPECIAL SPA IS WAITING FOR YOU IN THE CENTRAL GARDEN.
A BEAUTY SALON IS ALSO AVAILABLE. PLEASE ENJOY THEM AT YOUR LEISURE. ☆
HEARTY RECEPTION
THEY'VE CHANGED COMPLETELY. TODAY THEY'RE REALLY GOING ALL-OUT.
THOSE TWO...
They said that for Tamaki's sake, they would serve Michelle with the utmost generosity.
HUNNY IS VISITING 1-A FOR SOME REASON.
TWITCH
OH, I'M SORRY...
THIS TEA DOESN'T SUIT MY TASTE.

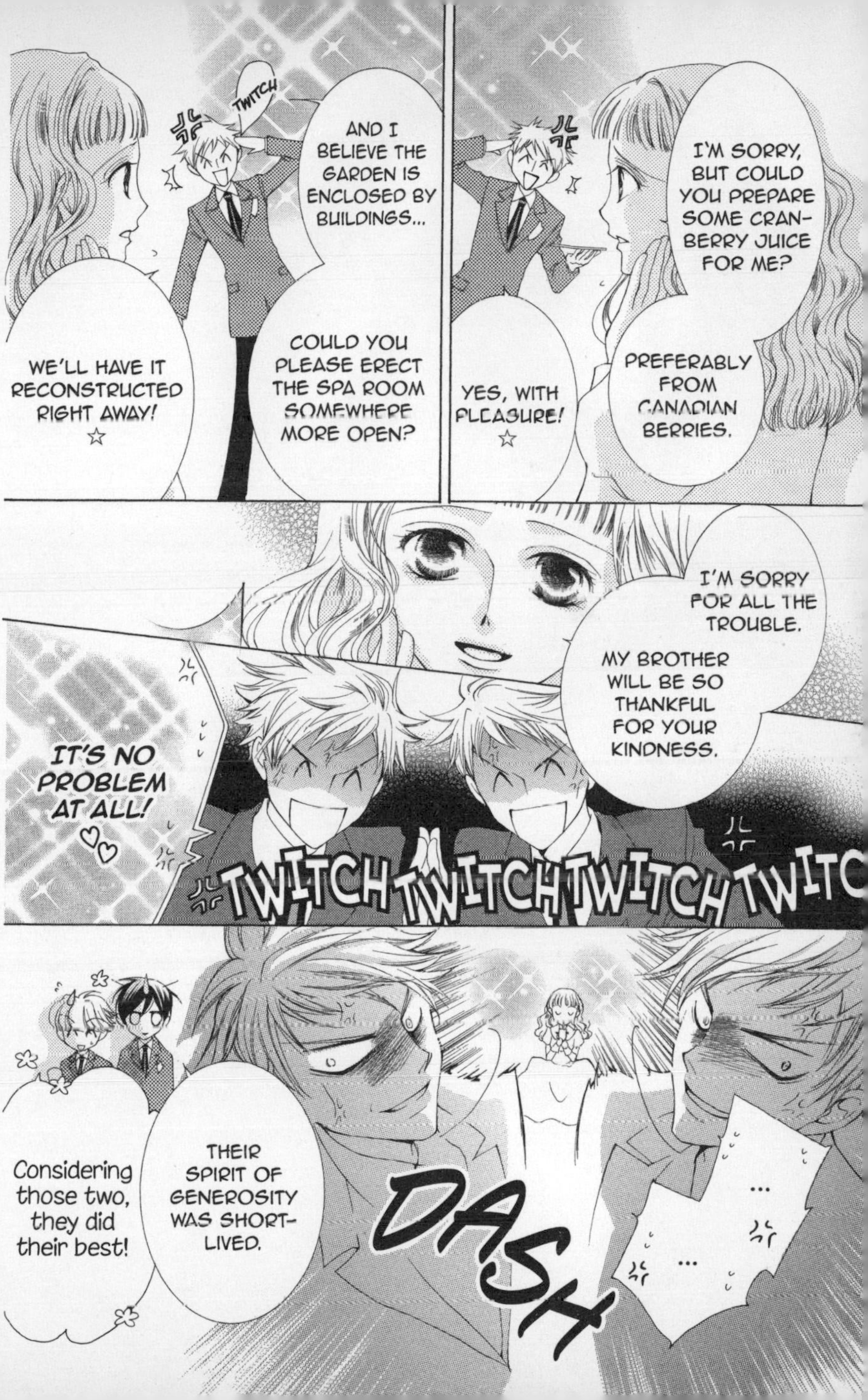
I'M SORRY, BUT COULD YOU PREPARE SOME CRAN-BERRY JUICE FOR ME?
PREFERABLY FROM CANADIAN BERRIES.
YES, WITH PLEASURE! ☆
TWITCH
AND I BELIEVE THE GARDEN IS ENCLOSED BY BUILDINGS...
COULD YOU PLEASE ERECT THE SPA ROOM SOMEWHERE MORE OPEN?
WE'LL HAVE IT RECONSTRUCTED RIGHT AWAY! ☆
I'M SORRY FOR ALL THE TROUBLE.
MY BROTHER WILL BE SO THANKFUL FOR YOUR KINDNESS.
IT'S NO PROBLEM AT ALL!
TWITCH TWITCH TWITCH TWITC
...
...
DASH
THEIR SPIRIT OF GENEROSITY WAS SHORT-LIVED.
Considering those two, they did their best!

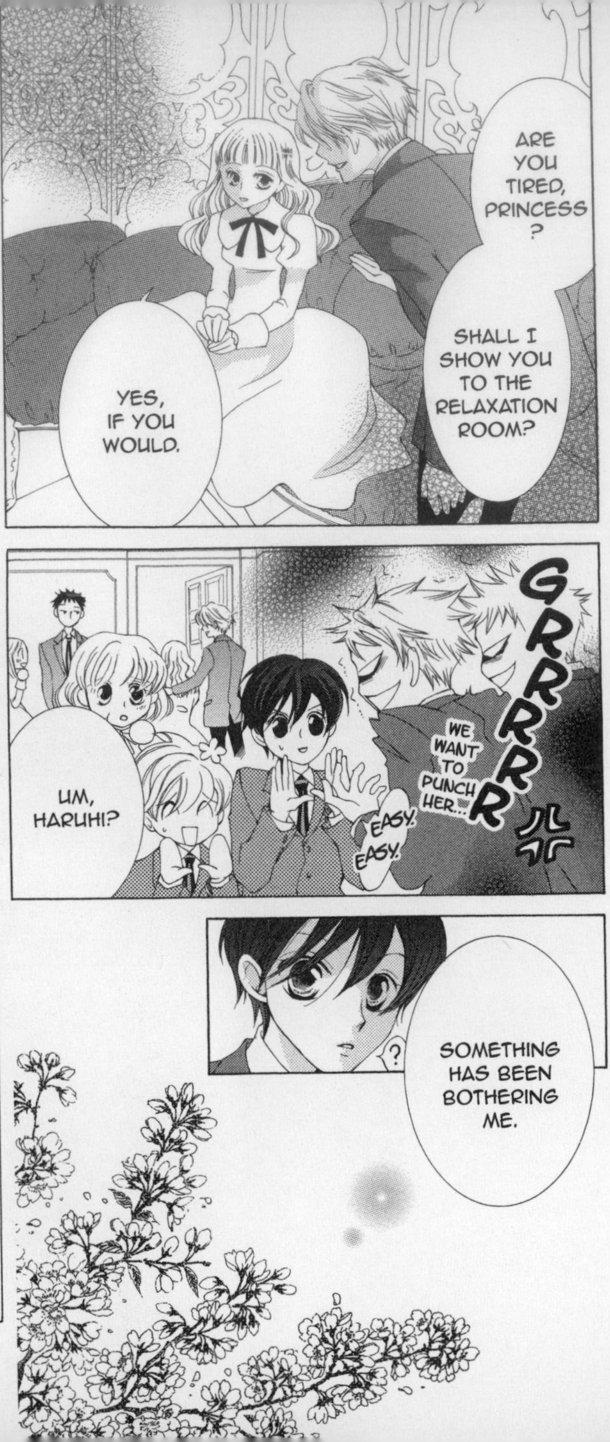
ARE YOU TIRED, PRINCESS?
SHALL I SHOW YOU TO THE RELAXATION ROOM?
YES, IF YOU WOULD.
GRRRRR
WE WANT TO PUNCH HER...
EASY. EASY.
UM, HARUHI?
?
SOMETHING HAS BEEN BOTHERING ME.

3

WELL, LET'S TALK ABOUT THE ANIME. THE ANIME... HOW WONDERFUL IT IS!! THOSE OF YOU WHO LIVE OUTSIDE THE BROADCAST AREA, GET SATELLITE TV OR BUY THE DVD, BUT BY ALL MEANS WATCH IT!! YOU MUST WATCH IT!!! IT IS SO AWESOME THAT I FEEL BAD FOR ANYONE WHO WATCHES THE ANIMATION AND THEN READS THE ORIGINAL MANGA. I WANT TO RELEASE A FAN BOOK OR SOMETHING... I'VE BECOME A CRAZY FAN. MAYBE EVEN A MANIAC!

"IT'S GOT TO BE MORE INTERESTING!" "IT WOULD BE SO MUCH BETTER IF ONLY I COULD DRAW PRETTIER PICTURES!" I'M ALWAYS SUFFERING FROM THESE INTERNAL STRUGGLES OVER *HOST CLUB*, SO I'M VERY HAPPY THAT IT ALL CAME TRUE WITH THE ANIME. IN FACT, I'M REALLY THANKFUL FOR THE INCREASING AMOUNT OF WORK, RESPONSES, AND VARIOUS PLANS THAT HAVE ARISEN SINCE THE ANIME STARTED.

(CONTINUES)

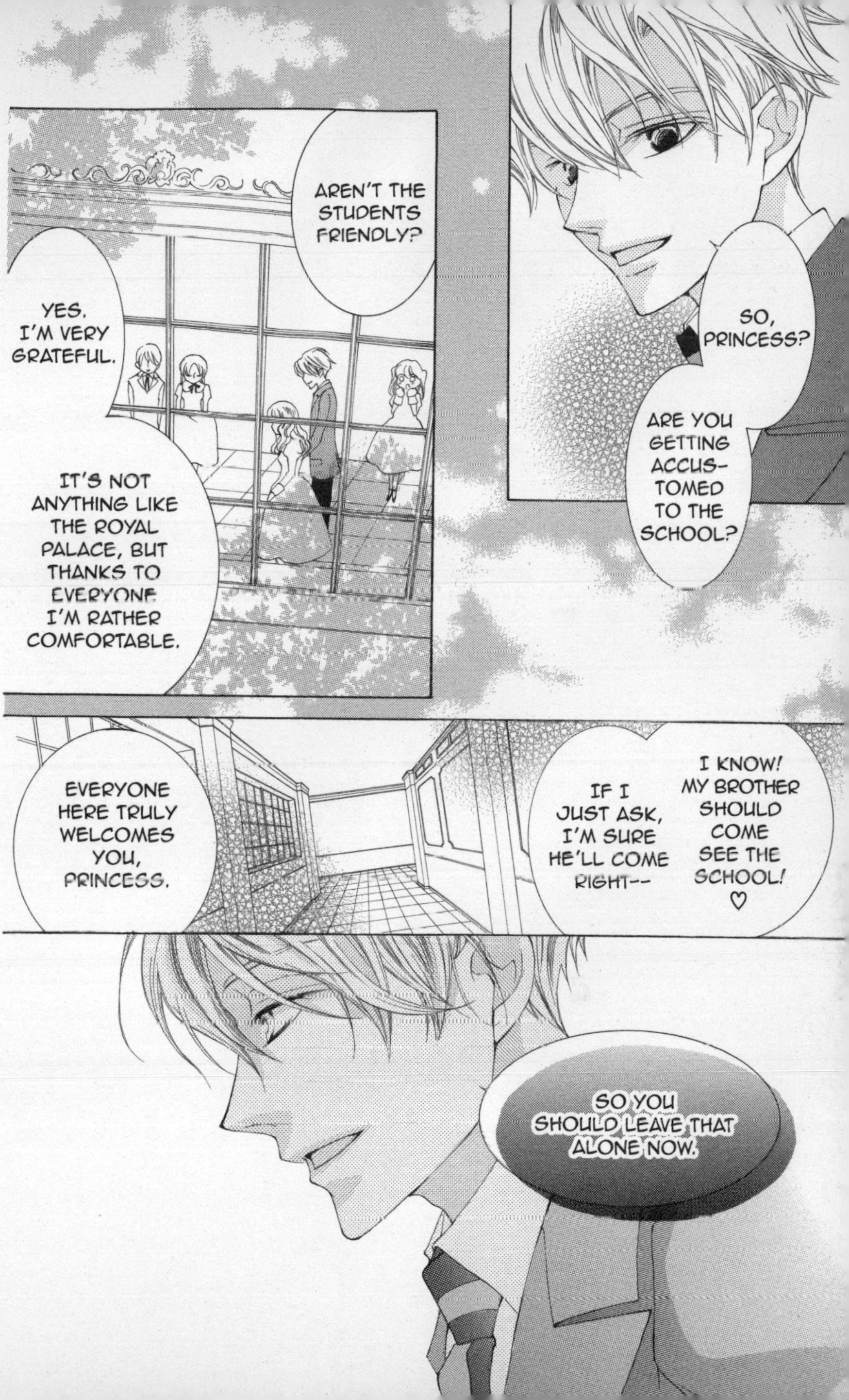
SO, PRINCESS?
ARE YOU GETTING ACCUS-TOMED TO THE SCHOOL?
AREN'T THE STUDENTS FRIENDLY?
YES. I'M VERY GRATEFUL.
IT'S NOT ANYTHING LIKE THE ROYAL PALACE, BUT THANKS TO EVERYONE I'M RATHER COMFORTABLE.
I KNOW! MY BROTHER SHOULD COME SEE THE SCHOOL! ♡
IF I JUST ASK, I'M SURE HE'LL COME RIGHT--
EVERYONE HERE TRULY WELCOMES YOU, PRINCESS.
SO YOU SHOULD LEAVE THAT ALONE NOW.

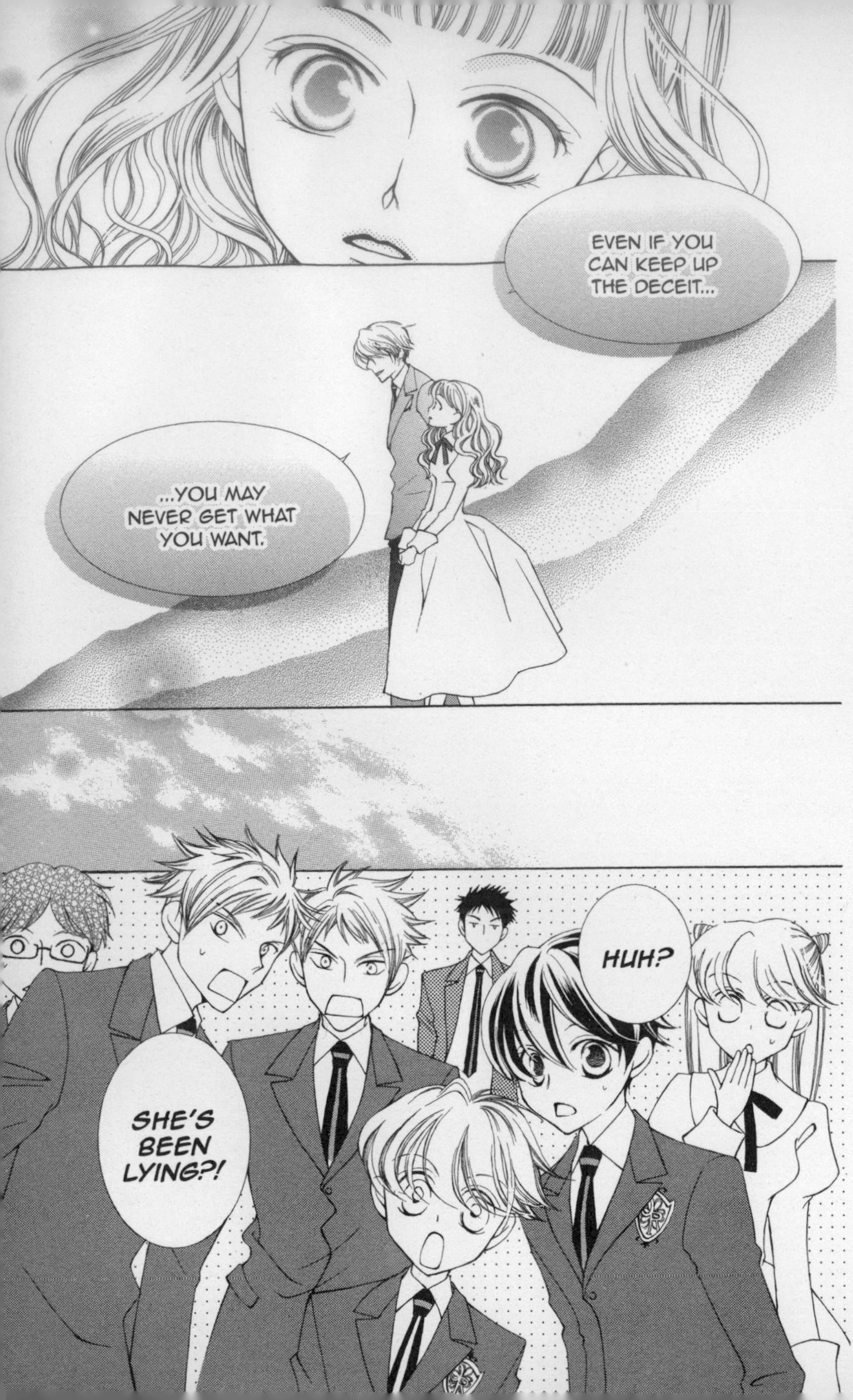
EVEN IF YOU CAN KEEP UP THE DECEIT...
...YOU MAY NEVER GET WHAT YOU WANT.
HUH?
SHE'S BEEN LYING?!

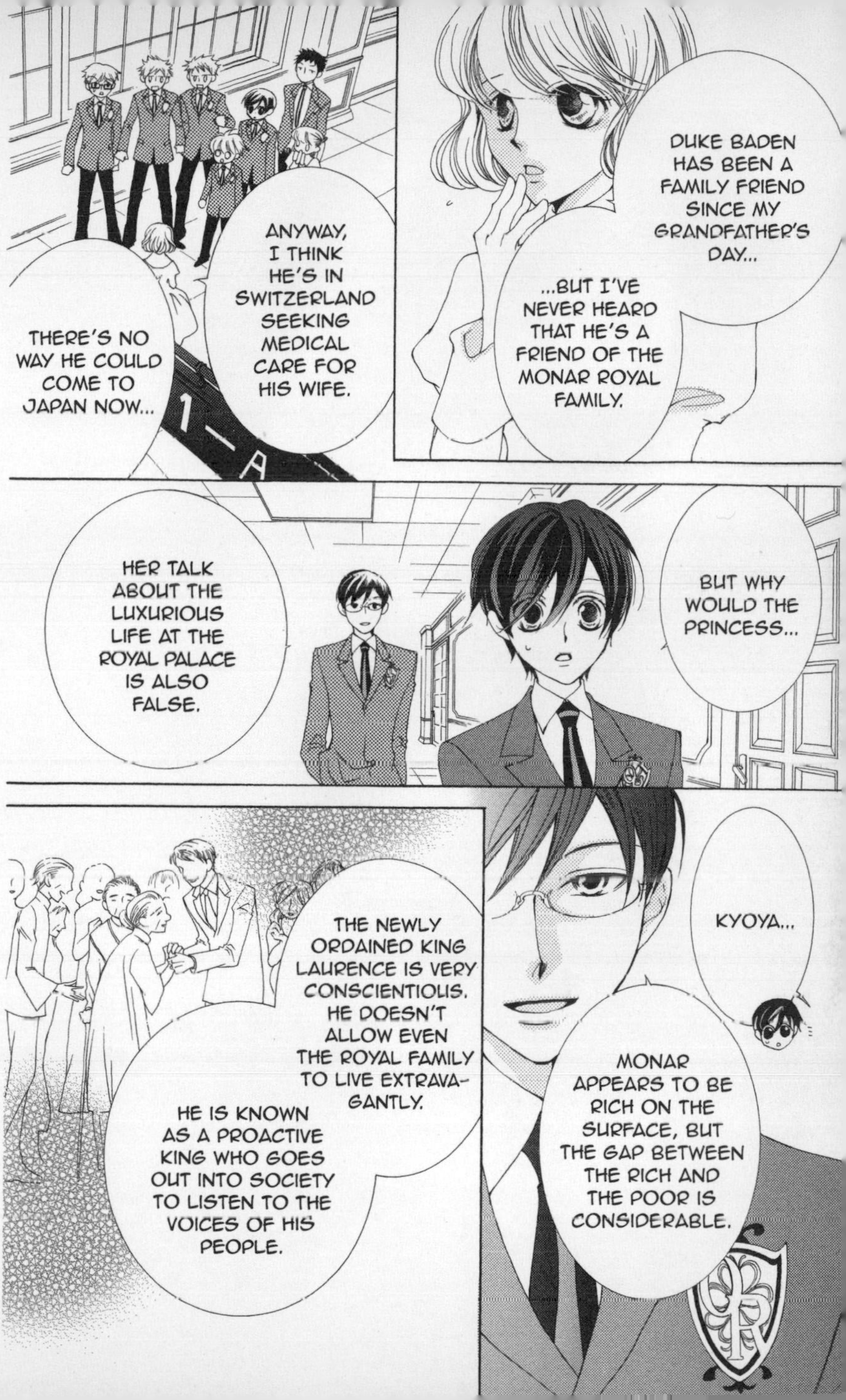
DUKE BADEN HAS BEEN A FAMILY FRIEND SINCE MY GRANDFATHER'S DAY...
...BUT I'VE NEVER HEARD THAT HE'S A FRIEND OF THE MONAR ROYAL FAMILY.
ANYWAY, I THINK HE'S IN SWITZERLAND SEEKING MEDICAL CARE FOR HIS WIFE.
THERE'S NO WAY HE COULD COME TO JAPAN NOW...
1-A
BUT WHY WOULD THE PRINCESS...
HER TALK ABOUT THE LUXURIOUS LIFE AT THE ROYAL PALACE IS ALSO FALSE.
KYOYA...
MONAR APPEARS TO BE RICH ON THE SURFACE, BUT THE GAP BETWEEN THE RICH AND THE POOR IS CONSIDERABLE.
THE NEWLY ORDAINED KING LAURENCE IS VERY CONSCIENTIOUS. HE DOESN'T ALLOW EVEN THE ROYAL FAMILY TO LIVE EXTRAVA-GANTLY.
HE IS KNOWN AS A PROACTIVE KING WHO GOES OUT INTO SOCIETY TO LISTEN TO THE VOICES OF HIS PEOPLE.

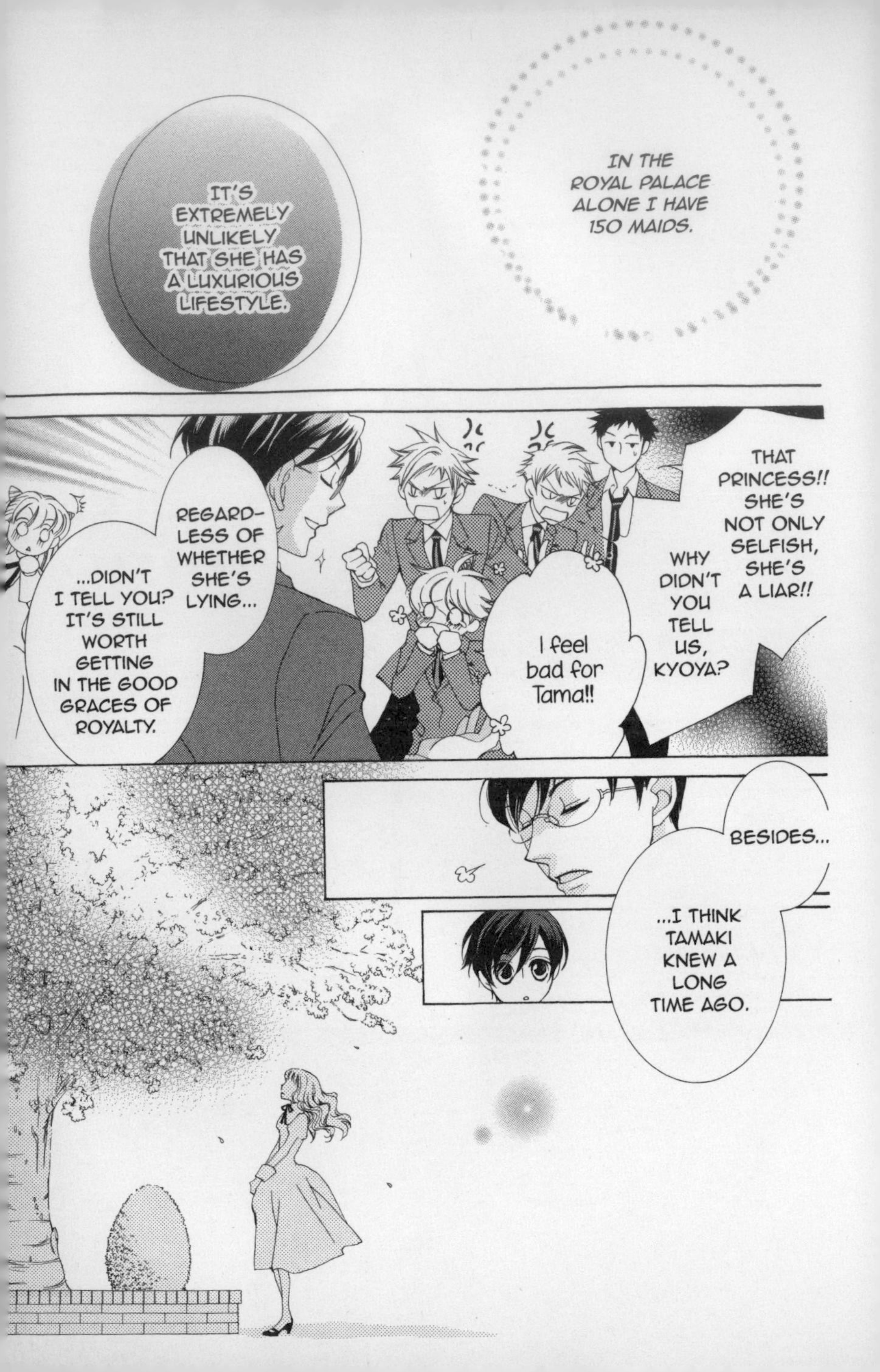
IN THE ROYAL PALACE ALONE I HAVE 150 MAIDS.
IT'S EXTREMELY UNLIKELY THAT SHE HAS A LUXURIOUS LIFESTYLE.
THAT PRINCESS!! SHE'S NOT ONLY SELFISH, SHE'S A LIAR!!
WHY DIDN'T YOU TELL US, KYOYA?
I feel bad for Tama!!
REGARD-LESS OF WHETHER SHE'S LYING...
...DIDN'T I TELL YOU? IT'S STILL WORTH GETTING IN THE GOOD GRACES OF ROYALTY.
BESIDES...
...I THINK TAMAKI KNEW A LONG TIME AGO.

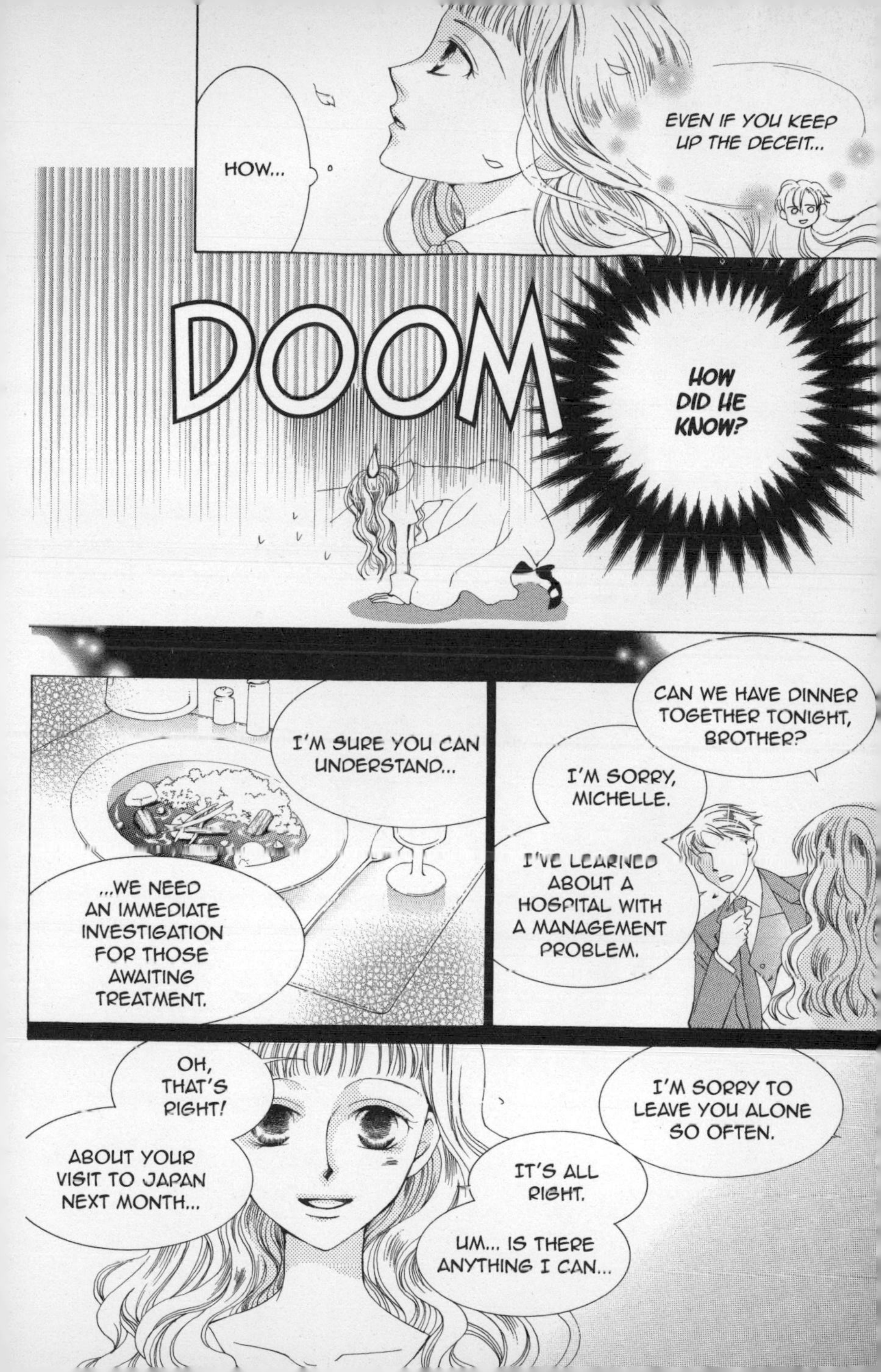
EVEN IF YOU KEEP UP THE DECEIT...
HOW...
HOW DID HE KNOW?
DOOM
CAN WE HAVE DINNER TOGETHER TONIGHT, BROTHER?
I'M SORRY, MICHELLE.
I'VE LEARNED ABOUT A HOSPITAL WITH A MANAGEMENT PROBLEM.
I'M SURE YOU CAN UNDERSTAND...
...WE NEED AN IMMEDIATE INVESTIGATION FOR THOSE AWAITING TREATMENT.
I'M SORRY TO LEAVE YOU ALONE SO OFTEN.
IT'S ALL RIGHT.
UM... IS THERE ANYTHING I CAN...
OH, THAT'S RIGHT!
ABOUT YOUR VISIT TO JAPAN NEXT MONTH...

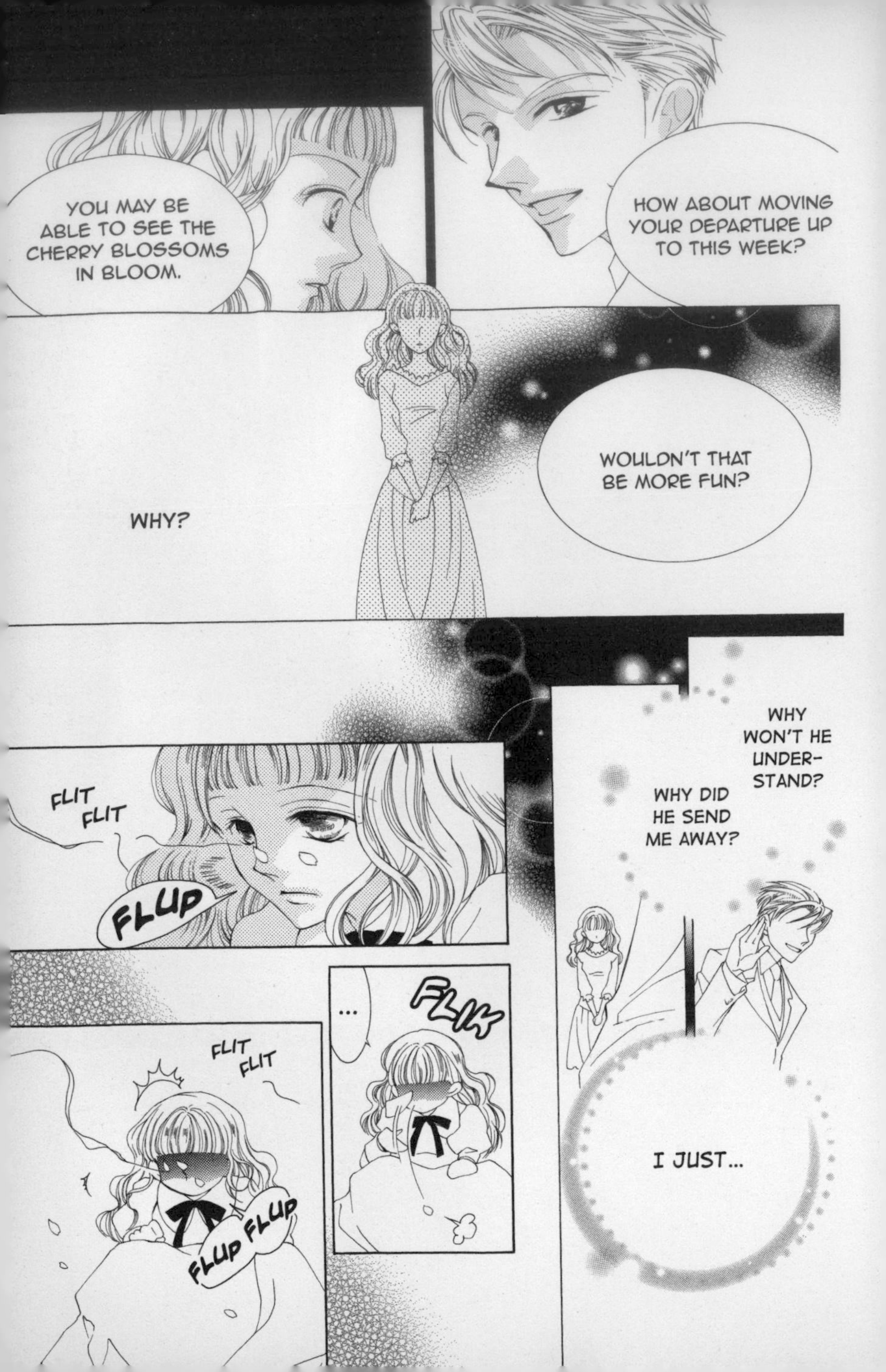
HOW ABOUT MOVING YOUR DEPARTURE UP TO THIS WEEK?
YOU MAY BE ABLE TO SEE THE CHERRY BLOSSOMS IN BLOOM.
WOULDN'T THAT BE MORE FUN?
WHY?
WHY WON'T HE UNDER-STAND?
WHY DID HE SEND ME AWAY?
I JUST...
FLIT FLIT
FLUP
...
FLIK
FLIT FLIT
FLUP FLUP

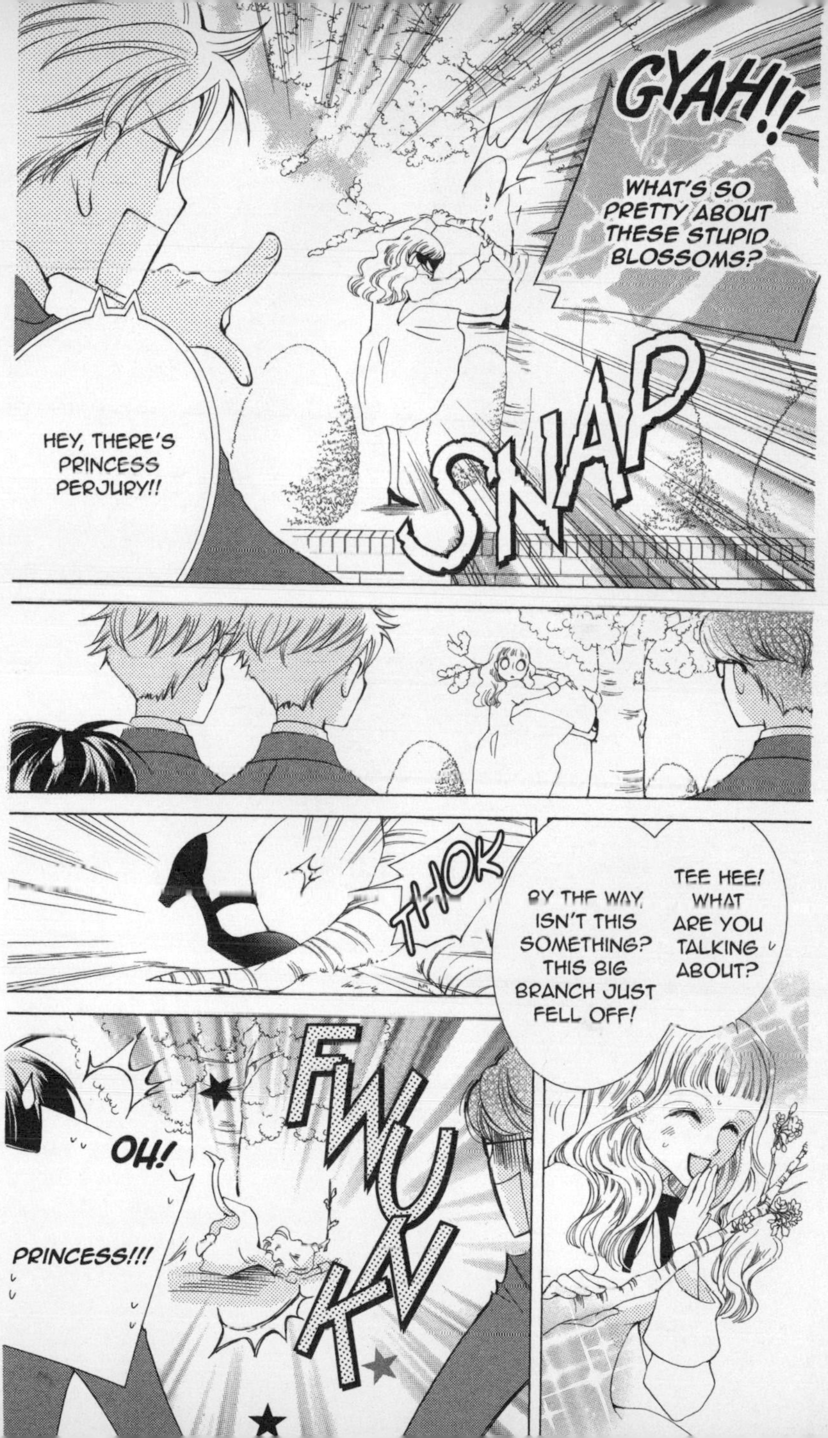
GYAH!!
WHAT'S SO PRETTY ABOUT THESE STUPID BLOSSOMS?
SNAP
HEY, THERE'S PRINCESS PERJURY!!
TEE HEE! WHAT ARE YOU TALKING ABOUT?
BY THE WAY, ISN'T THIS SOMETHING? THIS BIG BRANCH JUST FELL OFF!
THOK
FWUNK
OH!
PRINCESS!!!

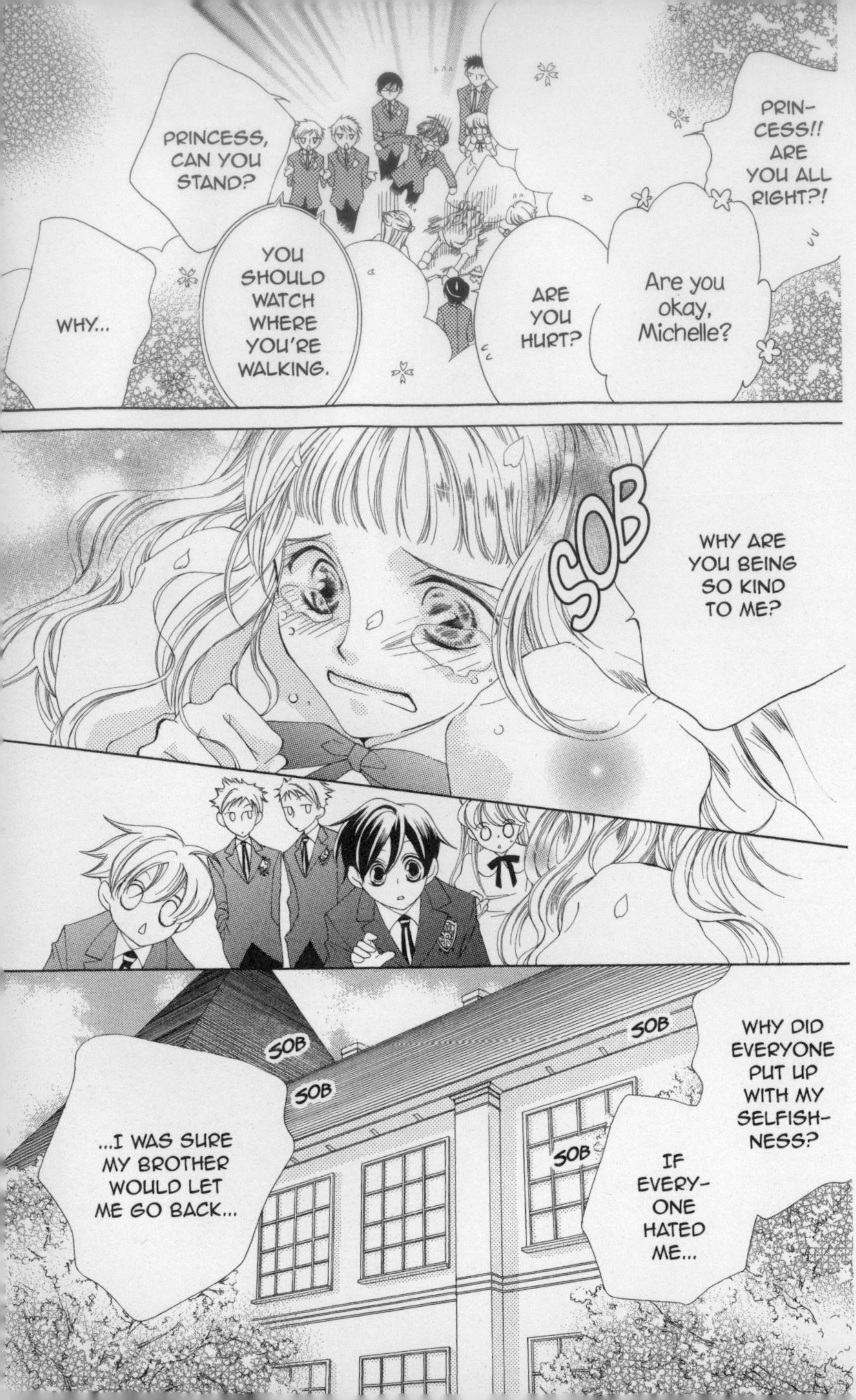

PRINCESS!! ARE YOU ALL RIGHT?!
Are you okay, Michelle?
ARE YOU HURT?
PRINCESS, CAN YOU STAND?
YOU SHOULD WATCH WHERE YOU'RE WALKING.
WHY...
SOB
WHY ARE YOU BEING SO KIND TO ME?
WHY DID EVERYONE PUT UP WITH MY SELFISHNESS?
IF EVERYONE HATED ME...
SOB
SOB
SOB
SOB
...I WAS SURE MY BROTHER WOULD LET ME GO BACK...

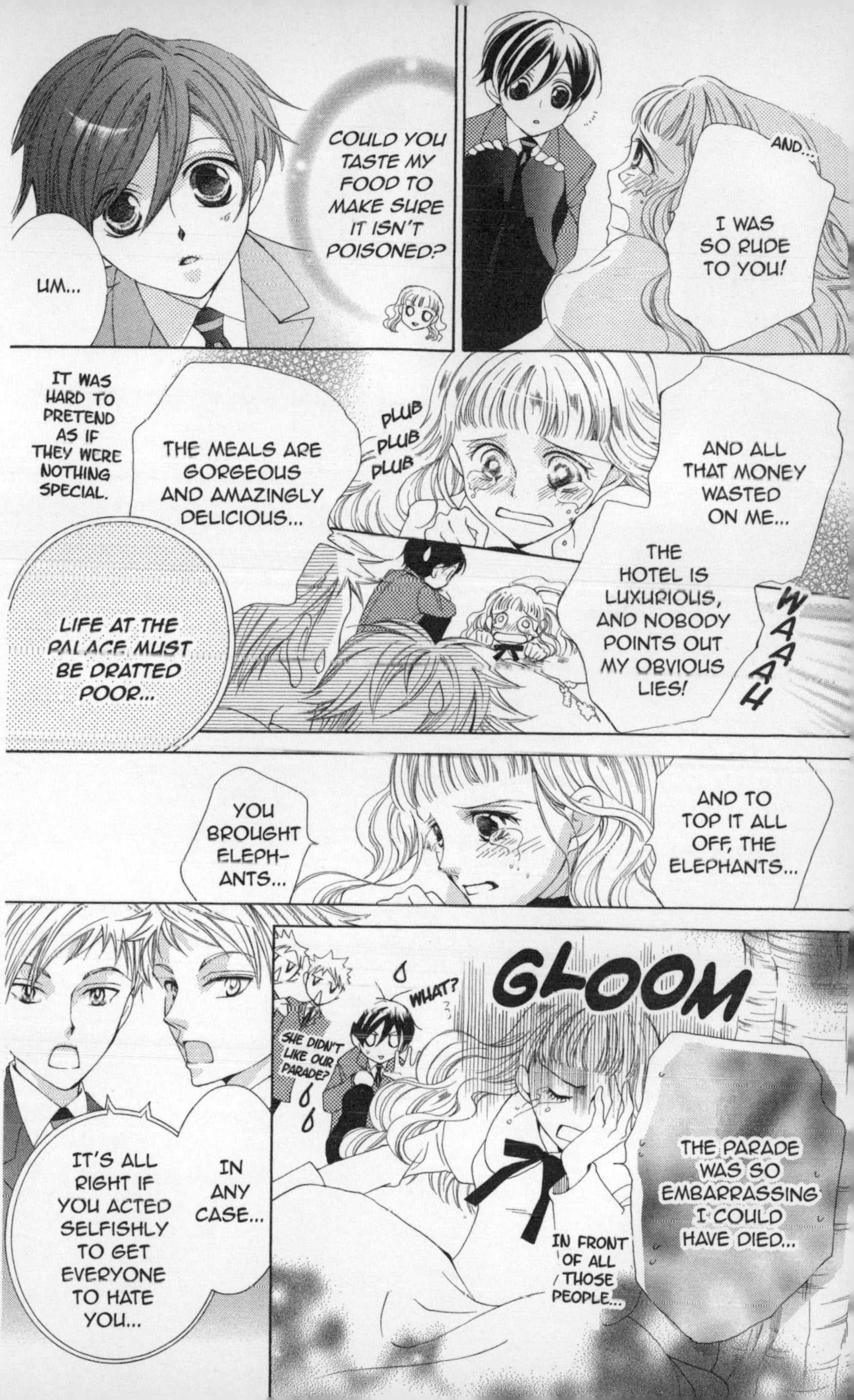
AND...
I WAS SO RUDE TO YOU!
COULD YOU TASTE MY FOOD TO MAKE SURE IT ISN'T POISONED?
UM...
AND ALL THAT MONEY WASTED ON ME...
THE MEALS ARE GORGEOUS AND AMAZINGLY DELICIOUS...
PLUB PLUB PLUB
IT WAS HARD TO PRETEND AS IF THEY WERE NOTHING SPECIAL.
THE HOTEL IS LUXURIOUS, AND NOBODY POINTS OUT MY OBVIOUS LIES!
WAAAAH
LIFE AT THE PALACE MUST BE DRATTED POOR...
AND TO TOP IT ALL OFF, THE ELEPHANTS...
YOU BROUGHT ELEPHANTS...
GLOOM
THE PARADE WAS SO EMBARRASSING I COULD HAVE DIED...
IN FRONT OF ALL THOSE PEOPLE...
WHAT?
SHE DIDN'T LIKE OUR PARADE?
IN ANY CASE...
IT'S ALL RIGHT IF YOU ACTED SELFISHLY TO GET EVERYONE TO HATE YOU...

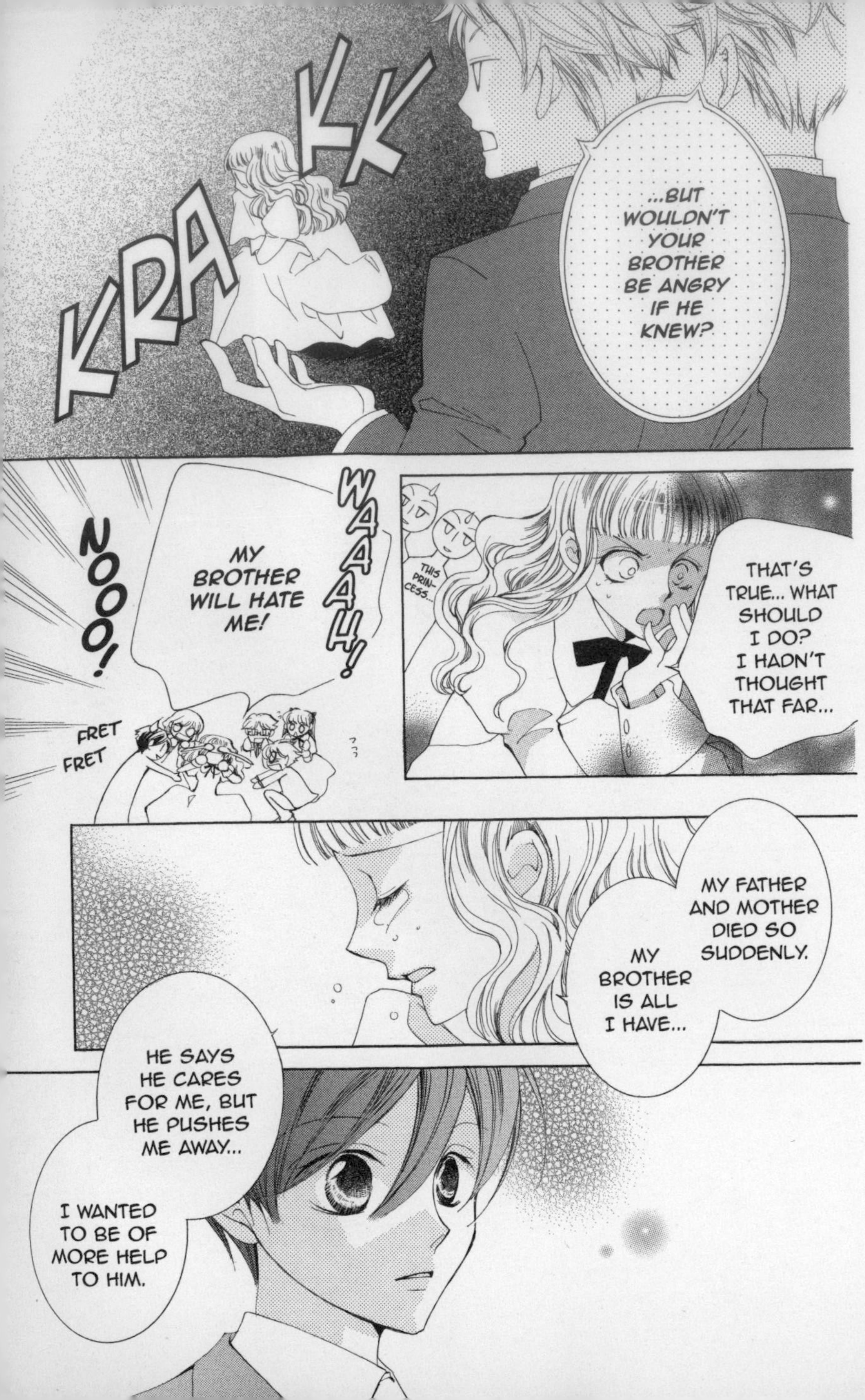
...BUT WOULDN'T YOUR BROTHER BE ANGRY IF HE KNEW?
KRAKK
THAT'S TRUE... WHAT SHOULD I DO? I HADN'T THOUGHT THAT FAR...
THIS PRINCESS...
WAAAH!
MY BROTHER WILL HATE ME!
NOOOO!
FRET FRET
MY FATHER AND MOTHER DIED SO SUDDENLY.
MY BROTHER IS ALL I HAVE...
HE SAYS HE CARES FOR ME, BUT HE PUSHES ME AWAY...
I WANTED TO BE OF MORE HELP TO HIM.

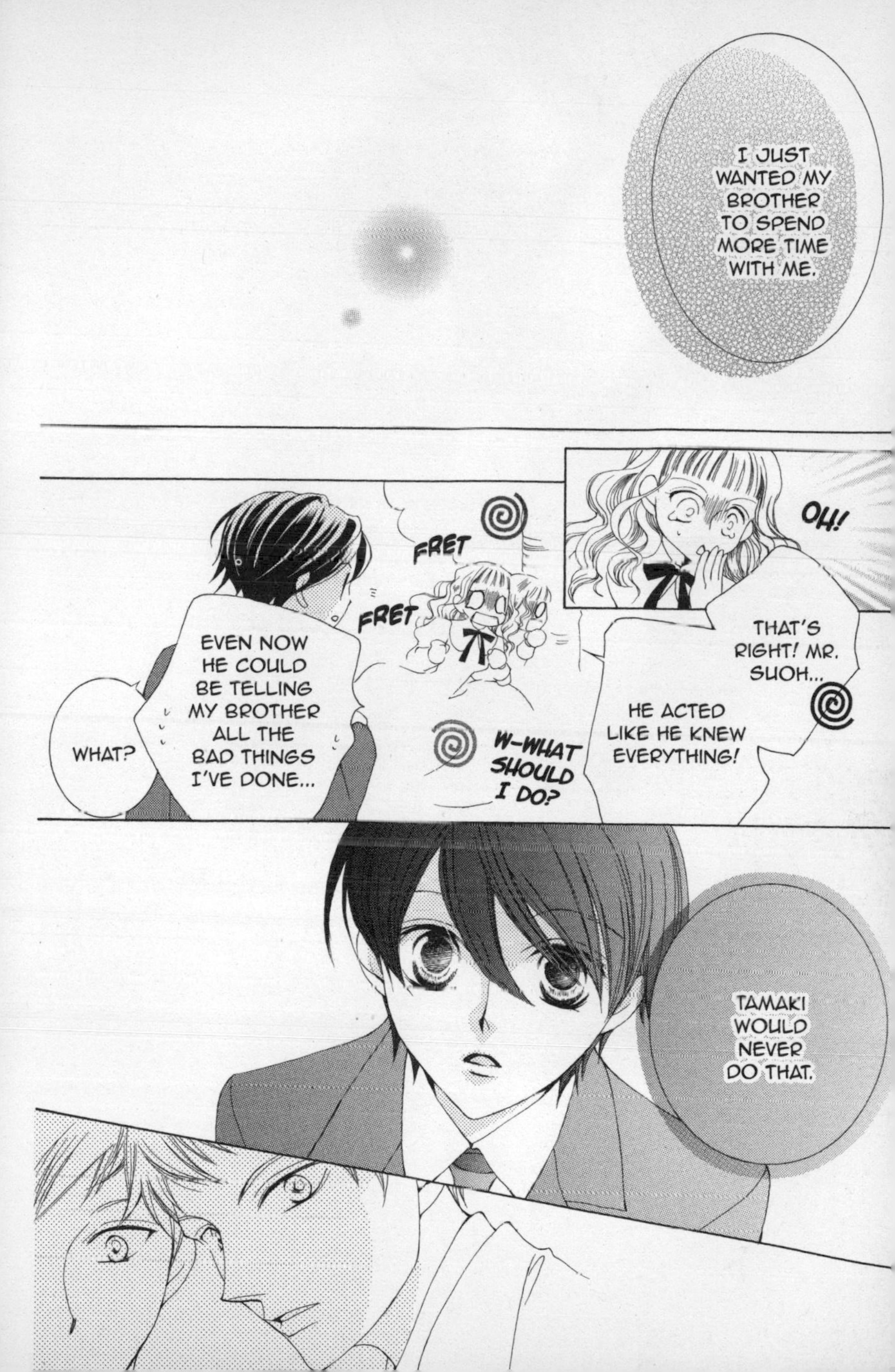
I JUST WANTED MY BROTHER TO SPEND MORE TIME WITH ME.
OH!
THAT'S RIGHT! MR. SUOH...
HE ACTED LIKE HE KNEW EVERYTHING!
W-WHAT SHOULD I DO?
FRET
FRET
EVEN NOW HE COULD BE TELLING MY BROTHER ALL THE BAD THINGS I'VE DONE...
WHAT?
TAMAKI WOULD NEVER DO THAT.

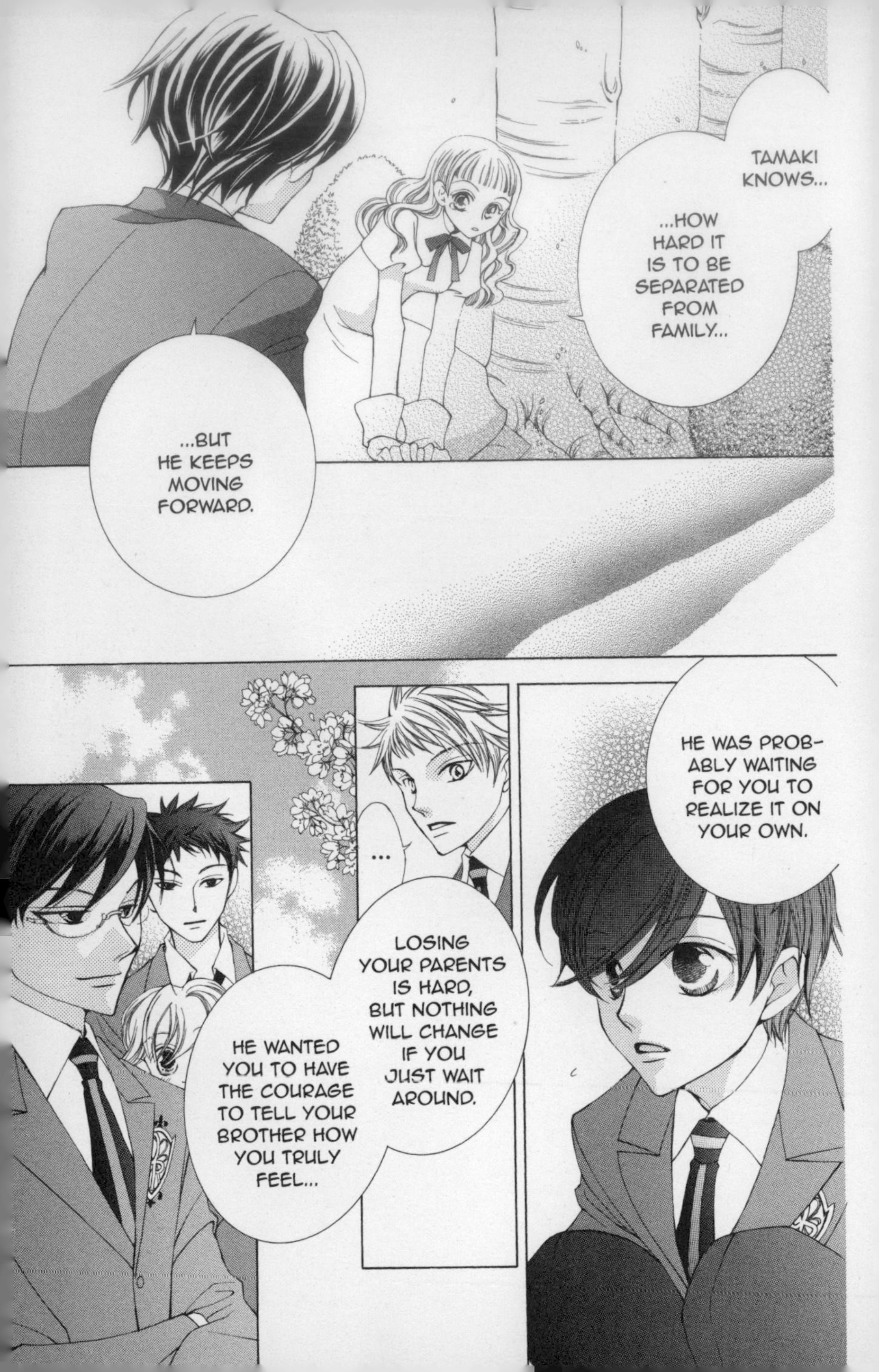
TAMAKI KNOWS...
...HOW HARD IT IS TO BE SEPARATED FROM FAMILY...
...BUT HE KEEPS MOVING FORWARD.
HE WAS PROB-ABLY WAITING FOR YOU TO REALIZE IT ON YOUR OWN.
...
LOSING YOUR PARENTS IS HARD, BUT NOTHING WILL CHANGE IF YOU JUST WAIT AROUND.
HE WANTED YOU TO HAVE THE COURAGE TO TELL YOUR BROTHER HOW YOU TRULY FEEL...

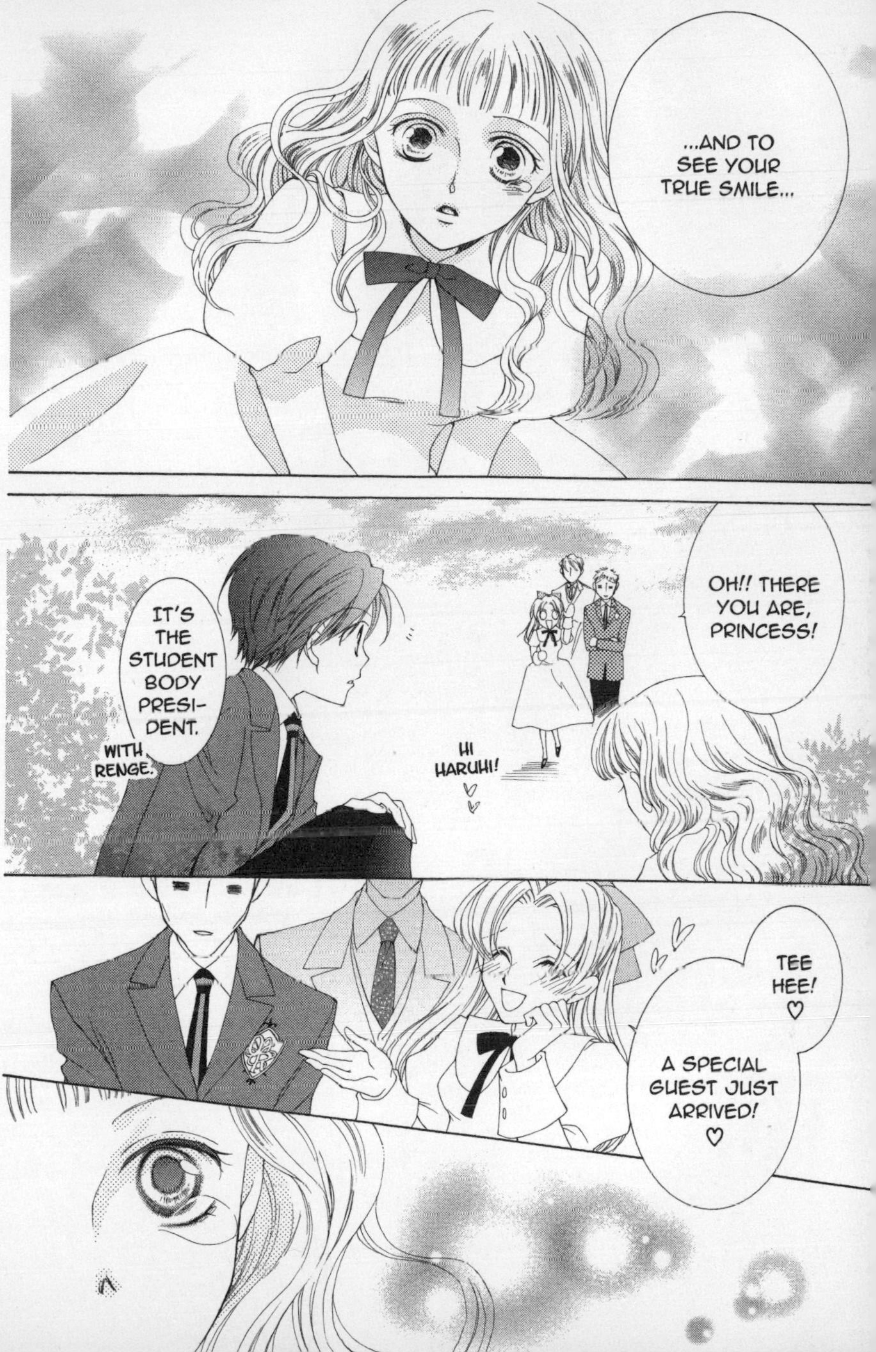
...AND TO SEE YOUR TRUE SMILE...
OH!! THERE YOU ARE, PRINCESS!
HI HARUHI! ♡ ♡
IT'S THE STUDENT BODY PRESI- DENT.
WITH RENGE.
TEE HEE! ♡
A SPECIAL GUEST JUST ARRIVED! ♡

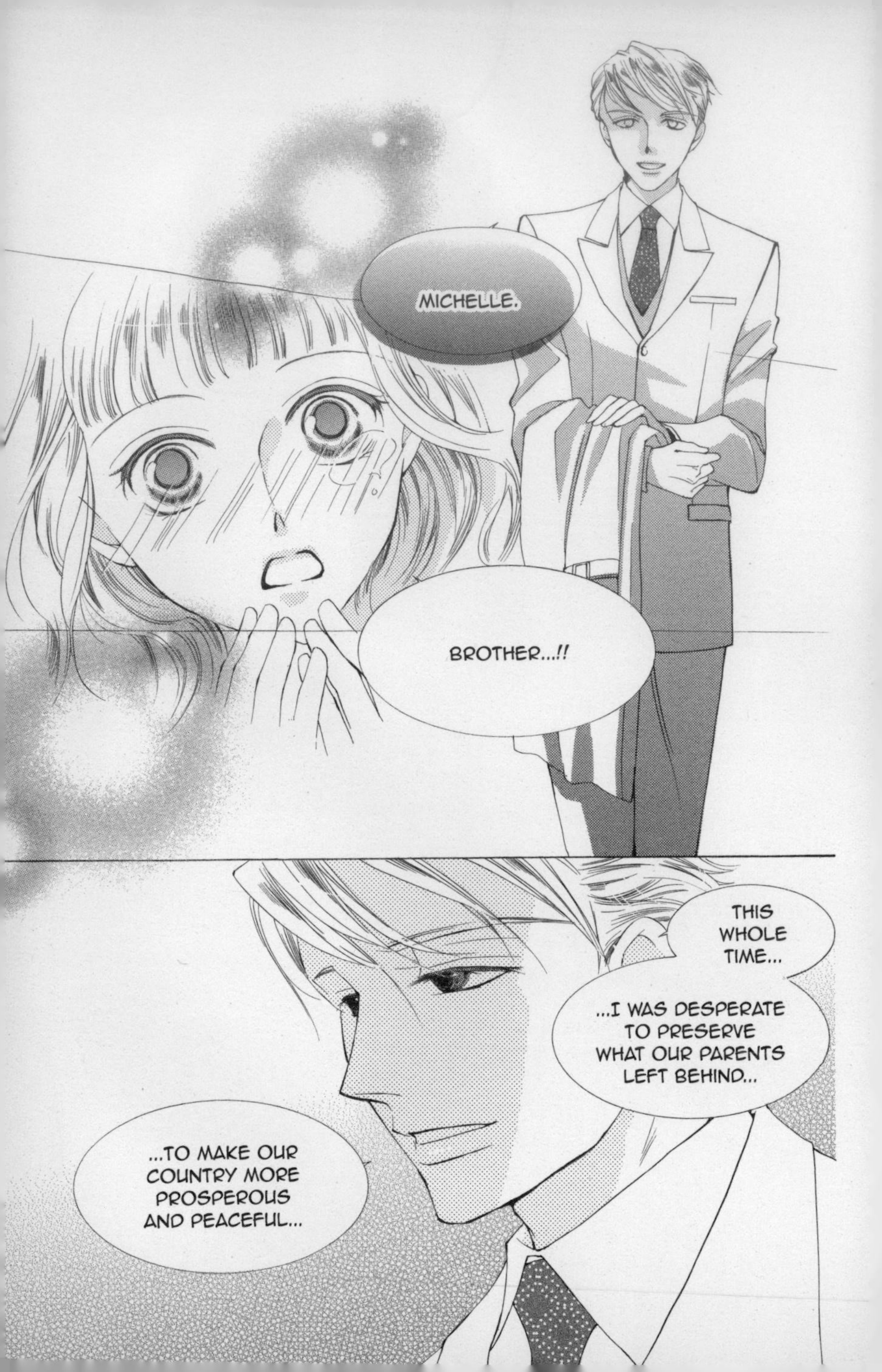
MICHELLE.
BROTHER...!!
THIS WHOLE TIME...
...I WAS DESPERATE TO PRESERVE WHAT OUR PARENTS LEFT BEHIND...
...TO MAKE OUR COUNTRY MORE PROSPEROUS AND PEACEFUL...

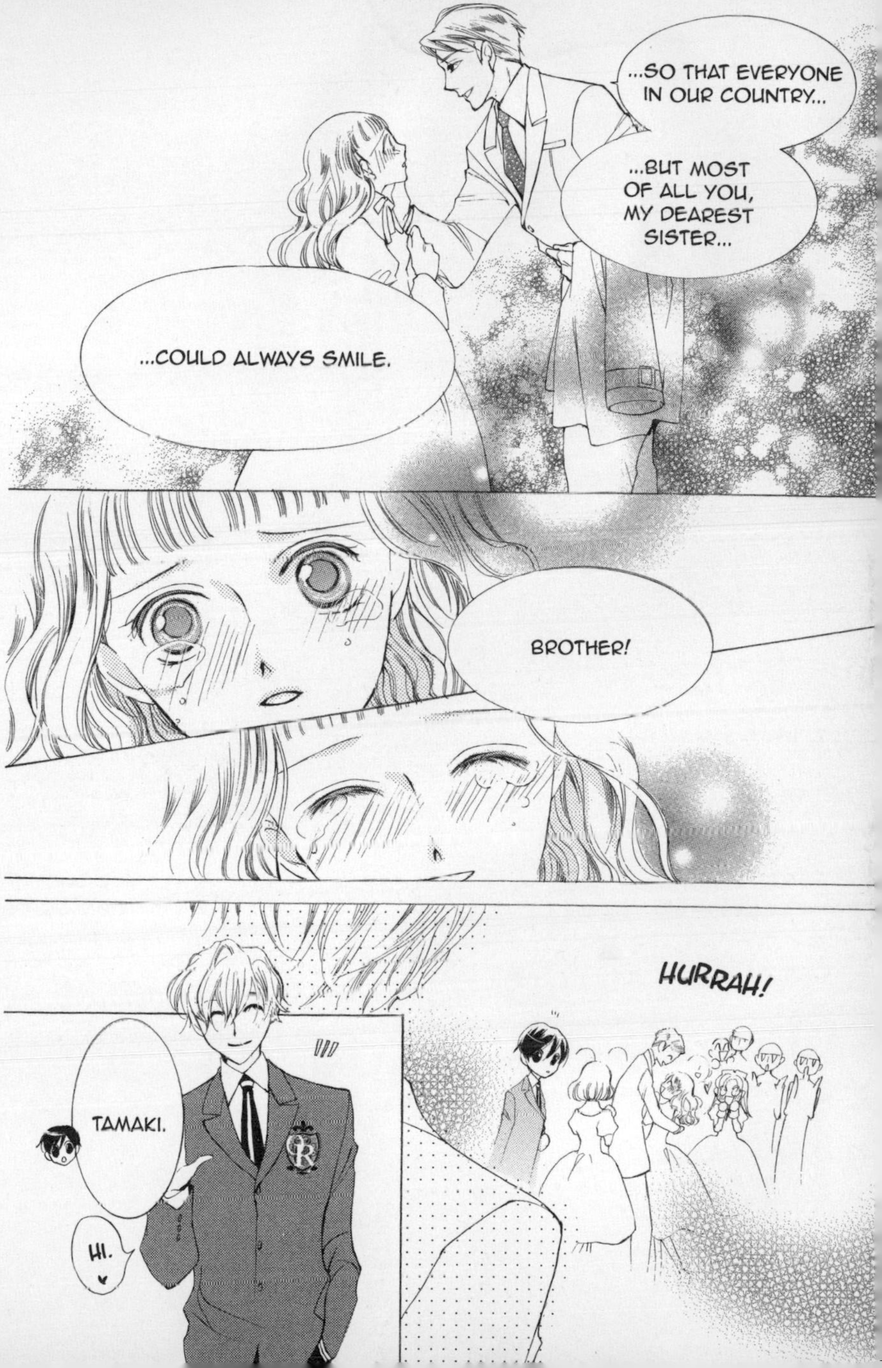
...SO THAT EVERYONE IN OUR COUNTRY...
...BUT MOST OF ALL YOU, MY DEAREST SISTER...
...COULD ALWAYS SMILE.
BROTHER!
HURRAH!
TAMAKI.
HI.

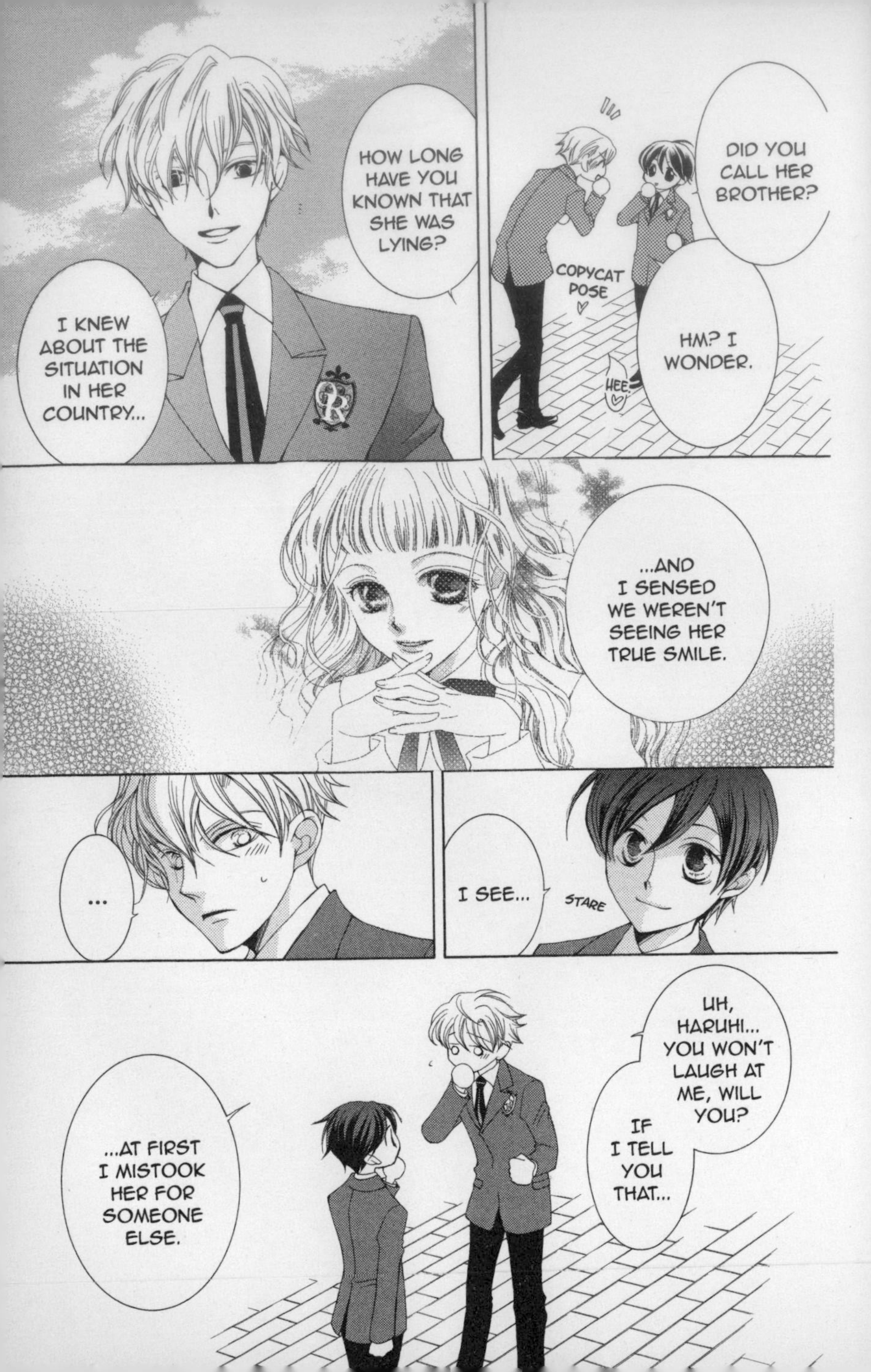
DID YOU CALL HER BROTHER?
HM? I WONDER.
COPYCAT POSE
HEE!
HOW LONG HAVE YOU KNOWN THAT SHE WAS LYING?
I KNEW ABOUT THE SITUATION IN HER COUNTRY...
...AND I SENSED WE WEREN'T SEEING HER TRUE SMILE.
I SEE...
STARE
...
UH, HARUHI... YOU WON'T LAUGH AT ME, WILL YOU?
IF I TELL YOU THAT...
...AT FIRST I MISTOOK HER FOR SOMEONE ELSE.

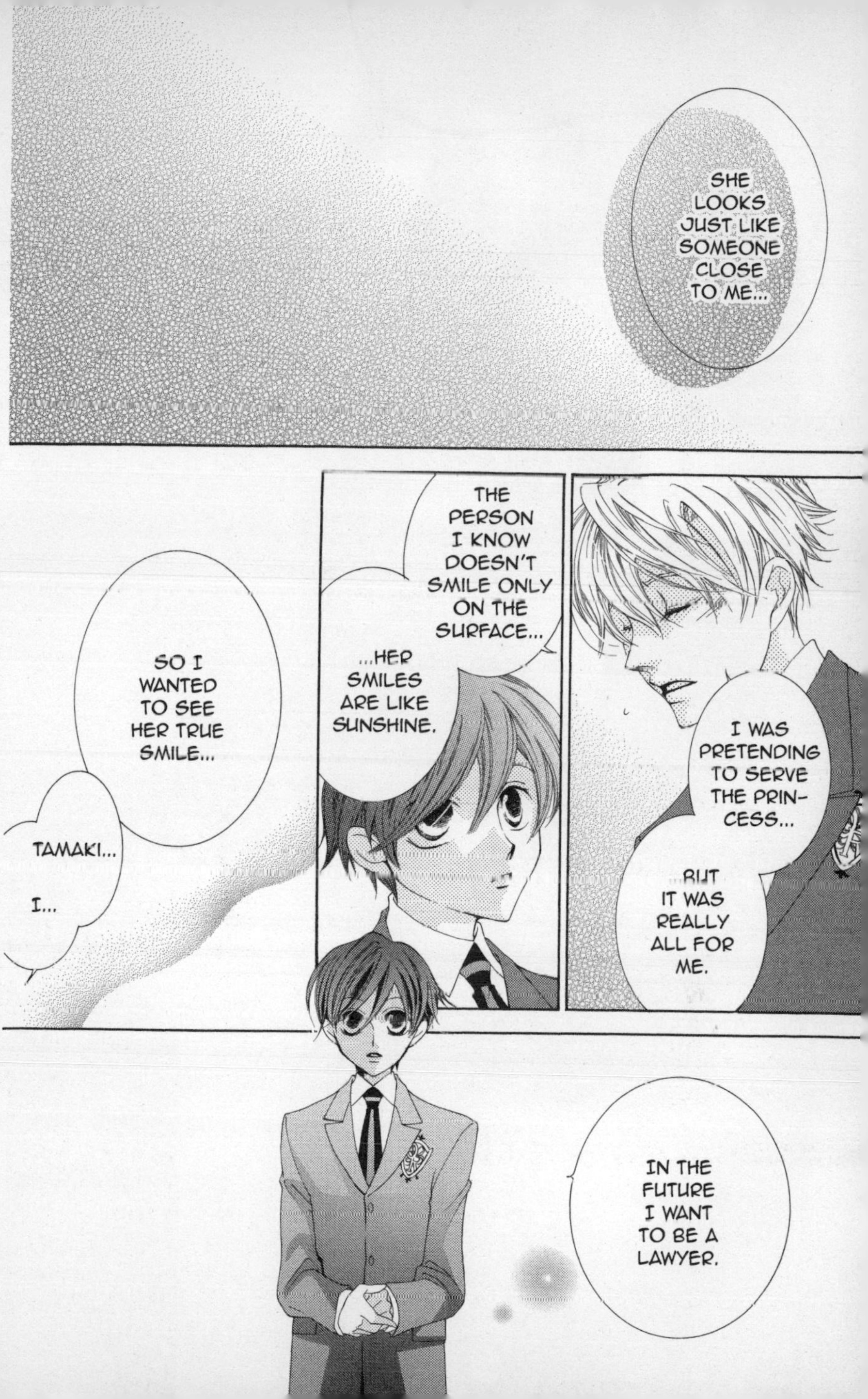
SHE LOOKS JUST LIKE SOMEONE CLOSE TO ME...
I WAS PRETENDING TO SERVE THE PRINCESS...
...BUT IT WAS REALLY ALL FOR ME.
THE PERSON I KNOW DOESN'T SMILE ONLY ON THE SURFACE...
...HER SMILES ARE LIKE SUNSHINE.
SO I WANTED TO SEE HER TRUE SMILE...
TAMAKI...
I...
IN THE FUTURE I WANT TO BE A LAWYER.

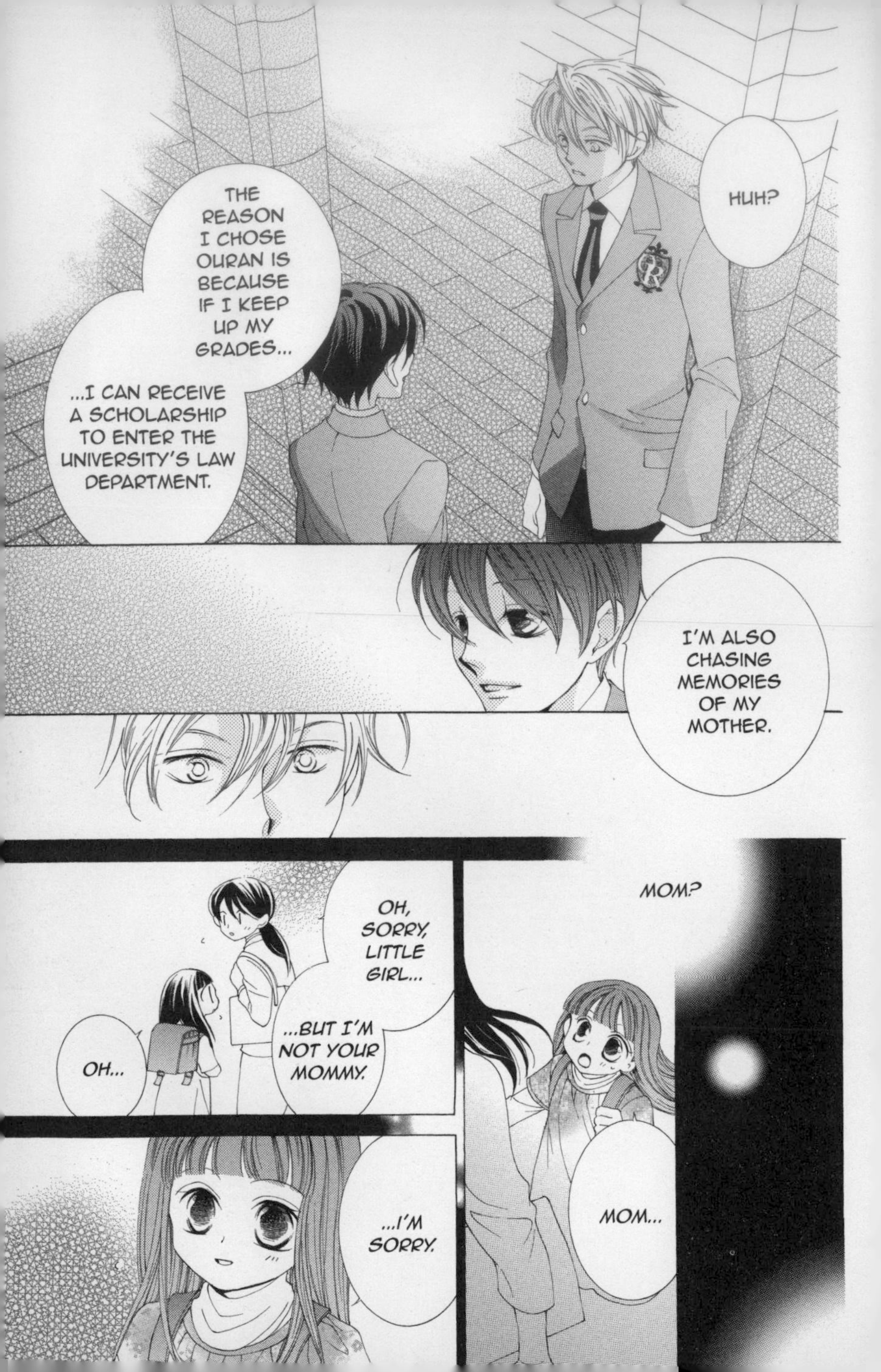
HUH?
THE REASON I CHOSE OURAN IS BECAUSE IF I KEEP UP MY GRADES...
...I CAN RECEIVE A SCHOLARSHIP TO ENTER THE UNIVERSITY'S LAW DEPARTMENT.
I'M ALSO CHASING MEMORIES OF MY MOTHER.
MOM?
MOM...
OH, SORRY, LITTLE GIRL...
...BUT I'M NOT YOUR MOMMY.
OH...
...I'M SORRY.

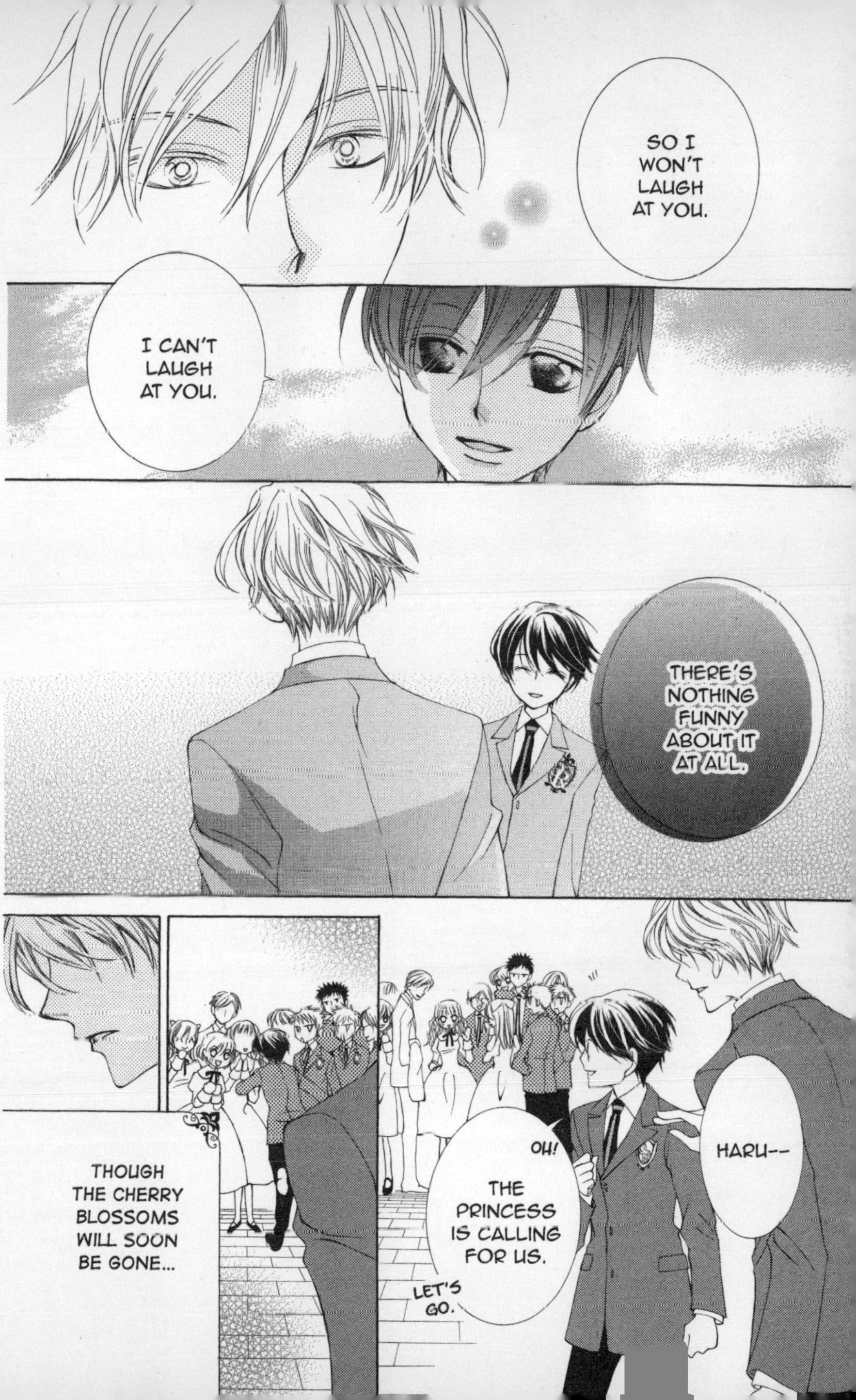
SO I WON'T LAUGH AT YOU.
I CAN'T LAUGH AT YOU.
THERE'S NOTHING FUNNY ABOUT IT AT ALL.
HARU--
OH!
THE PRINCESS IS CALLING FOR US.
LET'S GO.
THOUGH THE CHERRY BLOSSOMS WILL SOON BE GONE...

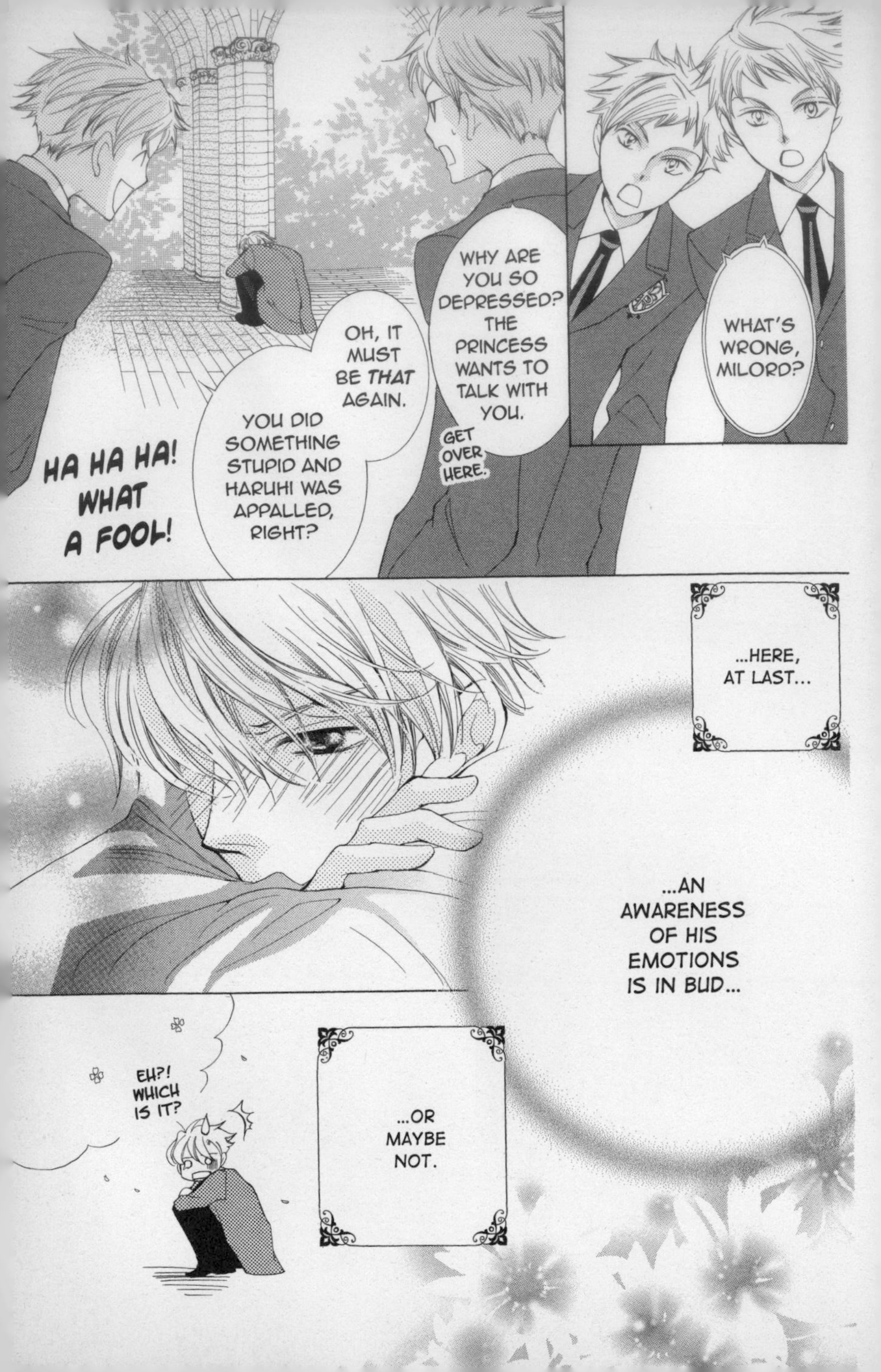
WHAT'S WRONG, MILORD?
WHY ARE YOU SO DEPRESSED? THE PRINCESS WANTS TO TALK WITH YOU.
GET OVER HERE.
OH, IT MUST BE *THAT* AGAIN.
YOU DID SOMETHING STUPID AND HARUHI WAS APPALLED, RIGHT?
HA HA HA! WHAT A FOOL!
...HERE, AT LAST...
...AN AWARENESS OF HIS EMOTIONS IS IN BUD...
...OR MAYBE NOT.
EH?! WHICH IS IT?

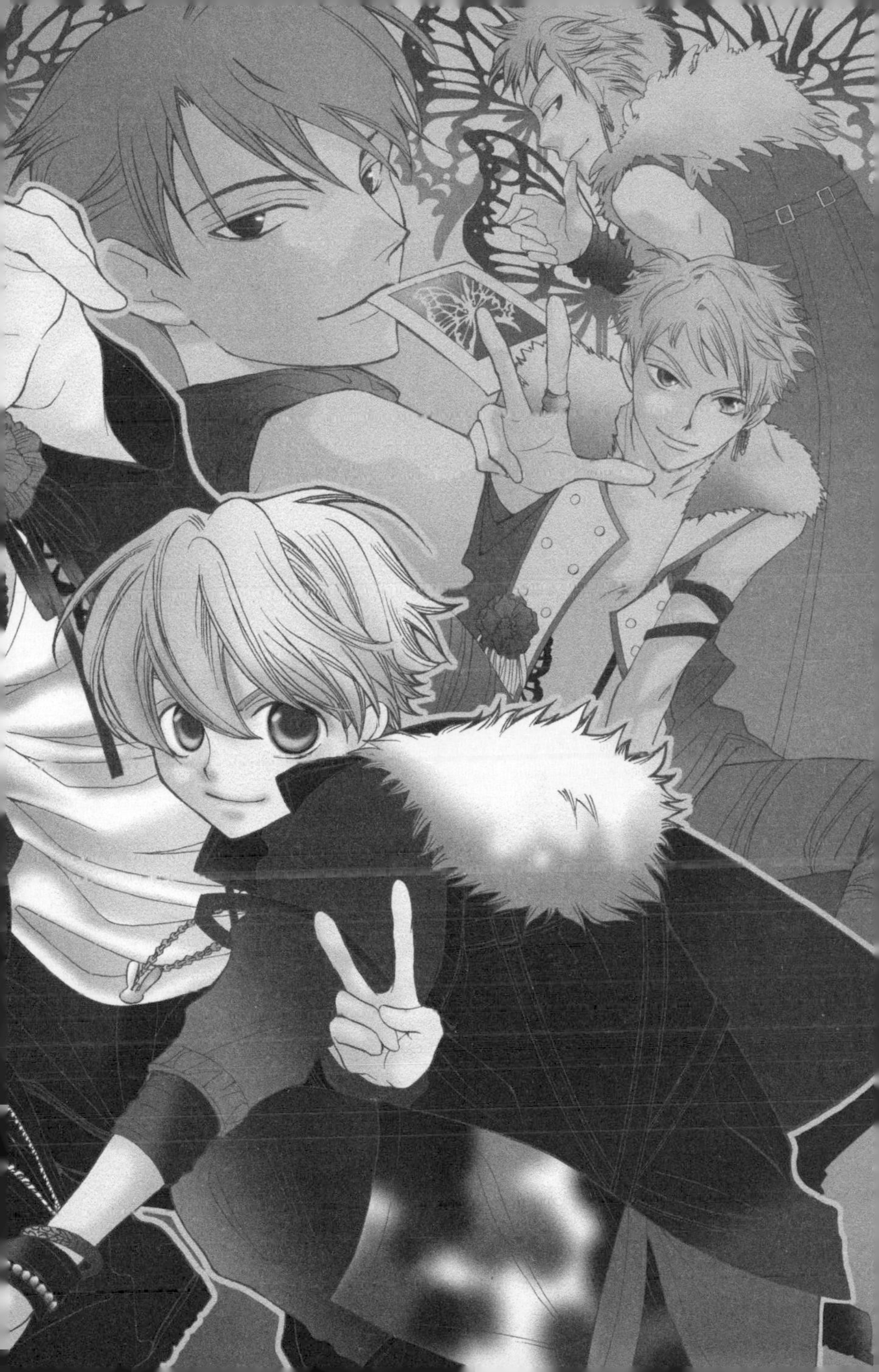

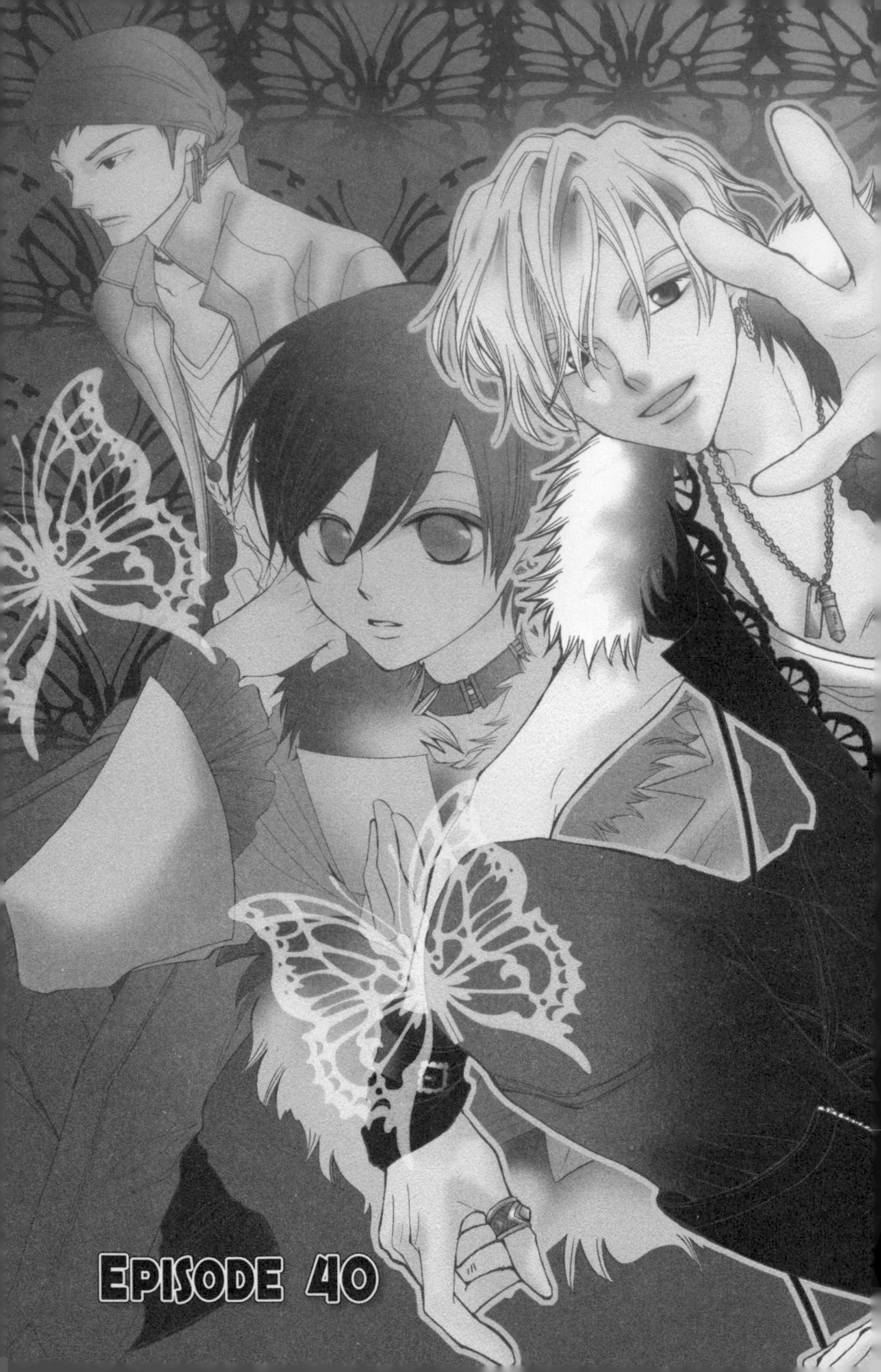
EPISODE 40

GUEST ROOM: FAXES ②

SPECIAL THANKS TO SHINOBU AMANO!!

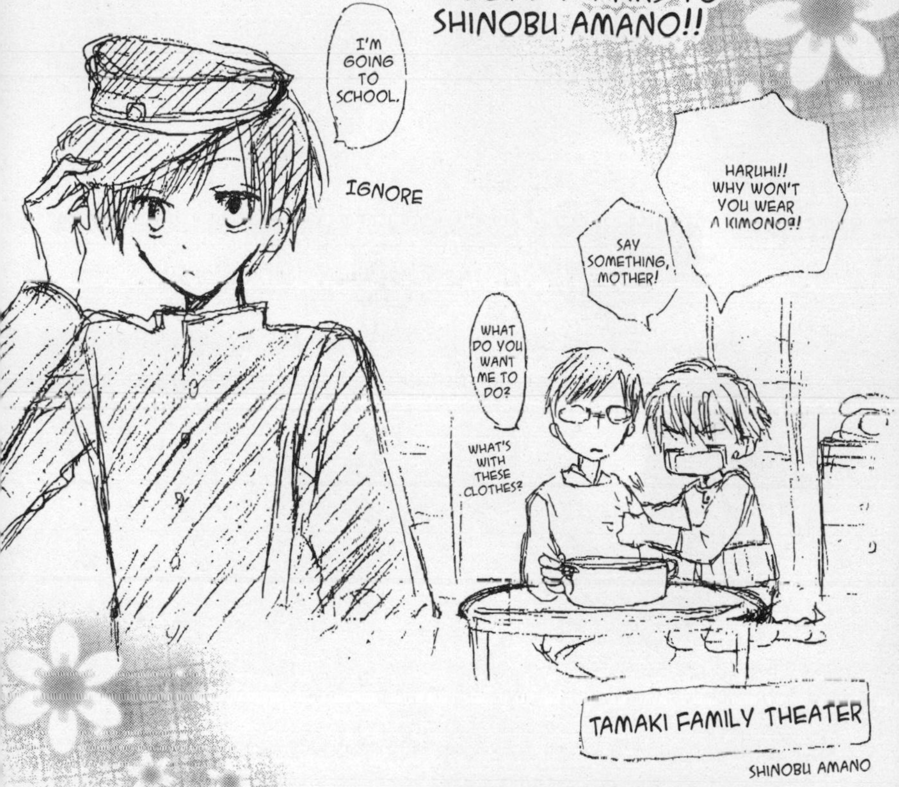
HARUHI!! WHY WON'T YOU WEAR A KIMONO?!
SAY SOMETHING, MOTHER!
WHAT DO YOU WANT ME TO DO?
WHAT'S WITH THESE CLOTHES?
I'M GOING TO SCHOOL.
IGNORE
TAMAKI FAMILY THEATER
SHINOBU AMANO

I GOT THIS SUOH FAMILY FAX FROM SHINOBU AMANO, WHO DRAWS FOR *LALA*!! PLEASE PAY SPECIAL ATTENTION TO KYOYA IN AN APRON (LAUGH). I WONDER WHAT'S IN THAT POT--MISO SOUP? I'D LIKE TO TRY IT!

THANK YOU FOR SUCH A CUTE FAX!! I'LL NEVER FORGET MY SHOCK WHEN I FIRST SAW SHINOBU AMANO... SHE IS EXTREMELY PRETTY!!!! (THERE ARE LOTS OF PRETTY MANGAKA AT *LALA*, BUT SHINOBU IS FAMOUS FOR BEING AN ABSOLUTE BEAUTY.) THE MANGA SHE DRAWS ARE SO POWERFUL AND RICH IN EMOTION.

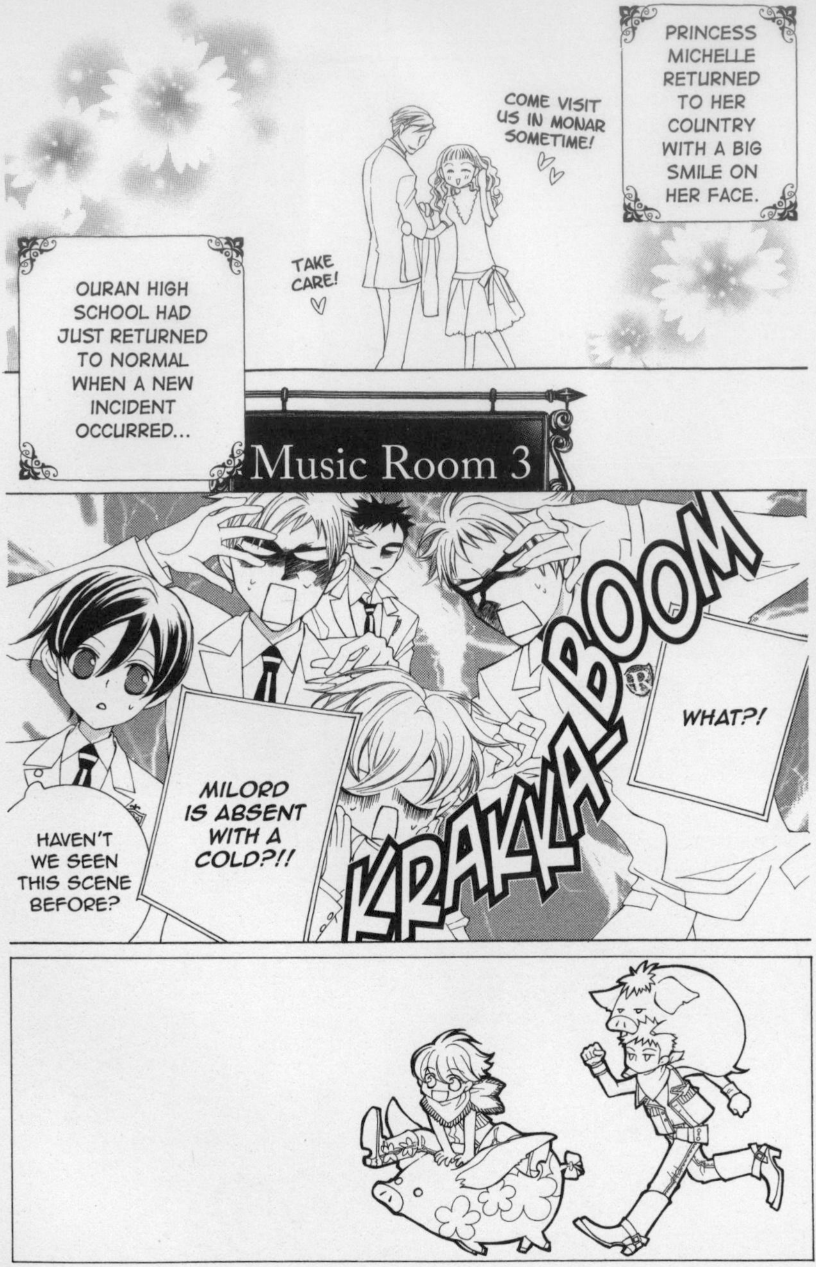
PRINCESS MICHELLE RETURNED TO HER COUNTRY WITH A BIG SMILE ON HER FACE.
COME VISIT US IN MONAR SOMETIME!
TAKE CARE!
OURAN HIGH SCHOOL HAD JUST RETURNED TO NORMAL WHEN A NEW INCIDENT OCCURRED...
Music Room 3
KRAKKA BOOM
WHAT?!
MILORD IS ABSENT WITH A COLD?!!
HAVEN'T WE SEEN THIS SCENE BEFORE?

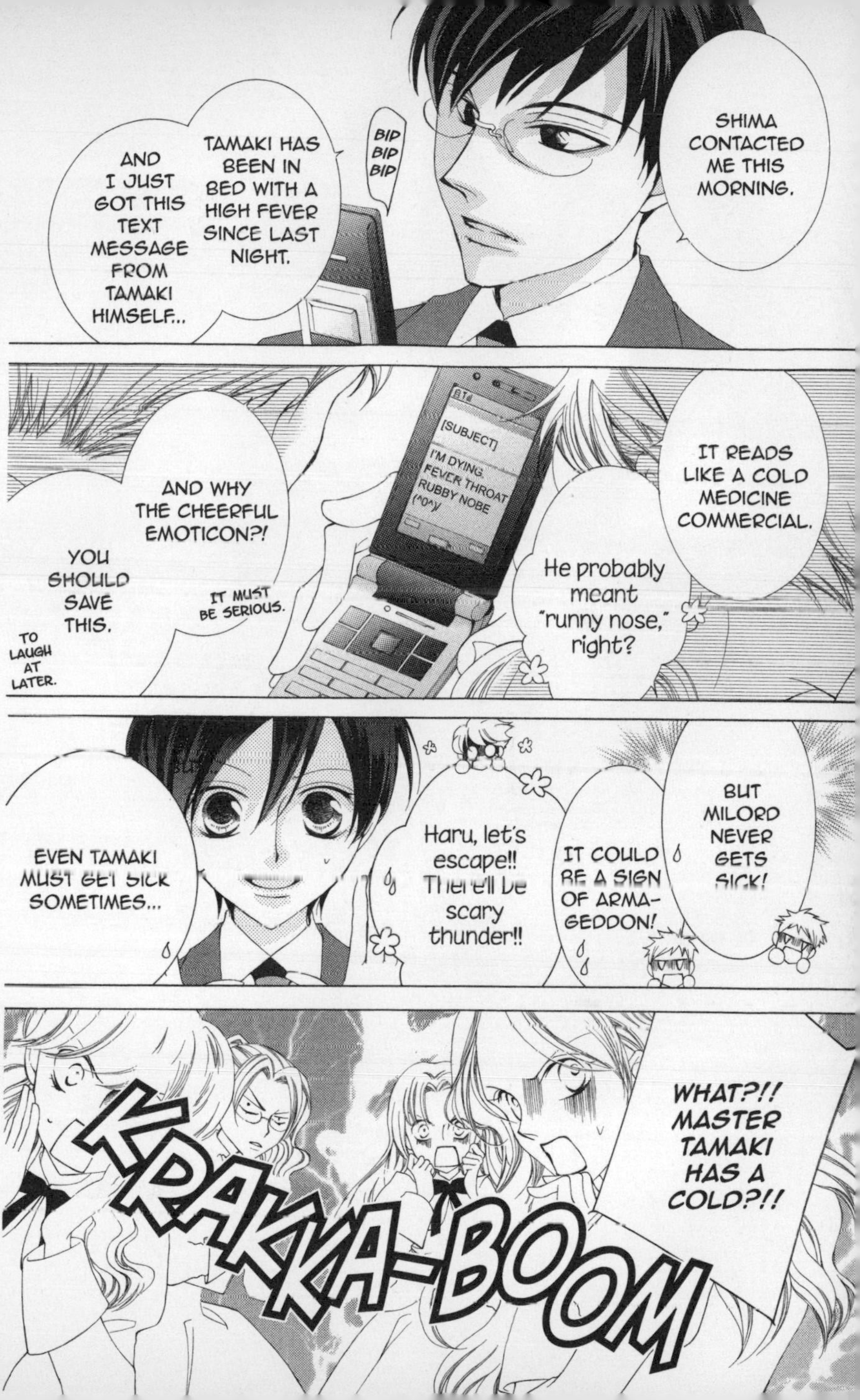
SHIMA CONTACTED ME THIS MORNING.
BIP BIP BIP
TAMAKI HAS BEEN IN BED WITH A HIGH FEVER SINCE LAST NIGHT.
AND I JUST GOT THIS TEXT MESSAGE FROM TAMAKI HIMSELF...
IT READS LIKE A COLD MEDICINE COMMERCIAL.
He probably meant "runny nose," right?
[SUBJECT]
I'M DYING. FEVER THROAT RUBBY NOBE (^o^)/
AND WHY THE CHEERFUL EMOTICON?!
IT MUST BE SERIOUS.
YOU SHOULD SAVE THIS.
TO LAUGH AT LATER.
BUT MILORD NEVER GETS SICK!
IT COULD BE A SIGN OF ARMA-GEDDON!
Haru, let's escape!! There'll be scary thunder!!
EVEN TAMAKI MUST GET SICK SOMETIMES...
WHAT?!! MASTER TAMAKI HAS A COLD?!!
KRAKKA-BOOM

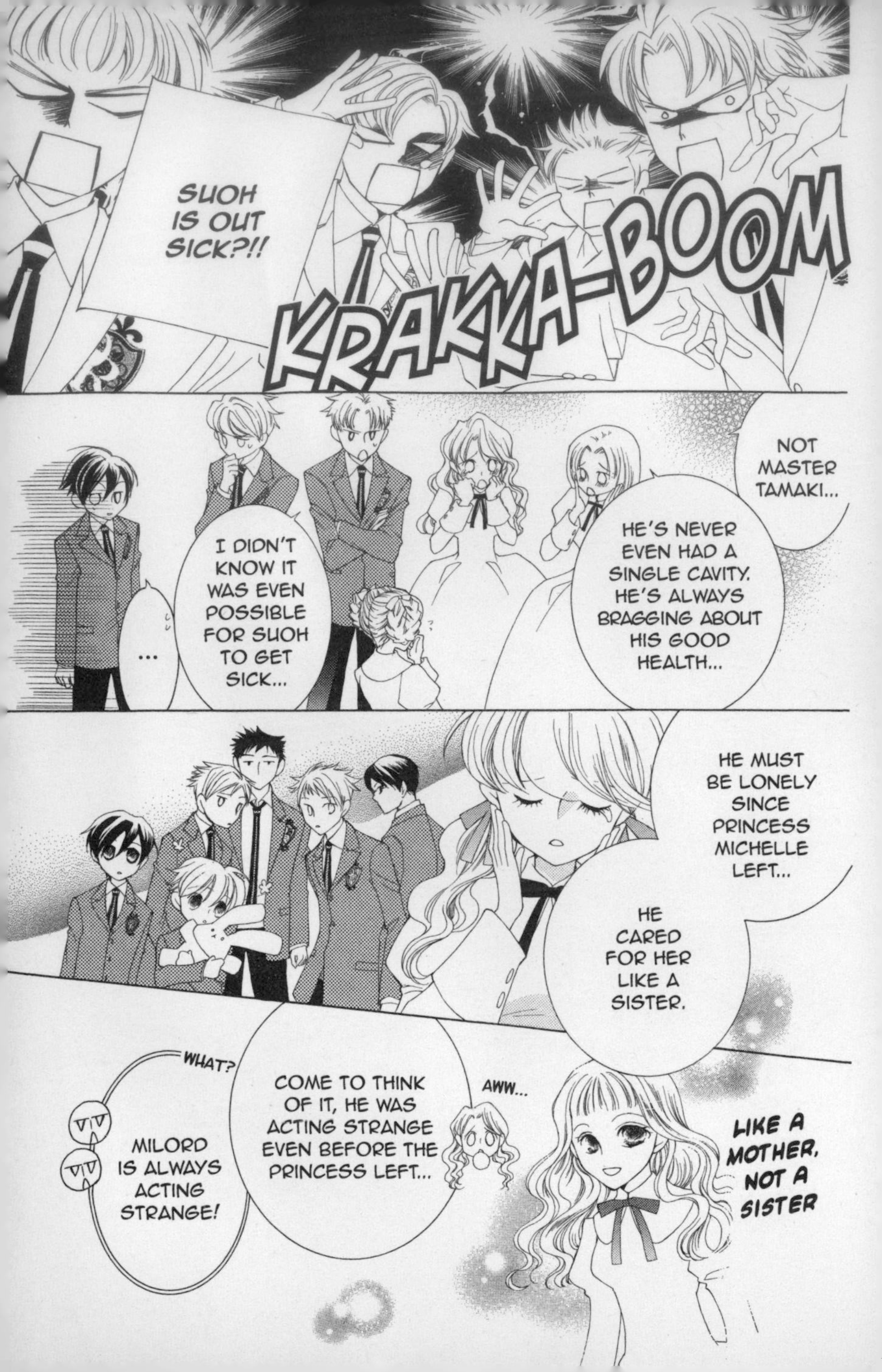
SUOH IS OUT SICK?!!
KRAKKA-BOOM
NOT MASTER TAMAKI...
HE'S NEVER EVEN HAD A SINGLE CAVITY. HE'S ALWAYS BRAGGING ABOUT HIS GOOD HEALTH...
I DIDN'T KNOW IT WAS EVEN POSSIBLE FOR SUOH TO GET SICK...
...
HE MUST BE LONELY SINCE PRINCESS MICHELLE LEFT...
HE CARED FOR HER LIKE A SISTER.
LIKE A MOTHER, NOT A SISTER
AWW...
COME TO THINK OF IT, HE WAS ACTING STRANGE EVEN BEFORE THE PRINCESS LEFT...
WHAT?
MILORD IS ALWAYS ACTING STRANGE!

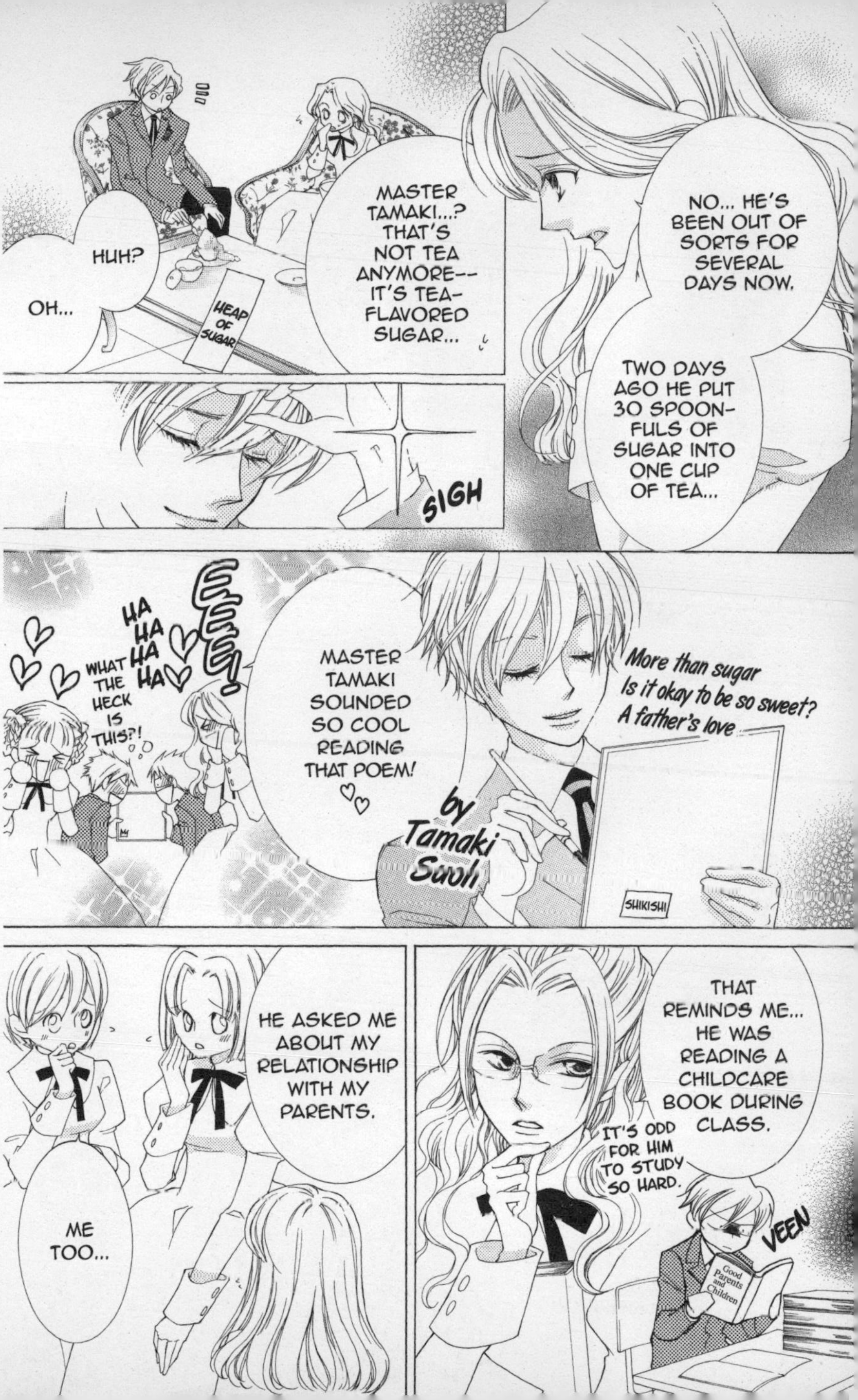
NO... HE'S BEEN OUT OF SORTS FOR SEVERAL DAYS NOW.
TWO DAYS AGO HE PUT 30 SPOONFULS OF SUGAR INTO ONE CUP OF TEA...
MASTER TAMAKI...? THAT'S NOT TEA ANYMORE-- IT'S TEA-FLAVORED SUGAR...
HEAP OF SUGAR
HUH?
OH...
SIGH
More than sugar
Is it okay to be so sweet?
A father's love
by Tamaki Suoh
SHIKISHI
MASTER TAMAKI SOUNDED SO COOL READING THAT POEM!
EEEE!
HA HA HA HA
WHAT THE HECK IS THIS?!
THAT REMINDS ME... HE WAS READING A CHILDCARE BOOK DURING CLASS.
IT'S ODD FOR HIM TO STUDY SO HARD.
VEEN
Good Parents and Children
HE ASKED ME ABOUT MY RELATIONSHIP WITH MY PARENTS.
ME TOO...

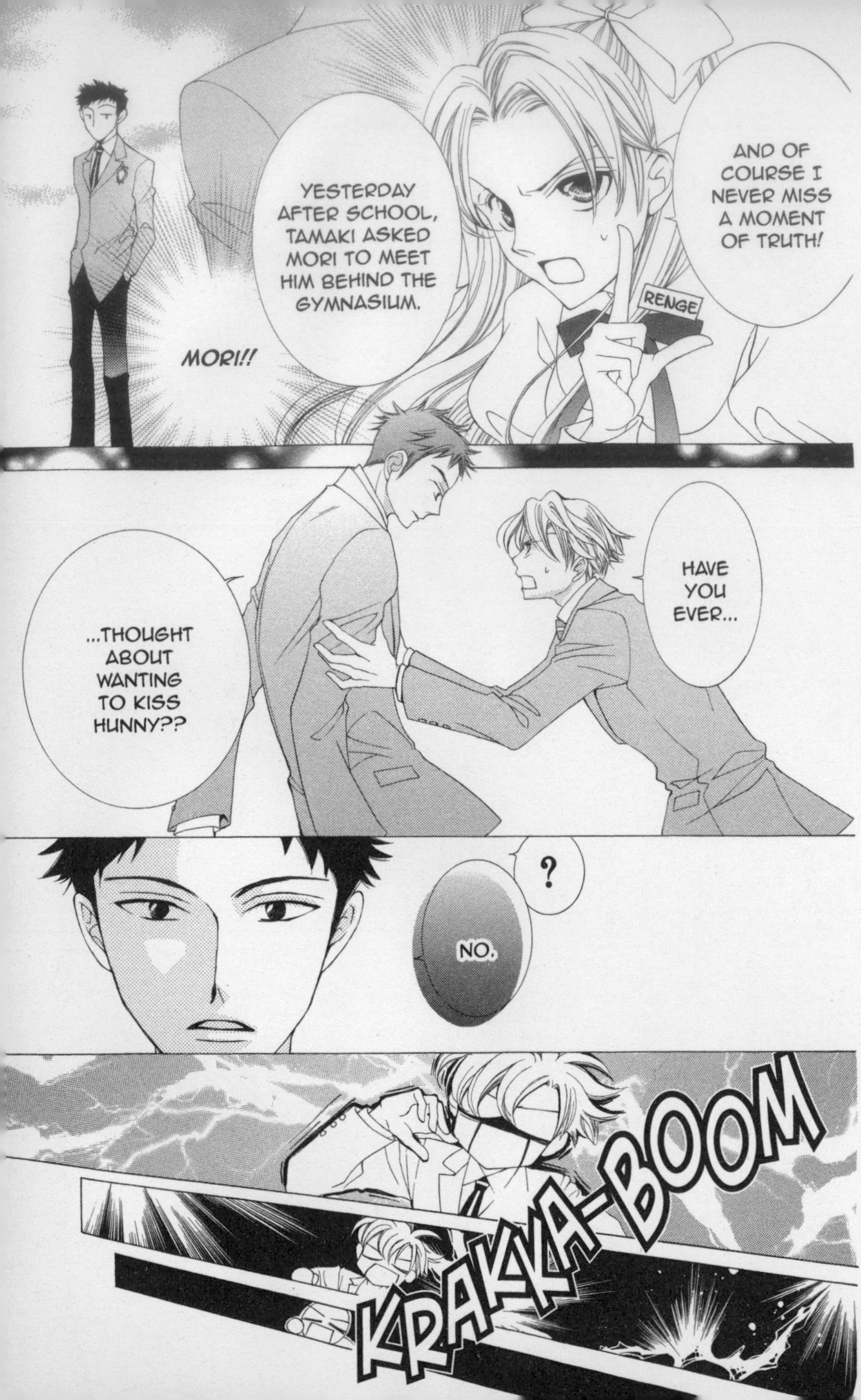
AND OF COURSE I NEVER MISS A MOMENT OF TRUTH!
RENGE
YESTERDAY AFTER SCHOOL, TAMAKI ASKED MORI TO MEET HIM BEHIND THE GYMNASIUM.
MORI!!
HAVE YOU EVER...
...THOUGHT ABOUT WANTING TO KISS HUNNY??
?
NO.
KRAKA-BOOM

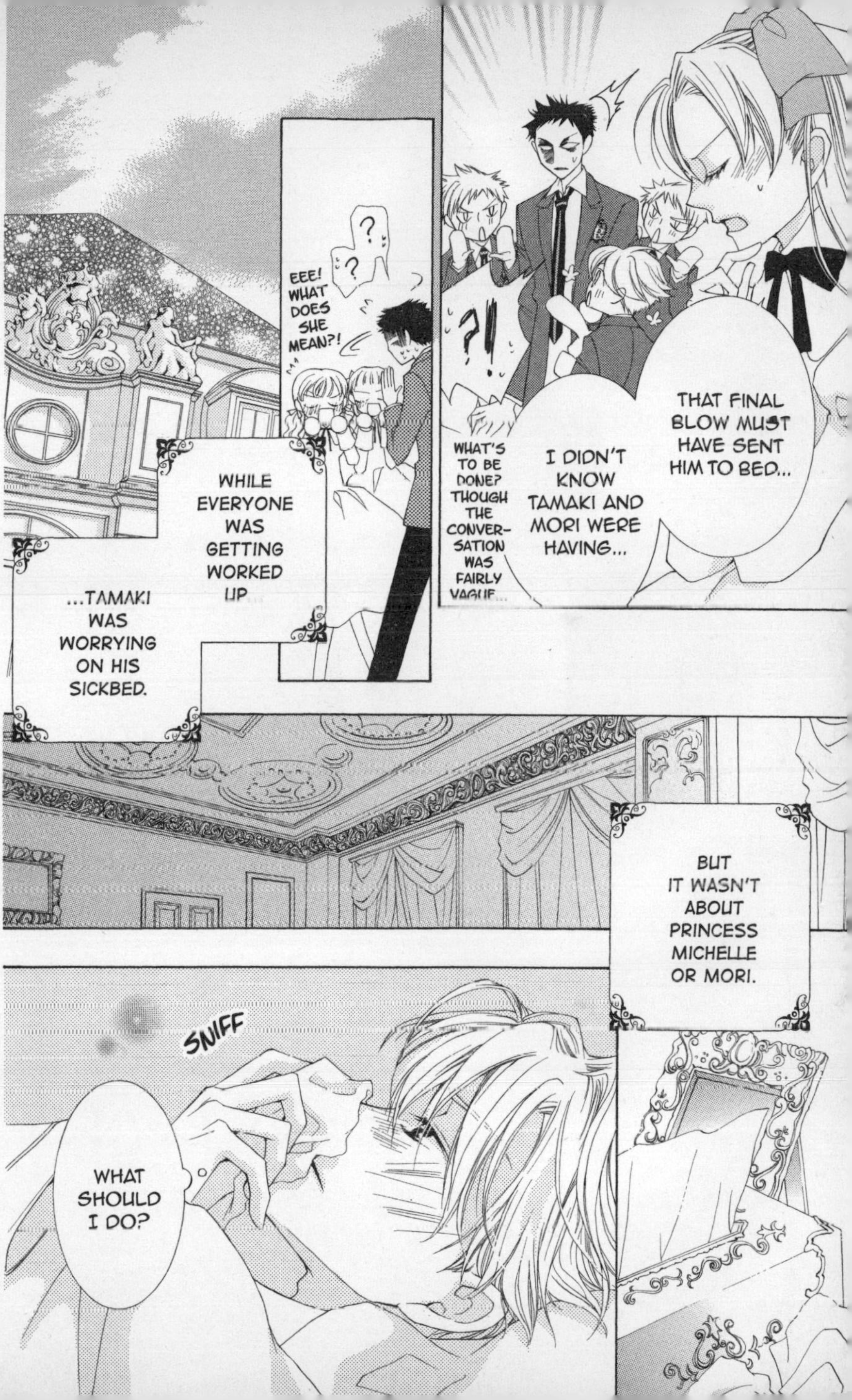
THAT FINAL BLOW MUST HAVE SENT HIM TO BED...
?!
I DIDN'T KNOW TAMAKI AND MORI WERE HAVING...
WHAT'S TO BE DONE? THOUGH THE CONVERSATION WAS FAIRLY VAGUE...
?
?
EEE! WHAT DOES SHE MEAN?!
WHILE EVERYONE WAS GETTING WORKED UP...
...TAMAKI WAS WORRYING ON HIS SICKBED.
BUT IT WASN'T ABOUT PRINCESS MICHELLE OR MORI.
SNIFF
WHAT SHOULD I DO?

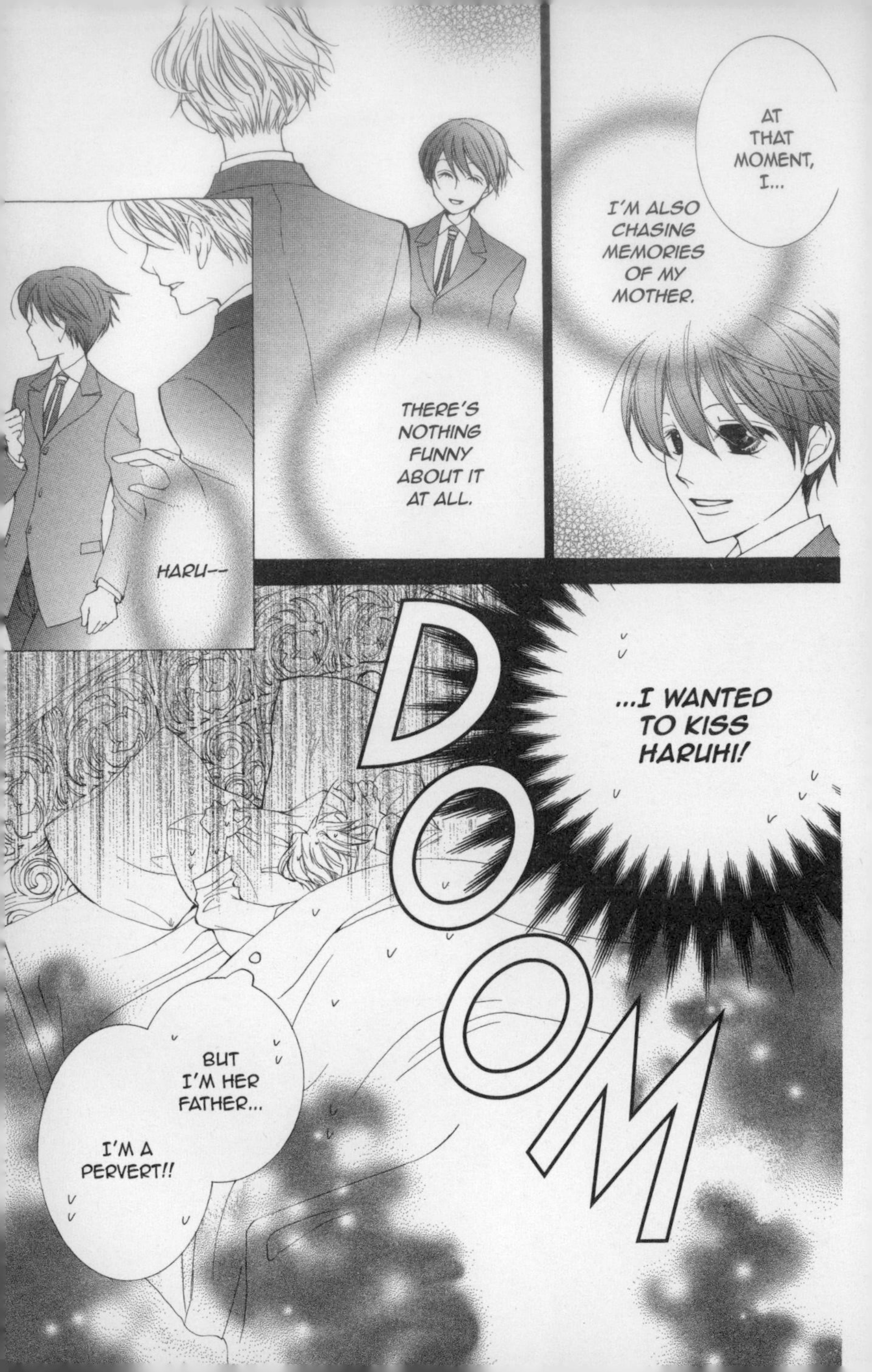
AT THAT MOMENT, I...
I'M ALSO CHASING MEMORIES OF MY MOTHER.
THERE'S NOTHING FUNNY ABOUT IT AT ALL.
HARU--
...I WANTED TO KISS HARUHI!
DOOM
BUT I'M HER FATHER...
I'M A PERVERT!!

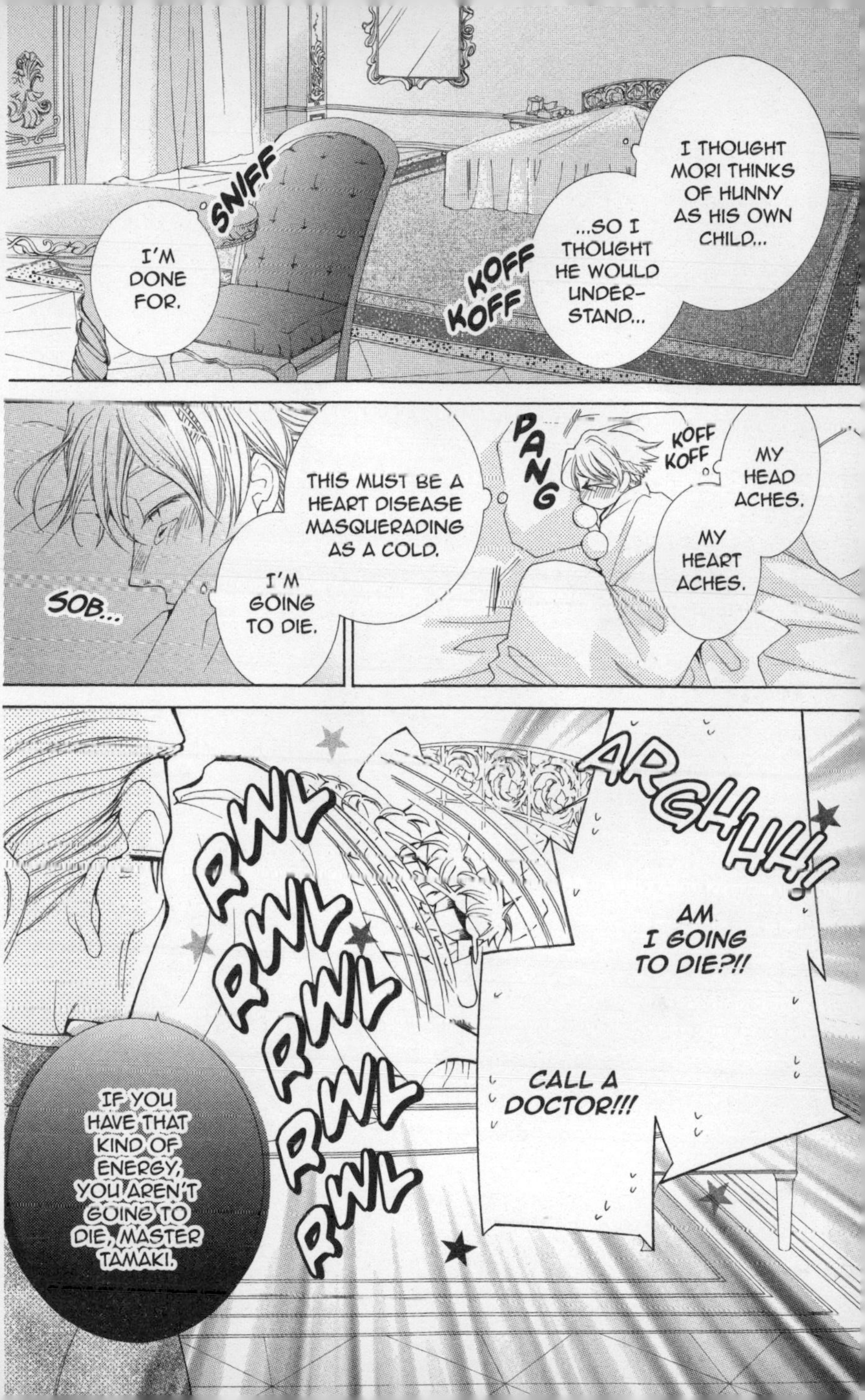
I THOUGHT MORI THINKS OF HUNNY AS HIS OWN CHILD...
...SO I THOUGHT HE WOULD UNDER-STAND...
KOFF KOFF
SNIFF
I'M DONE FOR.
MY HEAD ACHES.
MY HEART ACHES.
KOFF KOFF
PANG
THIS MUST BE A HEART DISEASE MASQUERADING AS A COLD.
I'M GOING TO DIE.
SOB...
ARGHHH!
AM I GOING TO DIE?!!
CALL A DOCTOR!!!
RWL RWL RWL RWL RWL RWL
IF YOU HAVE THAT KIND OF ENERGY, YOU AREN'T GOING TO DIE, MASTER TAMAKI.

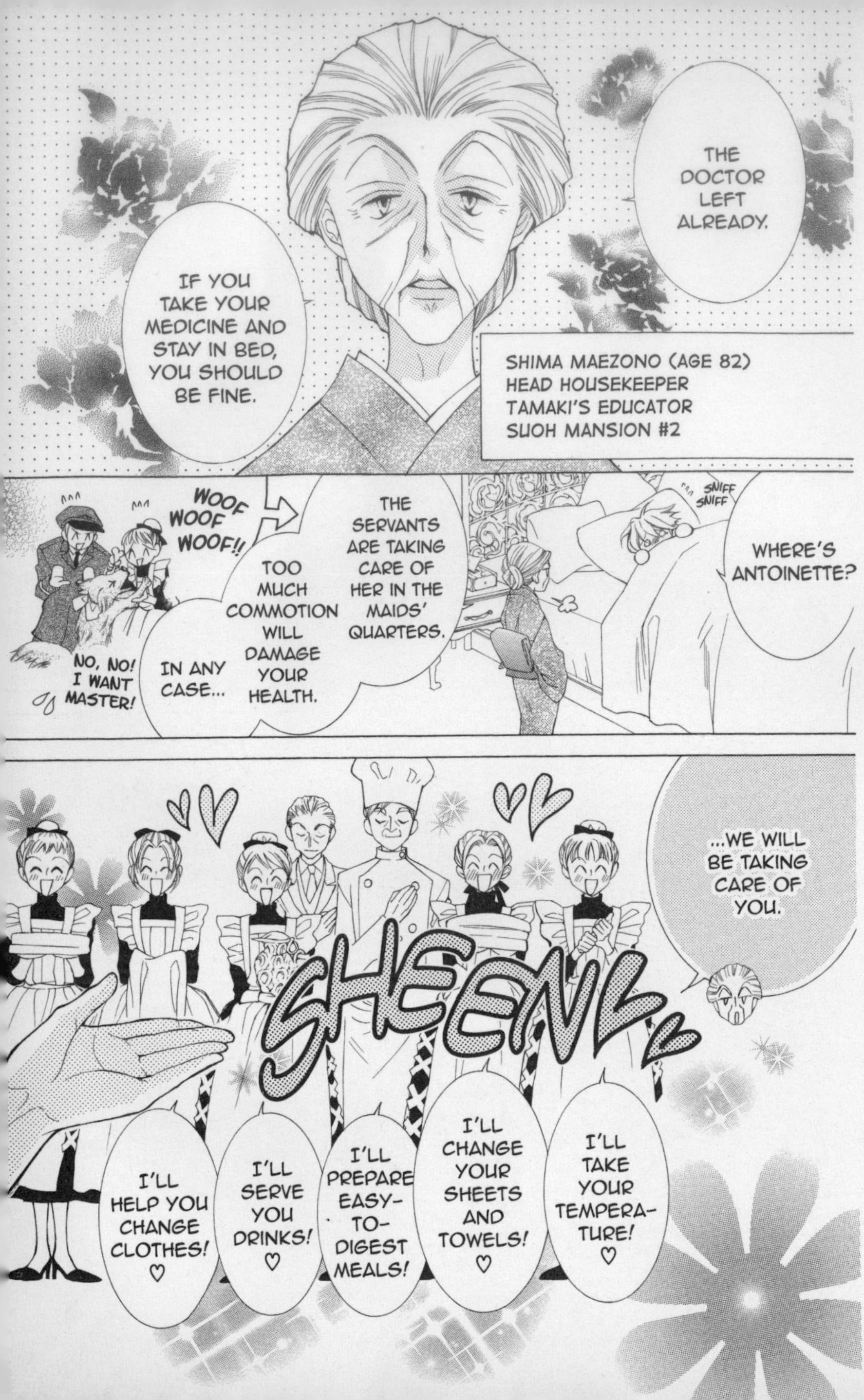
THE DOCTOR LEFT ALREADY.
IF YOU TAKE YOUR MEDICINE AND STAY IN BED, YOU SHOULD BE FINE.
SHIMA MAEZONO (AGE 82)
HEAD HOUSEKEEPER
TAMAKI'S EDUCATOR
SUOH MANSION #2
SNIFF SNIFF
WHERE'S ANTOINETTE?
THE SERVANTS ARE TAKING CARE OF HER IN THE MAIDS' QUARTERS.
WOOF WOOF WOOF!!
NO, NO! I WANT MASTER!
TOO MUCH COMMOTION WILL DAMAGE YOUR HEALTH.
IN ANY CASE...
...WE WILL BE TAKING CARE OF YOU.
SHEEN!
I'LL TAKE YOUR TEMPERA-TURE! ♡
I'LL CHANGE YOUR SHEETS AND TOWELS! ♡
I'LL PREPARE EASY-TO-DIGEST MEALS!
I'LL SERVE YOU DRINKS! ♡
I'LL HELP YOU CHANGE CLOTHES! ♡

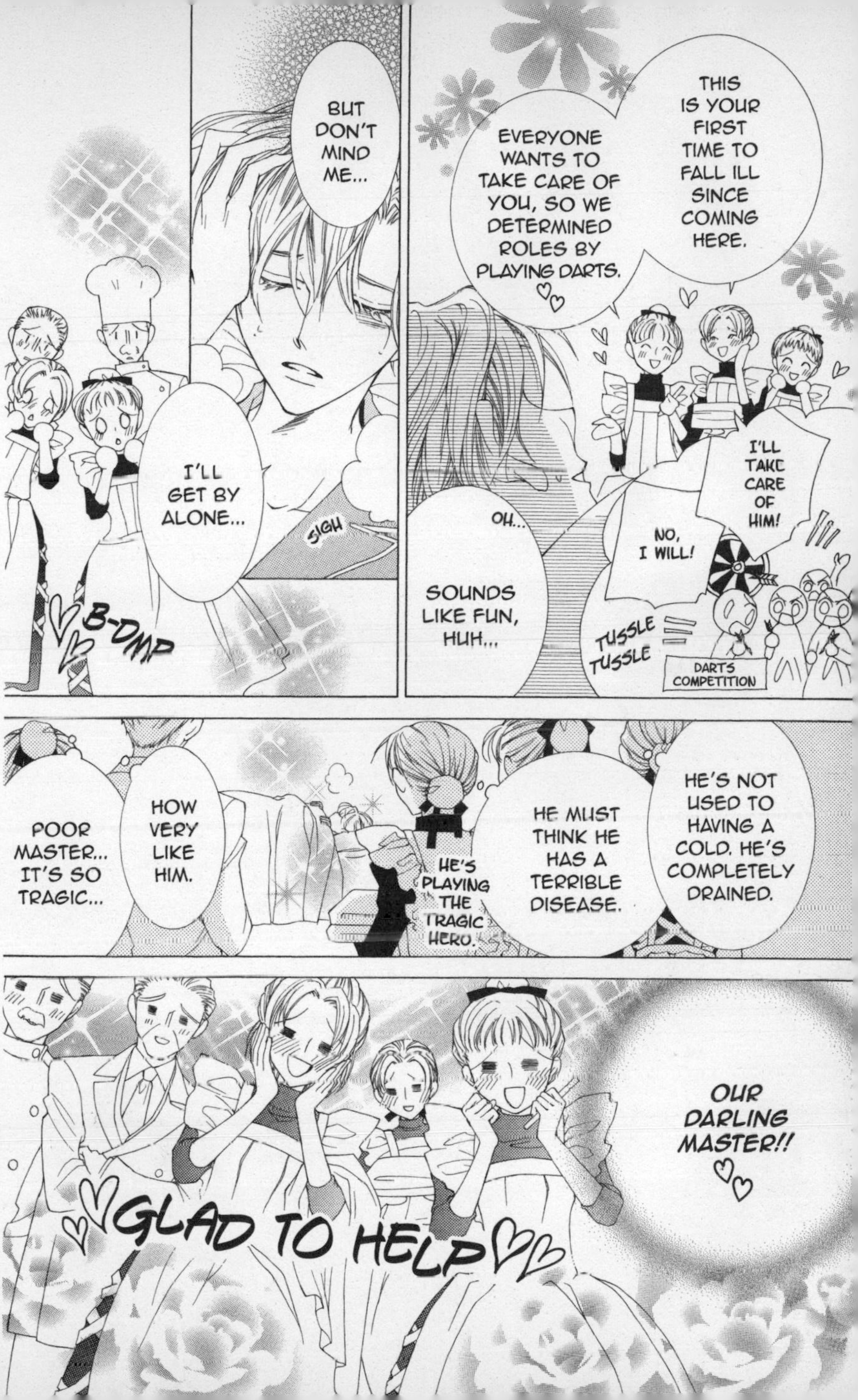
THIS IS YOUR FIRST TIME TO FALL ILL SINCE COMING HERE.
EVERYONE WANTS TO TAKE CARE OF YOU, SO WE DETERMINED ROLES BY PLAYING DARTS. ♡♡
I'LL TAKE CARE OF HIM!
NO, I WILL!
TUSSLE TUSSLE
DARTS COMPETITION
OH...
SOUNDS LIKE FUN, HUH...
BUT DON'T MIND ME...
I'LL GET BY ALONE...
SIGH
♡B-DMP♡
HE'S NOT USED TO HAVING A COLD. HE'S COMPLETELY DRAINED.
HE MUST THINK HE HAS A TERRIBLE DISEASE.
HE'S PLAYING THE TRAGIC HERO.
HOW VERY LIKE HIM.
POOR MASTER... IT'S SO TRAGIC...
OUR DARLING MASTER!! ♡♡
♡GLAD TO HELP♡

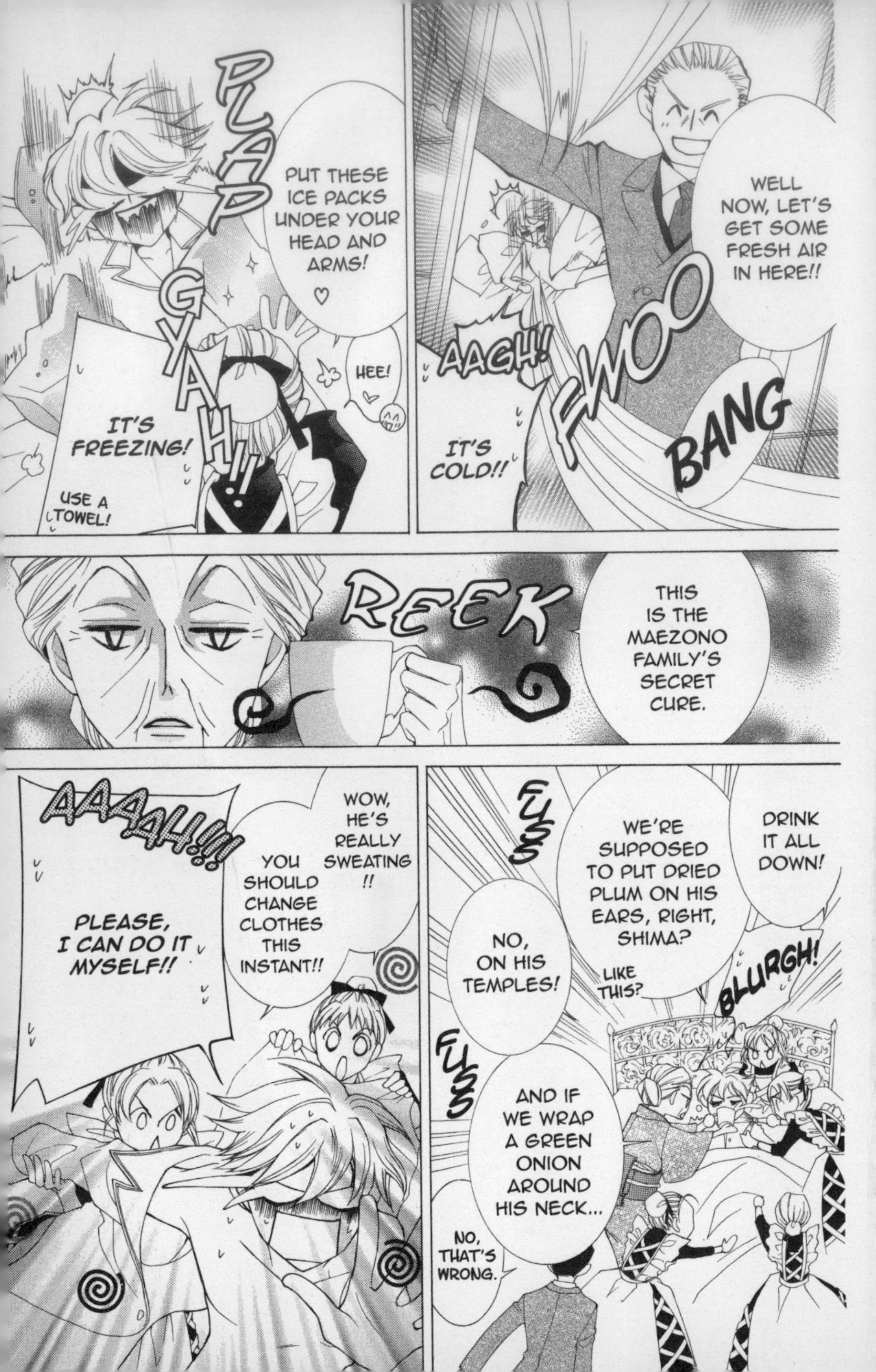
WELL NOW, LET'S GET SOME FRESH AIR IN HERE!!
FWOO
BANG
AAGH!
IT'S COLD!!
PLAP
PUT THESE ICE PACKS UNDER YOUR HEAD AND ARMS! ♡
HEE!
GYAAH!!
IT'S FREEZING!
USE A TOWEL!
REEK
THIS IS THE MAEZONO FAMILY'S SECRET CURE.
DRINK IT ALL DOWN!
FUSS
WE'RE SUPPOSED TO PUT DRIED PLUM ON HIS EARS, RIGHT, SHIMA?
BLURGH!
LIKE THIS?
NO, ON HIS TEMPLES!
FUSS
AND IF WE WRAP A GREEN ONION AROUND HIS NECK...
NO, THAT'S WRONG.
WOW, HE'S REALLY SWEATING!!
YOU SHOULD CHANGE CLOTHES THIS INSTANT!!
AAAAH!!!!
PLEASE, I CAN DO IT MYSELF!!

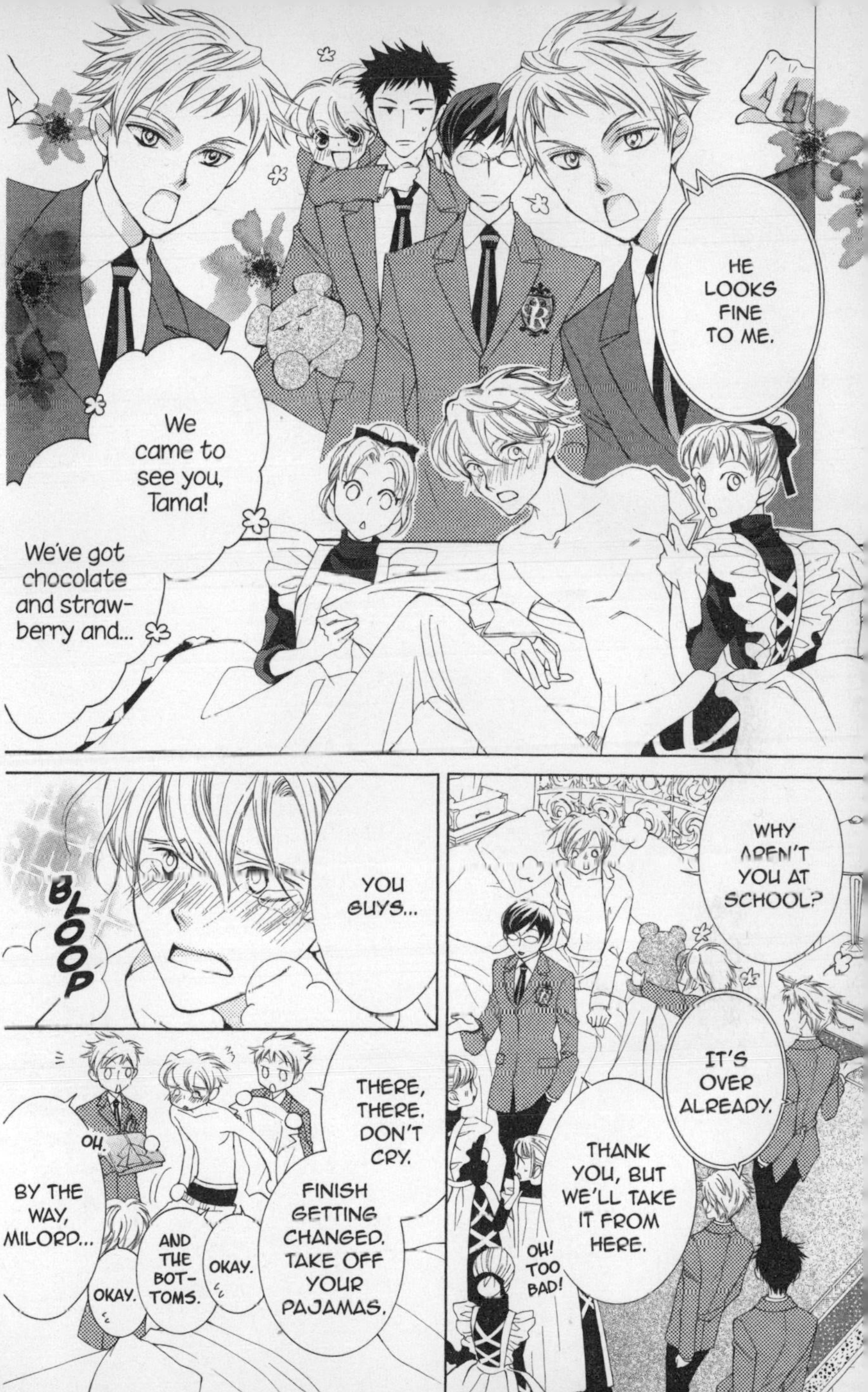
HE LOOKS FINE TO ME.
We came to see you, Tama!
We've got chocolate and straw-berry and...
WHY AREN'T YOU AT SCHOOL?
IT'S OVER ALREADY.
THANK YOU, BUT WE'LL TAKE IT FROM HERE.
OH! TOO BAD!
BLOOP
YOU GUYS...
THERE, THERE. DON'T CRY.
FINISH GETTING CHANGED. TAKE OFF YOUR PAJAMAS.
OKAY.
AND THE BOT-TOMS.
OKAY.
OH.
BY THE WAY, MILORD...

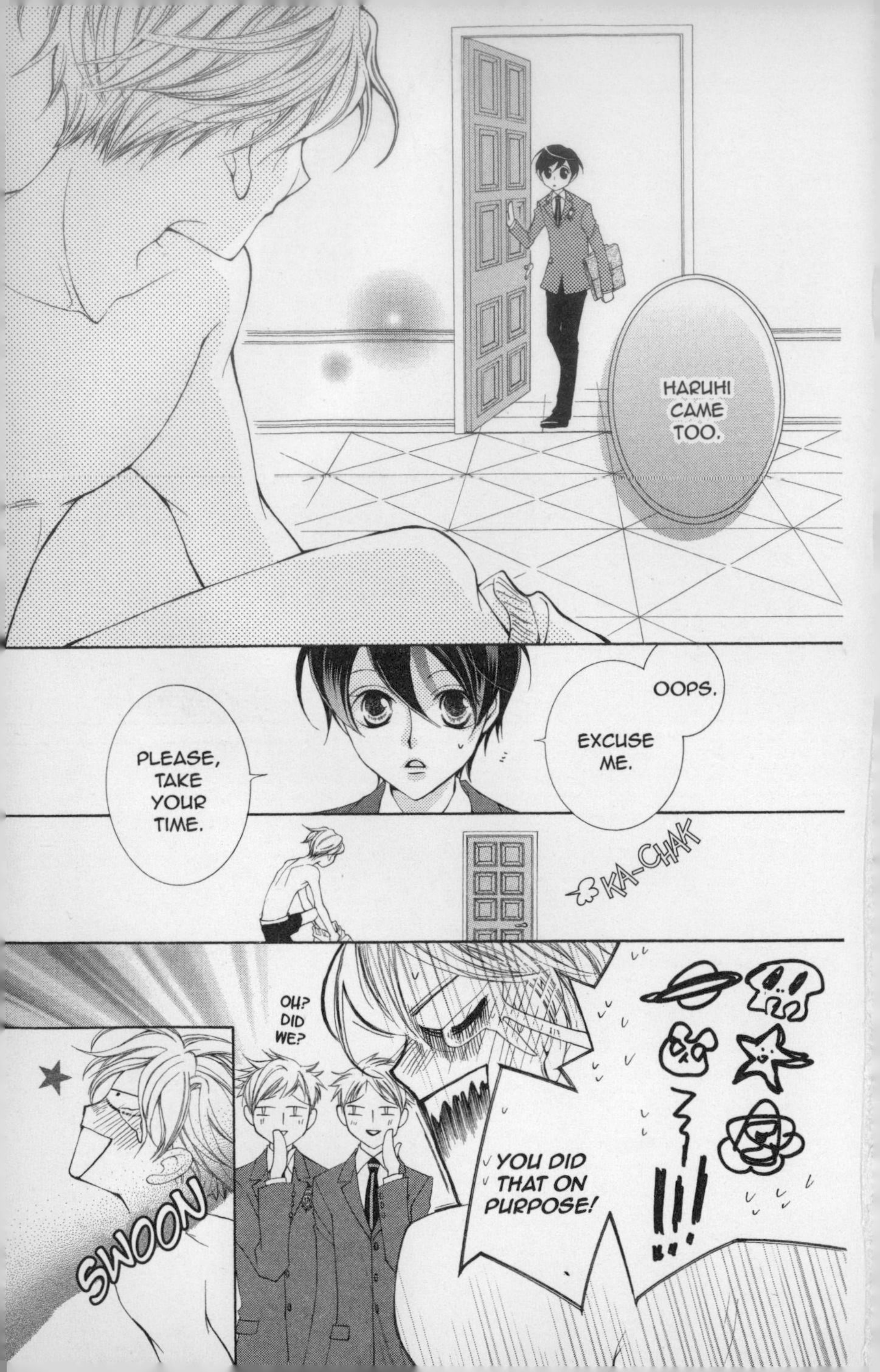
HARUHI CAME TOO.
OOPS.
EXCUSE ME.
PLEASE, TAKE YOUR TIME.
KA-CHAK
YOU DID THAT ON PURPOSE!
OH? DID WE?
SWOON

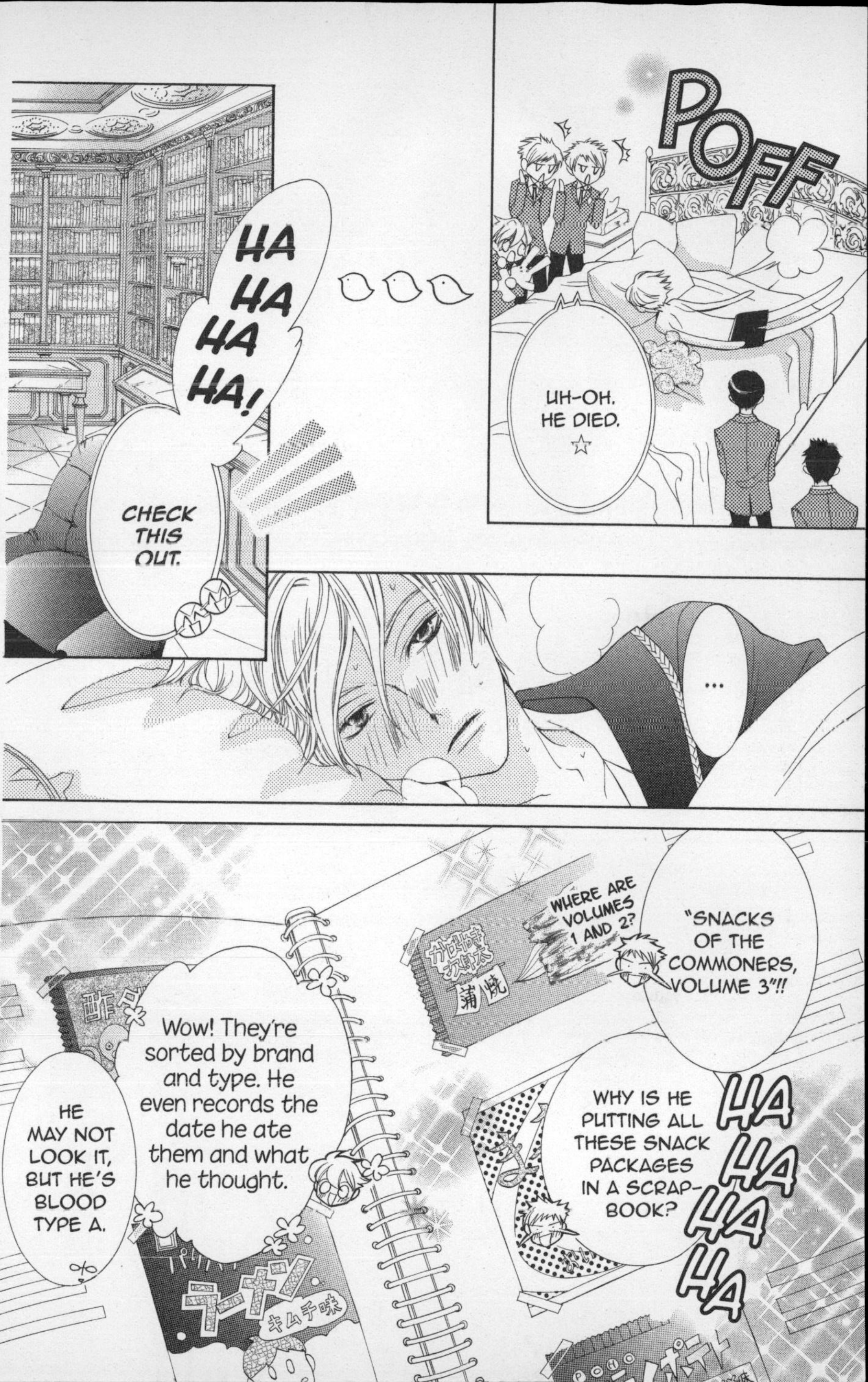
POFF
UH-OH. HE DIED. ☆
HA HA HA HA!
CHECK THIS OUT.
...
"SNACKS OF THE COMMONERS, VOLUME 3"!!
WHERE ARE VOLUMES 1 AND 2?
WHY IS HE PUTTING ALL THESE SNACK PACKAGES IN A SCRAP-BOOK?
HA HA HA HA
Wow! They're sorted by brand and type. He even records the date he ate them and what he thought.
HE MAY NOT LOOK IT, BUT HE'S BLOOD TYPE A.

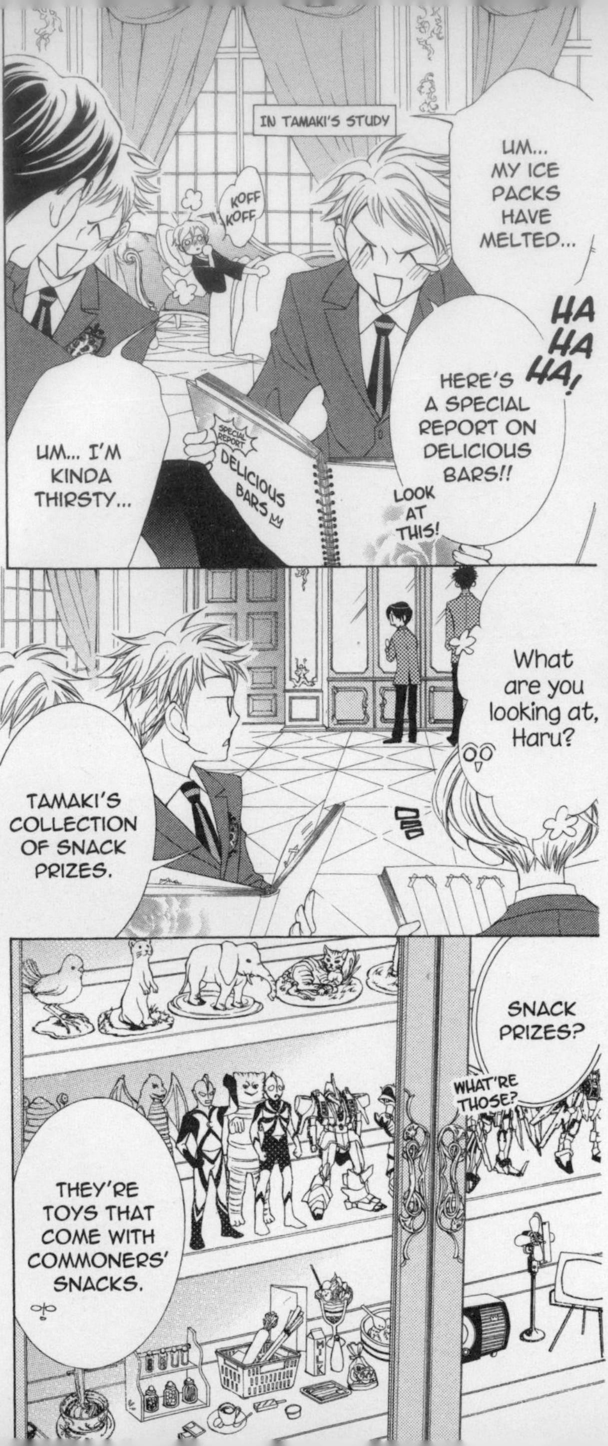
IN TAMAKI'S STUDY
UM... MY ICE PACKS HAVE MELTED...
HA HA HA!
HERE'S A SPECIAL REPORT ON DELICIOUS BARS!!
LOOK AT THIS!
SPECIAL REPORT
DELICIOUS BARS
KOFF KOFF
UM... I'M KINDA THIRSTY...
What are you looking at, Haru?
TAMAKI'S COLLECTION OF SNACK PRIZES.
SNACK PRIZES?
WHAT'RE THOSE?
THEY'RE TOYS THAT COME WITH COMMONERS' SNACKS.
MILK

4

AS EVERYTHING GOT BIGGER AND BIGGER, I WAS THE ONLY ONE WHO COULDN'T KEEP UP. WHO SAID ANYTHING MORE MIGHT BE DIFFICULT...? (YES, I DID...) I'M VERY SELFISH. BUT I ACCEPTED BECAUSE THERE IS NO GREATER PRIVILEGE THAN BEING OFFERED AN ANIME PRODUCTION... IT WAS REALLY GREAT!!!!! THAT'S WHAT I THINK NOW. HA HA!!! (I'M SO SELFISH!)

IN ADDITION TO THE SPLENDID QUALITY OF THE ANIME, ALL THE STAFF MEMBERS ARE REALLY GREAT PEOPLE. *HOST CLUB* ANIME...!!

DIRECTOR IGARASHI EMAILS ME A LOT EVEN WHEN HE'S BUSY, AND SCRIPTWRITER ENOKIDO ASKS, "IS THE SCRIPT OKAY?" EVERY TIME WE MEET. COMPANY PRESIDENT MINAMI OF BONES AND I HAVE THE SAME BLOOD TYPE AND HOROSCOPE (NOT REALLY IMPORTANT), AND OYABU LOOKS REALLY GOOD IN GLASSES!!! EVEN THOUGH EVERYONE IS SO BUSY THEY'RE VERY KIND. OYABU WAS THE ONE WHO CAME UP WITH THE NAMES FOR THE CUSTOMERS!

(BECAUSE I NEVER DID...)

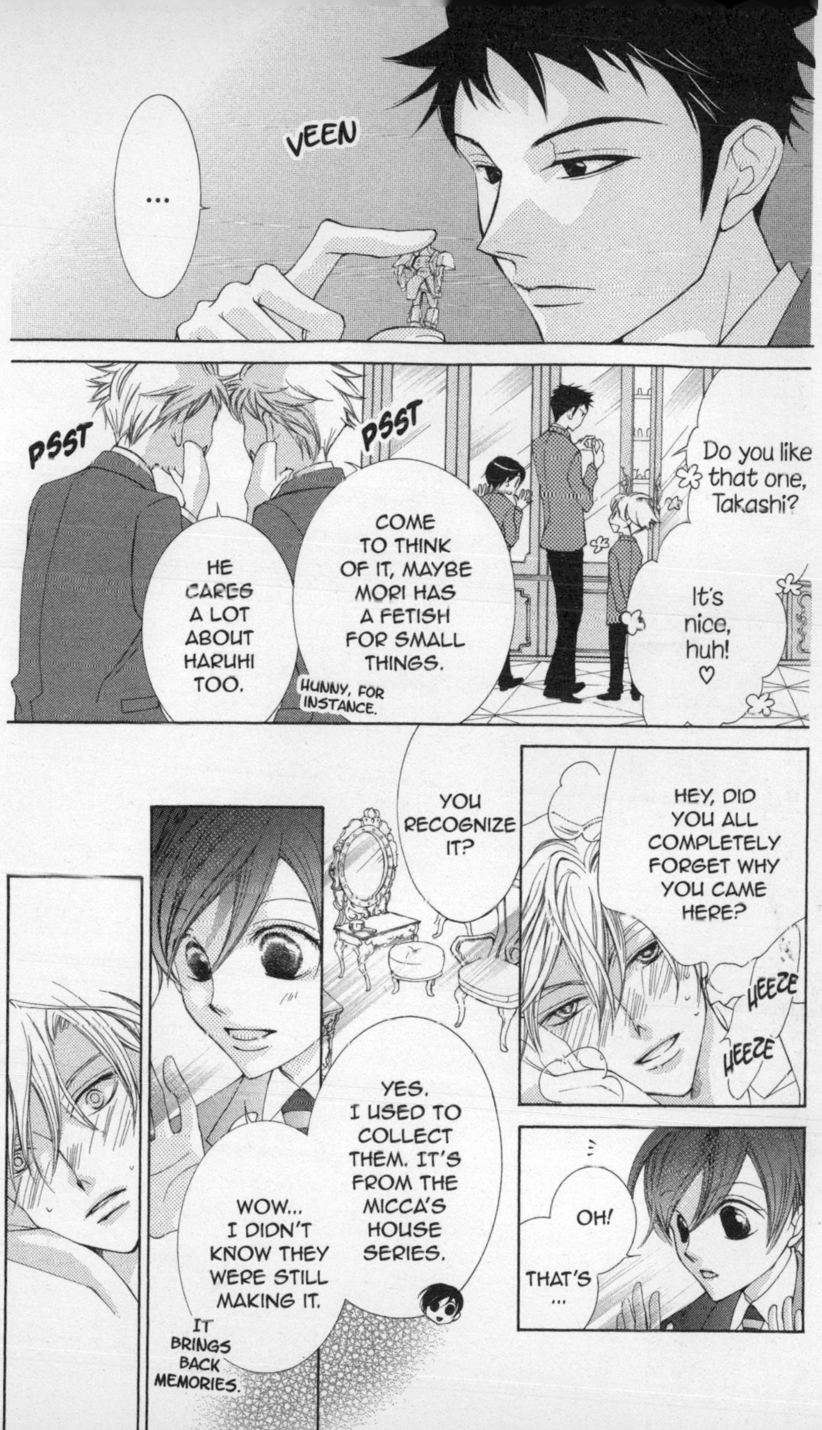
VEEN
...
Do you like that one, Takashi?
It's nice, huh! ♡
PSST
COME TO THINK OF IT, MAYBE MORI HAS A FETISH FOR SMALL THINGS.
HUNNY, FOR INSTANCE.
PSST
HE CARES A LOT ABOUT HARUHI TOO.
HEY, DID YOU ALL COMPLETELY FORGET WHY YOU CAME HERE?
HEEZE
HEEZE
OH!
THAT'S ...
YOU RECOGNIZE IT?
YES. I USED TO COLLECT THEM. IT'S FROM THE MICCA'S HOUSE SERIES.
WOW... I DIDN'T KNOW THEY WERE STILL MAKING IT.
IT BRINGS BACK MEMORIES.

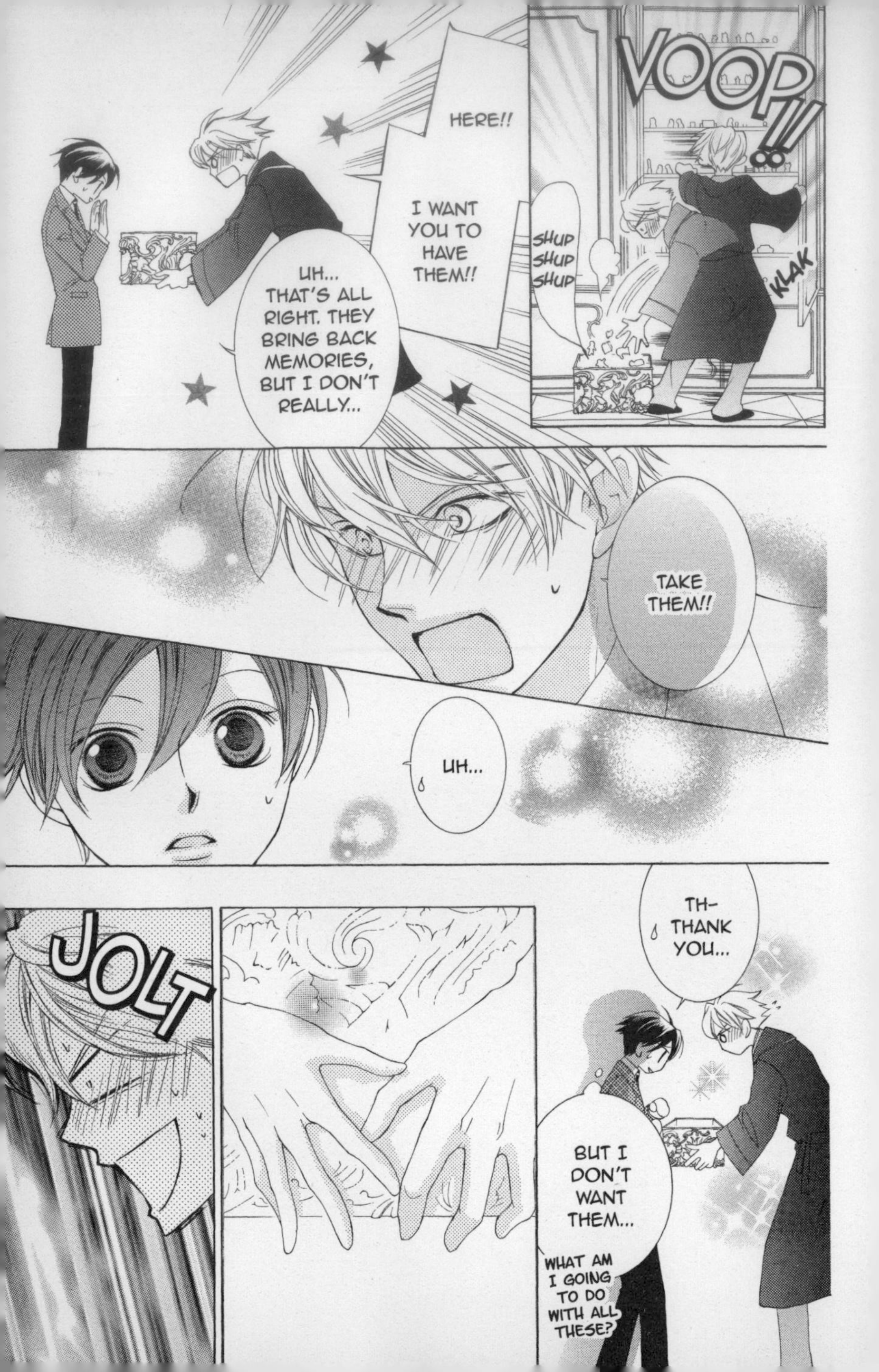
VOOP!!
SHUP SHUP SHUP
KLAK
HERE!!
I WANT YOU TO HAVE THEM!!
UH... THAT'S ALL RIGHT. THEY BRING BACK MEMORIES, BUT I DON'T REALLY...
TAKE THEM!!
UH...
TH- THANK YOU...
BUT I DON'T WANT THEM...
WHAT AM I GOING TO DO WITH ALL THESE?
JOLT

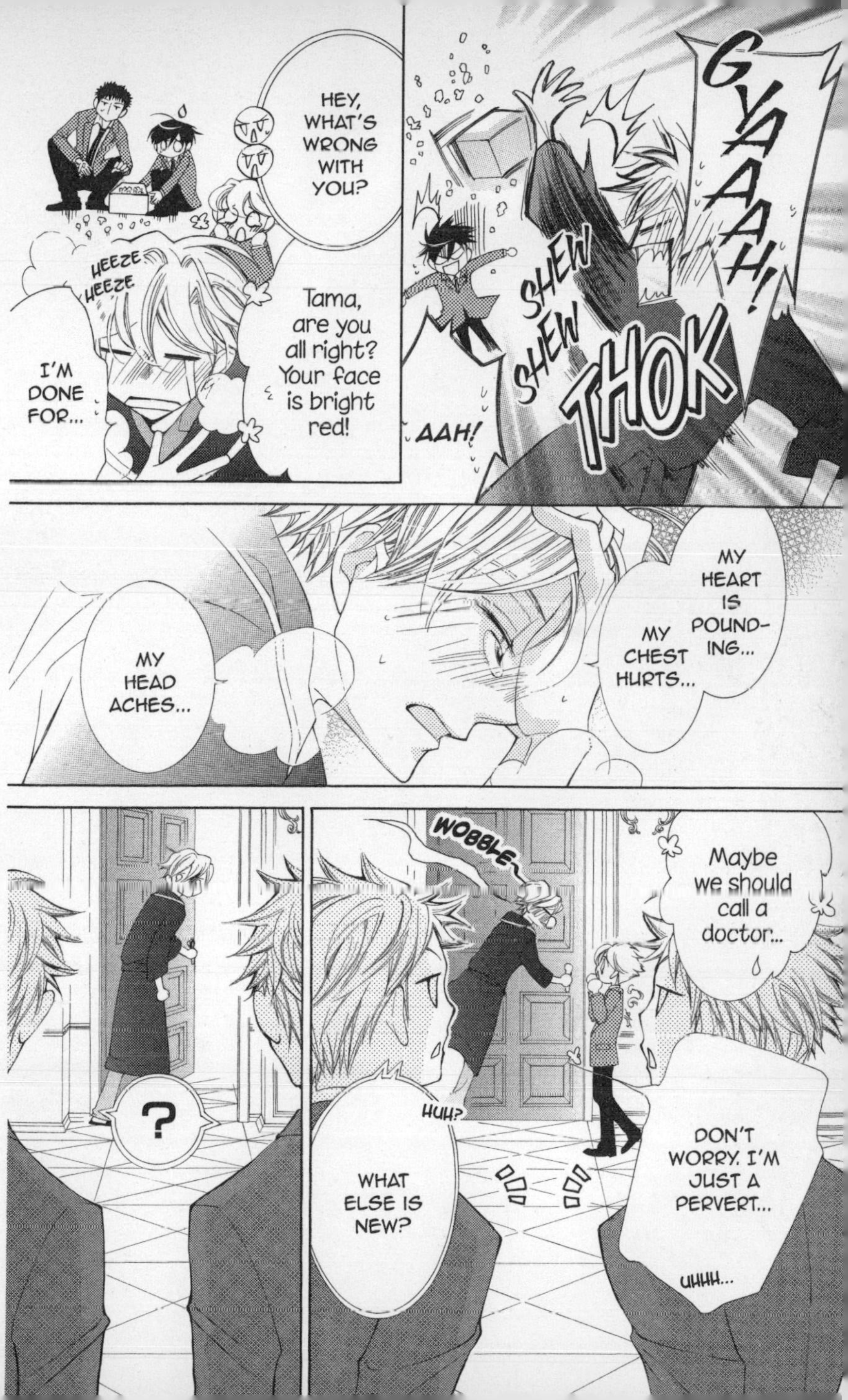
GYAAAH!
SHEW SHEW
THOK
AAH!
HEY, WHAT'S WRONG WITH YOU?
Tama, are you all right? Your face is bright red!
HEEZE HEEZE
I'M DONE FOR...
MY HEART IS POUNDING...
MY CHEST HURTS...
MY HEAD ACHES...
WOBBLE
Maybe we should call a doctor...
DON'T WORRY. I'M JUST A PERVERT...
UHHH...
HUH?
WHAT ELSE IS NEW?
?

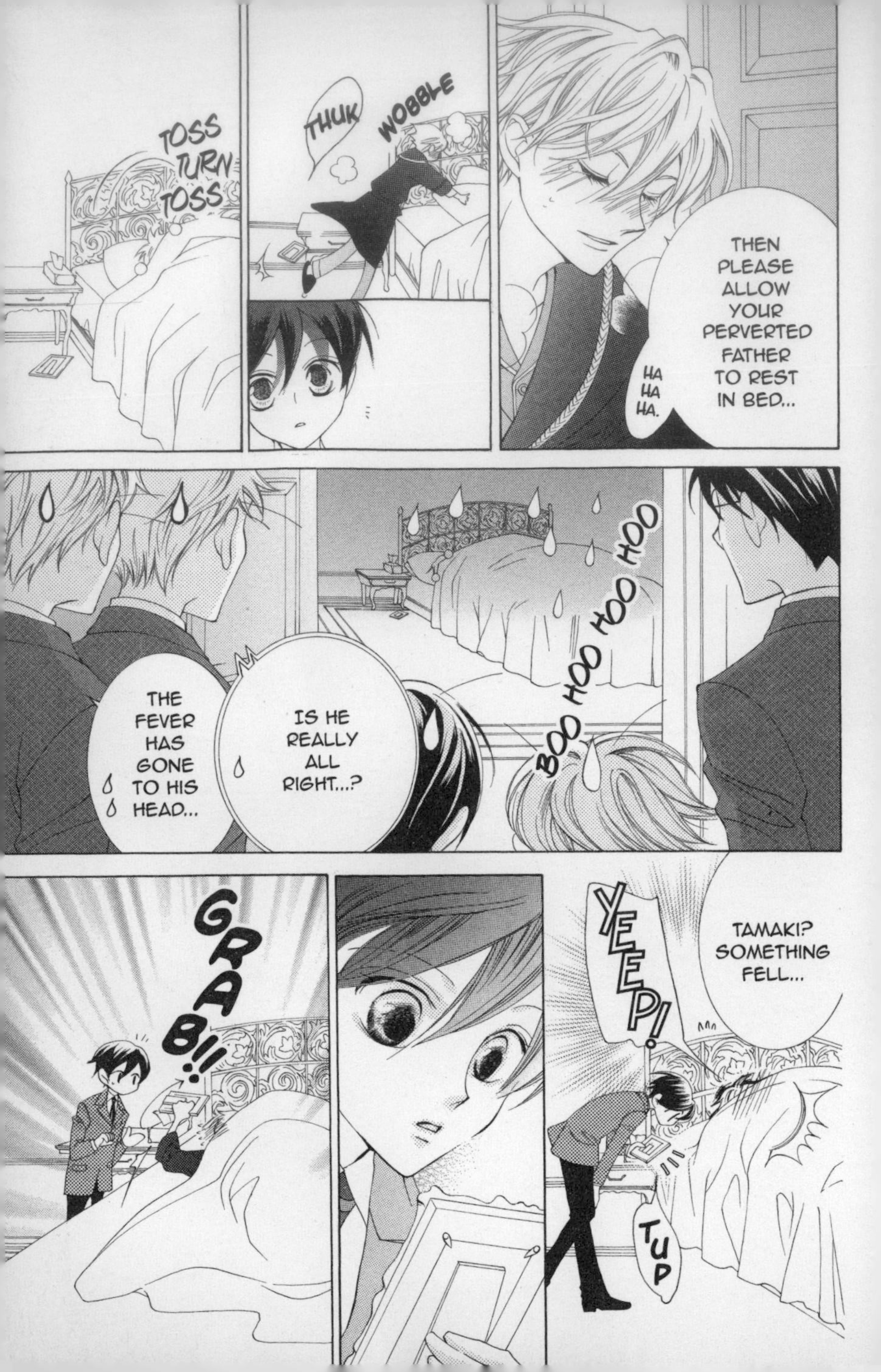
THEN PLEASE ALLOW YOUR PERVERTED FATHER TO REST IN BED...
HA HA HA.
THUK
WOBBLE
TOSS TURN TOSS
BOO HOO HOO HOO
IS HE REALLY ALL RIGHT...?
THE FEVER HAS GONE TO HIS HEAD...
TAMAKI? SOMETHING FELL...
YEEP!
TUP
GRAB!!

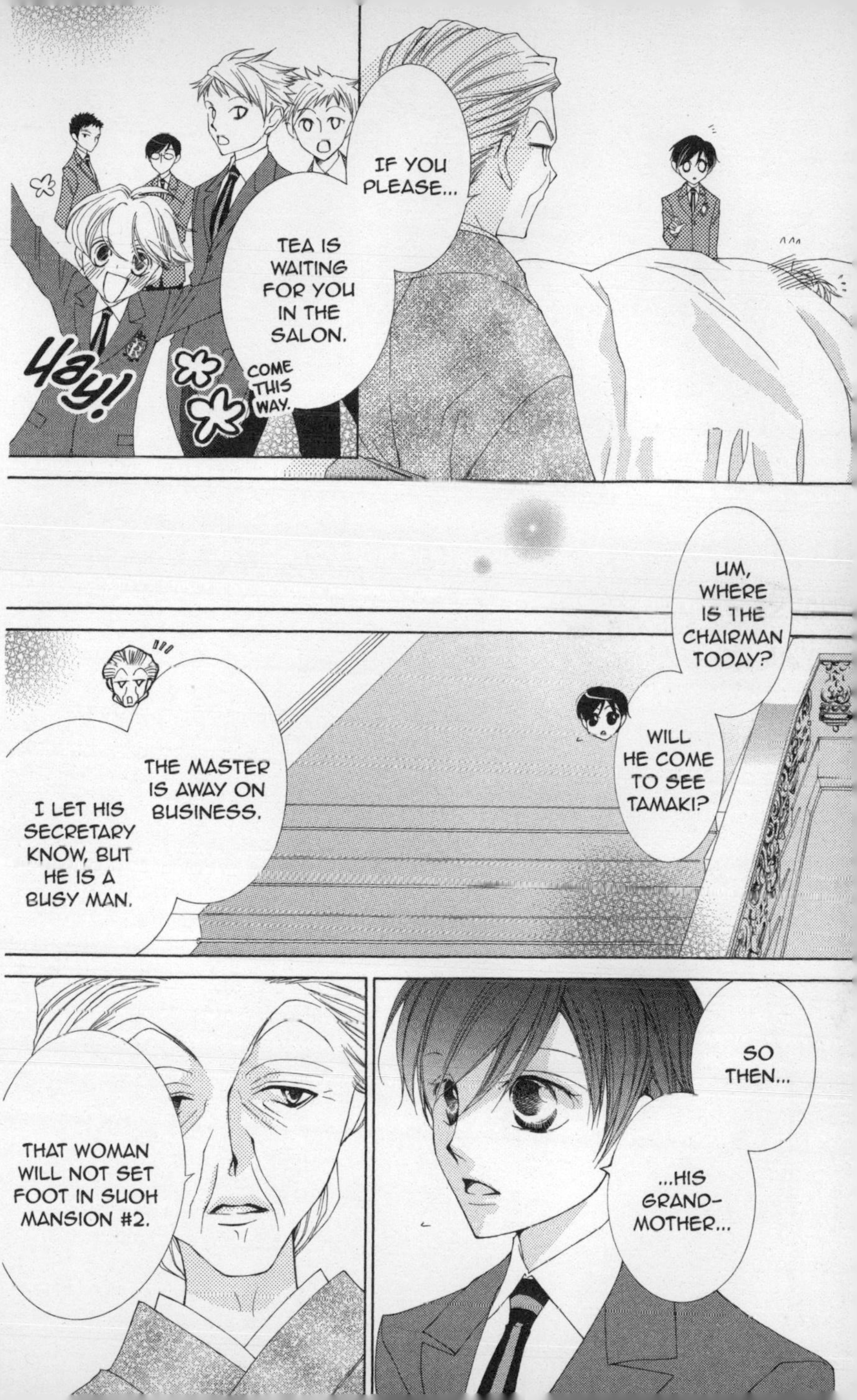
IF YOU PLEASE...
TEA IS WAITING FOR YOU IN THE SALON.
COME THIS WAY.
Yay!
UM, WHERE IS THE CHAIRMAN TODAY?
WILL HE COME TO SEE TAMAKI?
THE MASTER IS AWAY ON BUSINESS.
I LET HIS SECRETARY KNOW, BUT HE IS A BUSY MAN.
SO THEN...
...HIS GRAND-MOTHER...
THAT WOMAN WILL NOT SET FOOT IN SUOH MANSION #2.

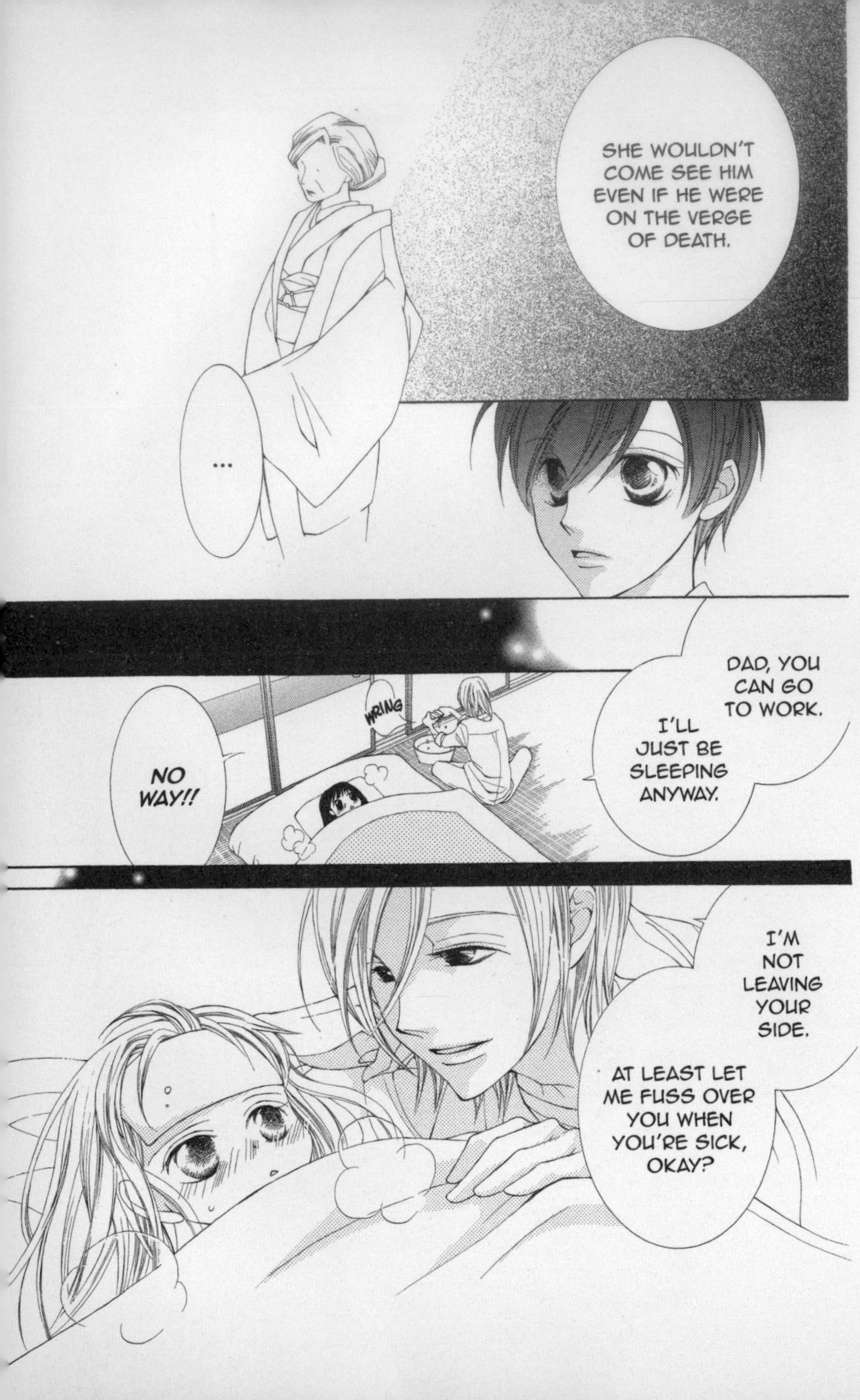
SHE WOULDN'T COME SEE HIM EVEN IF HE WERE ON THE VERGE OF DEATH.
...
DAD, YOU CAN GO TO WORK.
I'LL JUST BE SLEEPING ANYWAY.
WRING
NO WAY!!
I'M NOT LEAVING YOUR SIDE.
AT LEAST LET ME FUSS OVER YOU WHEN YOU'RE SICK, OKAY?

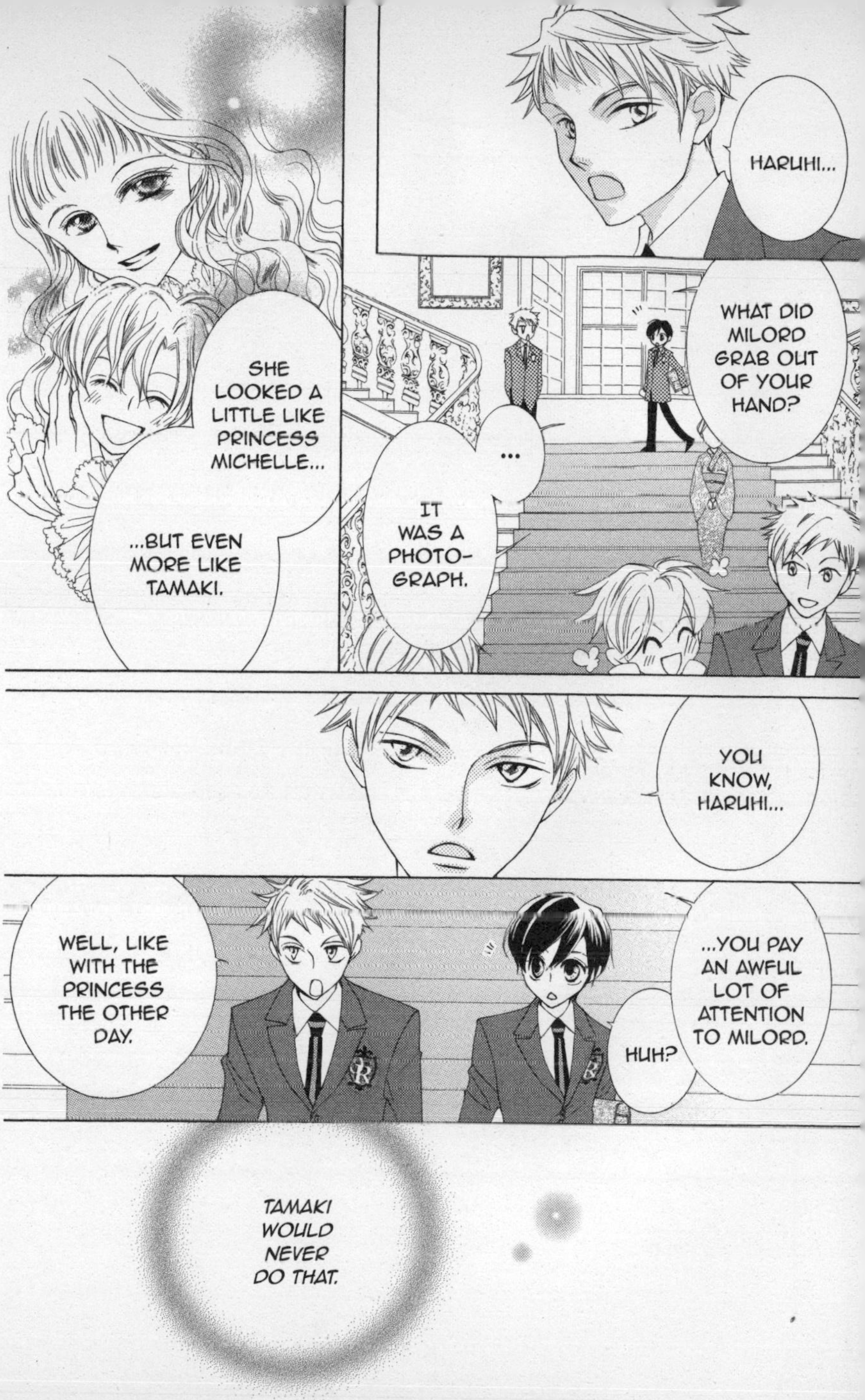
HARUHI...
WHAT DID MILORD GRAB OUT OF YOUR HAND?
...
IT WAS A PHOTOGRAPH.
SHE LOOKED A LITTLE LIKE PRINCESS MICHELLE...
...BUT EVEN MORE LIKE TAMAKI.
YOU KNOW, HARUHI...
...YOU PAY AN AWFUL LOT OF ATTENTION TO MILORD.
HUH?
WELL, LIKE WITH THE PRINCESS THE OTHER DAY.
TAMAKI WOULD NEVER DO THAT.

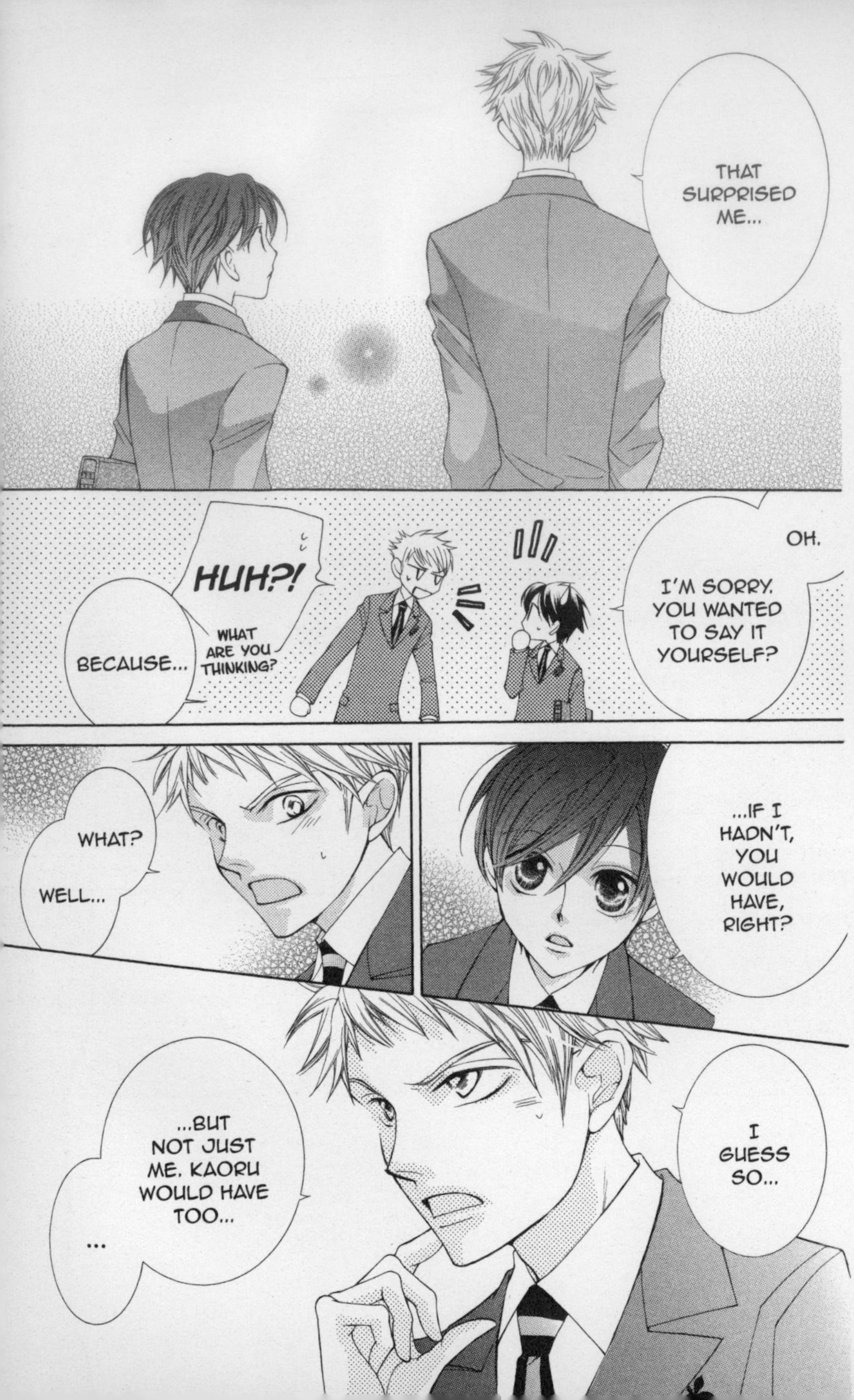
THAT SURPRISED ME...
OH.
I'M SORRY. YOU WANTED TO SAY IT YOURSELF?
HUH?!
WHAT ARE YOU THINKING?
BECAUSE...
...IF I HADN'T, YOU WOULD HAVE, RIGHT?
WHAT?
WELL...
I GUESS SO...
...BUT NOT JUST ME. KAORU WOULD HAVE TOO...
...

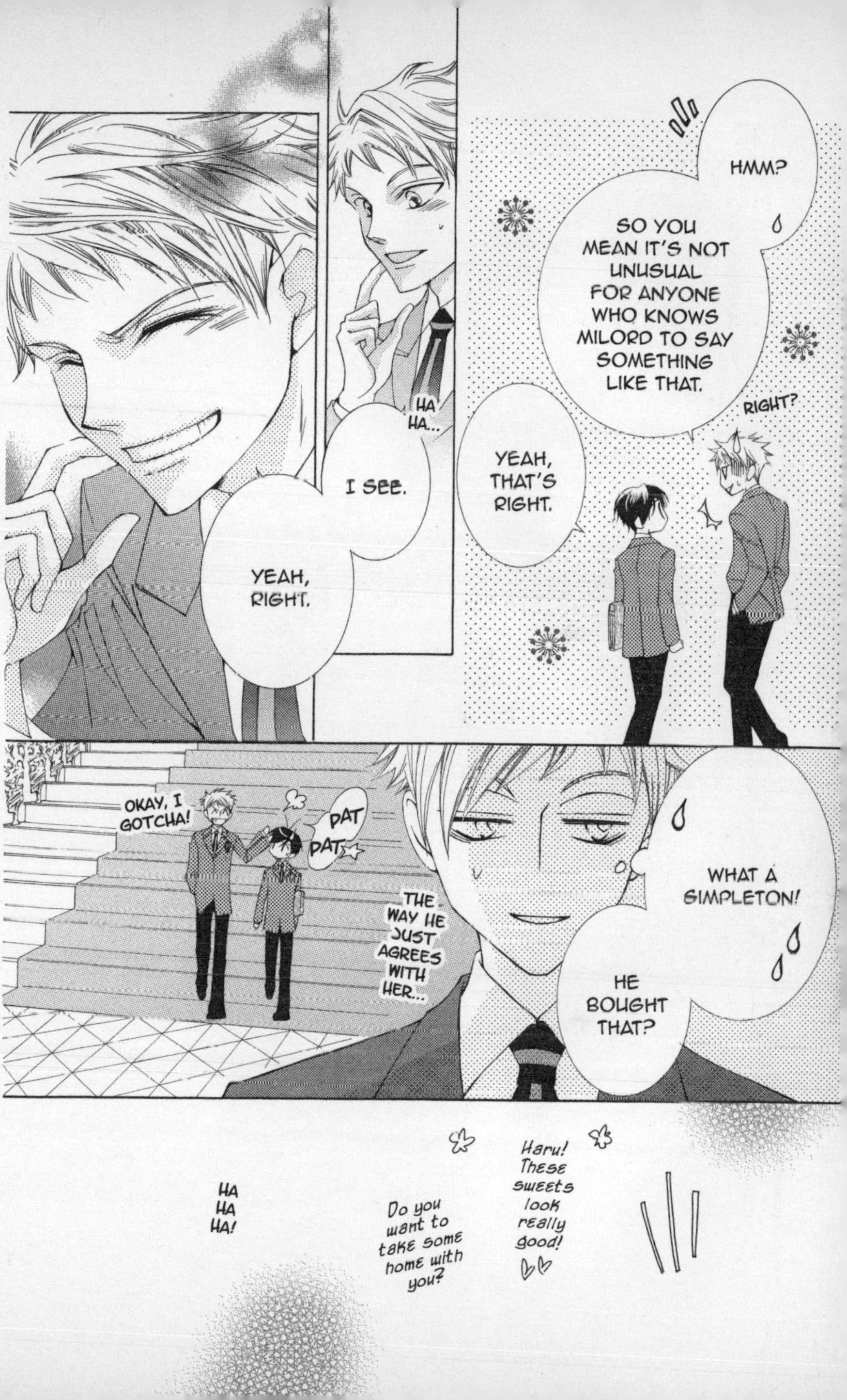
HMM?
SO YOU MEAN IT'S NOT UNUSUAL FOR ANYONE WHO KNOWS MILORD TO SAY SOMETHING LIKE THAT.
RIGHT?
YEAH, THAT'S RIGHT.
HA HA...
I SEE.
YEAH, RIGHT.
WHAT A SIMPLETON!
HE BOUGHT THAT?
THE WAY HE JUST AGREES WITH HER...
PAT PAT
OKAY, I GOTCHA!
Haru! These sweets look really good!
Do you want to take some home with you?
HA HA HA!

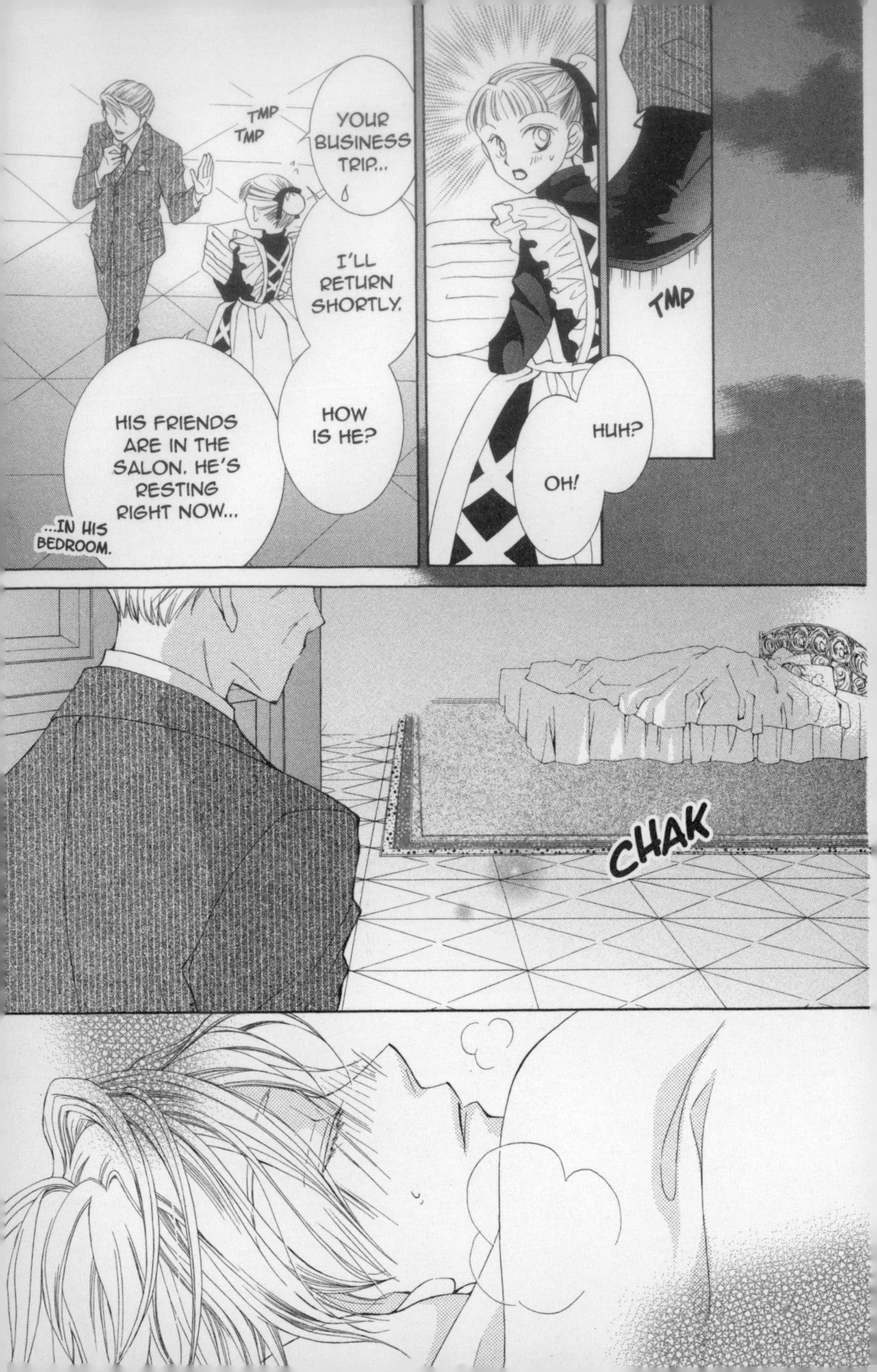
TMP
HUH?
OH!
YOUR BUSINESS TRIP...
TMP TMP
I'LL RETURN SHORTLY.
HOW IS HE?
HIS FRIENDS ARE IN THE SALON. HE'S RESTING RIGHT NOW...
...IN HIS BEDROOM.
CHAK

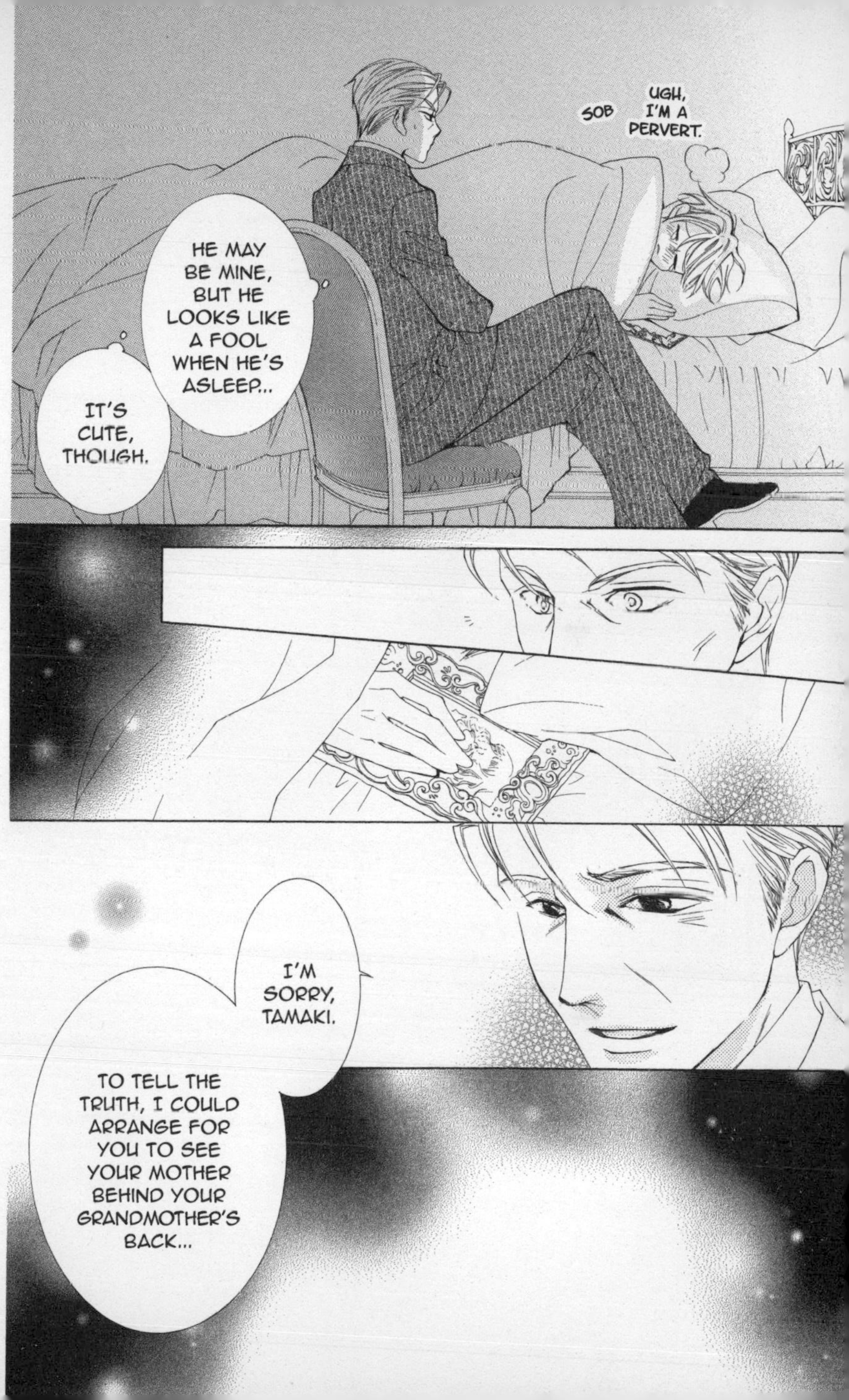
UGH, I'M A PERVERT.
SOB
HE MAY BE MINE, BUT HE LOOKS LIKE A FOOL WHEN HE'S ASLEEP...
IT'S CUTE, THOUGH.
I'M SORRY, TAMAKI.
TO TELL THE TRUTH, I COULD ARRANGE FOR YOU TO SEE YOUR MOTHER BEHIND YOUR GRANDMOTHER'S BACK...

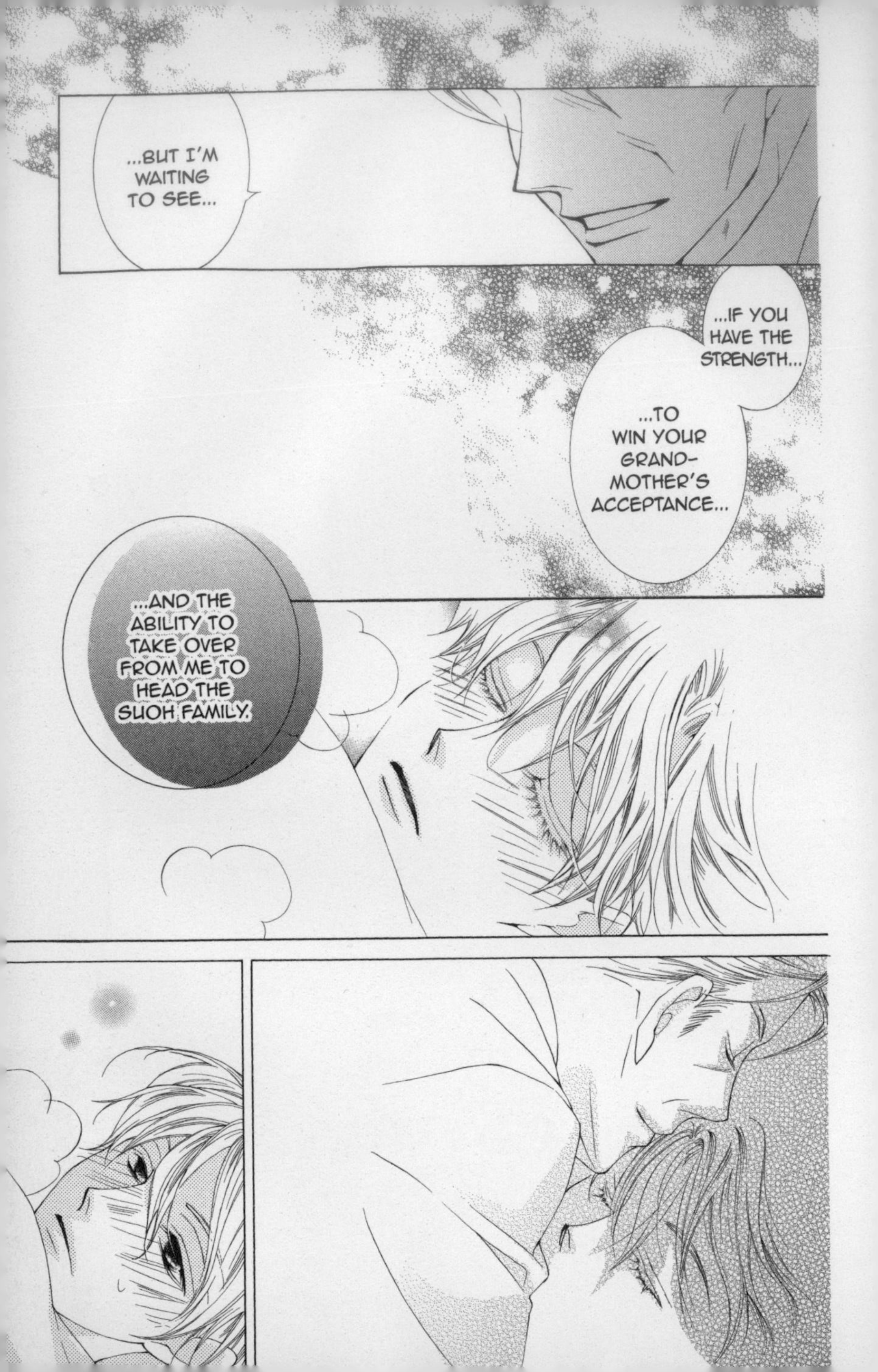
...BUT I'M WAITING TO SEE...
...IF YOU HAVE THE STRENGTH...
...TO WIN YOUR GRAND-MOTHER'S ACCEPTANCE...
...AND THE ABILITY TO TAKE OVER FROM ME TO HEAD THE SUOH FAMILY.

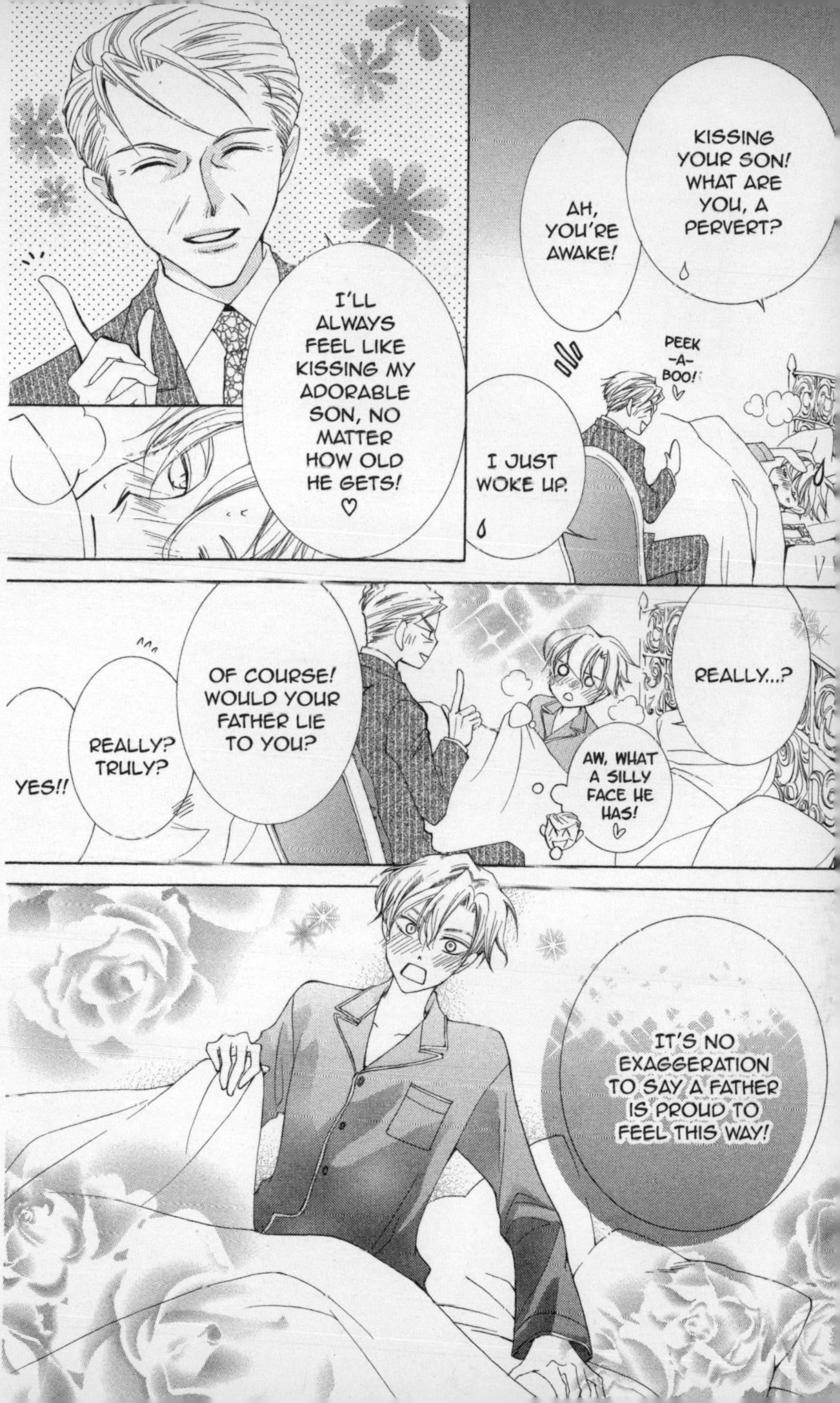
KISSING YOUR SON! WHAT ARE YOU, A PERVERT?
AH, YOU'RE AWAKE!
PEEK-A-BOO! ♡
I JUST WOKE UP.
I'LL ALWAYS FEEL LIKE KISSING MY ADORABLE SON, NO MATTER HOW OLD HE GETS! ♡
REALLY...?
AW, WHAT A SILLY FACE HE HAS! ♡
OF COURSE! WOULD YOUR FATHER LIE TO YOU?
REALLY? TRULY?
YES!!
IT'S NO EXAGGERATION TO SAY A FATHER IS PROUD TO FEEL THIS WAY!

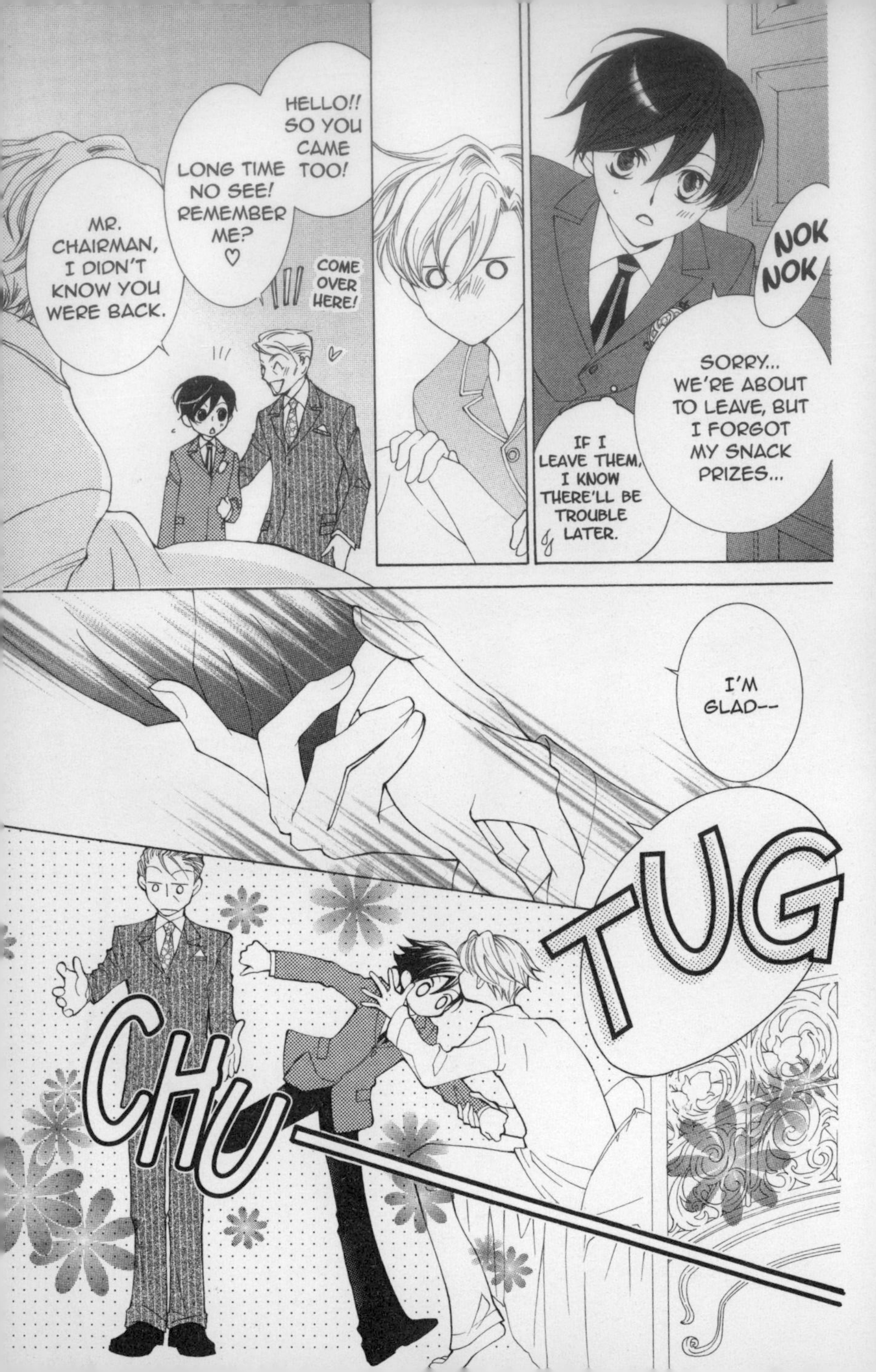
NOK NOK
SORRY... WE'RE ABOUT TO LEAVE, BUT I FORGOT MY SNACK PRIZES...
IF I LEAVE THEM, I KNOW THERE'LL BE TROUBLE LATER.
HELLO!! SO YOU CAME TOO!
LONG TIME NO SEE! REMEMBER ME? ♡
MR. CHAIRMAN, I DIDN'T KNOW YOU WERE BACK.
COME OVER HERE!
I'M GLAD--
TUG
CHU

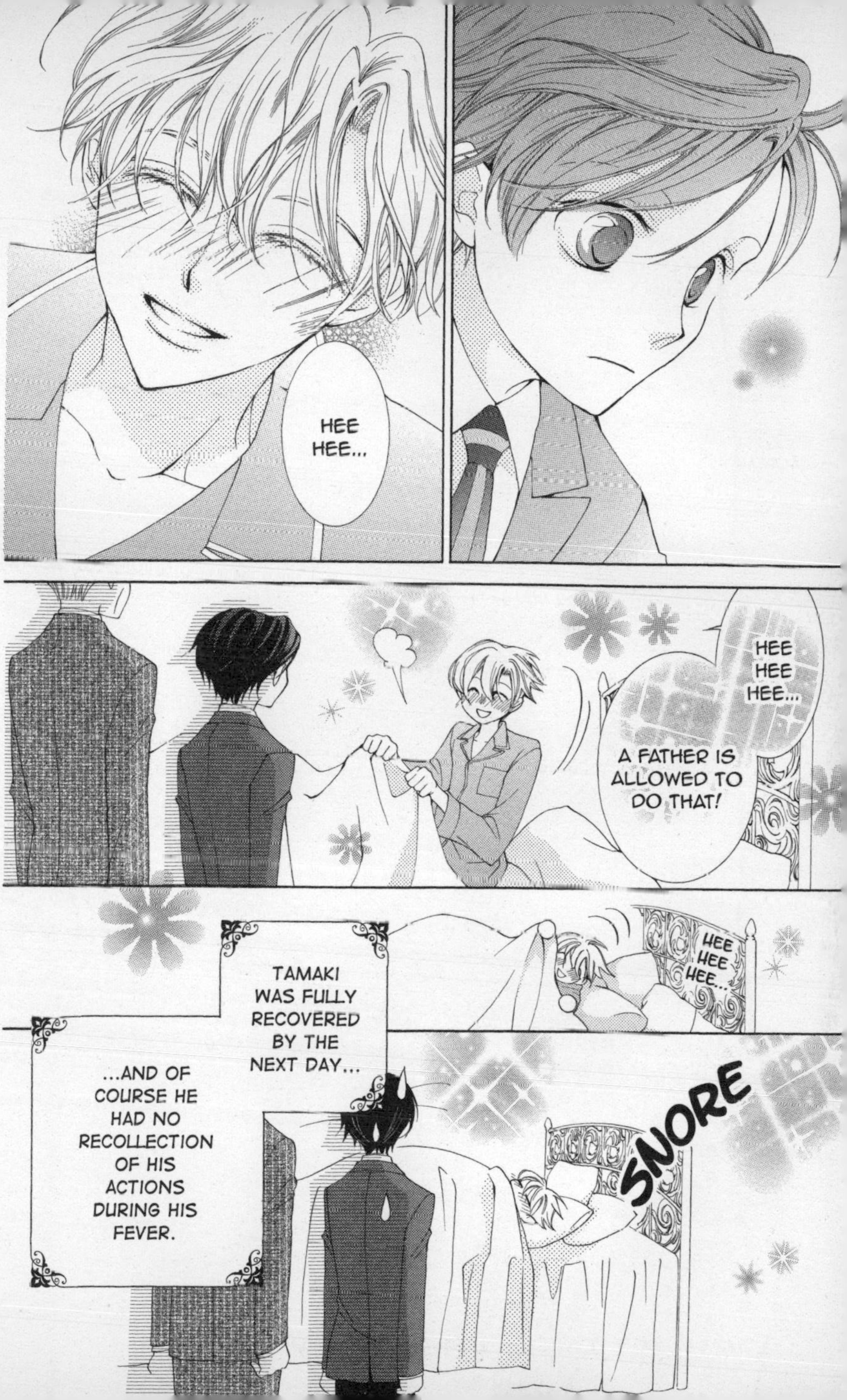
HEE HEE...
HEE HEE HEE...
A FATHER IS ALLOWED TO DO THAT!
HEE HEE HEE...
TAMAKI WAS FULLY RECOVERED BY THE NEXT DAY...
SNORE
...AND OF COURSE HE HAD NO RECOLLECTION OF HIS ACTIONS DURING HIS FEVER.

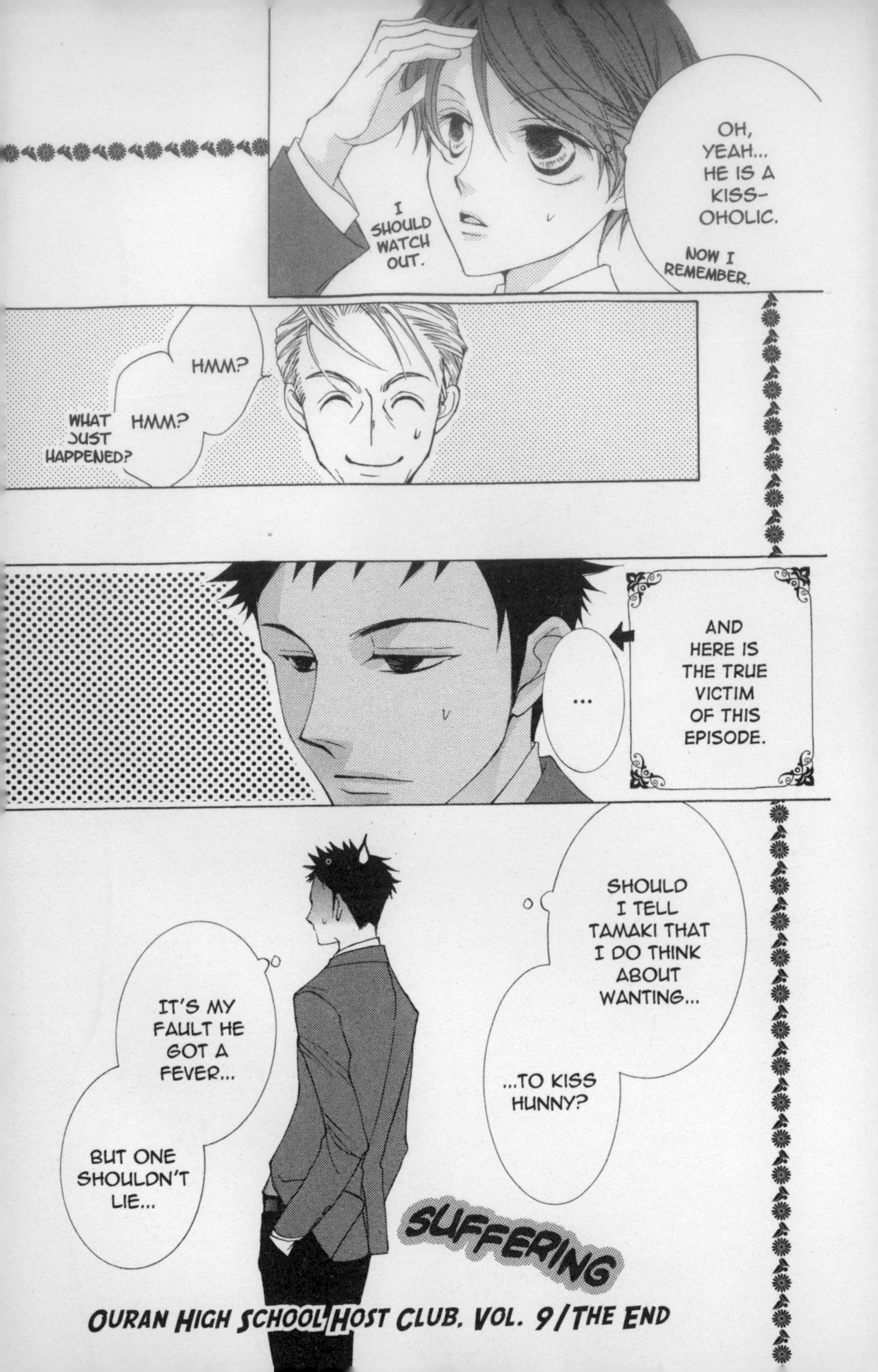

OH, YEAH... HE IS A KISS-OHOLIC.
NOW I REMEMBER.
I SHOULD WATCH OUT.
HMM?
HMM?
WHAT JUST HAPPENED?
AND HERE IS THE TRUE VICTIM OF THIS EPISODE.
...
SHOULD I TELL TAMAKI THAT I DO THINK ABOUT WANTING...
...TO KISS HUNNY?
IT'S MY FAULT HE GOT A FEVER...
BUT ONE SHOULDN'T LIE...
SUFFERING
OURAN HIGH SCHOOL HOST CLUB, VOL. 9/THE END

GUEST ROOM: FAXES ③

SPECIAL THANKS TO ASUKA IZUMI!!

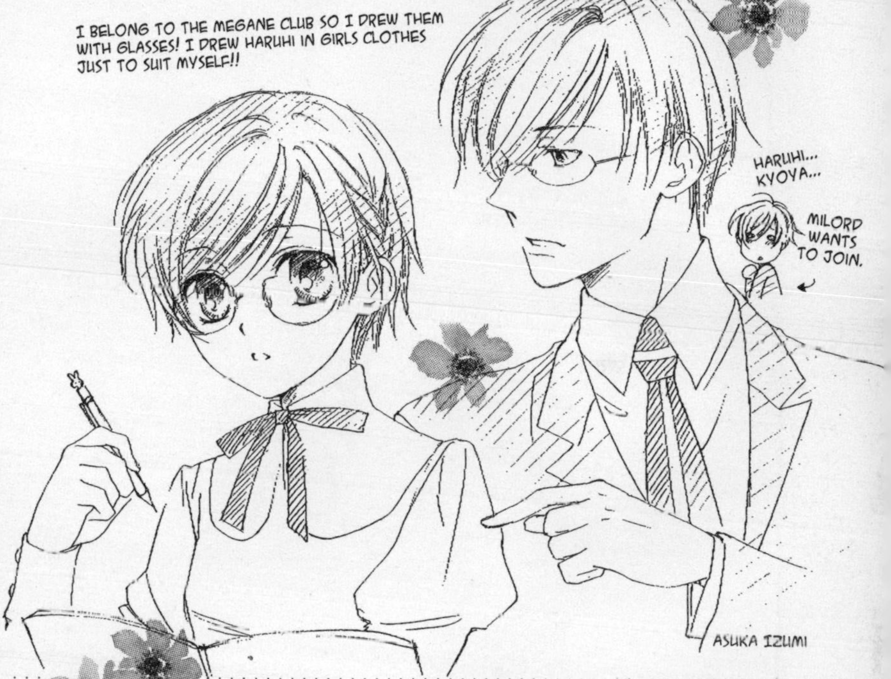
I BELONG TO THE MEGANE CLUB SO I DREW THEM WITH GLASSES! I DREW HARUHI IN GIRLS CLOTHES JUST TO SUIT MYSELF!!
HARUHI... KYOYA...
MILORD WANTS TO JOIN.
ASUKA IZUMI

ASUKA IZUMI DRAWS FOR *LALA* TOO! WE FIRST MET BEFORE HER DEBUT WHEN SHE CAME TO HELP ME OUT, AND I BECAME AN INSTANT FAN AFTER READING HER PRIZE-WINNING *PRINCE LIZARD*!! KYOYA LOOKS SO GENTLE!! IT SEEMS THE ARTIST'S PERSONALITY IS REFLECTED IN HER DRAWINGS... I LEARNED FOR THE FIRST TIME WITH THIS FAX THAT ASUKA BELONGS TO THE MEGANE CLUB (MEGANE LOVE!) (LAUGH). TELL ME ALL ABOUT IT SOMETIME! ♡

Extra Episode: The Host Club's Operation for Modest Happiness

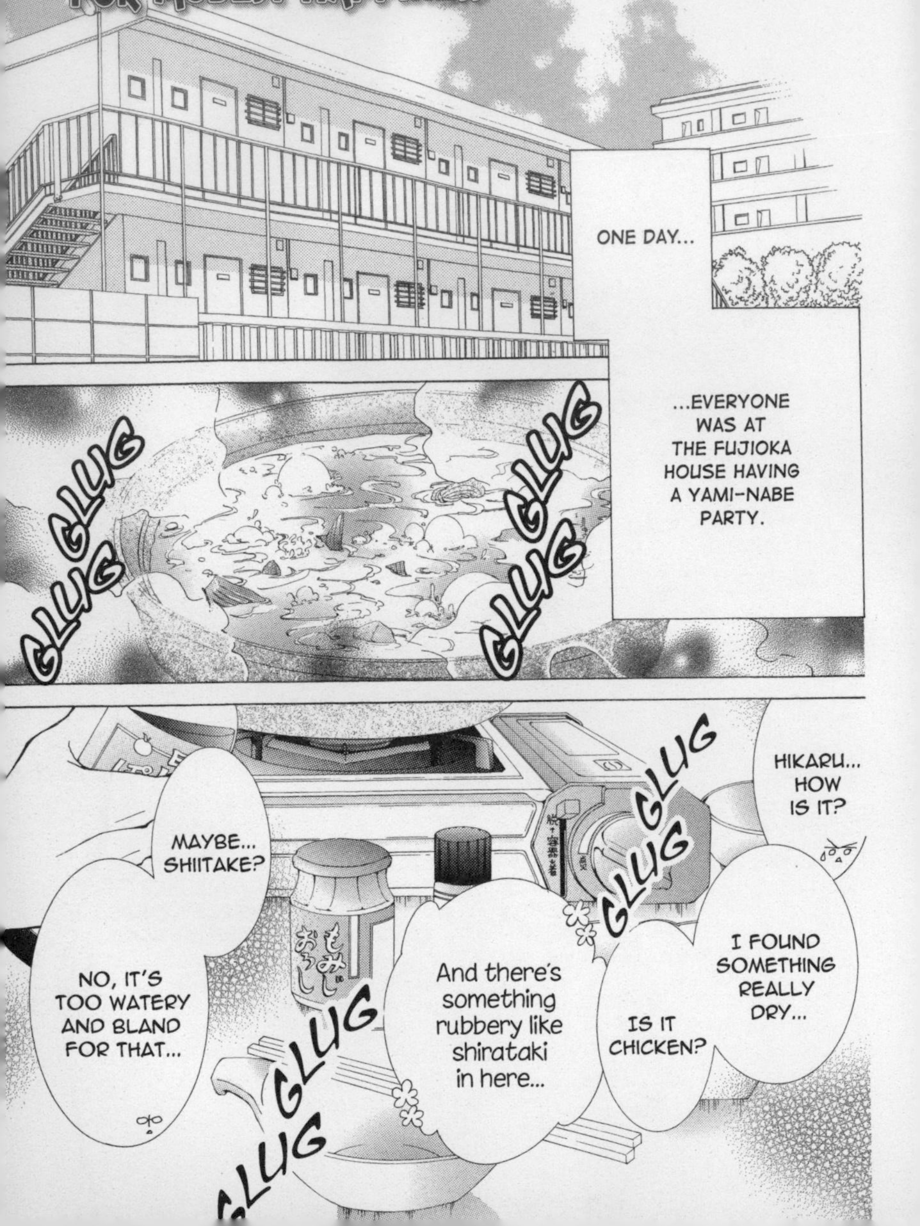
ONE DAY...
...EVERYONE WAS AT THE FUJIOKA HOUSE HAVING A YAMI-NABE PARTY.
GLUG GLUG
GLUG GLUG
HIKARU... HOW IS IT?
I FOUND SOMETHING REALLY DRY...
IS IT CHICKEN?
GLUG GLUG
And there's something rubbery like shirataki in here...
もみじおろし
MAYBE... SHIITAKE?
NO, IT'S TOO WATERY AND BLAND FOR THAT...
GLUG GLUG

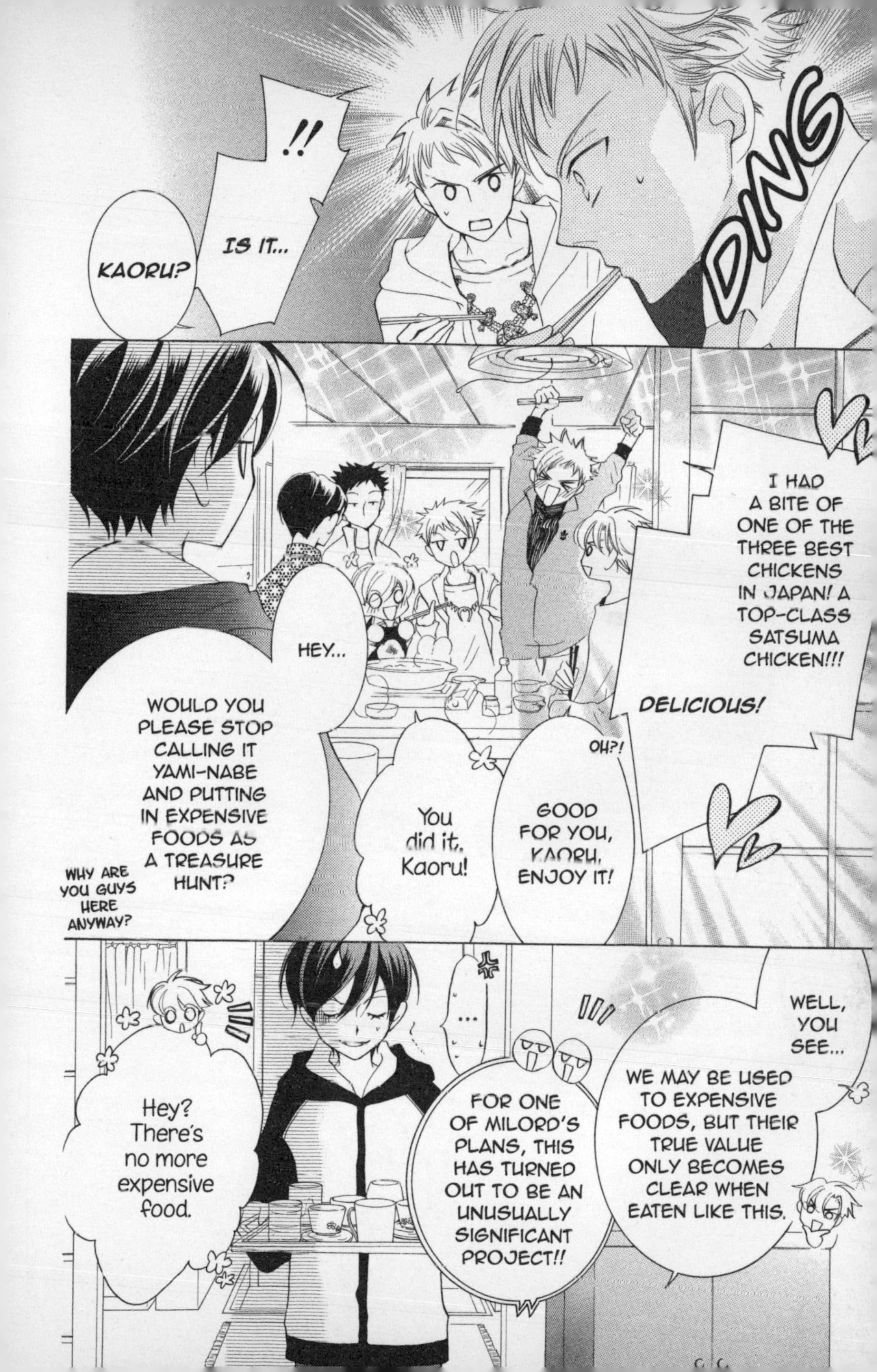
DING
!!
IS IT...
KAORU?
I HAD A BITE OF ONE OF THE THREE BEST CHICKENS IN JAPAN! A TOP-CLASS SATSUMA CHICKEN!!!
DELICIOUS!
OH?!
GOOD FOR YOU, KAORU, ENJOY IT!
You did it, Kaoru!
HEY...
WOULD YOU PLEASE STOP CALLING IT YAMI-NABE AND PUTTING IN EXPENSIVE FOODS AS A TREASURE HUNT?
WHY ARE YOU GUYS HERE ANYWAY?
WELL, YOU SEE...
WE MAY BE USED TO EXPENSIVE FOODS, BUT THEIR TRUE VALUE ONLY BECOMES CLEAR WHEN EATEN LIKE THIS.
FOR ONE OF MILORD'S PLANS, THIS HAS TURNED OUT TO BE AN UNUSUALLY SIGNIFICANT PROJECT!!
...
Hey? There's no more expensive food.

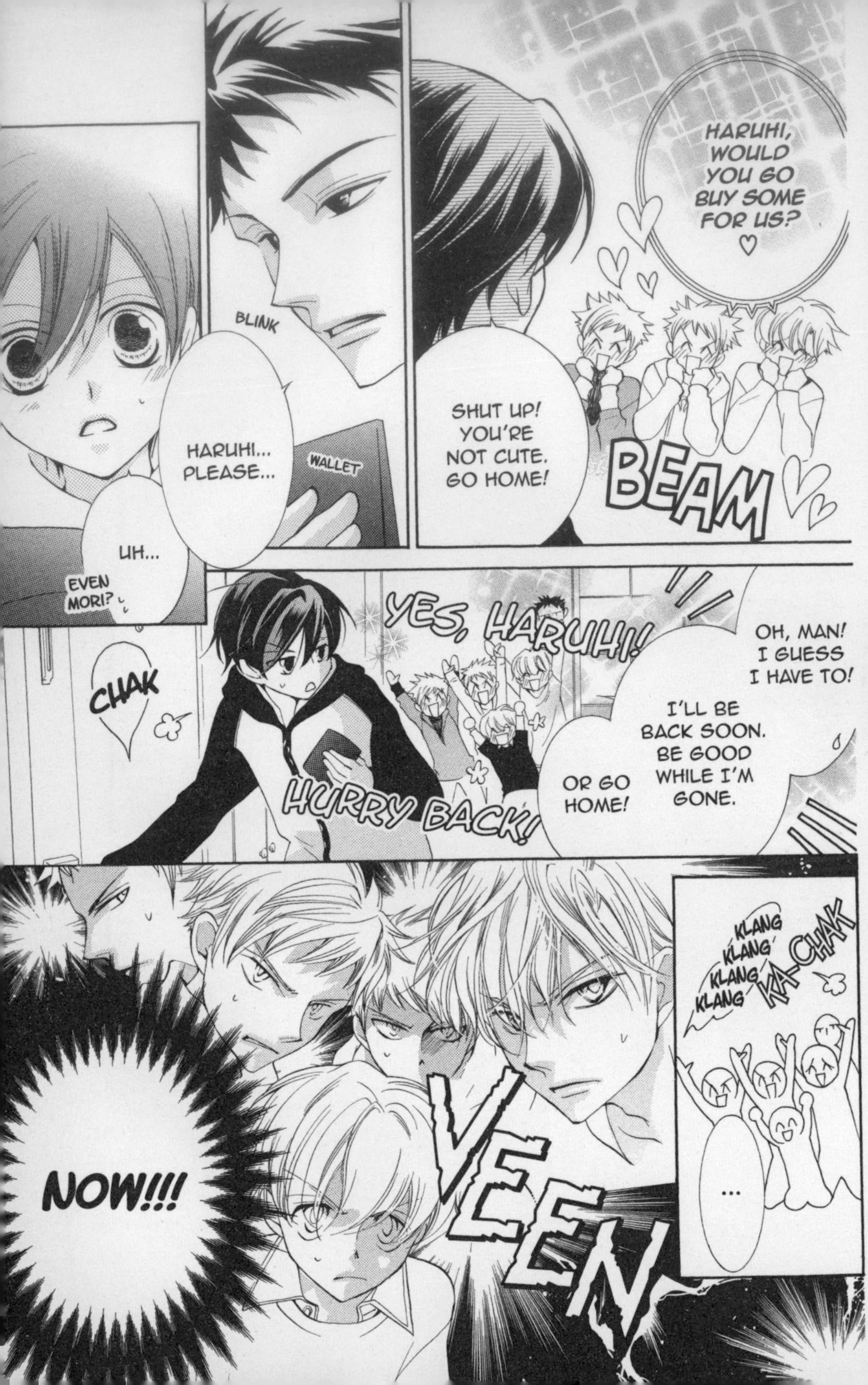
HARUHI, WOULD YOU GO BUY SOME FOR US?
BEAM
SHUT UP! YOU'RE NOT CUTE. GO HOME!
BLINK
HARUHI... PLEASE...
WALLET
UH...
EVEN MORI?
OH, MAN! I GUESS I HAVE TO!
I'LL BE BACK SOON. BE GOOD WHILE I'M GONE.
OR GO HOME!
YES, HARUHI!
HURRY BACK!
CHAK
KLANG KLANG KLANG KLANG
KA-CHAK
...
VEEN
NOW!!!

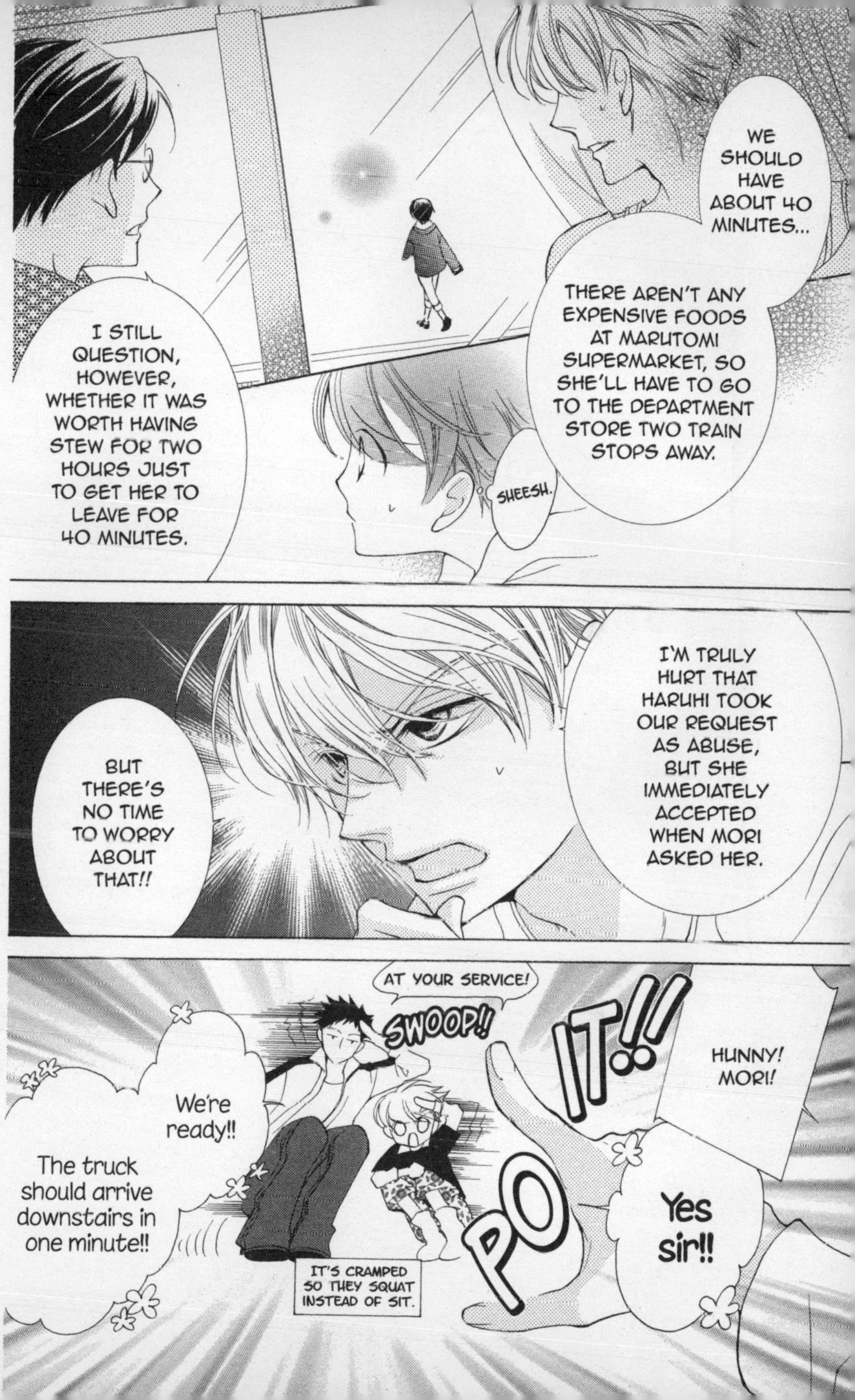
WE SHOULD HAVE ABOUT 40 MINUTES...
THERE AREN'T ANY EXPENSIVE FOODS AT MARUTOMI SUPERMARKET, SO SHE'LL HAVE TO GO TO THE DEPARTMENT STORE TWO TRAIN STOPS AWAY.
SHEESH.
I STILL QUESTION, HOWEVER, WHETHER IT WAS WORTH HAVING STEW FOR TWO HOURS JUST TO GET HER TO LEAVE FOR 40 MINUTES.
I'M TRULY HURT THAT HARUHI TOOK OUR REQUEST AS ABUSE, BUT SHE IMMEDIATELY ACCEPTED WHEN MORI ASKED HER.
BUT THERE'S NO TIME TO WORRY ABOUT THAT!!
HUNNY! MORI!
POIT!!
Yes sir!!
AT YOUR SERVICE!
SWOOP!!
We're ready!!
The truck should arrive downstairs in one minute!!
IT'S CRAMPED SO THEY SQUAT INSTEAD OF SIT.

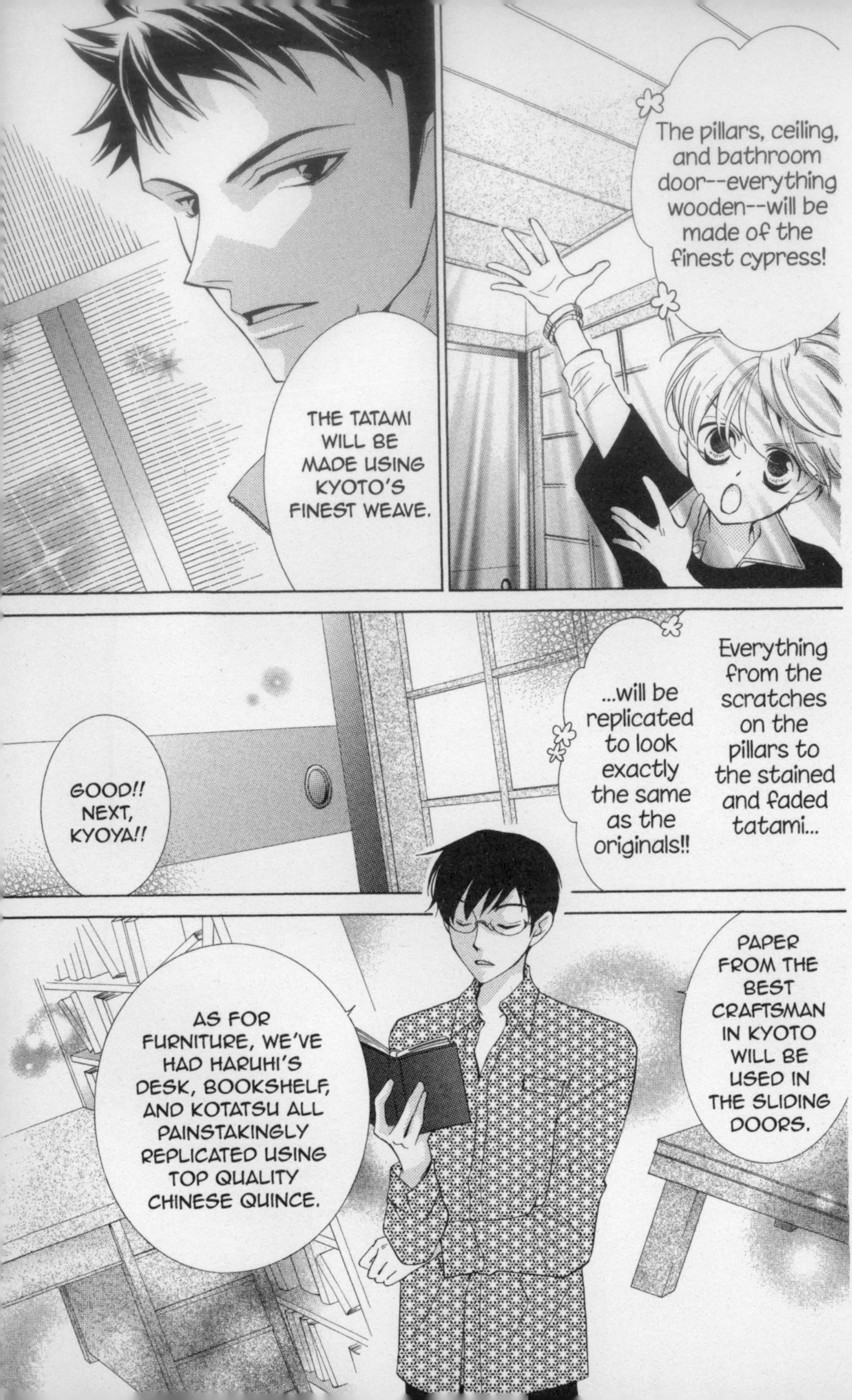
The pillars, ceiling, and bathroom door--everything wooden--will be made of the finest cypress!
THE TATAMI WILL BE MADE USING KYOTO'S FINEST WEAVE.
Everything from the scratches on the pillars to the stained and faded tatami...
...will be replicated to look exactly the same as the originals!!
GOOD!! NEXT, KYOYA!!
PAPER FROM THE BEST CRAFTSMAN IN KYOTO WILL BE USED IN THE SLIDING DOORS.
AS FOR FURNITURE, WE'VE HAD HARUHI'S DESK, BOOKSHELF, AND KOTATSU ALL PAINSTAKINGLY REPLICATED USING TOP QUALITY CHINESE QUINCE.

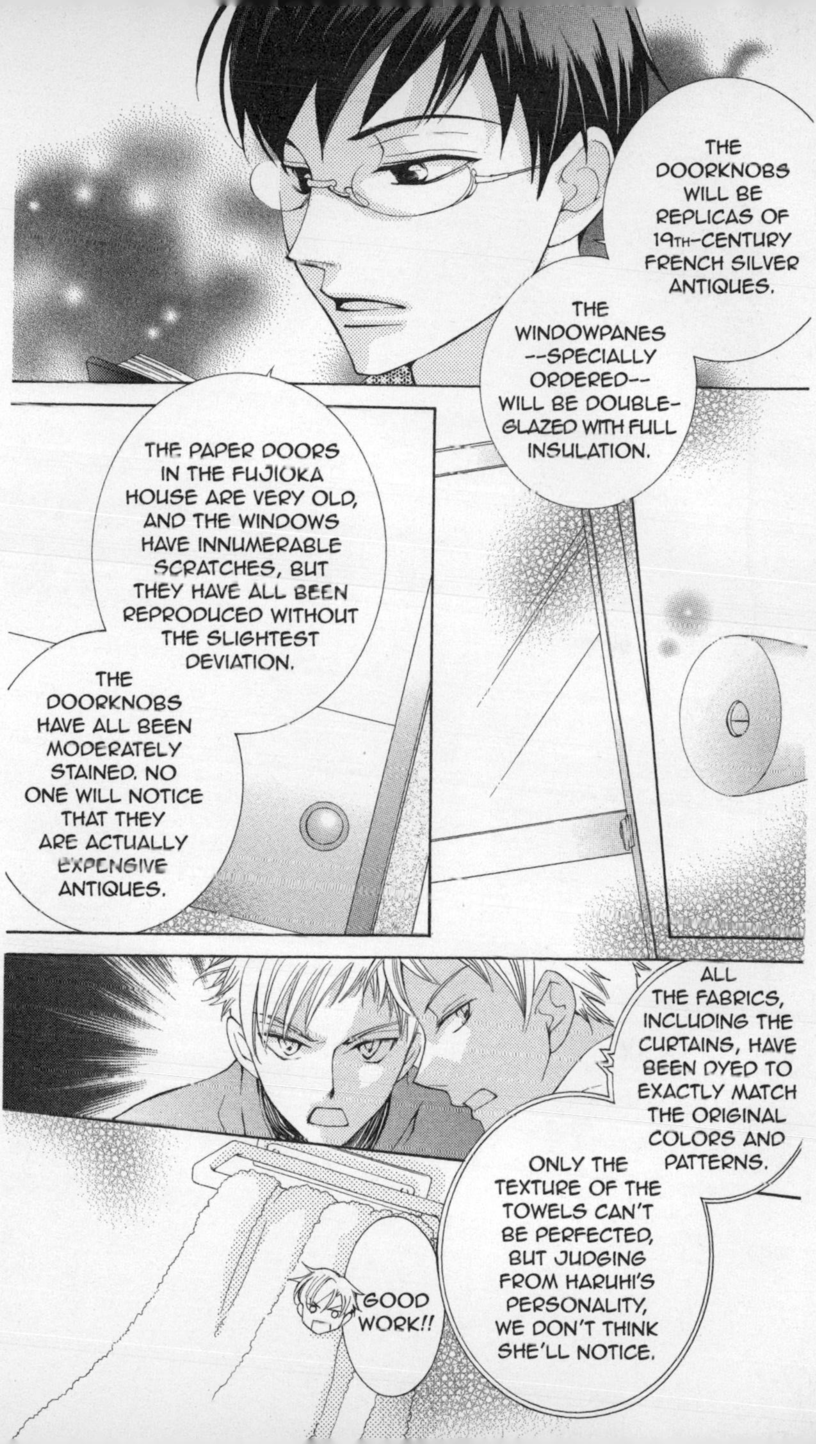
THE DOORKNOBS WILL BE REPLICAS OF 19TH-CENTURY FRENCH SILVER ANTIQUES.
THE WINDOWPANES --SPECIALLY ORDERED-- WILL BE DOUBLE-GLAZED WITH FULL INSULATION.
THE PAPER DOORS IN THE FUJIOKA HOUSE ARE VERY OLD, AND THE WINDOWS HAVE INNUMERABLE SCRATCHES, BUT THEY HAVE ALL BEEN REPRODUCED WITHOUT THE SLIGHTEST DEVIATION.
THE DOORKNOBS HAVE ALL BEEN MODERATELY STAINED. NO ONE WILL NOTICE THAT THEY ARE ACTUALLY EXPENSIVE ANTIQUES.
ALL THE FABRICS, INCLUDING THE CURTAINS, HAVE BEEN DYED TO EXACTLY MATCH THE ORIGINAL COLORS AND PATTERNS.
ONLY THE TEXTURE OF THE TOWELS CAN'T BE PERFECTED, BUT JUDGING FROM HARUHI'S PERSONALITY, WE DON'T THINK SHE'LL NOTICE.
GOOD WORK!!

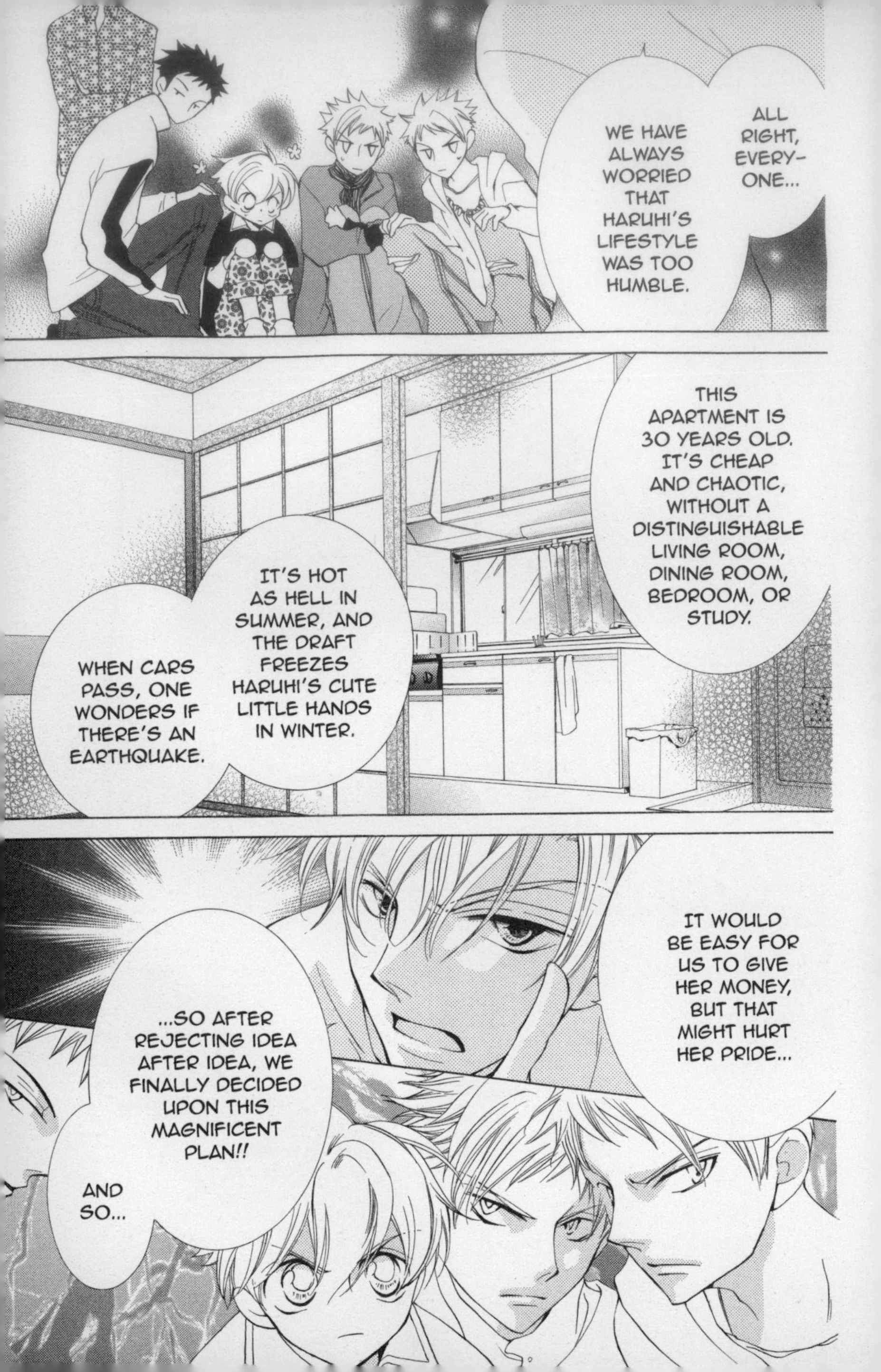
ALL RIGHT, EVERYONE...
WE HAVE ALWAYS WORRIED THAT HARUHI'S LIFESTYLE WAS TOO HUMBLE.
THIS APARTMENT IS 30 YEARS OLD. IT'S CHEAP AND CHAOTIC, WITHOUT A DISTINGUISHABLE LIVING ROOM, DINING ROOM, BEDROOM, OR STUDY.
IT'S HOT AS HELL IN SUMMER, AND THE DRAFT FREEZES HARUHI'S CUTE LITTLE HANDS IN WINTER.
WHEN CARS PASS, ONE WONDERS IF THERE'S AN EARTHQUAKE.
IT WOULD BE EASY FOR US TO GIVE HER MONEY, BUT THAT MIGHT HURT HER PRIDE...
...SO AFTER REJECTING IDEA AFTER IDEA, WE FINALLY DECIDED UPON THIS MAGNIFICENT PLAN!!
AND SO...

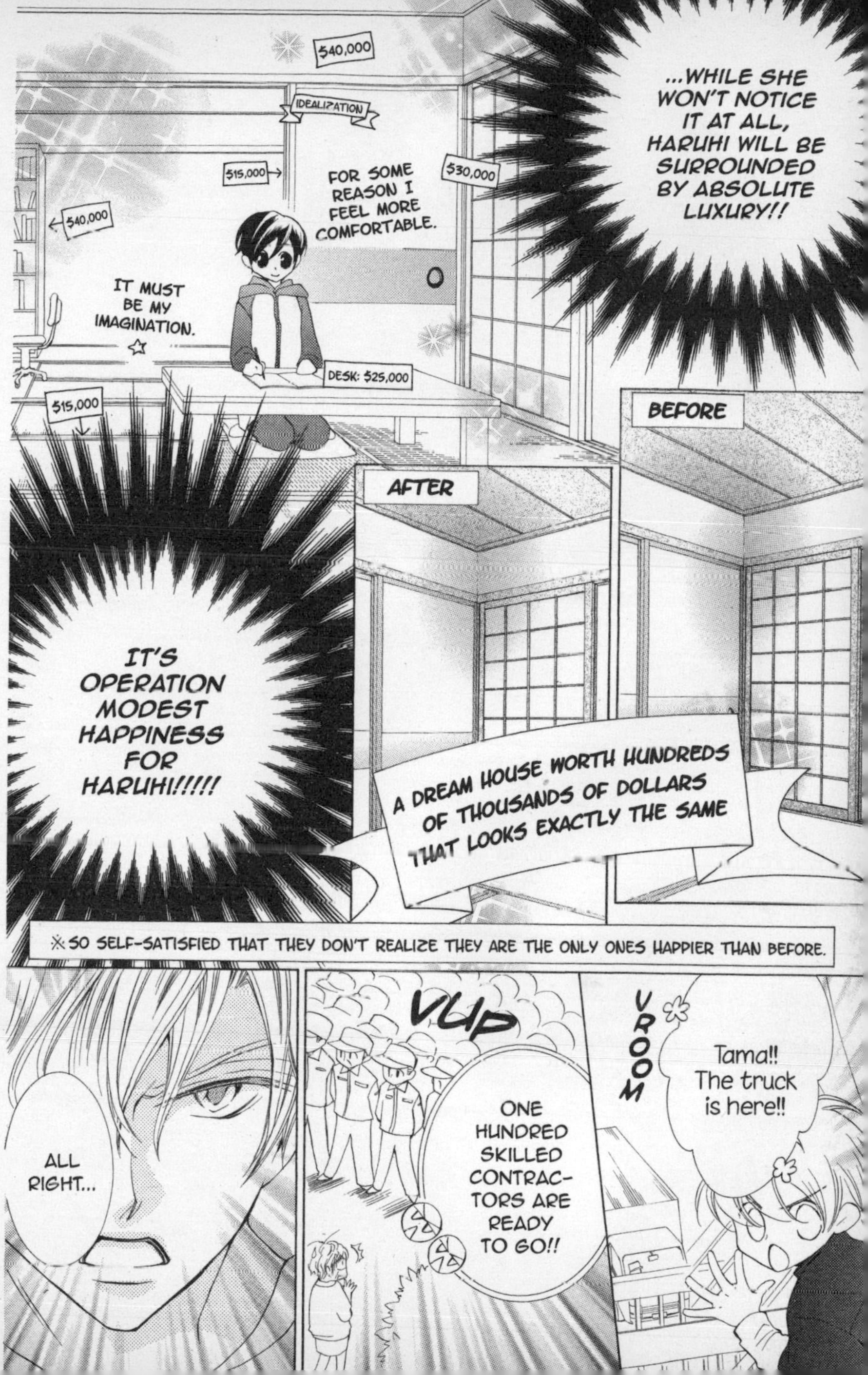
...WHILE SHE WON'T NOTICE IT AT ALL, HARUHI WILL BE SURROUNDED BY ABSOLUTE LUXURY!!
$40,000
IDEALIZATION
$30,000
$15,000
FOR SOME REASON I FEEL MORE COMFORTABLE.
$40,000
IT MUST BE MY IMAGINATION.
DESK: $25,000
$15,000
BEFORE
AFTER
A DREAM HOUSE WORTH HUNDREDS OF THOUSANDS OF DOLLARS THAT LOOKS EXACTLY THE SAME
IT'S OPERATION MODEST HAPPINESS FOR HARUHI!!!!!
※SO SELF-SATISFIED THAT THEY DON'T REALIZE THEY ARE THE ONLY ONES HAPPIER THAN BEFORE.
VROOM
Tama!! The truck is here!!
VUP
ONE HUNDRED SKILLED CONTRAC-TORS ARE READY TO GO!!
ALL RIGHT...

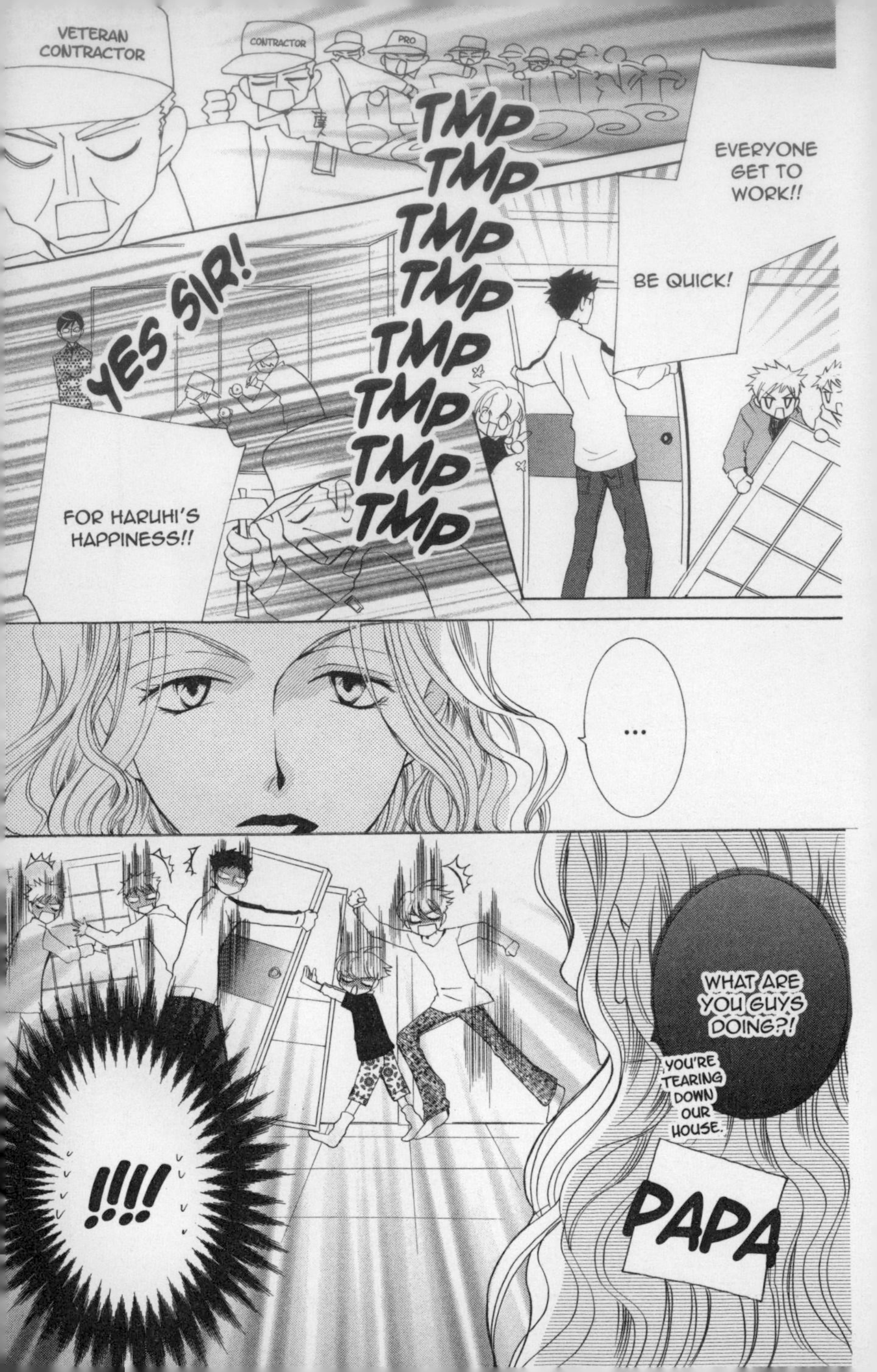
VETERAN CONTRACTOR
CONTRACTOR
PRO
EVERYONE GET TO WORK!!
TMP TMP TMP TMP TMP TMP TMP TMP
BE QUICK!
YES SIR!
FOR HARUHI'S HAPPINESS!!
...
WHAT ARE YOU GUYS DOING?!
YOU'RE TEARING DOWN OUR HOUSE.
PAPA
!!!!

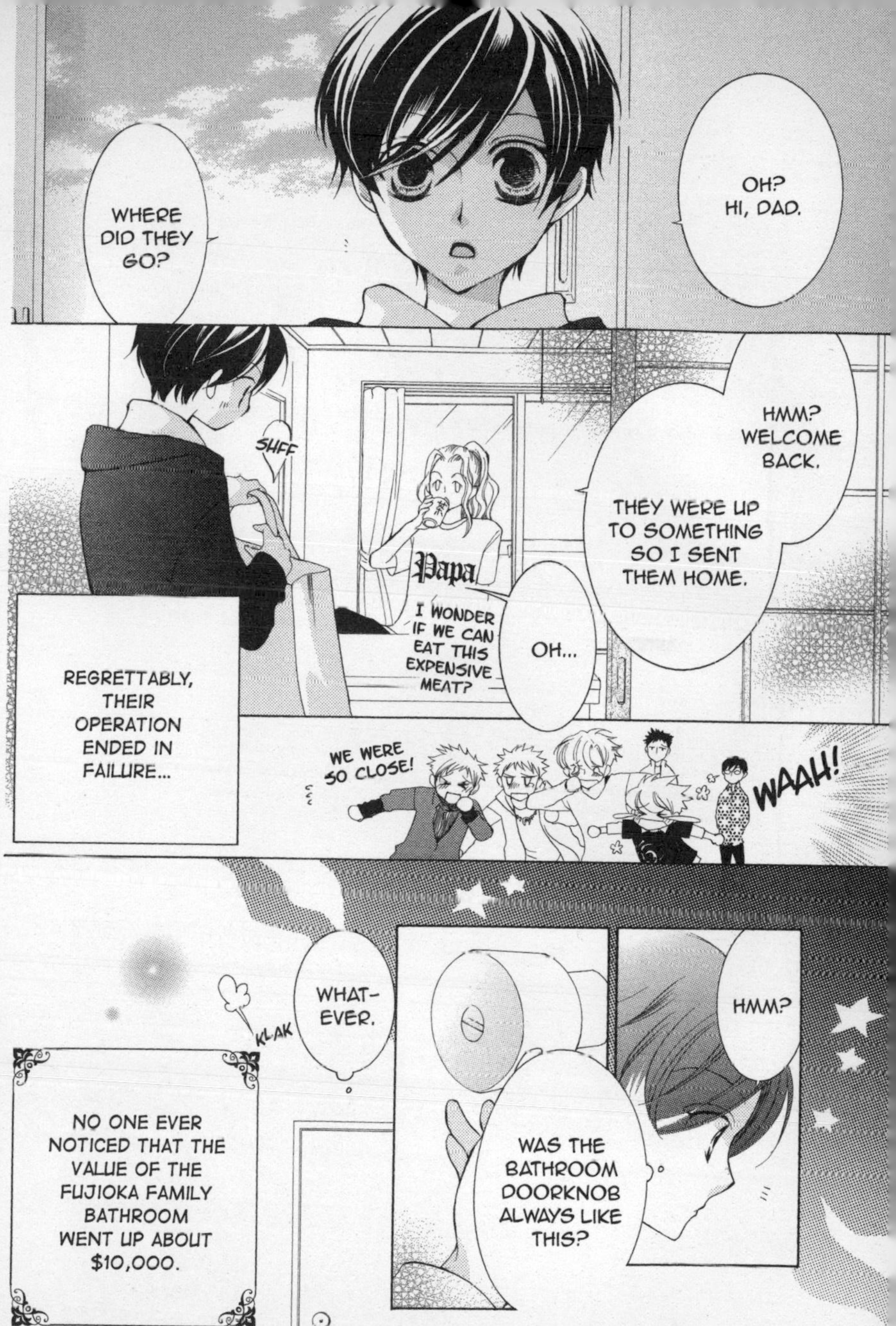
OH? HI, DAD.
WHERE DID THEY GO?
HMM? WELCOME BACK.
THEY WERE UP TO SOMETHING SO I SENT THEM HOME.
OH...
I WONDER IF WE CAN EAT THIS EXPENSIVE MEAT?
SHFF
Papa
WAAH!
WE WERE SO CLOSE!
REGRETTABLY, THEIR OPERATION ENDED IN FAILURE...
HMM?
WAS THE BATHROOM DOORKNOB ALWAYS LIKE THIS?
WHAT-EVER.
KLAK
NO ONE EVER NOTICED THAT THE VALUE OF THE FUJIOKA FAMILY BATHROOM WENT UP ABOUT $10,000.

Extra Episode: The Host Club's Operation for Modest Happiness/The End

FRENCH VERSION →

THESE ARE THE FRENCH AND ITALIAN VERSIONS OF HOST CLUB. WHAT IMPRESSES ME IS THE WAY THE SOUND EFFECTS HAVE BEEN REDRAWN BASED ON THE ONES I DREW!!

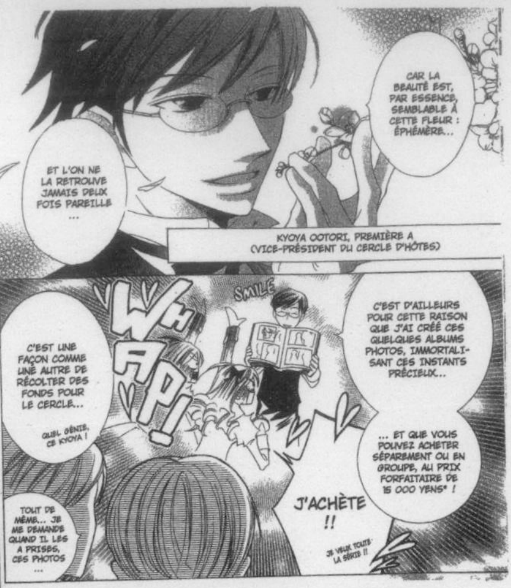
CAR LA BEAUTÉ EST, PAR ESSENCE, SEMBLABLE À CETTE FLEUR : ÉPHÉMÈRE...
ET L'ON NE LA RETROUVE JAMAIS DEUX FOIS PAREILLE ...
KYOYA OOTORI, PREMIÈRE A (VICE-PRÉSIDENT DU CERCLE D'HÔTES)
C'EST D'AILLEURS POUR CETTE RAISON QUE J'AI CRÉÉ CES QUELQUES ALBUMS PHOTOS, IMMORTALISANT CES INSTANTS PRÉCIEUX..
SMILE
WHAP!
C'EST UNE FAÇON COMME UNE AUTRE DE RÉCOLTER DES FONDS POUR LE CERCLE...
QUEL GÉNIE, CE KYOYA !
... ET QUE VOUS POUVEZ ACHETER SÉPARÉMENT OU EN GROUPE, AU PRIX FORFAITAIRE DE 15 000 YENS* !
J'ACHÈTE !!
JE VEUX TOUTE LA SÉRIE !!
TOUT DE MÊME... JE ME DEMANDE QUAND IL LES A PRISES, CES PHOTOS ...

「Host Club Le lycée de la séduction」

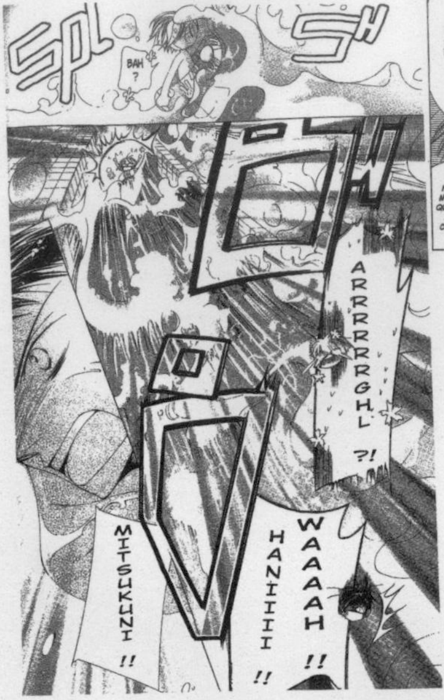
SH
SPL
BAH ?
ARRRRRRGHL ?!
WAAAAAH !!
HANIIIII !!
MITSUKUNI !!

← LIKE THESE PAGES. COMPARE THEM WITH THE JAPANESE MANGA. IT'S AMAZING!!

ITALIAN VERSION →

「Host Club Amore in affitto」

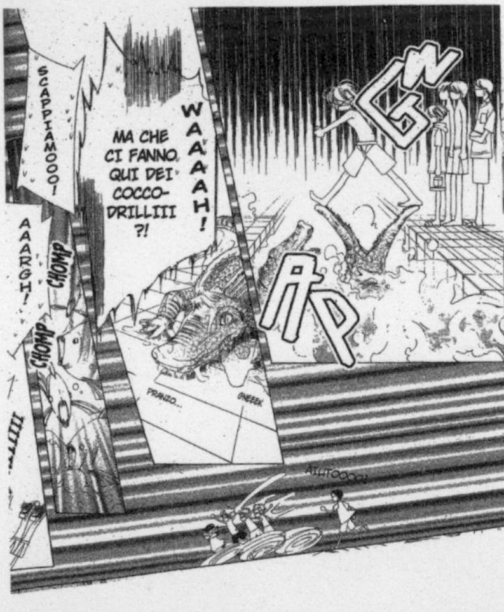
GN
AP
WAAAAAH!
MA CHE CI FANNO QUI DEI COCCO-DRILLIII ?!
SCAPPIAMOOO!
PRANZO...
GNEEEK
CHOMP
AAARGH!
CHOMP
AIUTOOOO!

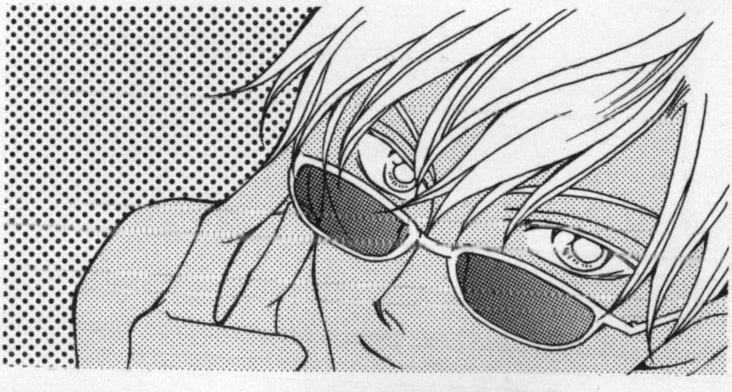

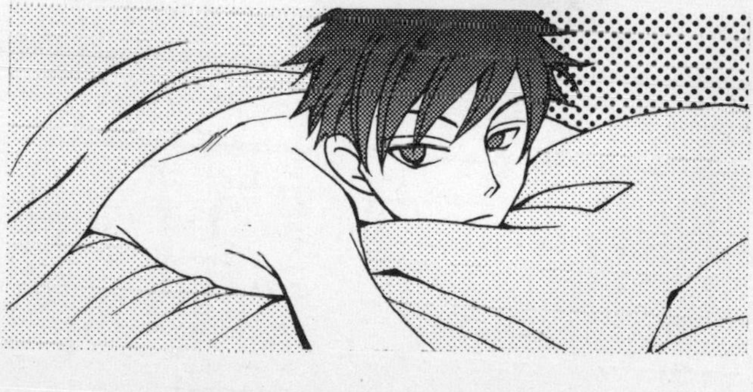

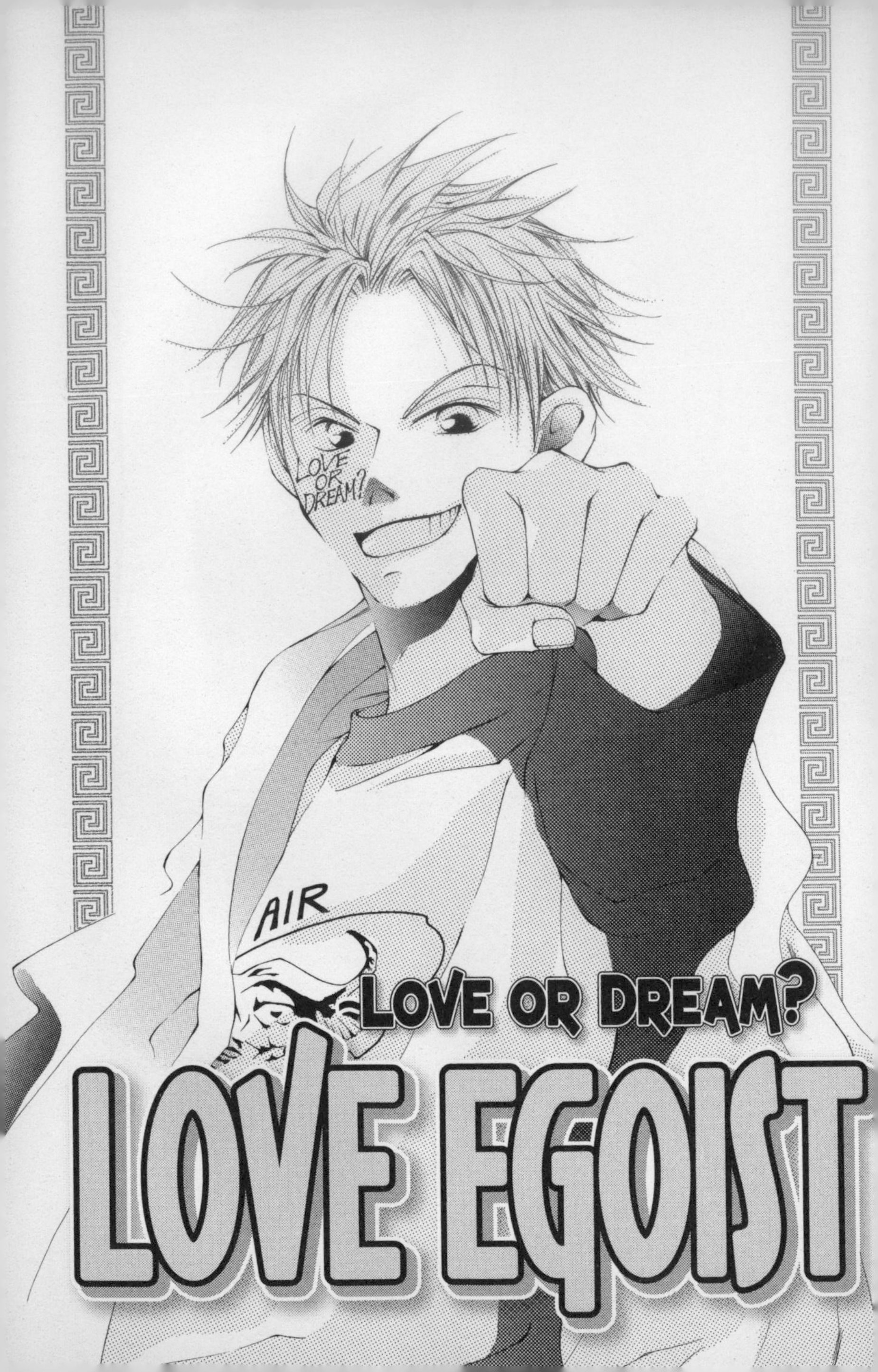
LOVE OR DREAM?
AIR
LOVE OR DREAM?
LOVE EGOIST

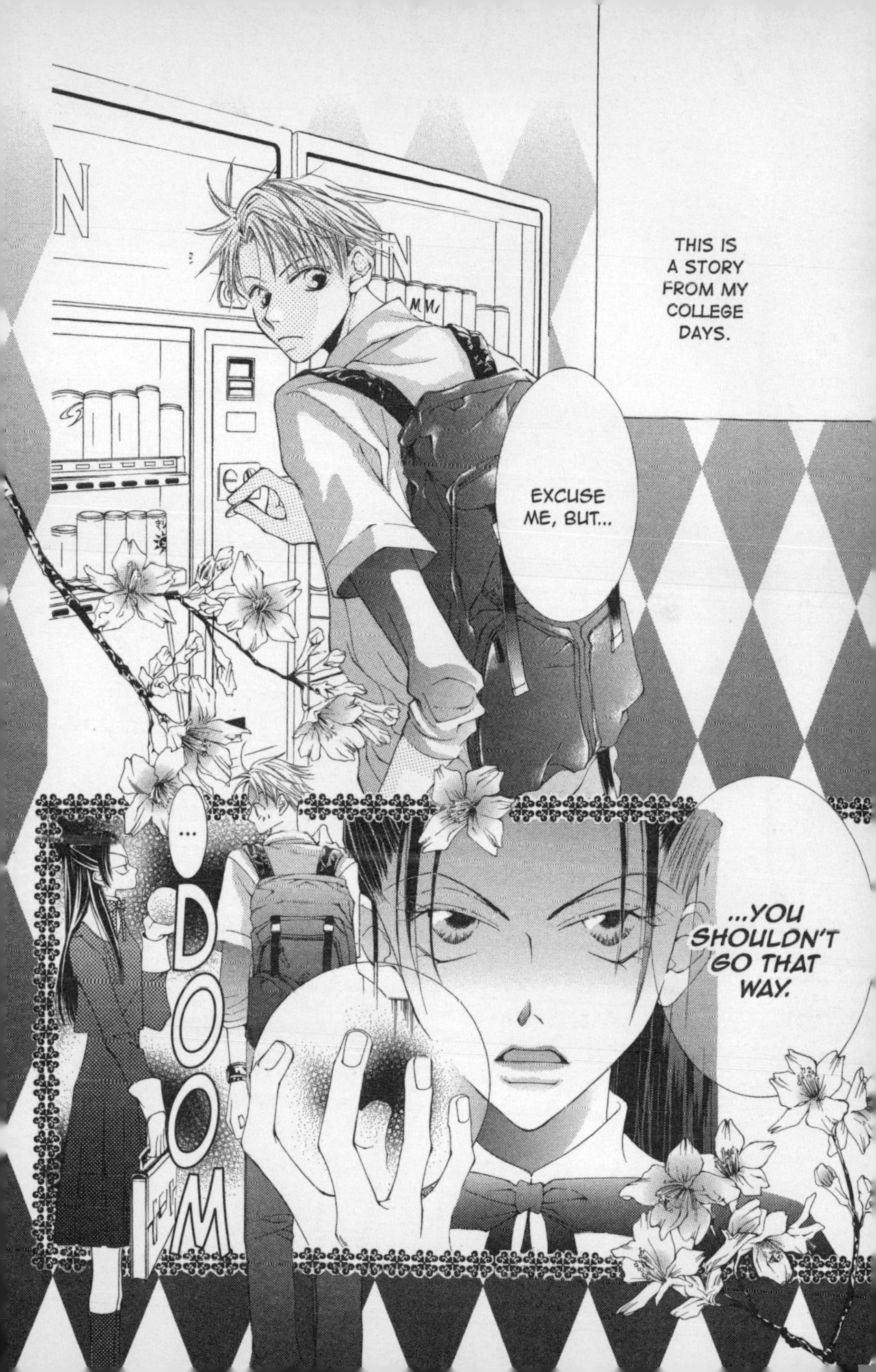
THIS IS A STORY FROM MY COLLEGE DAYS.
EXCUSE ME, BUT...
...YOU SHOULDN'T GO THAT WAY.
...
DOOM

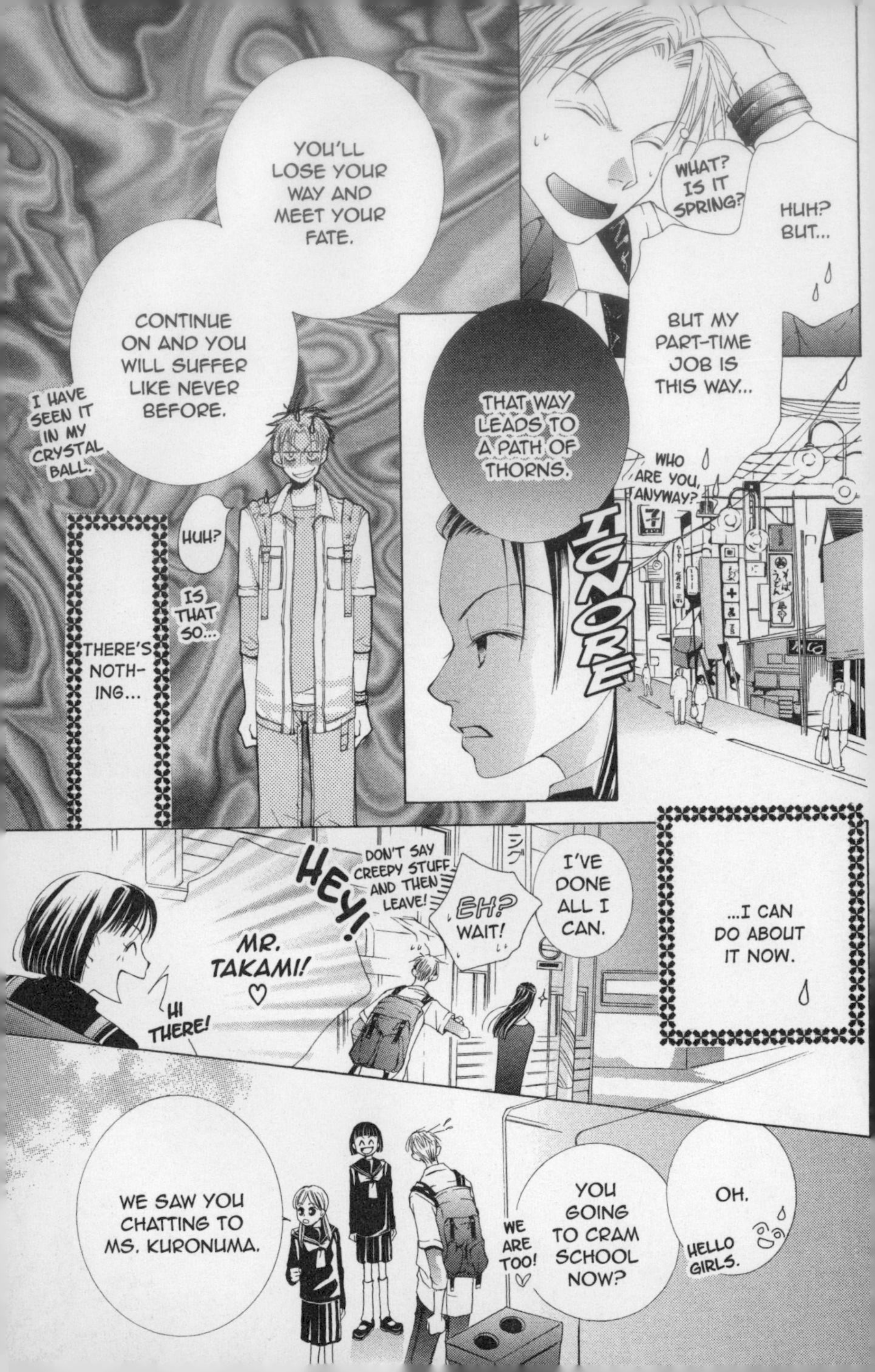
WHAT? IS IT SPRING?
HUH? BUT...
BUT MY PART-TIME JOB IS THIS WAY...
THAT WAY LEADS TO A PATH OF THORNS.
WHO ARE YOU, ANYWAY?
IGNORE
YOU'LL LOSE YOUR WAY AND MEET YOUR FATE.
CONTINUE ON AND YOU WILL SUFFER LIKE NEVER BEFORE.
I HAVE SEEN IT IN MY CRYSTAL BALL.
HUH?
IS THAT SO...
THERE'S NOTHING...
...I CAN DO ABOUT IT NOW.
I'VE DONE ALL I CAN.
EH? WAIT!
DON'T SAY CREEPY STUFF AND THEN LEAVE!
HEY!
MR. TAKAMI! ♡
HI THERE!
OH.
HELLO GIRLS.
YOU GOING TO CRAM SCHOOL NOW?
WE ARE TOO! ♡
WE SAW YOU CHATTING TO MS. KURONUMA.

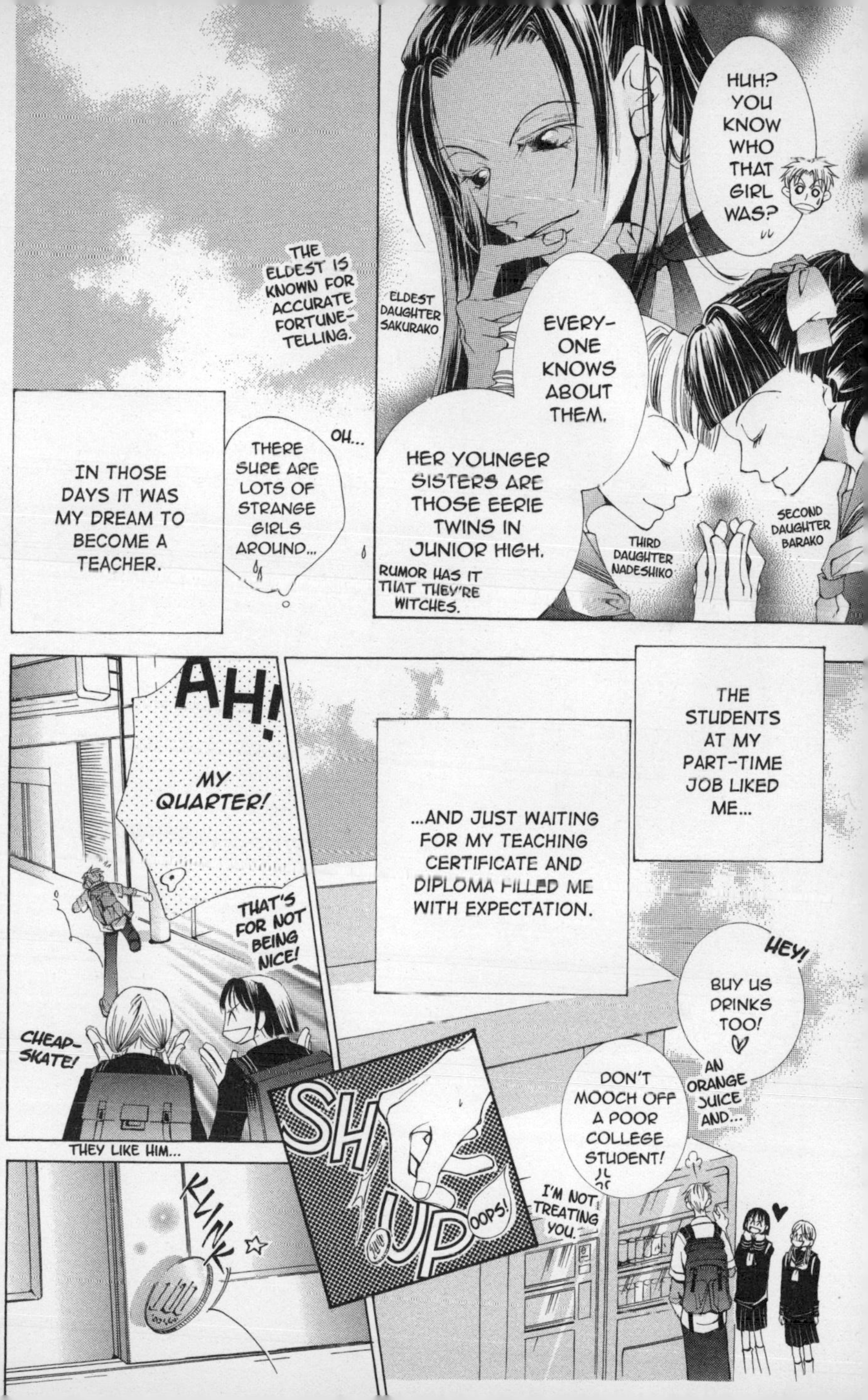
HUH? YOU KNOW WHO THAT GIRL WAS?
EVERY-ONE KNOWS ABOUT THEM.
ELDEST DAUGHTER SAKURAKO
HER YOUNGER SISTERS ARE THOSE EERIE TWINS IN JUNIOR HIGH.
SECOND DAUGHTER BARAKO
THIRD DAUGHTER NADESHIKO
RUMOR HAS IT THAT THEY'RE WITCHES.
THE ELDEST IS KNOWN FOR ACCURATE FORTUNE-TELLING.
OH...
THERE SURE ARE LOTS OF STRANGE GIRLS AROUND...
IN THOSE DAYS IT WAS MY DREAM TO BECOME A TEACHER.
THE STUDENTS AT MY PART-TIME JOB LIKED ME...
...AND JUST WAITING FOR MY TEACHING CERTIFICATE AND DIPLOMA FILLED ME WITH EXPECTATION.
HEY!
BUY US DRINKS TOO!
AN ORANGE JUICE AND...
DON'T MOOCH OFF A POOR COLLEGE STUDENT!
I'M NOT TREATING YOU.
SHUP
OOPS!
KLINK
AH!
MY QUARTER!
THAT'S FOR NOT BEING NICE!
CHEAP-SKATE!
THEY LIKE HIM...

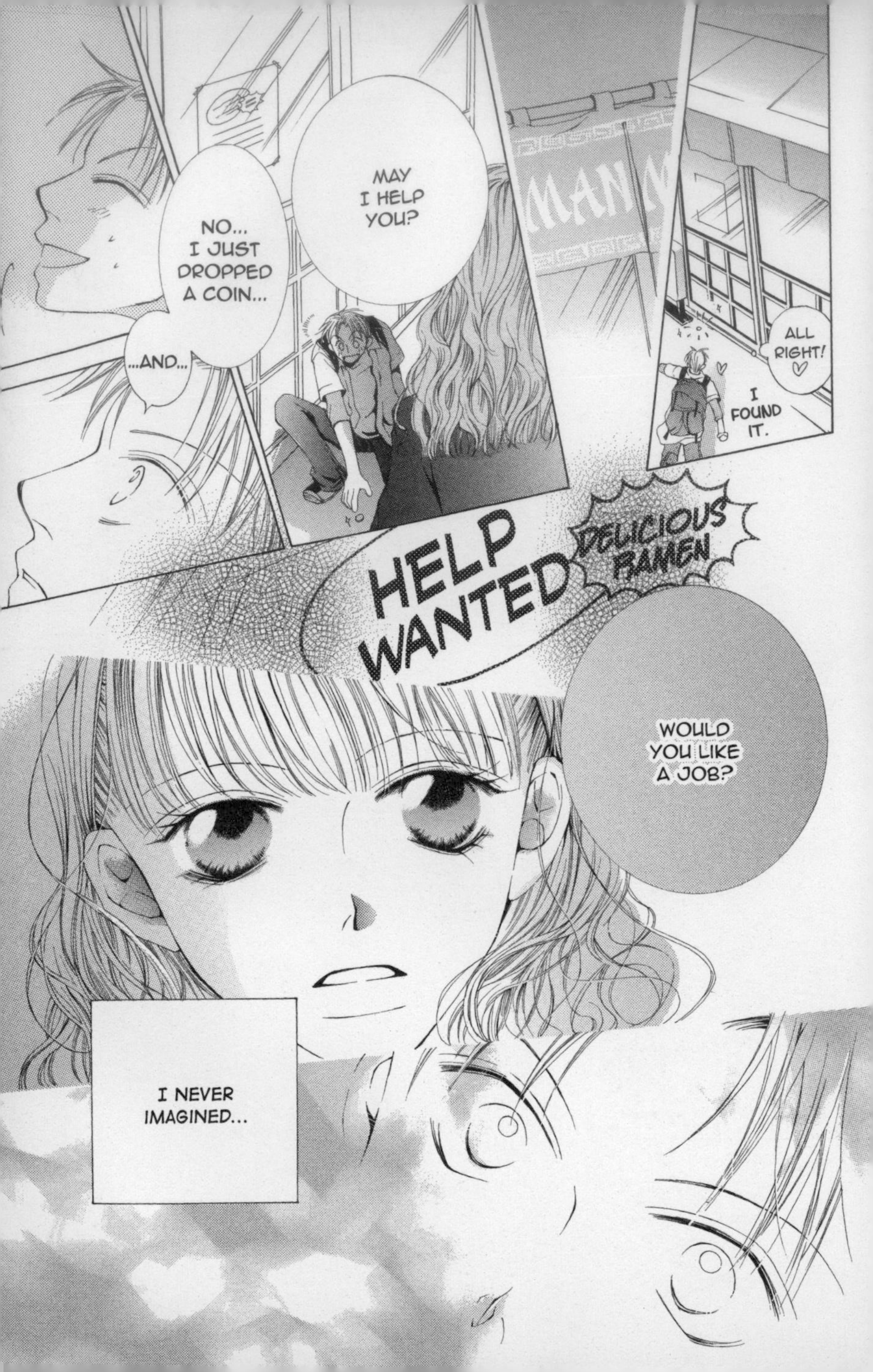
ALL RIGHT! ♡
I FOUND IT.
MAY I HELP YOU?
NO... I JUST DROPPED A COIN...
...AND...
HELP WANTED
DELICIOUS RAMEN
WOULD YOU LIKE A JOB?
I NEVER IMAGINED...

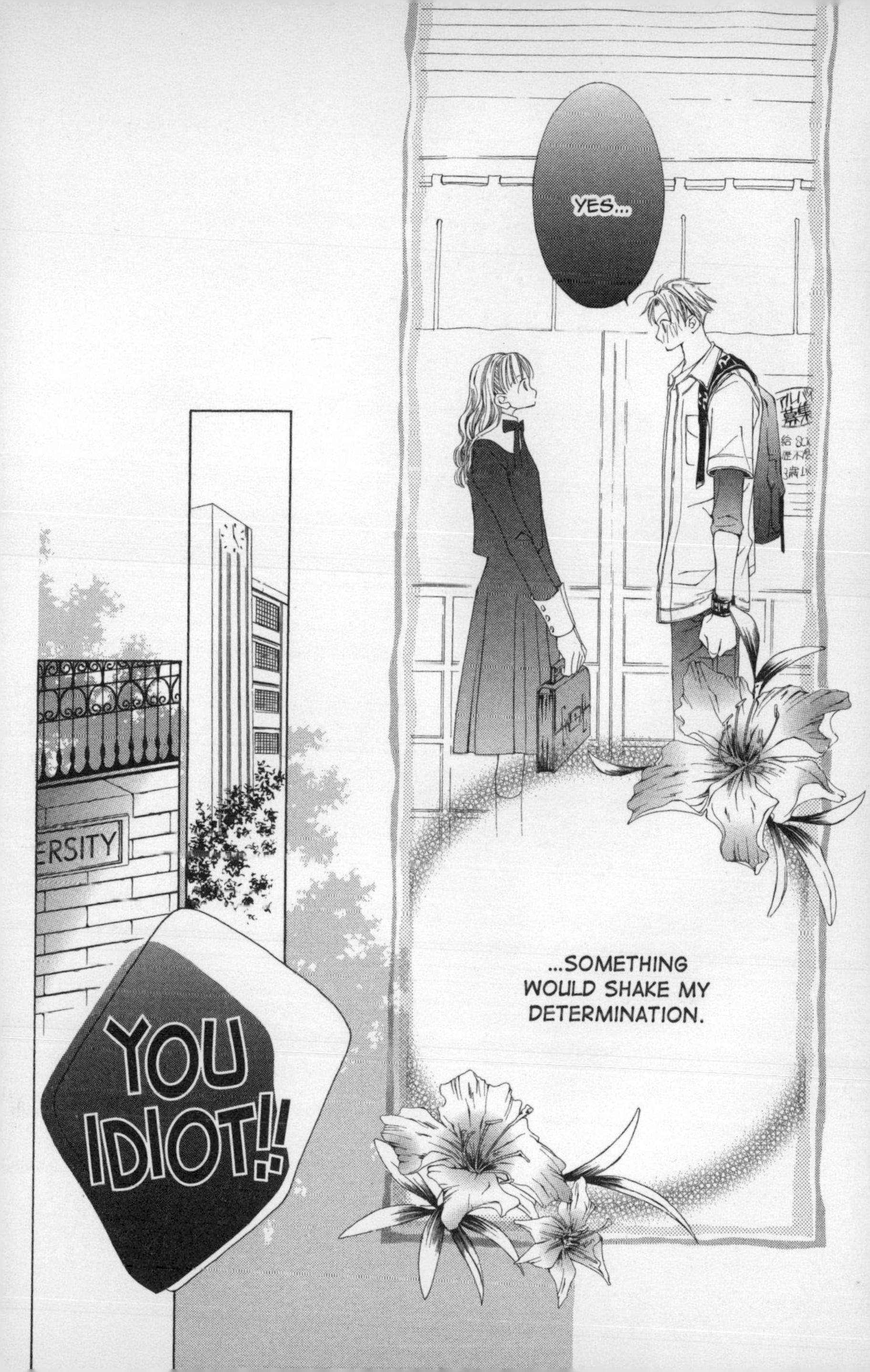
YES...
...SOMETHING WOULD SHAKE MY DETERMINATION.
ERSITY
YOU IDIOT!!

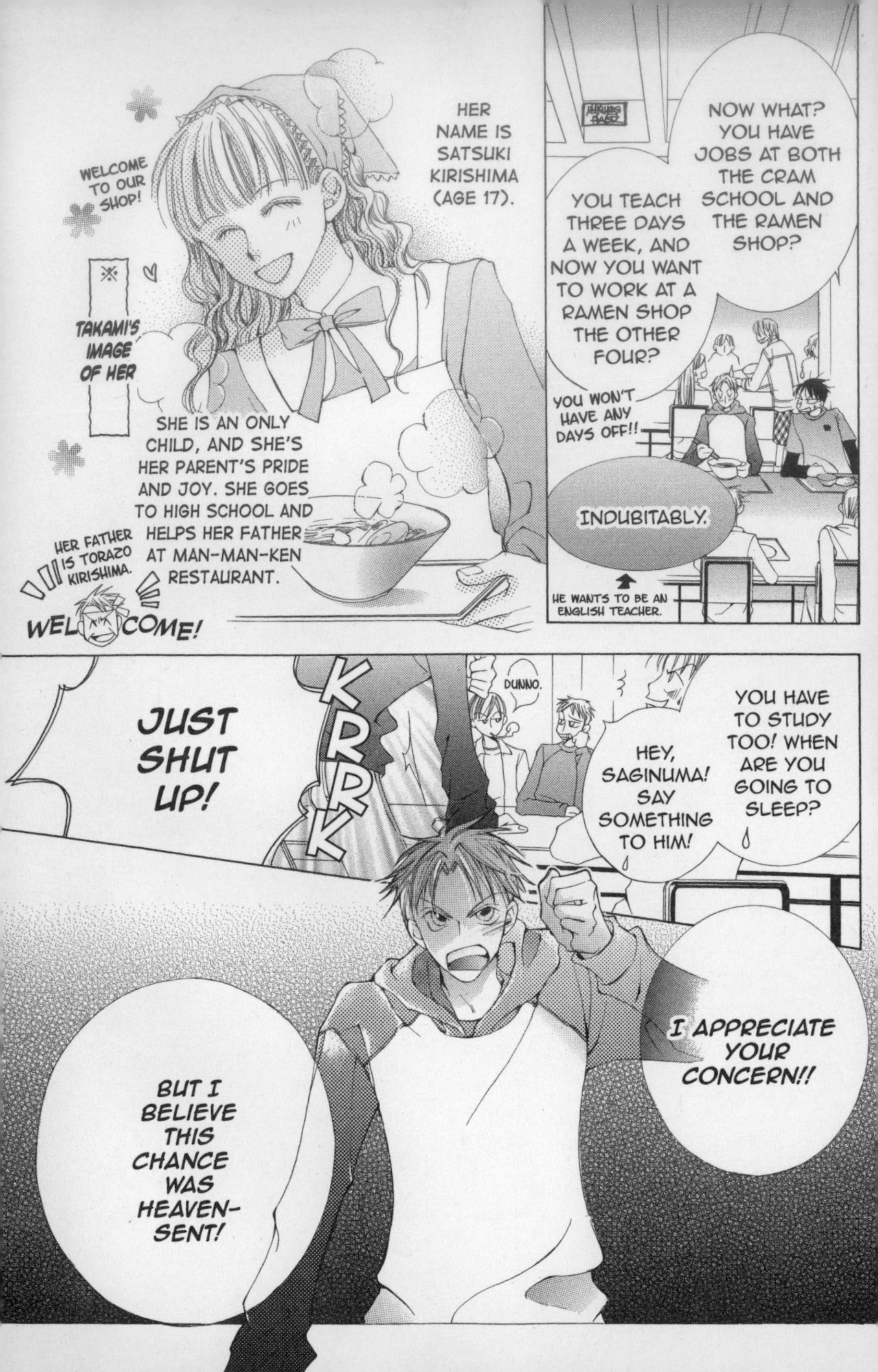
NOW WHAT? YOU HAVE JOBS AT BOTH THE CRAM SCHOOL AND THE RAMEN SHOP?
YOU TEACH THREE DAYS A WEEK, AND NOW YOU WANT TO WORK AT A RAMEN SHOP THE OTHER FOUR?
YOU WON'T HAVE ANY DAYS OFF!!
INDUBITABLY.
HE WANTS TO BE AN ENGLISH TEACHER.
HER NAME IS SATSUKI KIRISHIMA (AGE 17).
WELCOME TO OUR SHOP!
※ TAKAMI'S IMAGE OF HER
SHE IS AN ONLY CHILD, AND SHE'S HER PARENT'S PRIDE AND JOY. SHE GOES TO HIGH SCHOOL AND HELPS HER FATHER AT MAN-MAN-KEN RESTAURANT.
HER FATHER IS TORAZO KIRISHIMA.
WEL COME!
YOU HAVE TO STUDY TOO! WHEN ARE YOU GOING TO SLEEP?
HEY, SAGINUMA! SAY SOMETHING TO HIM!
DUNNO.
KRRK
JUST SHUT UP!
I APPRECIATE YOUR CONCERN!!
BUT I BELIEVE THIS CHANCE WAS HEAVEN-SENT!

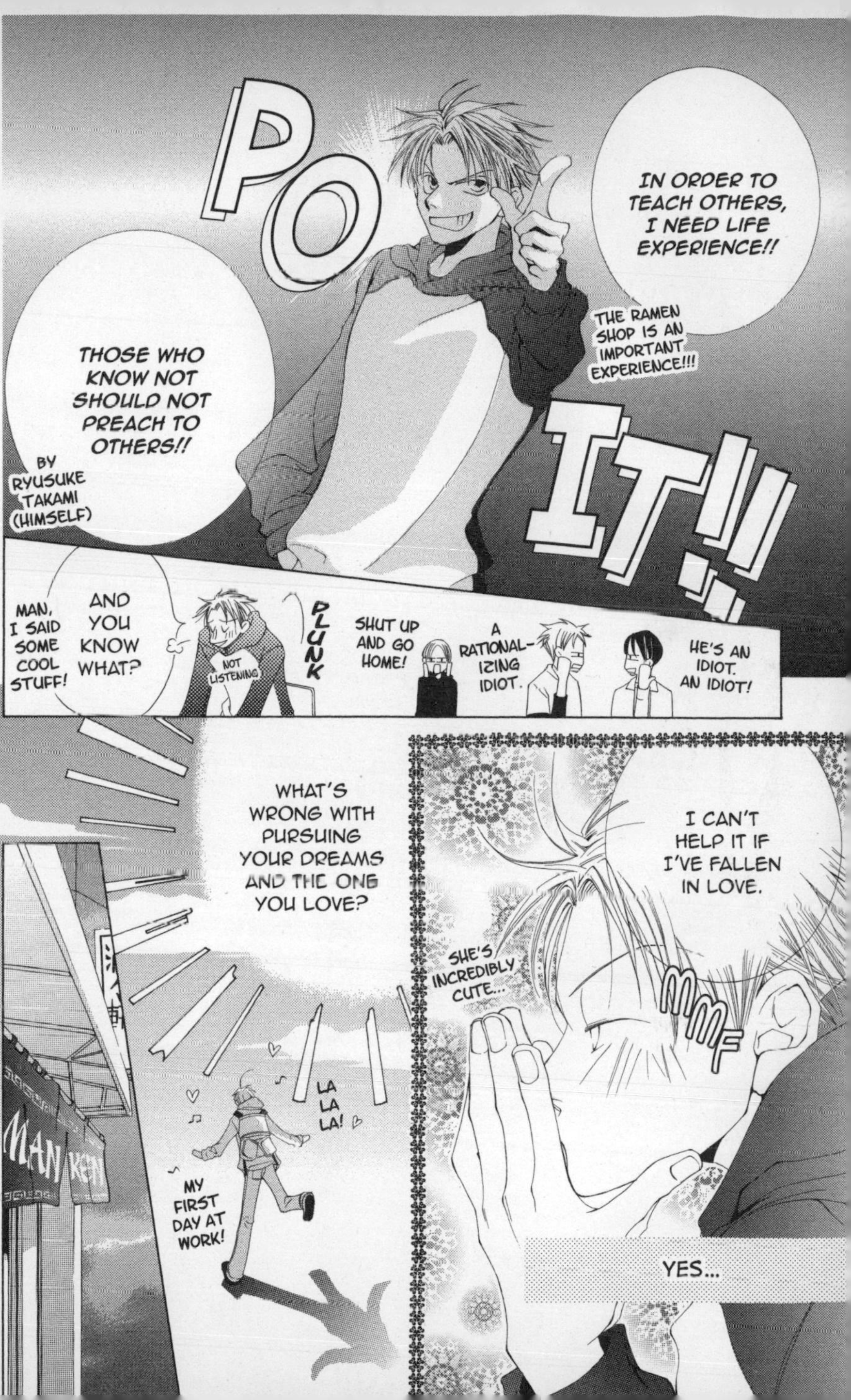
IN ORDER TO TEACH OTHERS, I NEED LIFE EXPERIENCE!!
THE RAMEN SHOP IS AN IMPORTANT EXPERIENCE!!!
THOSE WHO KNOW NOT SHOULD NOT PREACH TO OTHERS!!
BY RYUSUKE TAKAMI (HIMSELF)
PO
IT!!
HE'S AN IDIOT. AN IDIOT!
A RATIONAL-IZING IDIOT.
SHUT UP AND GO HOME!
PLUNK
NOT LISTENING
AND YOU KNOW WHAT?
MAN, I SAID SOME COOL STUFF!
I CAN'T HELP IT IF I'VE FALLEN IN LOVE.
SHE'S INCREDIBLY CUTE...
MMF
YES...
WHAT'S WRONG WITH PURSUING YOUR DREAMS AND THE ONE YOU LOVE?
LA LA LA!
MY FIRST DAY AT WORK!
MAN KEN

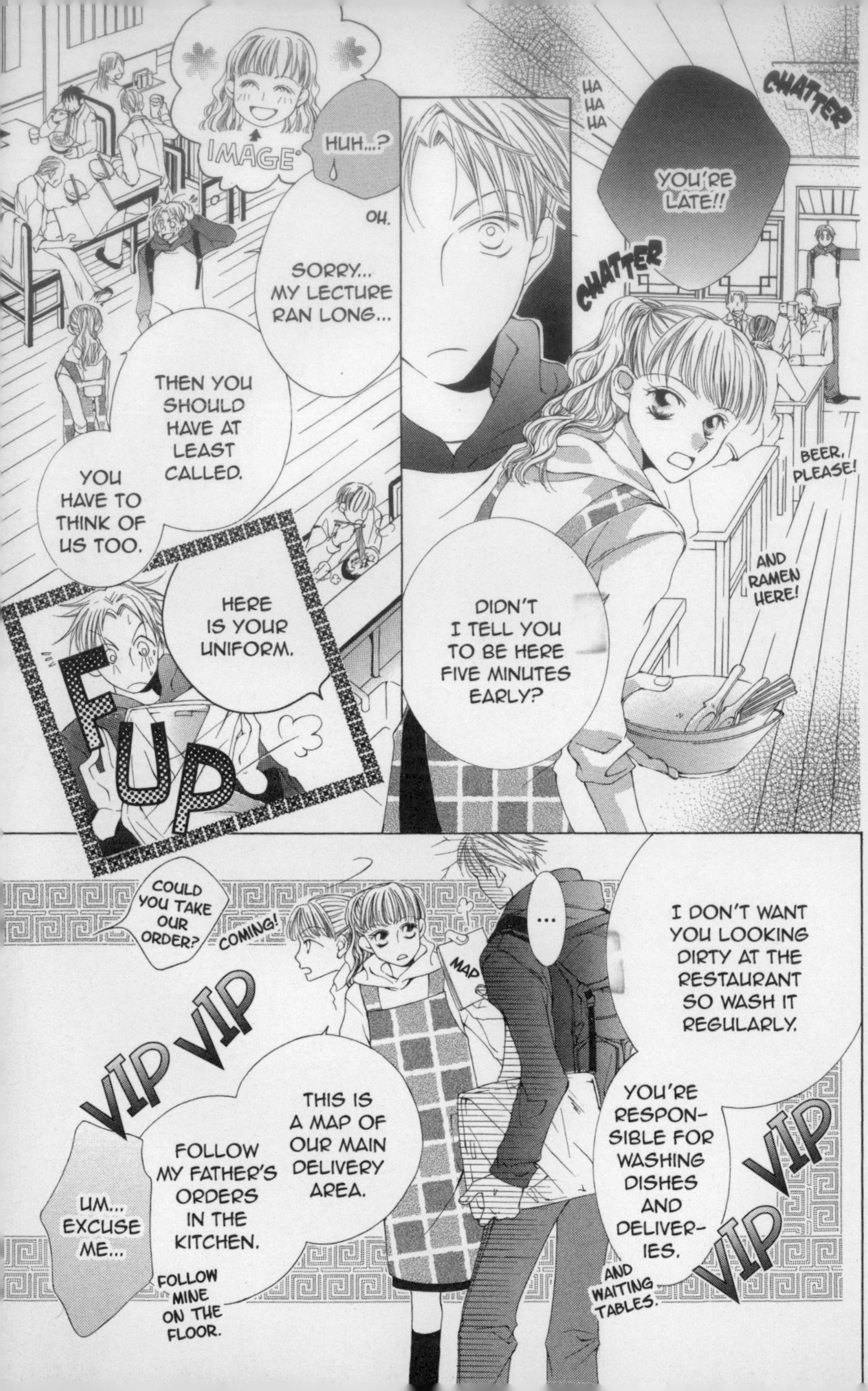
HA HA HA
CHATTER
YOU'RE LATE!!
CHATTER
BEER, PLEASE!
AND RAMEN HERE!
DIDN'T I TELL YOU TO BE HERE FIVE MINUTES EARLY?
HUH...?
OH.
SORRY... MY LECTURE RAN LONG...
IMAGE
THEN YOU SHOULD HAVE AT LEAST CALLED.
YOU HAVE TO THINK OF US TOO.
HERE IS YOUR UNIFORM.
FUP
I DON'T WANT YOU LOOKING DIRTY AT THE RESTAURANT SO WASH IT REGULARLY.
...
MAP
COULD YOU TAKE OUR ORDER?
COMING!
YOU'RE RESPONSIBLE FOR WASHING DISHES AND DELIVERIES.
AND WAITING TABLES.
VIP VIP
THIS IS A MAP OF OUR MAIN DELIVERY AREA.
FOLLOW MY FATHER'S ORDERS IN THE KITCHEN.
FOLLOW MINE ON THE FLOOR.
UM... EXCUSE ME...
VIP VIP

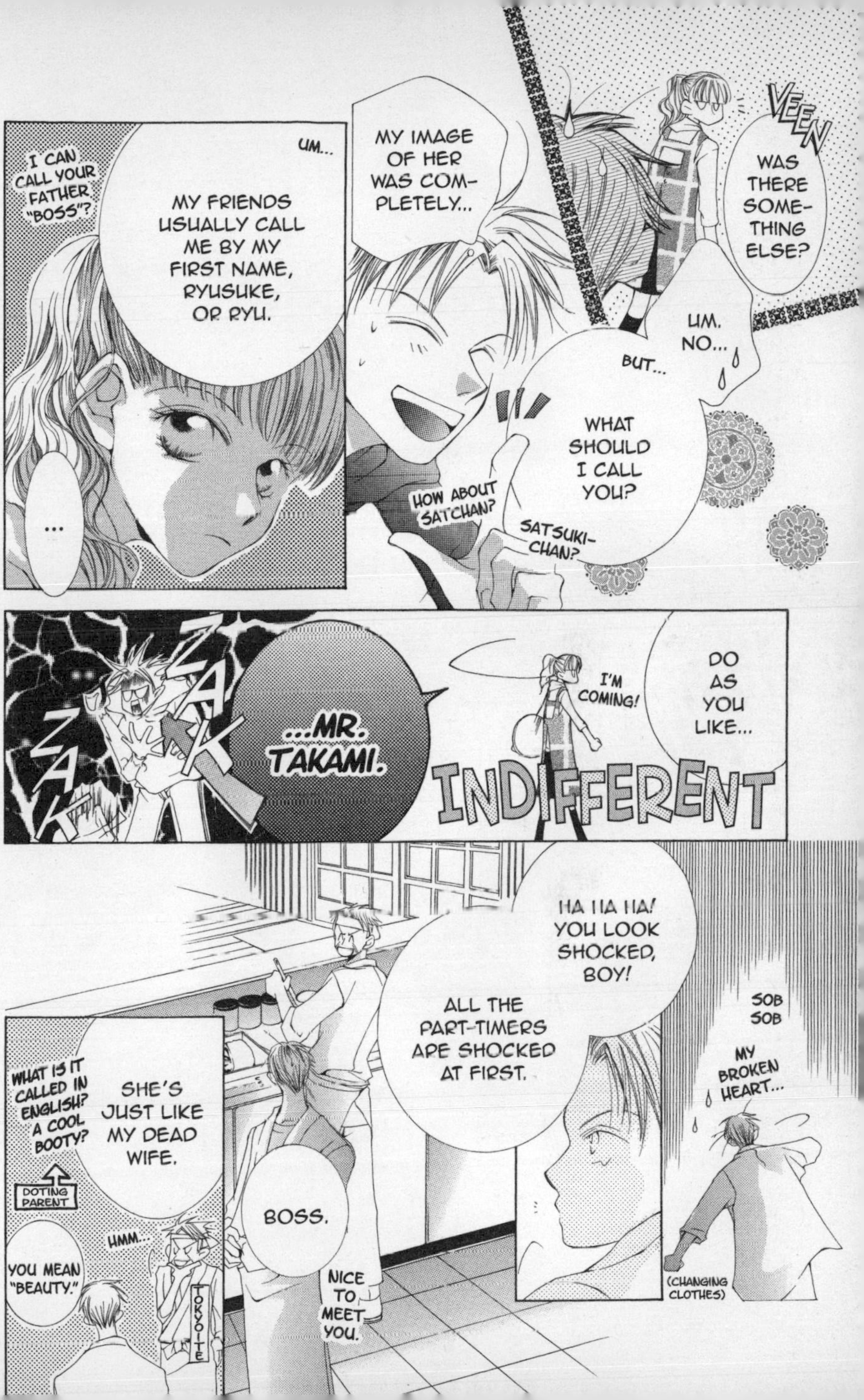
VEEN
WAS THERE SOME-THING ELSE?
UM. NO...
BUT...
WHAT SHOULD I CALL YOU?
SATSUKI-CHAN?
HOW ABOUT SATCHAN?
MY IMAGE OF HER WAS COM-PLETELY...
UM...
MY FRIENDS USUALLY CALL ME BY MY FIRST NAME, RYUSUKE, OR RYU.
I CAN CALL YOUR FATHER "BOSS"?
...
DO AS YOU LIKE...
I'M COMING!
INDIFFERENT
...MR. TAKAMI.
ZAK
ZAK
SOB SOB
MY BROKEN HEART...
(CHANGING CLOTHES)
HA HA HA! YOU LOOK SHOCKED, BOY!
ALL THE PART-TIMERS ARE SHOCKED AT FIRST.
BOSS.
NICE TO MEET YOU.
SHE'S JUST LIKE MY DEAD WIFE.
WHAT IS IT CALLED IN ENGLISH? A COOL BOOTY?
DOTING PARENT
HMM...
YOU MEAN "BEAUTY."
TOKYOITE

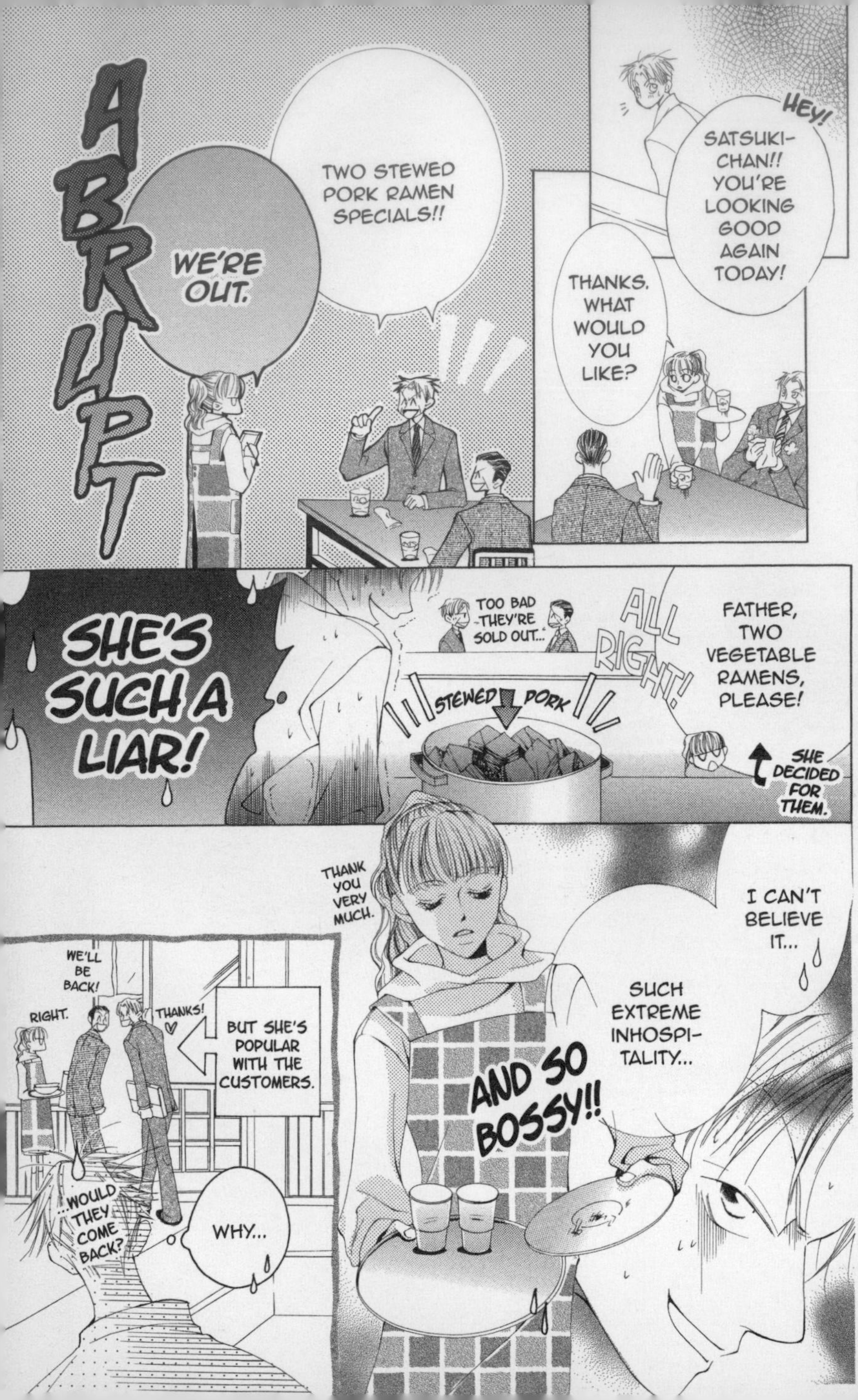
HEY!
SATSUKI-CHAN!! YOU'RE LOOKING GOOD AGAIN TODAY!
THANKS. WHAT WOULD YOU LIKE?
TWO STEWED PORK RAMEN SPECIALS!!
WE'RE OUT.
ABRUPT
FATHER, TWO VEGETABLE RAMENS, PLEASE!
SHE DECIDED FOR THEM.
ALL RIGHT!
STEWED PORK
TOO BAD THEY'RE SOLD OUT...
SHE'S SUCH A LIAR!
THANK YOU VERY MUCH.
I CAN'T BELIEVE IT...
SUCH EXTREME INHOSPI-TALITY...
AND SO BOSSY!!
BUT SHE'S POPULAR WITH THE CUSTOMERS.
THANKS!
WE'LL BE BACK!
RIGHT.
WHY...
...WOULD THEY COME BACK?

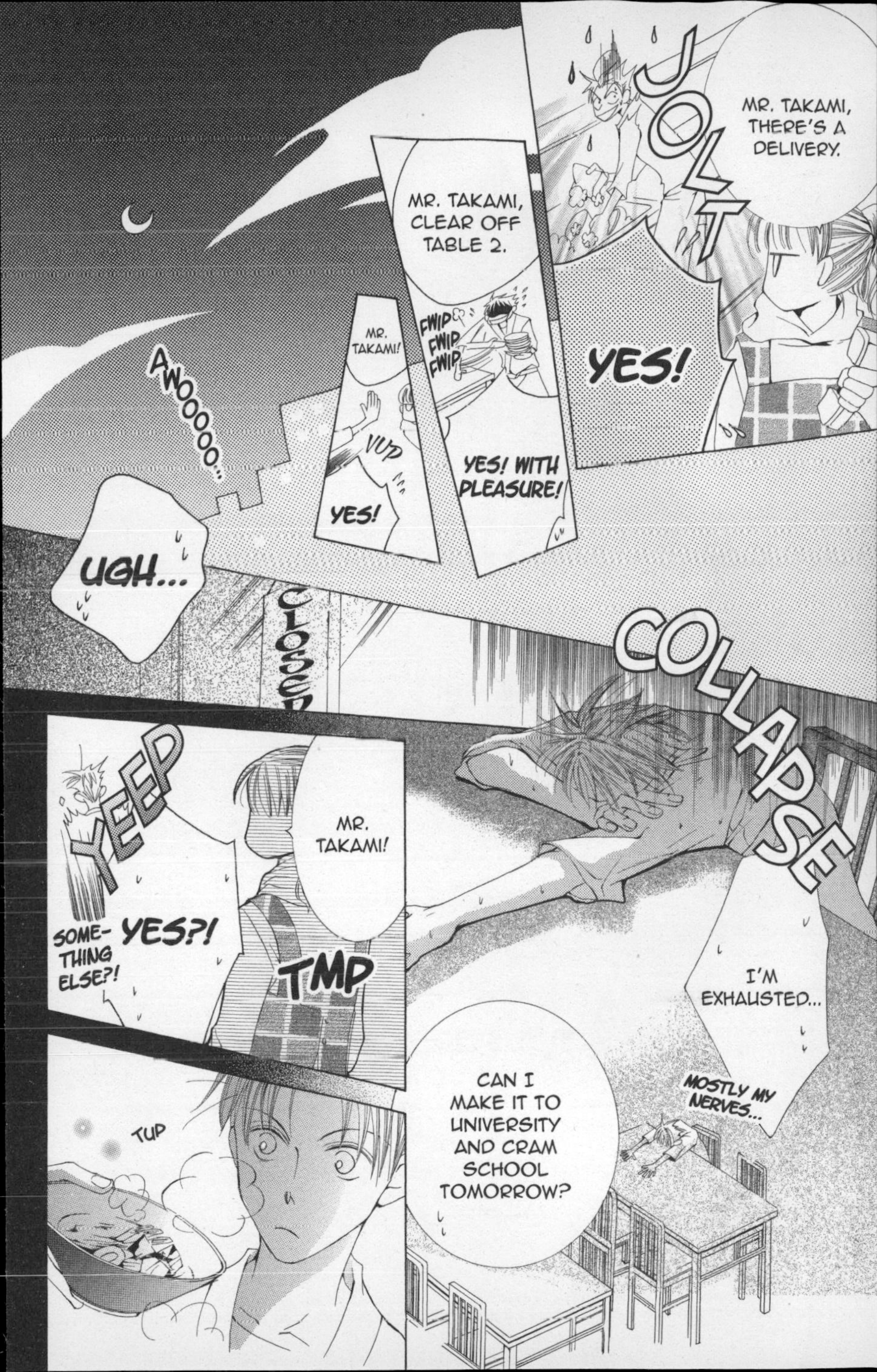
MR. TAKAMI, THERE'S A DELIVERY.
JOLT
YES!
MR. TAKAMI, CLEAR OFF TABLE 2.
FWIP FWIP FWIP
YES! WITH PLEASURE!
MR. TAKAMI!
VUP
YES!
AWOOOOOO...
UGH...
CLOSED
COLLAPSE
I'M EXHAUSTED...
MOSTLY MY NERVES...
CAN I MAKE IT TO UNIVERSITY AND CRAM SCHOOL TOMORROW?
MR. TAKAMI!
YEEP
TMP
YES?!
SOME-THING ELSE?!
TUP

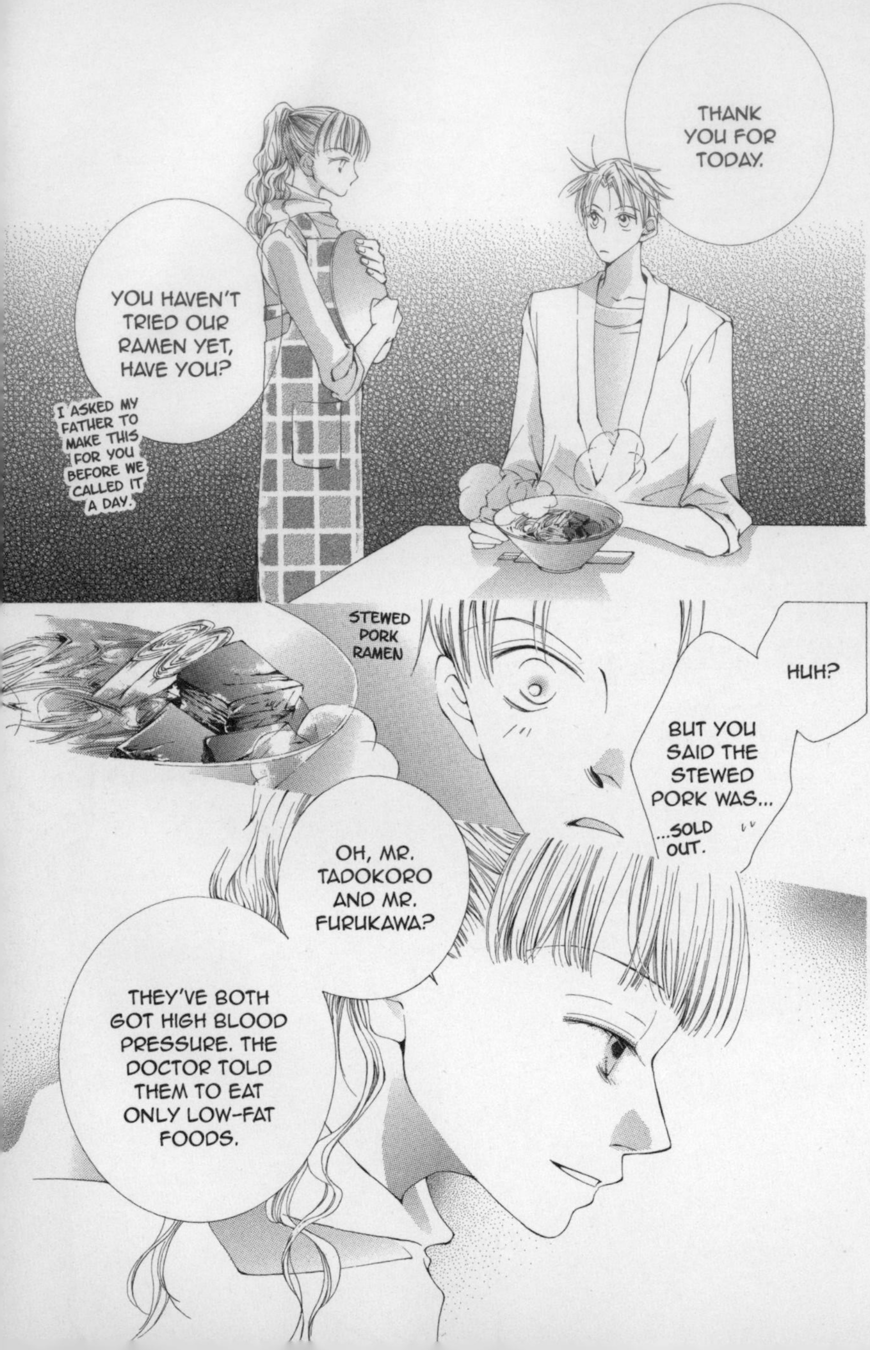
THANK YOU FOR TODAY.
YOU HAVEN'T TRIED OUR RAMEN YET, HAVE YOU?
I ASKED MY FATHER TO MAKE THIS FOR YOU BEFORE WE CALLED IT A DAY.
HUH?
BUT YOU SAID THE STEWED PORK WAS...
...SOLD OUT.
STEWED PORK RAMEN
OH, MR. TADOKORO AND MR. FURUKAWA?
THEY'VE BOTH GOT HIGH BLOOD PRESSURE. THE DOCTOR TOLD THEM TO EAT ONLY LOW-FAT FOODS.

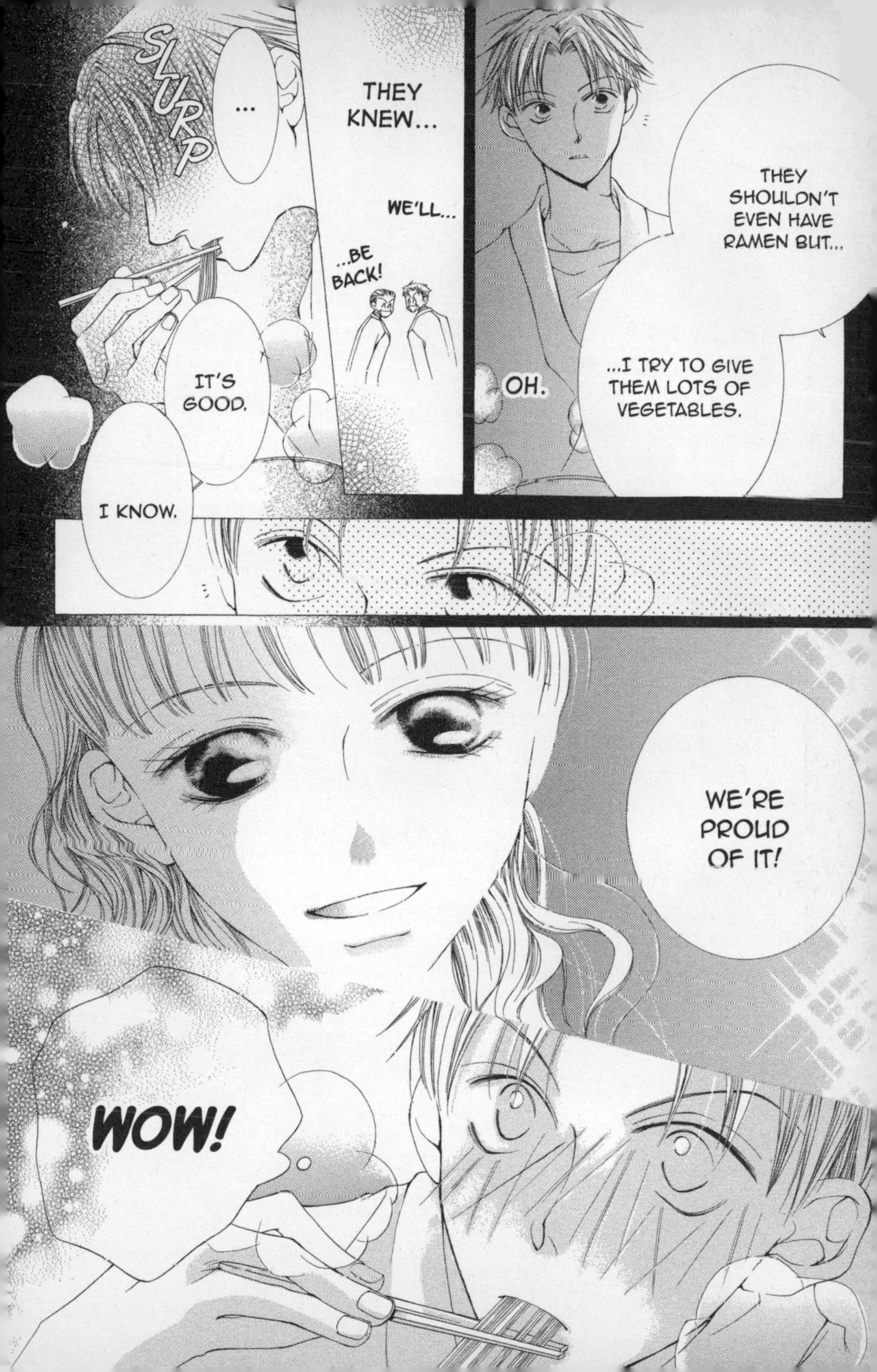
THEY SHOULDN'T EVEN HAVE RAMEN BUT...
...I TRY TO GIVE THEM LOTS OF VEGETABLES.
OH.
THEY KNEW...
WE'LL...
...BE BACK!
SLURP
...
IT'S GOOD.
I KNOW.
WE'RE PROUD OF IT!
WOW!

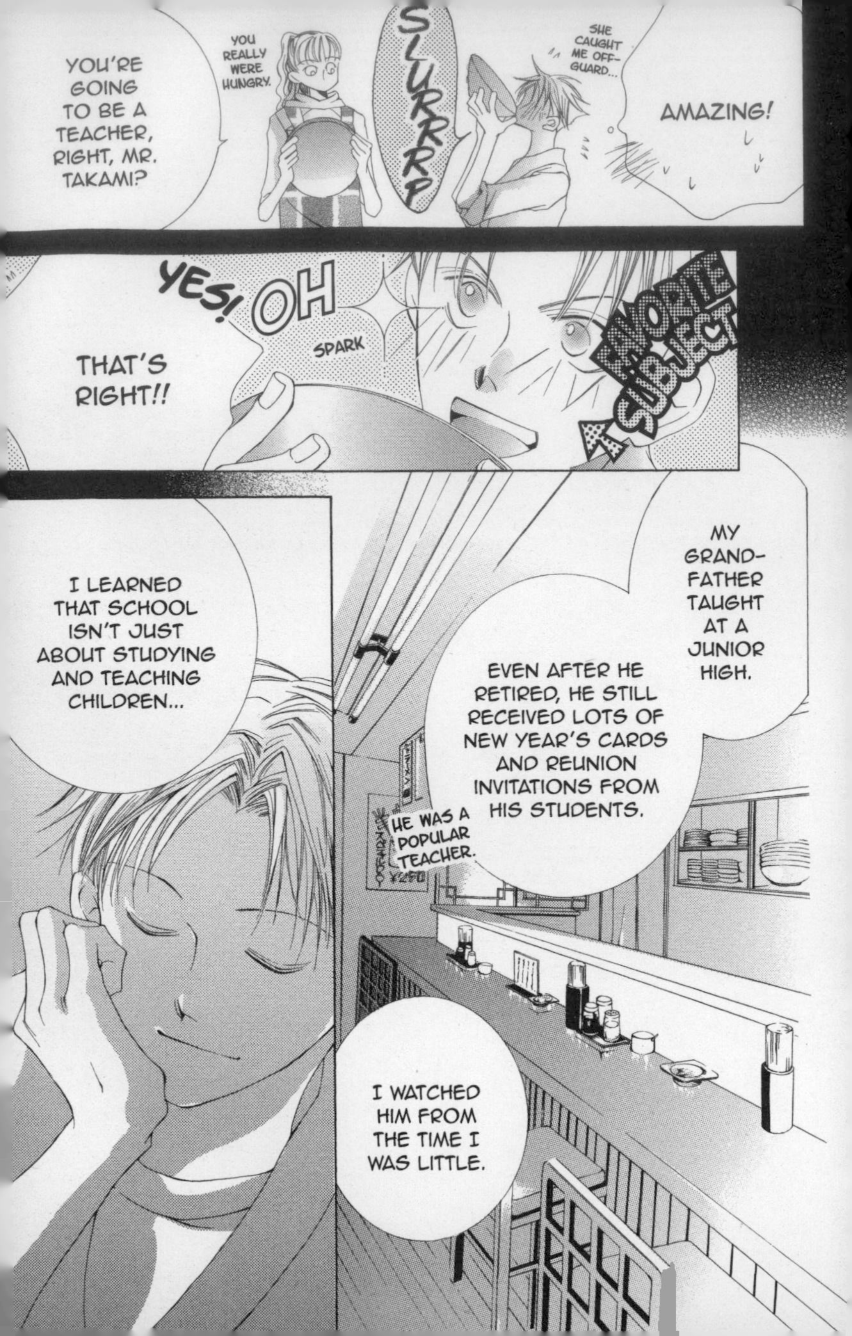
AMAZING!
SHE CAUGHT ME OFF-GUARD...
SLURRRP
YOU REALLY WERE HUNGRY.
YOU'RE GOING TO BE A TEACHER, RIGHT, MR. TAKAMI?
FAVORITE SUBJECT
SPARK
OH YES!
THAT'S RIGHT!!
MY GRANDFATHER TAUGHT AT A JUNIOR HIGH.
EVEN AFTER HE RETIRED, HE STILL RECEIVED LOTS OF NEW YEAR'S CARDS AND REUNION INVITATIONS FROM HIS STUDENTS.
HE WAS A POPULAR TEACHER.
I WATCHED HIM FROM THE TIME I WAS LITTLE.
I LEARNED THAT SCHOOL ISN'T JUST ABOUT STUDYING AND TEACHING CHILDREN...

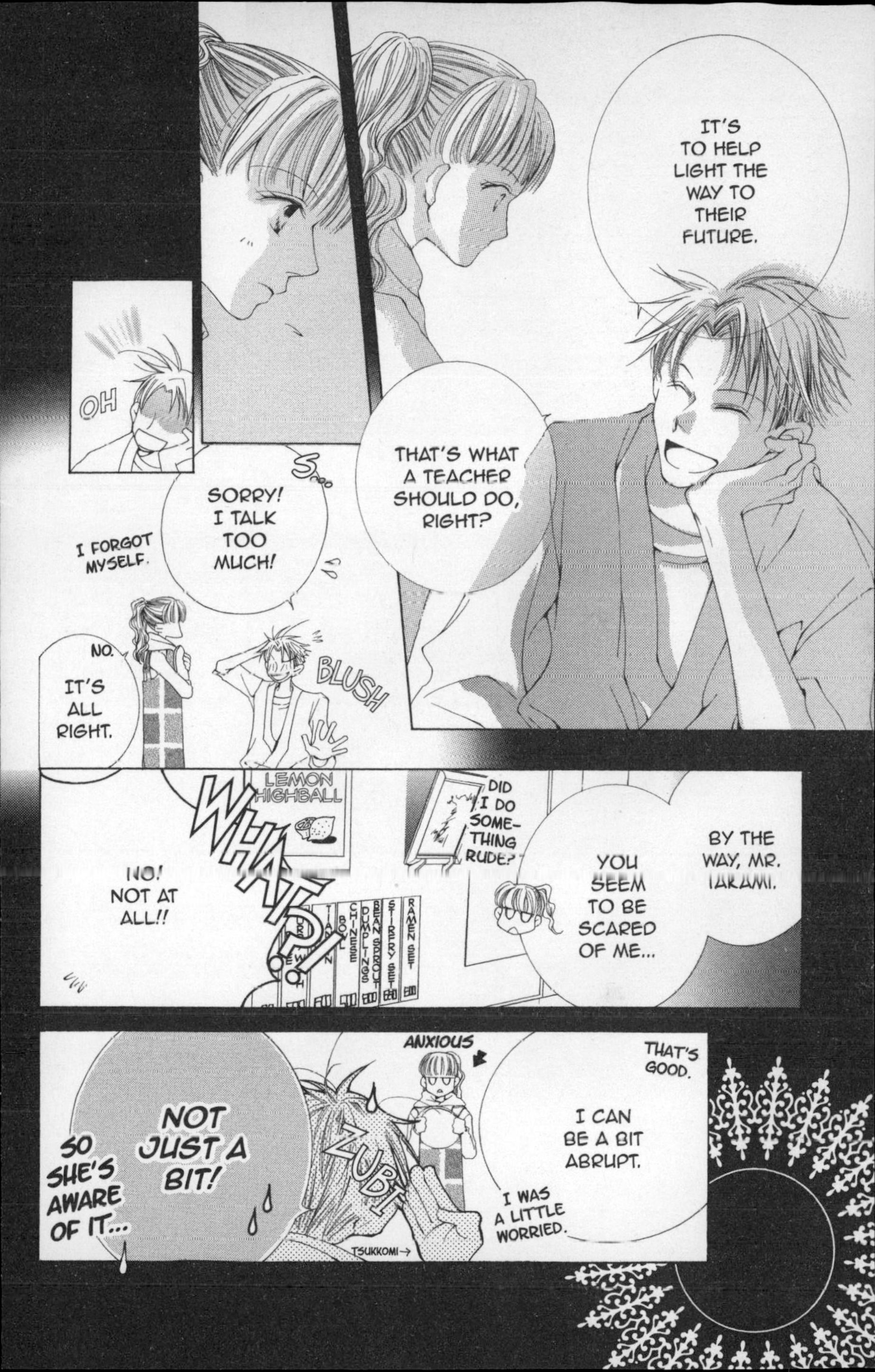
IT'S TO HELP LIGHT THE WAY TO THEIR FUTURE.
THAT'S WHAT A TEACHER SHOULD DO, RIGHT?
OH
S...
SORRY! I TALK TOO MUCH!
I FORGOT MYSELF.
NO.
IT'S ALL RIGHT.
BLUSH
BY THE WAY, MR. TAKAMI.
YOU SEEM TO BE SCARED OF ME...
DID I DO SOMETHING RUDE?
LEMON HIGHBALL
RAMEN SET
STIRFRY SET
BEAN SPROUT
DUMPLINGS
CHINESE BOWL
WHAT?!
NO! NOT AT ALL!!
THAT'S GOOD.
I CAN BE A BIT ABRUPT.
I WAS A LITTLE WORRIED.
ANXIOUS
ZUBI
TSUKKOMI→
NOT JUST A BIT!
SO SHE'S AWARE OF IT...

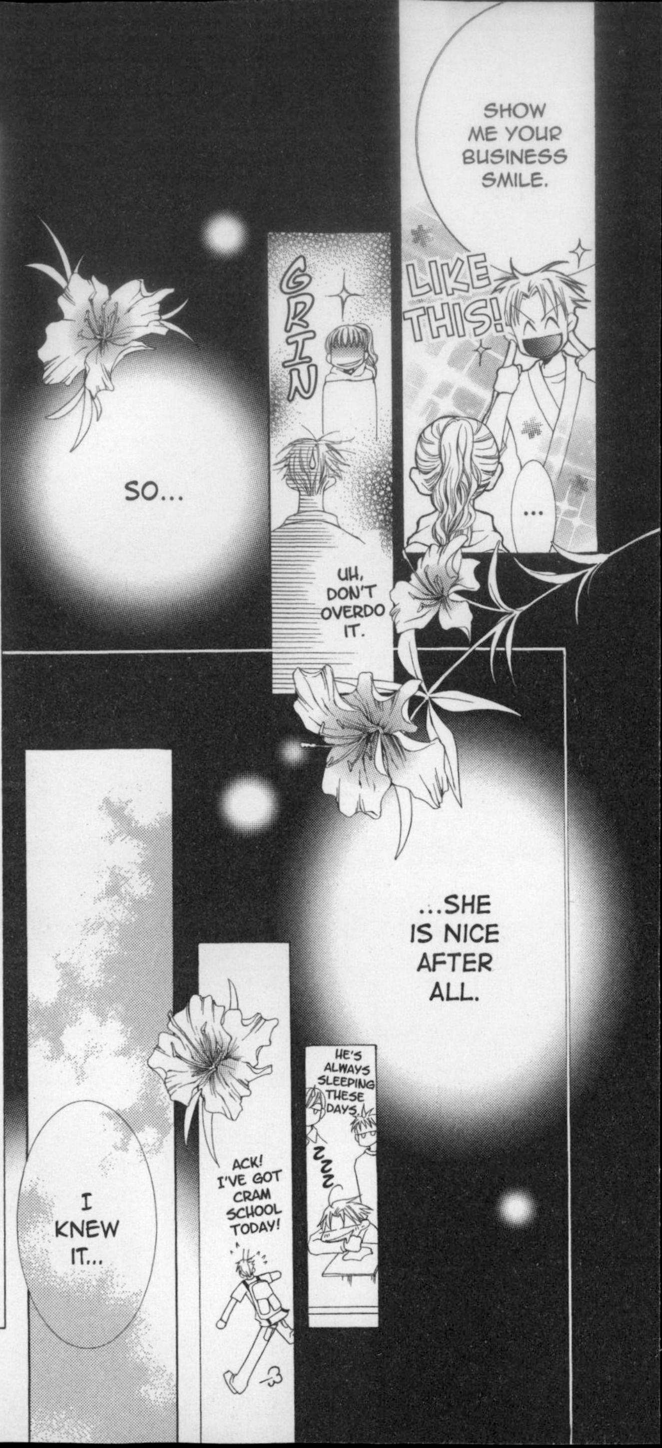
SHOW ME YOUR BUSINESS SMILE.
LIKE THIS!
...
GRIN
UH, DON'T OVERDO IT.
SO...
...SHE IS NICE AFTER ALL.
HE'S ALWAYS SLEEPING THESE DAYS.
ZZZ
ACK! I'VE GOT CRAM SCHOOL TODAY!
I KNEW IT...

5

✿EVERYONE AT NIPPON TELEVISION, CHARACTER DESIGNER KUMIKO TAKAHASHI (VERY NICE PERSON ☺), THE PEOPLE AT BONES, EVERYONE WHO CONTRIBUTED TO THE ANIME PRODUCTION--INCLUDING THE VOICE ACTORS!!--ARE ALL GREAT PEOPLE. AND WHAT AN AWESOME ANIME IT IS!!

✿AND YOU READERS, THANK YOU FOR ALL THE CONGRATULATIONS!♡♡♡ AFTER I INSERTED AN OPINION FROM A READER AT THE END OF THE PREVIOUS VOLUME, I GOT A LETTER FROM THE SAME PERSON SAYING, "YOU REALLY READ YOUR LETTERS!"

✿I ALWAYS READ THEM!!

✿OH, AND SPEAKING OF LETTERS, MR. MATSUKAZE, WHO PLAYED THE PART OF KYOYA IN THE *LALA* GIVEAWAY ANIME DVD, SAYS THAT KYOYA ISN'T VERY POPULAR, SO PLEASE WRITE A FAN LETTER SAYING THAT'S NOT TRUE!!!! (LAUGH) ADDRESS IT TO MR. MATSUKAZE!!

JUDGING FROM ALL THE LETTERS RECEIVED SO FAR, KYOYA RANKS ABOUT NUMBER ONE OR TWO, I THINK.

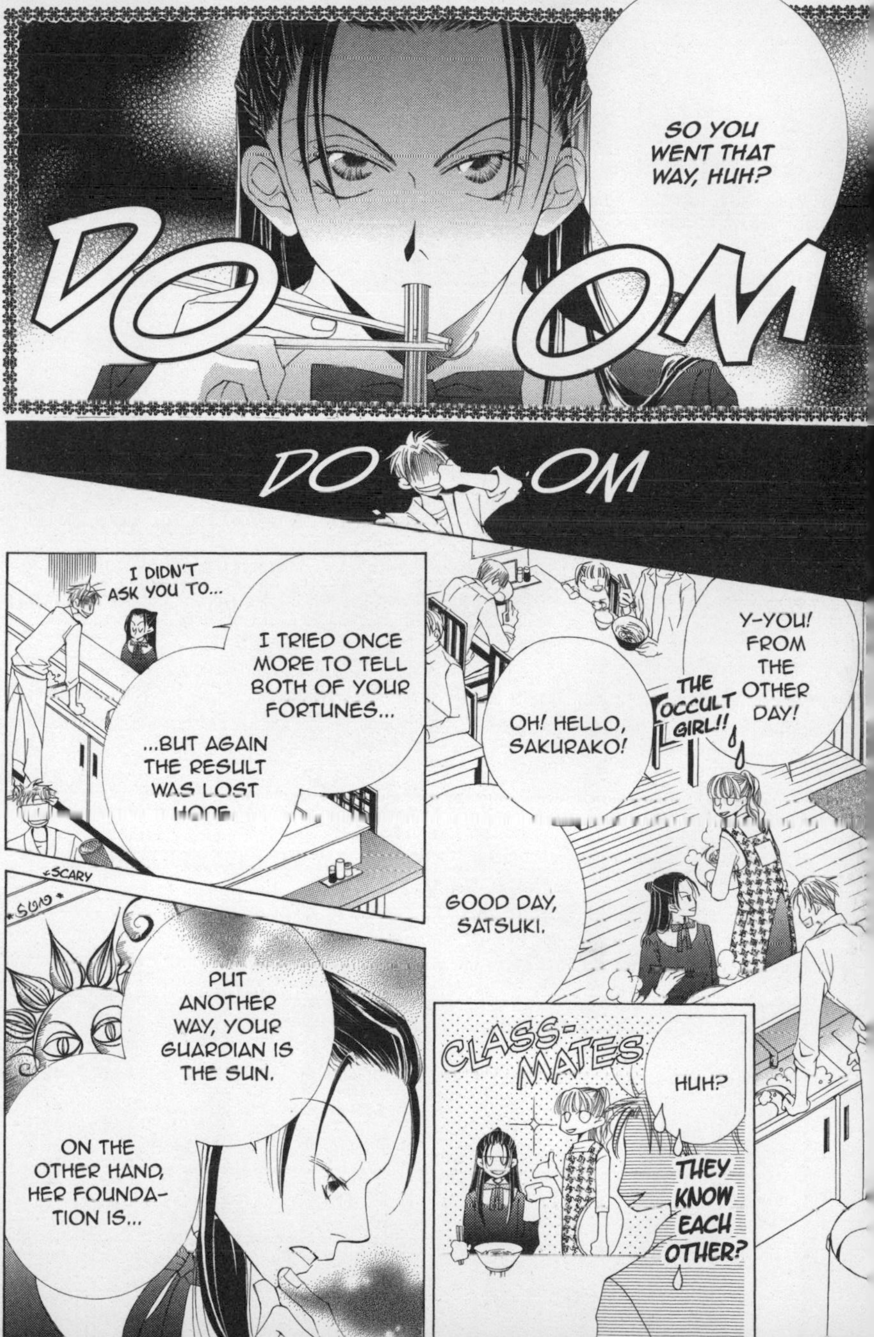
SO YOU WENT THAT WAY, HUH?
DO OM
DO OM
Y-YOU! FROM THE OTHER DAY!
THE OCCULT GIRL!!
OH! HELLO, SAKURAKO!
GOOD DAY, SATSUKI.
I DIDN'T ASK YOU TO...
I TRIED ONCE MORE TO TELL BOTH OF YOUR FORTUNES...
...BUT AGAIN THE RESULT WAS LOST HOPE
CLASS-MATES
HUH?
THEY KNOW EACH OTHER?
SCARY
SUN
PUT ANOTHER WAY, YOUR GUARDIAN IS THE SUN.
ON THE OTHER HAND, HER FOUNDATION IS...

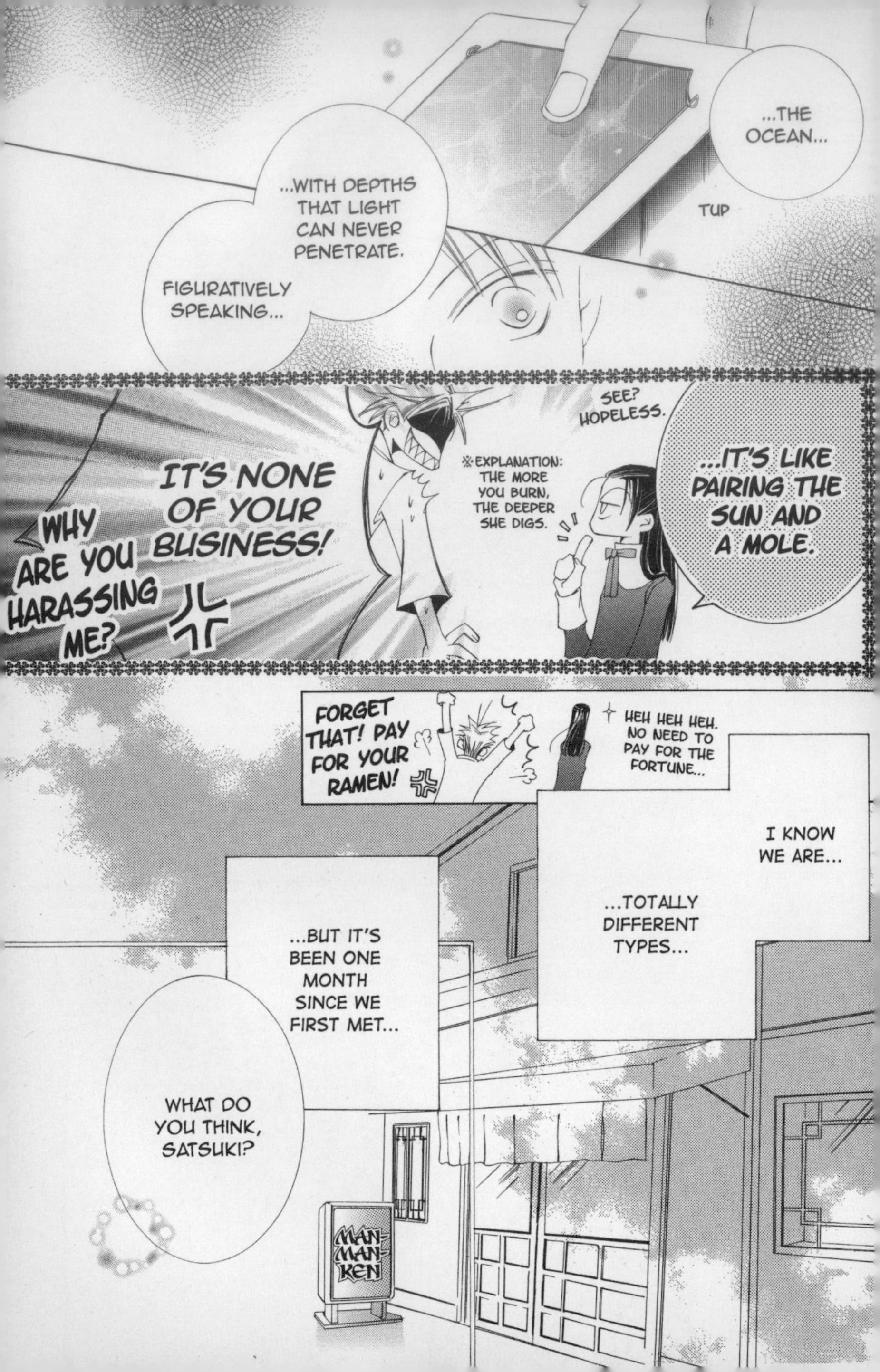

...THE OCEAN...
TUP
...WITH DEPTHS THAT LIGHT CAN NEVER PENETRATE.
FIGURATIVELY SPEAKING...
...IT'S LIKE PAIRING THE SUN AND A MOLE.
SEE? HOPELESS.
※EXPLANATION: THE MORE YOU BURN, THE DEEPER SHE DIGS.
IT'S NONE OF YOUR BUSINESS!
WHY ARE YOU HARASSING ME?
HEH HEH HEH. NO NEED TO PAY FOR THE FORTUNE...
FORGET THAT! PAY FOR YOUR RAMEN!
I KNOW WE ARE...
...TOTALLY DIFFERENT TYPES...
...BUT IT'S BEEN ONE MONTH SINCE WE FIRST MET...
WHAT DO YOU THINK, SATSUKI?
MAN-MAN-KEN

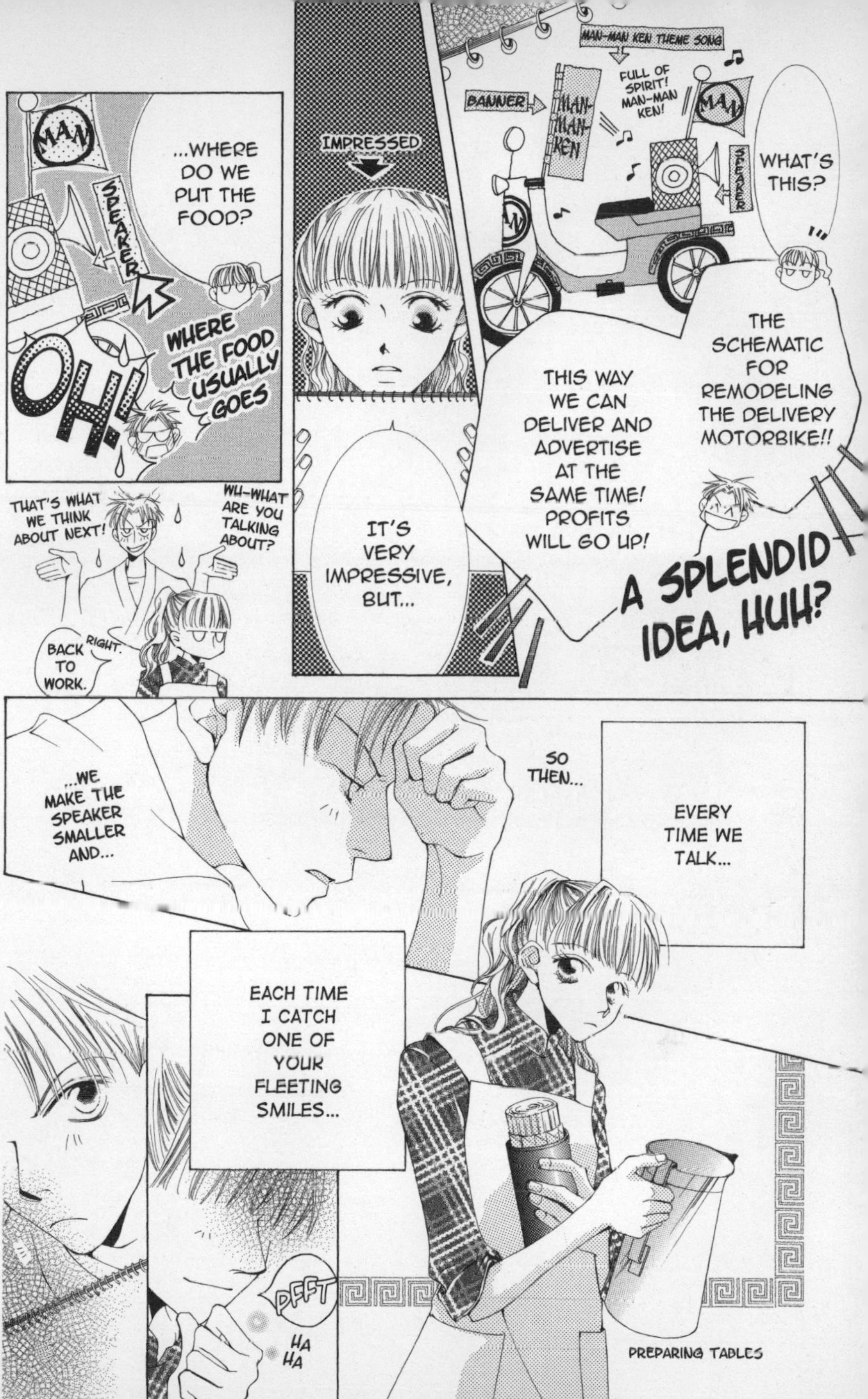
MAN-MAN KEN THEME SONG
FULL OF SPIRIT! MAN-MAN KEN!
BANNER
MAN-MAN-KEN
SPEAKER
WHAT'S THIS?
THE SCHEMATIC FOR REMODELING THE DELIVERY MOTORBIKE!!
THIS WAY WE CAN DELIVER AND ADVERTISE AT THE SAME TIME! PROFITS WILL GO UP!
A SPLENDID IDEA, HUH?
IMPRESSED
IT'S VERY IMPRESSIVE, BUT...
...WHERE DO WE PUT THE FOOD?
SPEAKER
WHERE THE FOOD USUALLY GOES
OH!
WU-WHAT ARE YOU TALKING ABOUT?
THAT'S WHAT WE THINK ABOUT NEXT!
RIGHT.
BACK TO WORK.
SO THEN...
...WE MAKE THE SPEAKER SMALLER AND...
EVERY TIME WE TALK...
PREPARING TABLES
EACH TIME I CATCH ONE OF YOUR FLEETING SMILES...
PFFT
HA HA

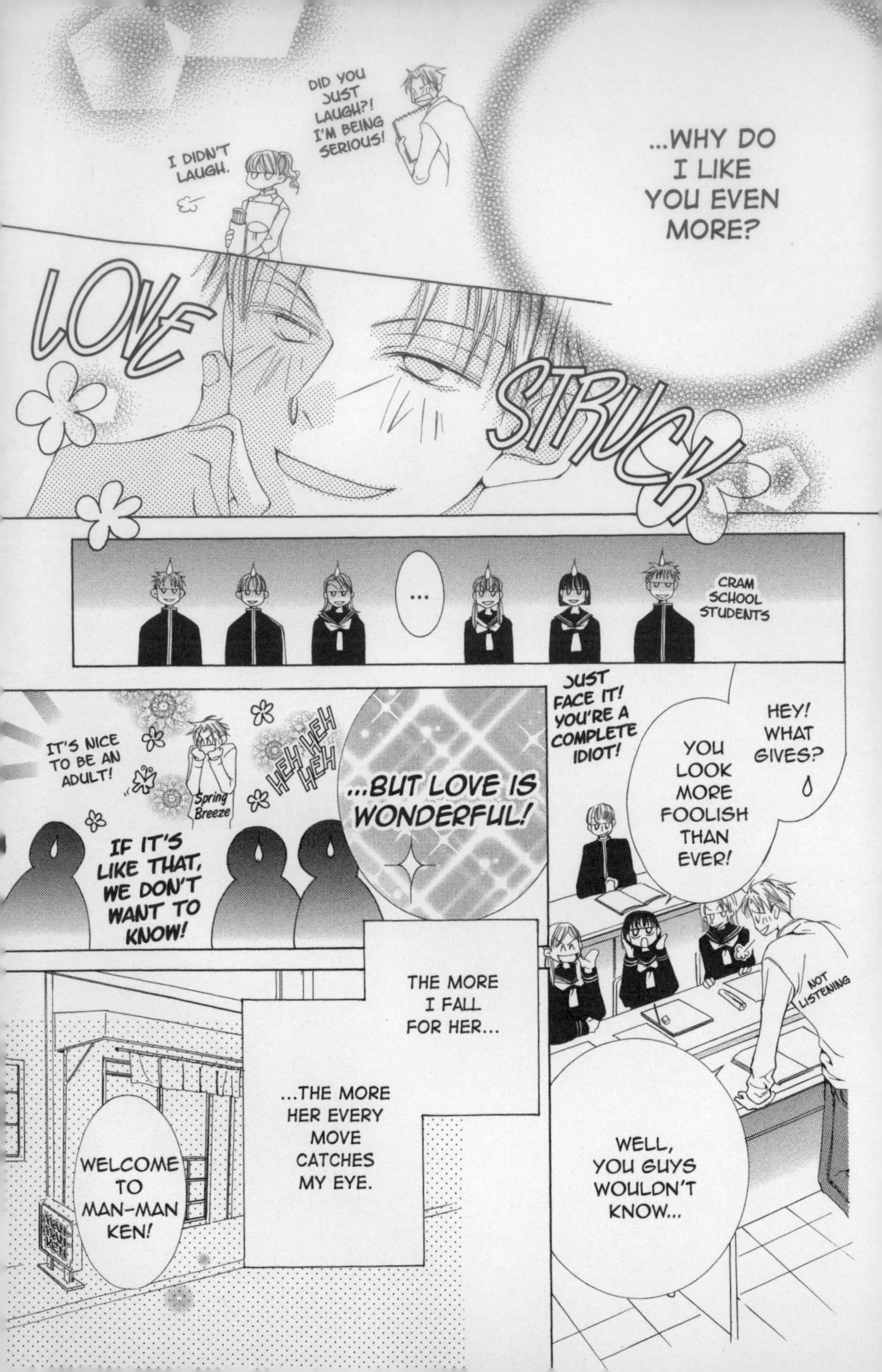
...WHY DO I LIKE YOU EVEN MORE?
DID YOU JUST LAUGH?! I'M BEING SERIOUS!
I DIDN'T LAUGH.
LOVE STRUCK
CRAM SCHOOL STUDENTS
...
HEY! WHAT GIVES?
YOU LOOK MORE FOOLISH THAN EVER!
JUST FACE IT! YOU'RE A COMPLETE IDIOT!
NOT LISTENING
WELL, YOU GUYS WOULDN'T KNOW...
...BUT LOVE IS WONDERFUL!
HEH HEH HEH
IT'S NICE TO BE AN ADULT!
Spring Breeze
IF IT'S LIKE THAT, WE DON'T WANT TO KNOW!
THE MORE I FALL FOR HER...
...THE MORE HER EVERY MOVE CATCHES MY EYE.
WELCOME TO MAN-MAN KEN!
MAN-MAN-KEN

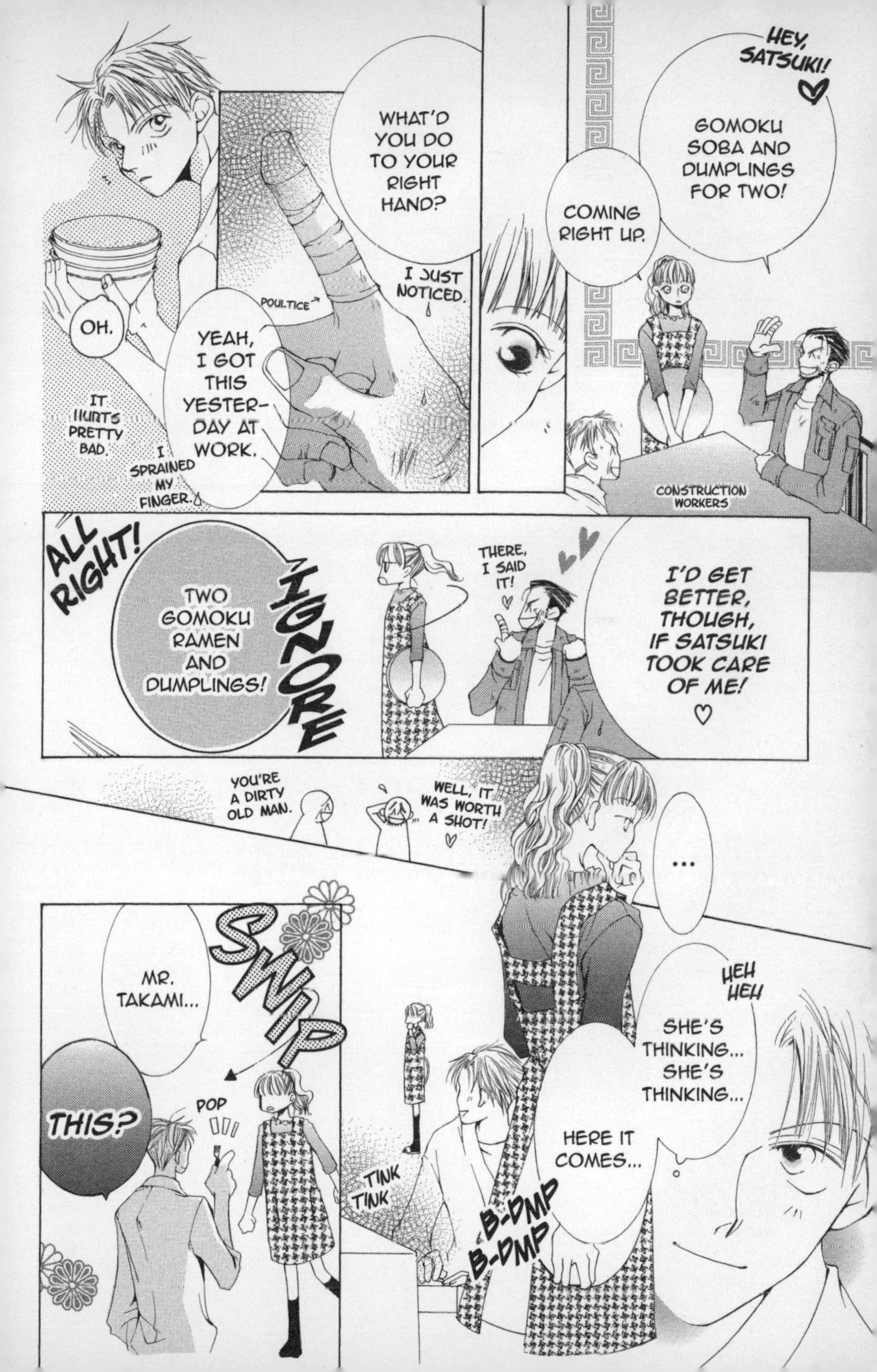
HEY, SATSUKI! ♥
GOMOKU SOBA AND DUMPLINGS FOR TWO!
COMING RIGHT UP.
CONSTRUCTION WORKERS
WHAT'D YOU DO TO YOUR RIGHT HAND?
I JUST NOTICED.
POULTICE
YEAH, I GOT THIS YESTER-DAY AT WORK.
OH.
I SPRAINED MY FINGER.
IT HURTS PRETTY BAD.
I'D GET BETTER, THOUGH, IF SATSUKI TOOK CARE OF ME! ♡
THERE, I SAID IT! ♡
IGNORE
TWO GOMOKU RAMEN AND DUMPLINGS!
ALL RIGHT!
WELL, IT WAS WORTH A SHOT! ♡
YOU'RE A DIRTY OLD MAN.
...
HEH HEH
SHE'S THINKING... SHE'S THINKING...
HERE IT COMES...
B-DMP B-DMP
TINK TINK
SWIP
MR. TAKAMI...
POP
THIS?

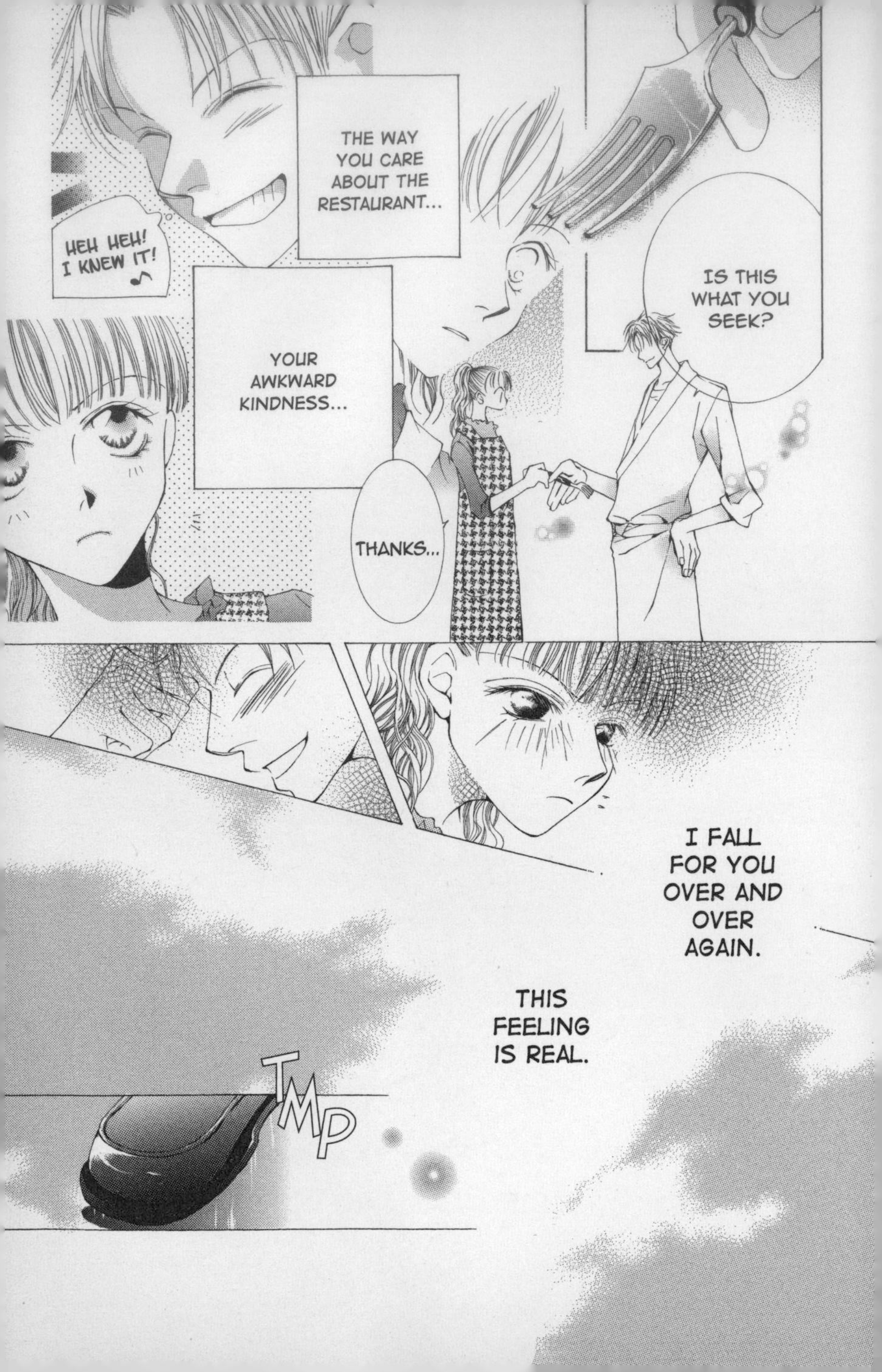
IS THIS WHAT YOU SEEK?
THANKS...
THE WAY YOU CARE ABOUT THE RESTAURANT...
HEH HEH! I KNEW IT! ♪
YOUR AWKWARD KINDNESS...
I FALL FOR YOU OVER AND OVER AGAIN.
THIS FEELING IS REAL.
TMP

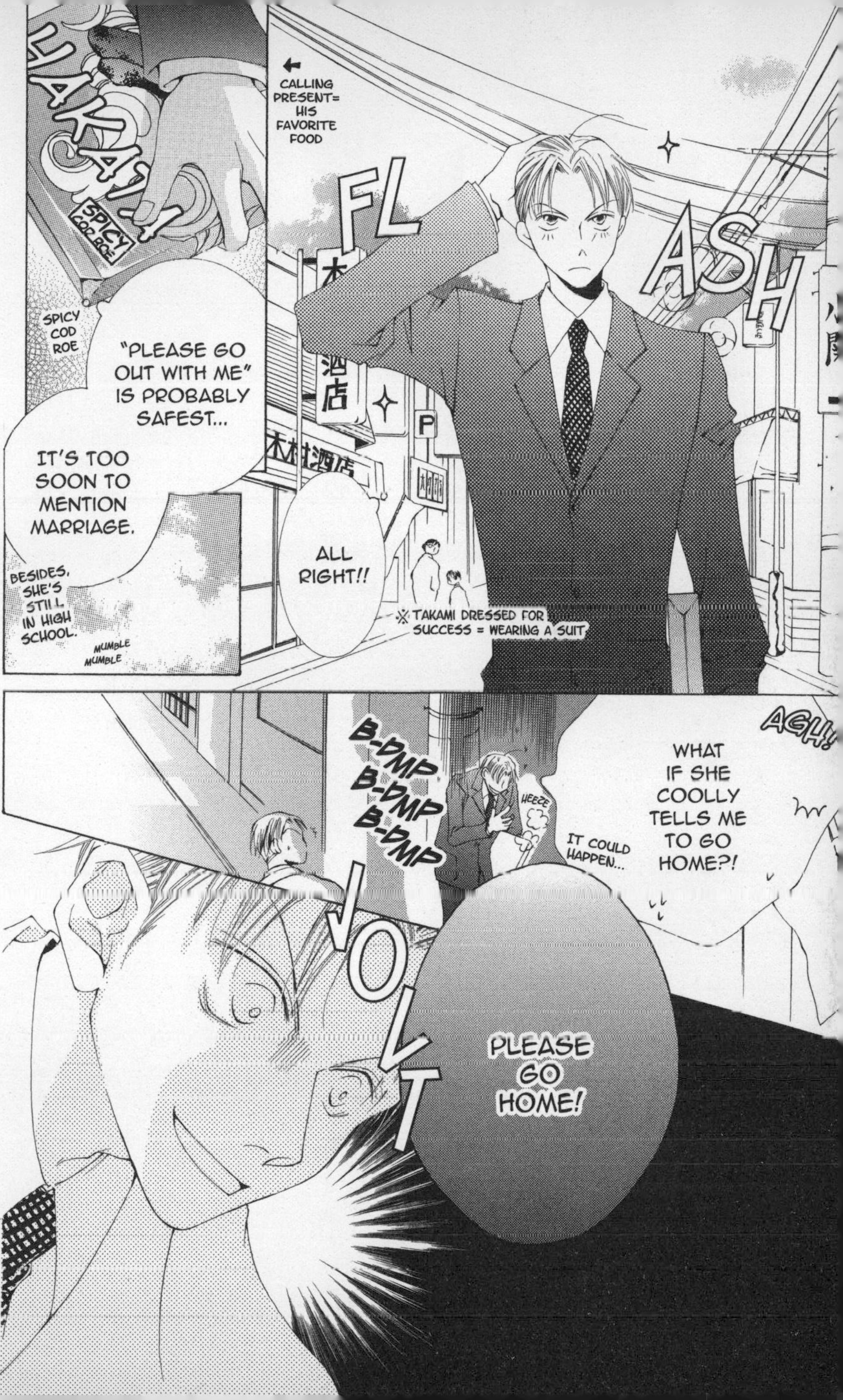
FL
ASH
ALL RIGHT!!
※TAKAMI DRESSED FOR SUCCESS = WEARING A SUIT
CALLING PRESENT= HIS FAVORITE FOOD
HAKATA
SPICY COD ROE
"PLEASE GO OUT WITH ME" IS PROBABLY SAFEST...
SPICY COD ROE
IT'S TOO SOON TO MENTION MARRIAGE.
BESIDES, SHE'S STILL IN HIGH SCHOOL.
MUMBLE MUMBLE
AGH!
WHAT IF SHE COOLLY TELLS ME TO GO HOME?!
IT COULD HAPPEN...
HEEZE
B-DMP B-DMP B-DMP
JOLT
PLEASE GO HOME!

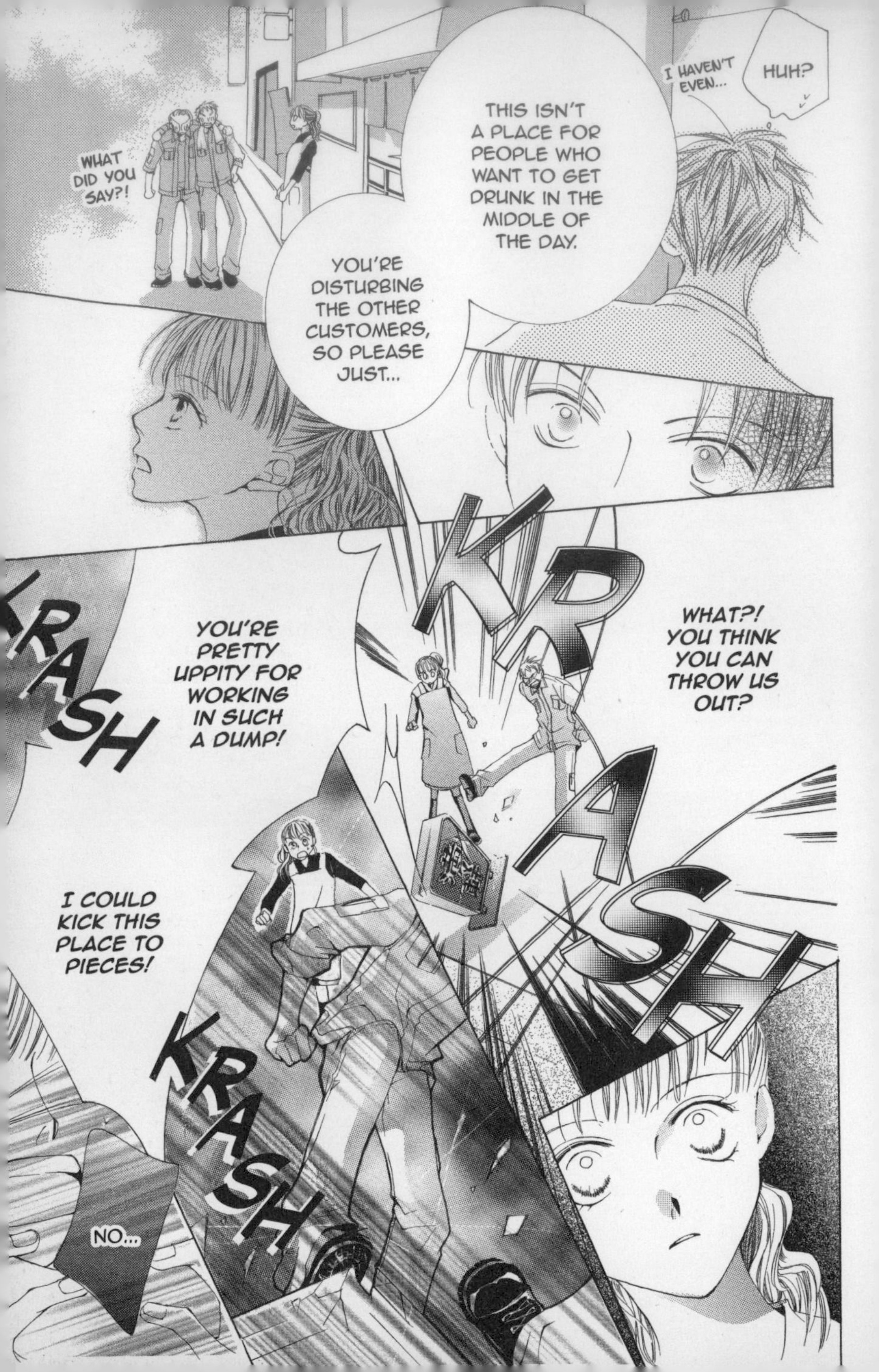
HUH?
I HAVEN'T EVEN...
WHAT DID YOU SAY?!
THIS ISN'T A PLACE FOR PEOPLE WHO WANT TO GET DRUNK IN THE MIDDLE OF THE DAY.
YOU'RE DISTURBING THE OTHER CUSTOMERS, SO PLEASE JUST...
WHAT?! YOU THINK YOU CAN THROW US OUT?
KRASH
YOU'RE PRETTY UPPITY FOR WORKING IN SUCH A DUMP!
KRASH
I COULD KICK THIS PLACE TO PIECES!
KRASH
NO...

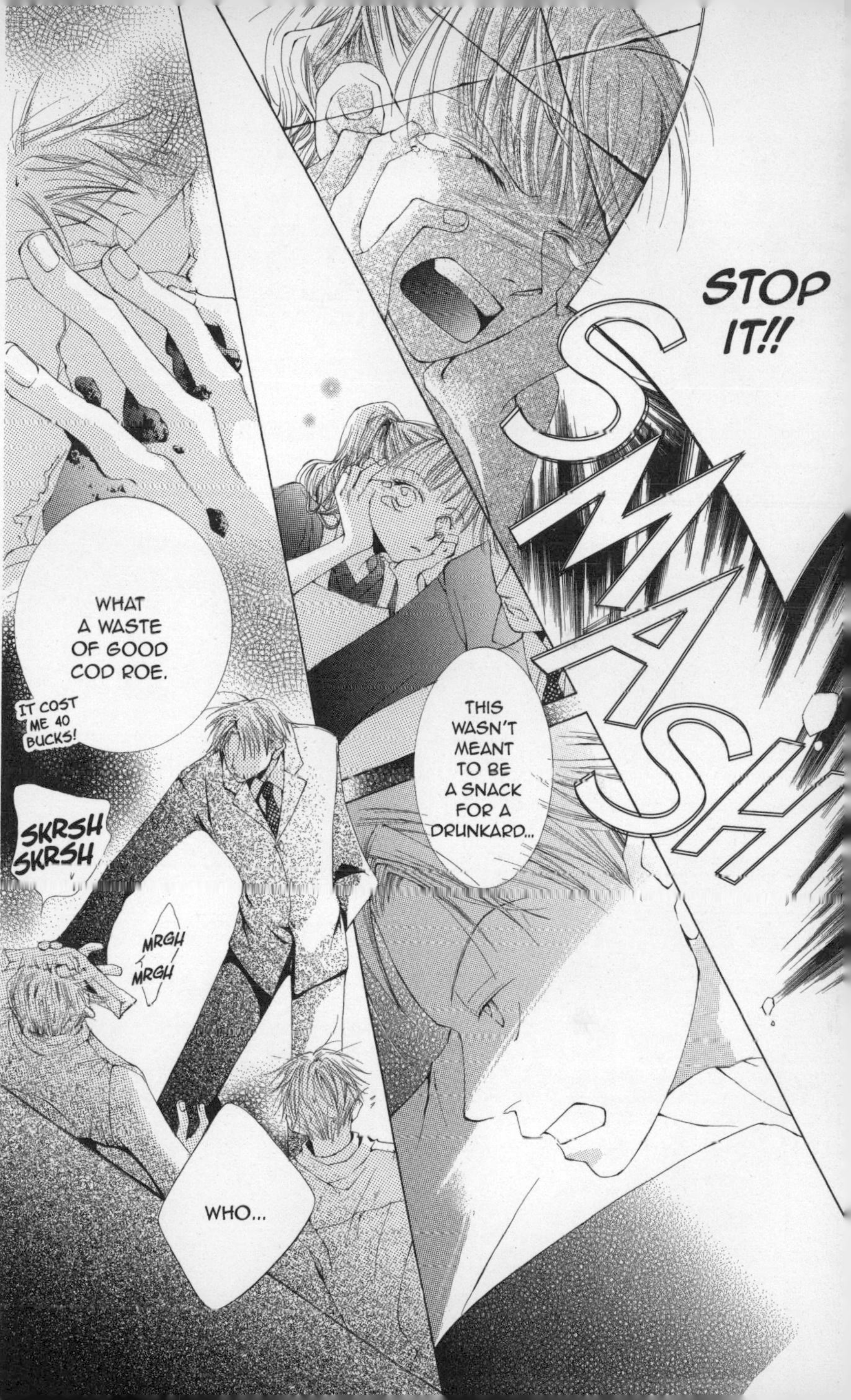
STOP IT!!
SMASH
THIS WASN'T MEANT TO BE A SNACK FOR A DRUNKARD...
WHAT A WASTE OF GOOD COD ROE.
IT COST ME 40 BUCKS!
SKRSH SKRSH
MRGH MRGH
WHO...

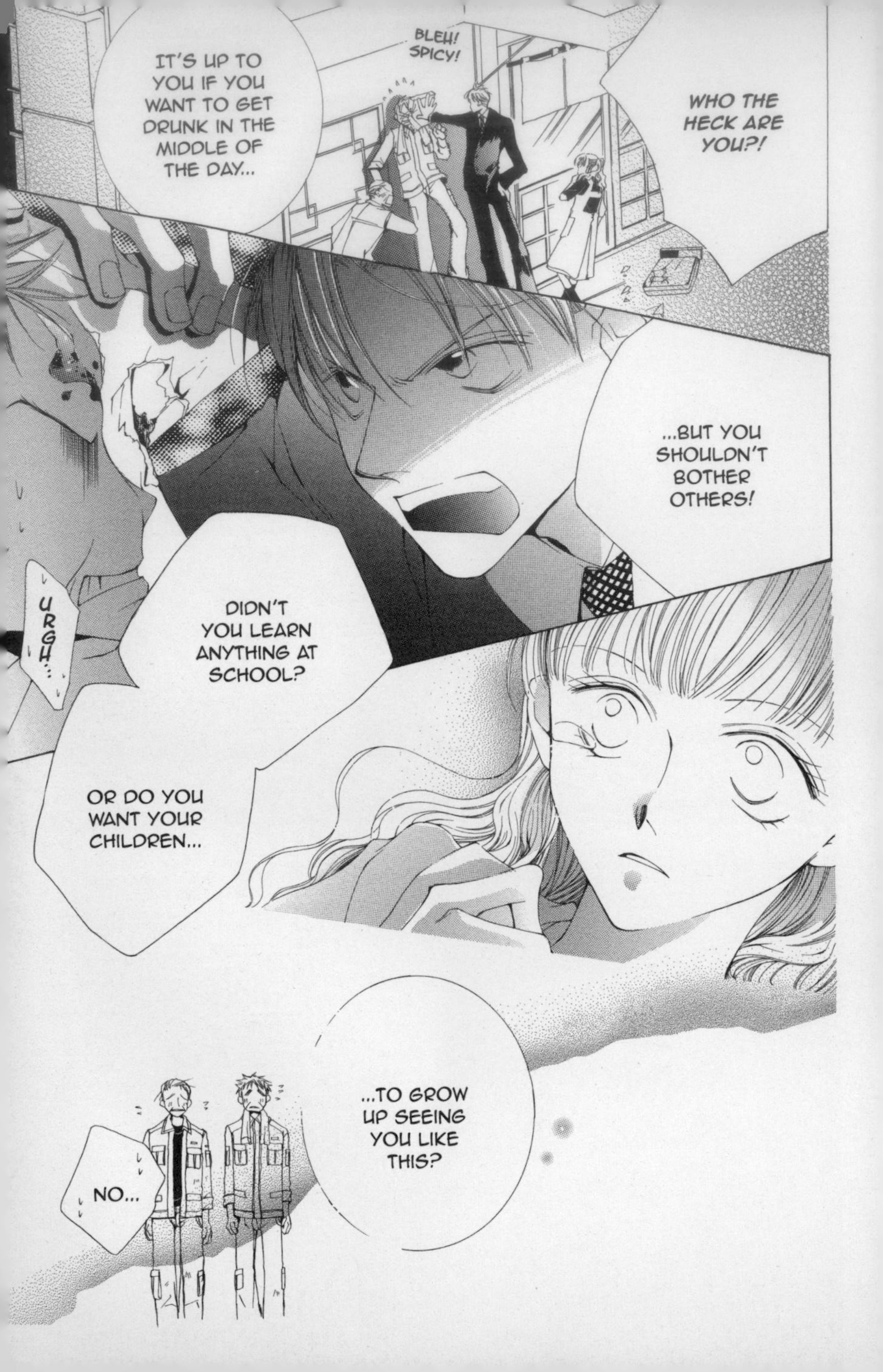
WHO THE HECK ARE YOU?!
BLEH! SPICY!
IT'S UP TO YOU IF YOU WANT TO GET DRUNK IN THE MIDDLE OF THE DAY...
...BUT YOU SHOULDN'T BOTHER OTHERS!
DIDN'T YOU LEARN ANYTHING AT SCHOOL?
URGH...
OR DO YOU WANT YOUR CHILDREN...
...TO GROW UP SEEING YOU LIKE THIS?
NO...

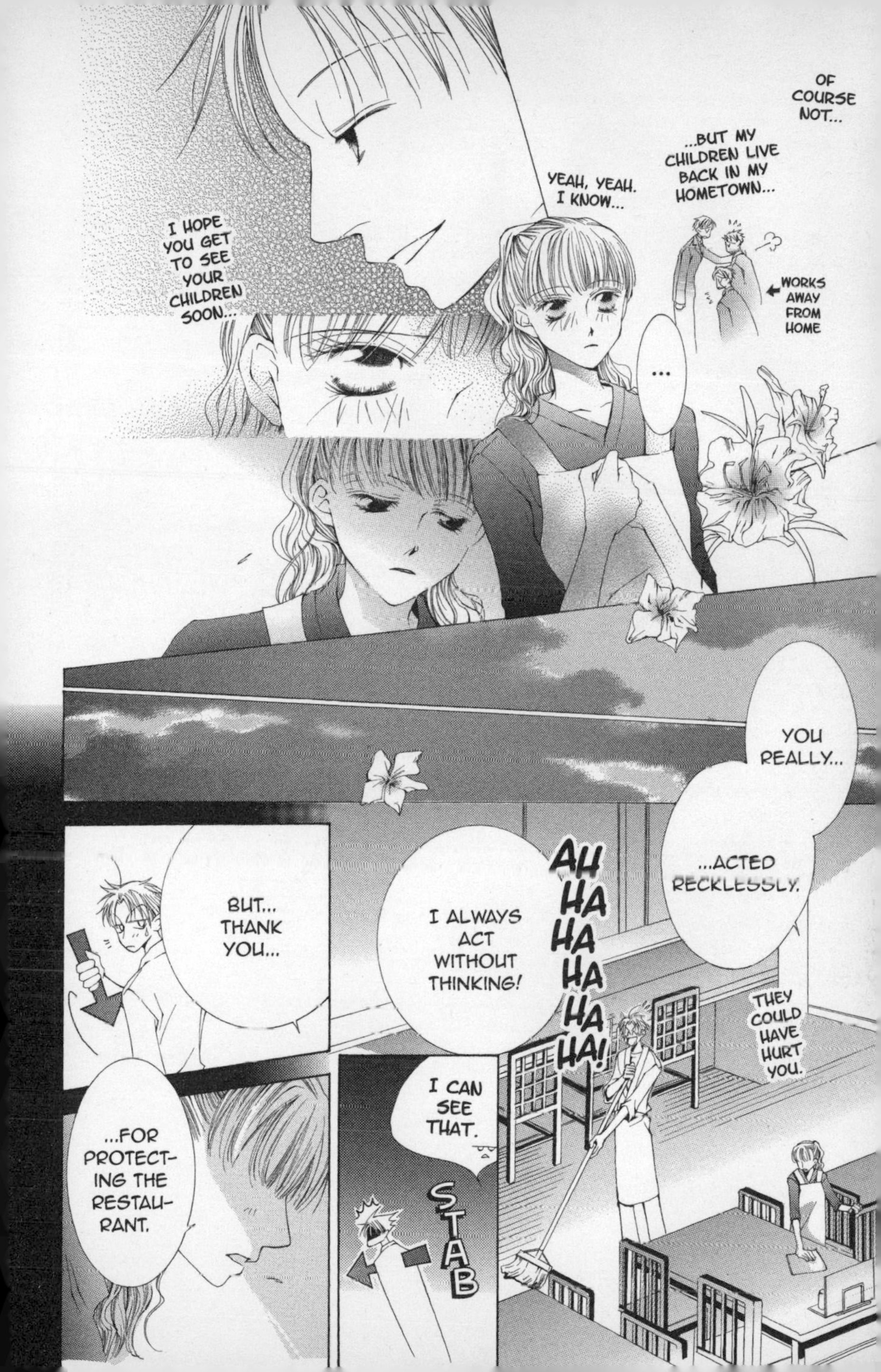
OF COURSE NOT...
...BUT MY CHILDREN LIVE BACK IN MY HOMETOWN...
WORKS AWAY FROM HOME
YEAH, YEAH. I KNOW...
I HOPE YOU GET TO SEE YOUR CHILDREN SOON...
...
YOU REALLY...
...ACTED RECKLESSLY.
THEY COULD HAVE HURT YOU.
AH HA HA HA HA HA HA!
I ALWAYS ACT WITHOUT THINKING!
I CAN SEE THAT.
STAB
BUT... THANK YOU...
...FOR PROTECTING THE RESTAURANT.

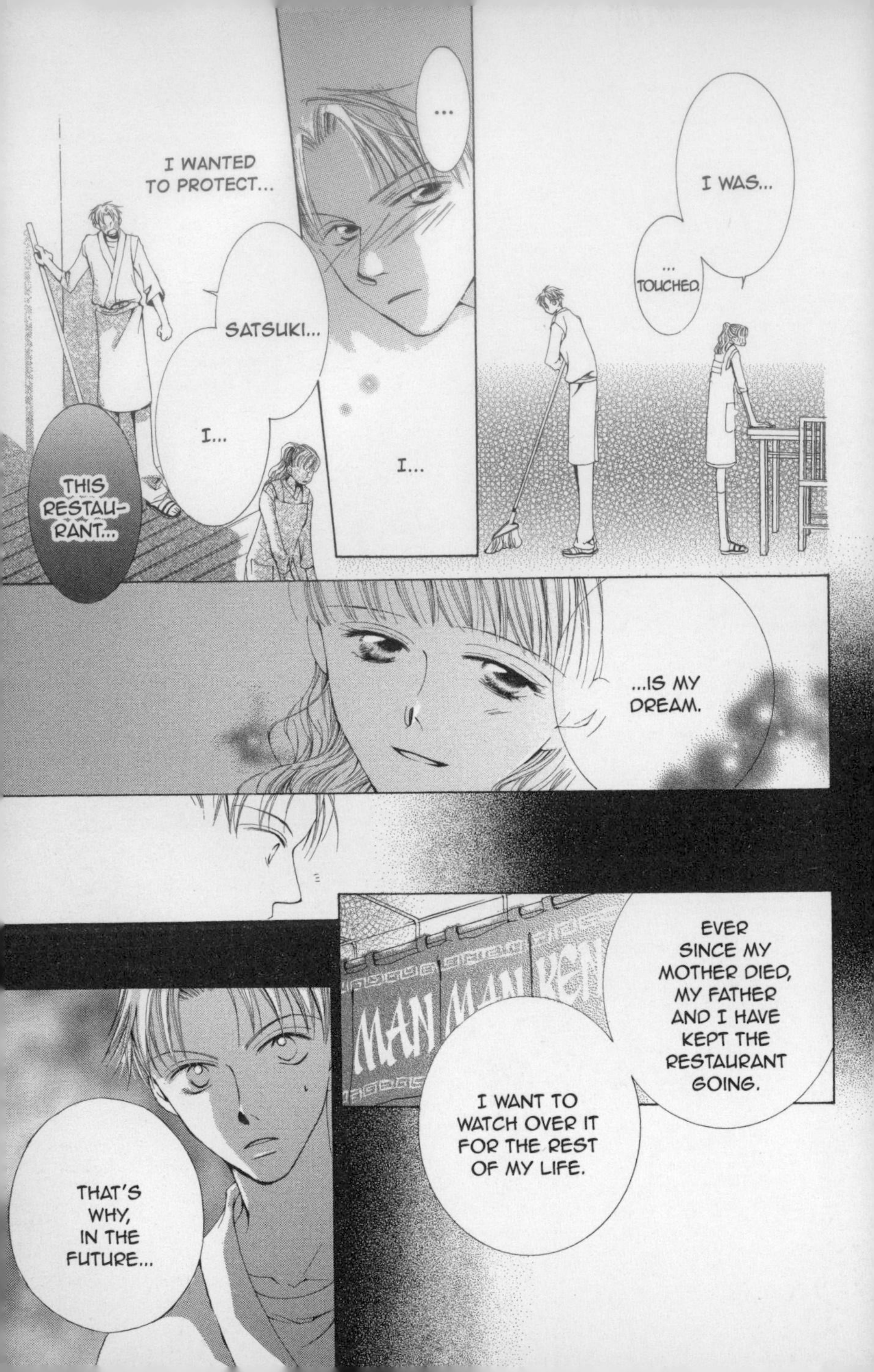
I WAS...
... TOUCHED.
...
I...
SATSUKI... I...
I WANTED TO PROTECT...
THIS RESTAURANT...
...IS MY DREAM.
EVER SINCE MY MOTHER DIED, MY FATHER AND I HAVE KEPT THE RESTAURANT GOING.
MAN MAN
I WANT TO WATCH OVER IT FOR THE REST OF MY LIFE.
THAT'S WHY, IN THE FUTURE...

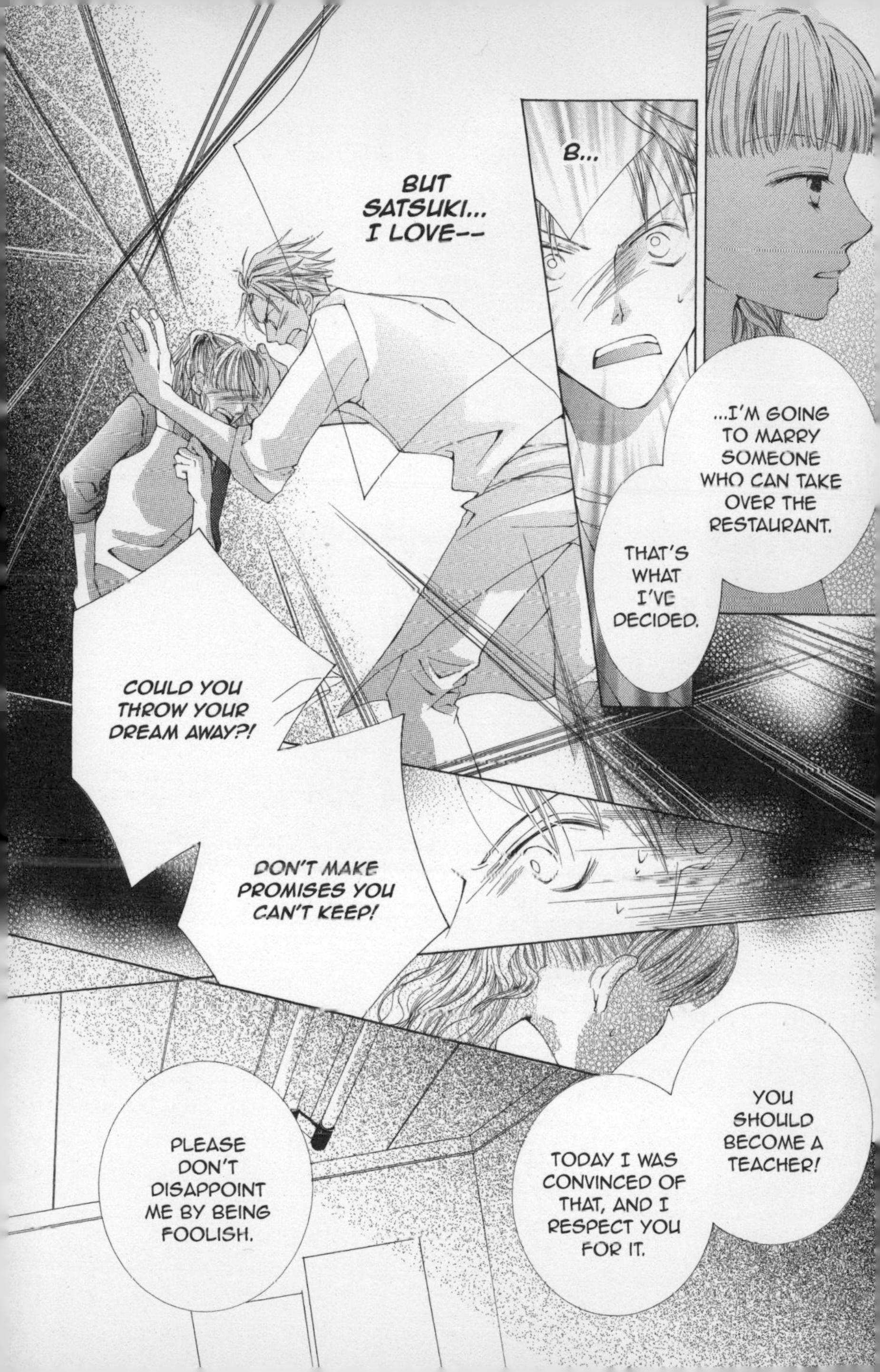
...I'M GOING TO MARRY SOMEONE WHO CAN TAKE OVER THE RESTAURANT.
THAT'S WHAT I'VE DECIDED.
B...
BUT SATSUKI... I LOVE--
COULD YOU THROW YOUR DREAM AWAY?!
DON'T MAKE PROMISES YOU CAN'T KEEP!
YOU SHOULD BECOME A TEACHER!
TODAY I WAS CONVINCED OF THAT, AND I RESPECT YOU FOR IT.
PLEASE DON'T DISAPPOINT ME BY BEING FOOLISH.

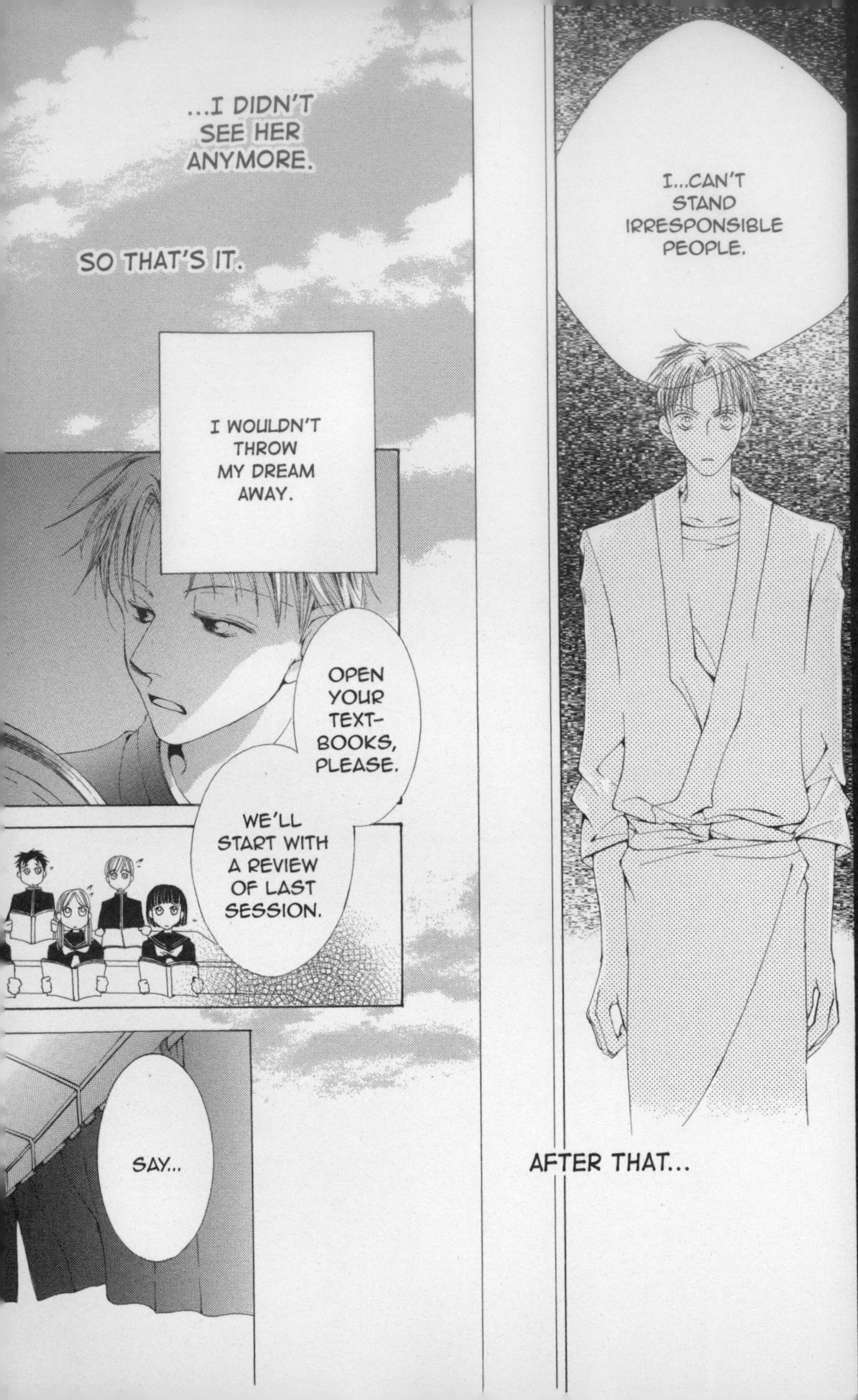
I...CAN'T STAND IRRESPONSIBLE PEOPLE.
AFTER THAT...
...I DIDN'T SEE HER ANYMORE.
SO THAT'S IT.
I WOULDN'T THROW MY DREAM AWAY.
OPEN YOUR TEXT-BOOKS, PLEASE.
WE'LL START WITH A REVIEW OF LAST SESSION.
SAY...

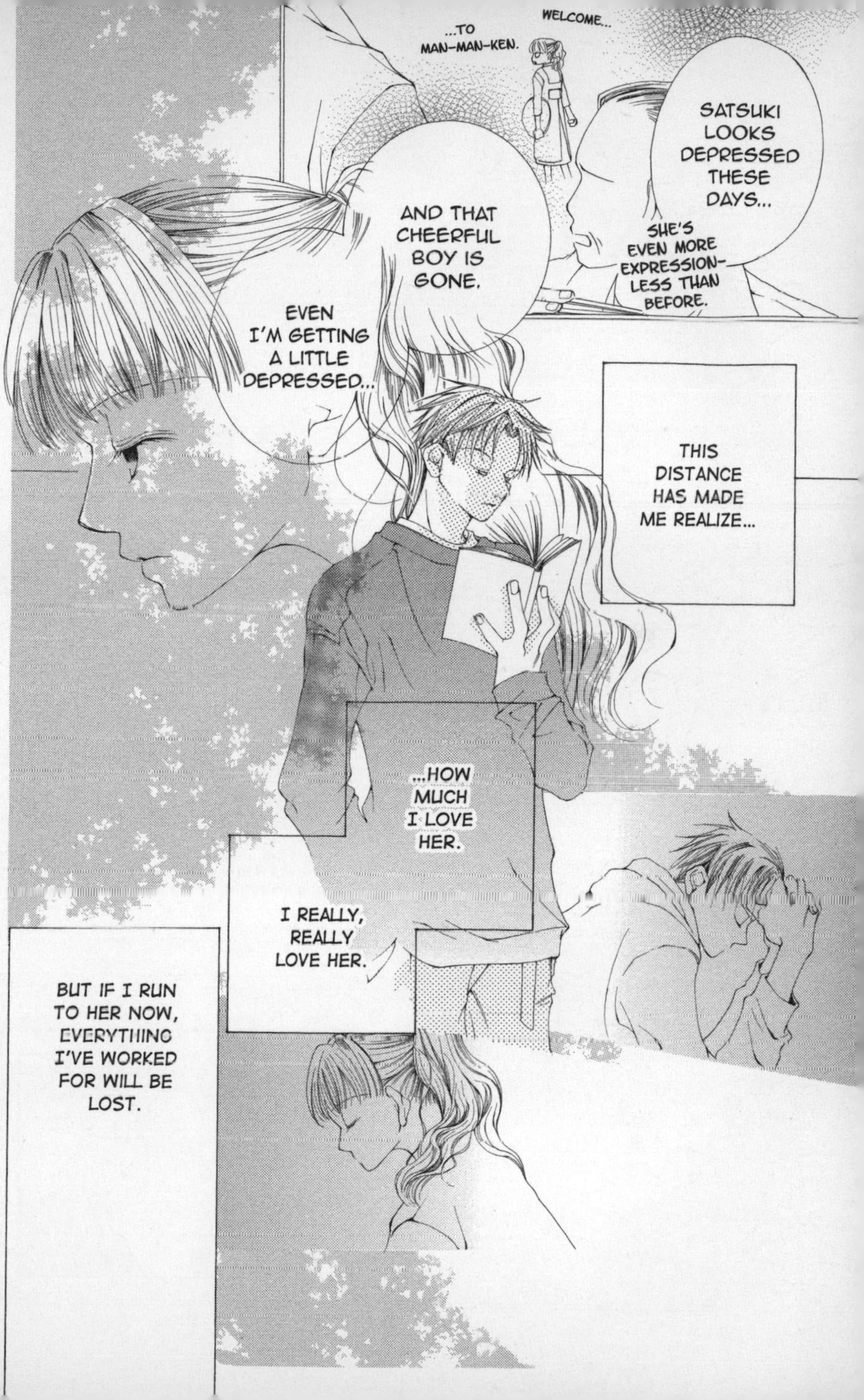
WELCOME...
...TO MAN-MAN-KEN.
SATSUKI LOOKS DEPRESSED THESE DAYS...
SHE'S EVEN MORE EXPRESSION-LESS THAN BEFORE.
AND THAT CHEERFUL BOY IS GONE.
EVEN I'M GETTING A LITTLE DEPRESSED...
THIS DISTANCE HAS MADE ME REALIZE...
...HOW MUCH I LOVE HER.
I REALLY, REALLY LOVE HER.
BUT IF I RUN TO HER NOW, EVERYTHING I'VE WORKED FOR WILL BE LOST.

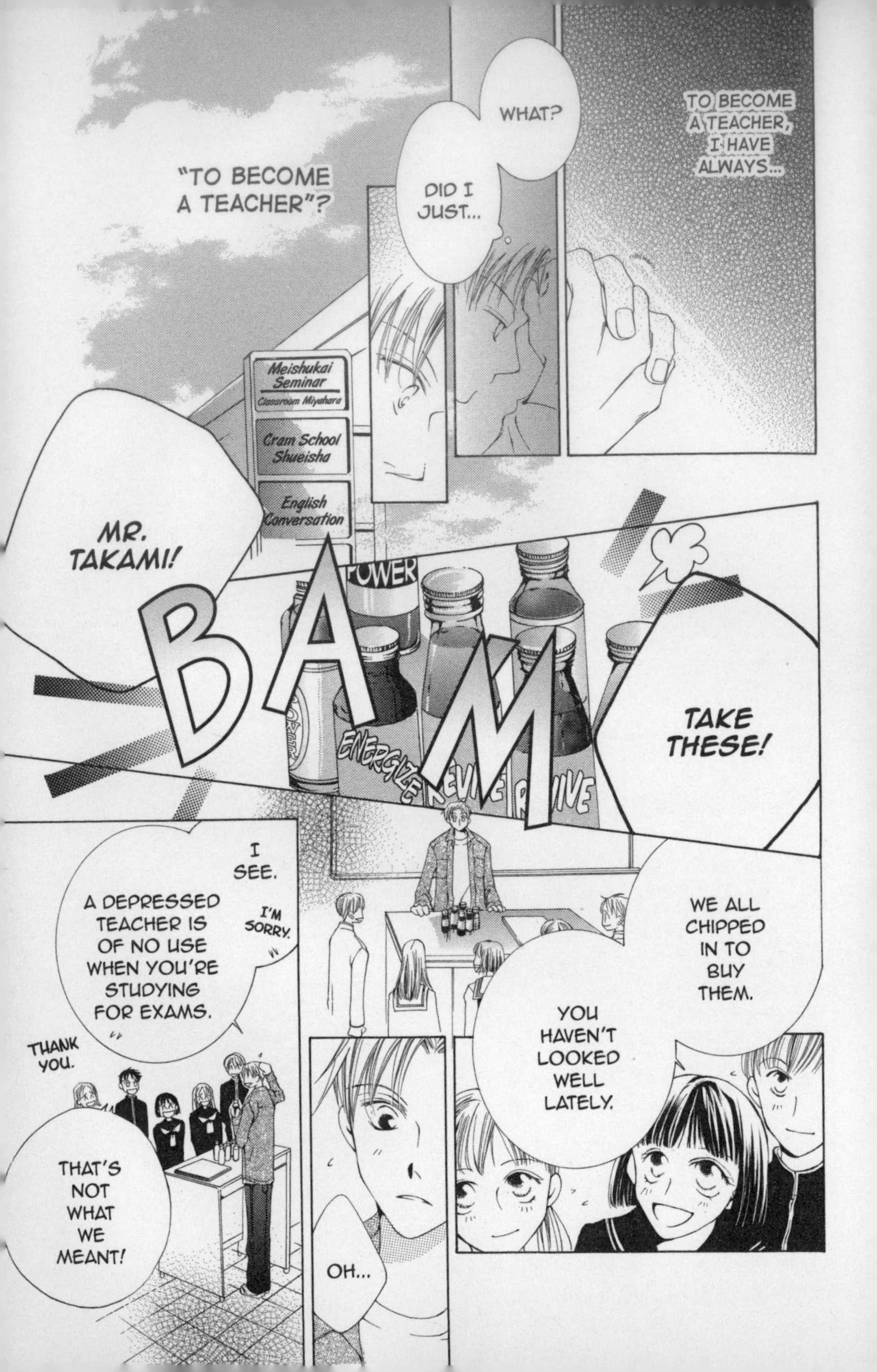
TO BECOME A TEACHER, I HAVE ALWAYS...
WHAT?
DID I JUST...
"TO BECOME A TEACHER"?
Meishukai Seminar
Classroom Miyahara
Cram School Shueisha
English Conversation
MR. TAKAMI!
TAKE THESE!
BAM
POWER
ENERGIZE
REVIVE
REVIVE
WE ALL CHIPPED IN TO BUY THEM.
YOU HAVEN'T LOOKED WELL LATELY.
OH...
I SEE.
A DEPRESSED TEACHER IS OF NO USE WHEN YOU'RE STUDYING FOR EXAMS.
I'M SORRY.
THANK YOU.
THAT'S NOT WHAT WE MEANT!

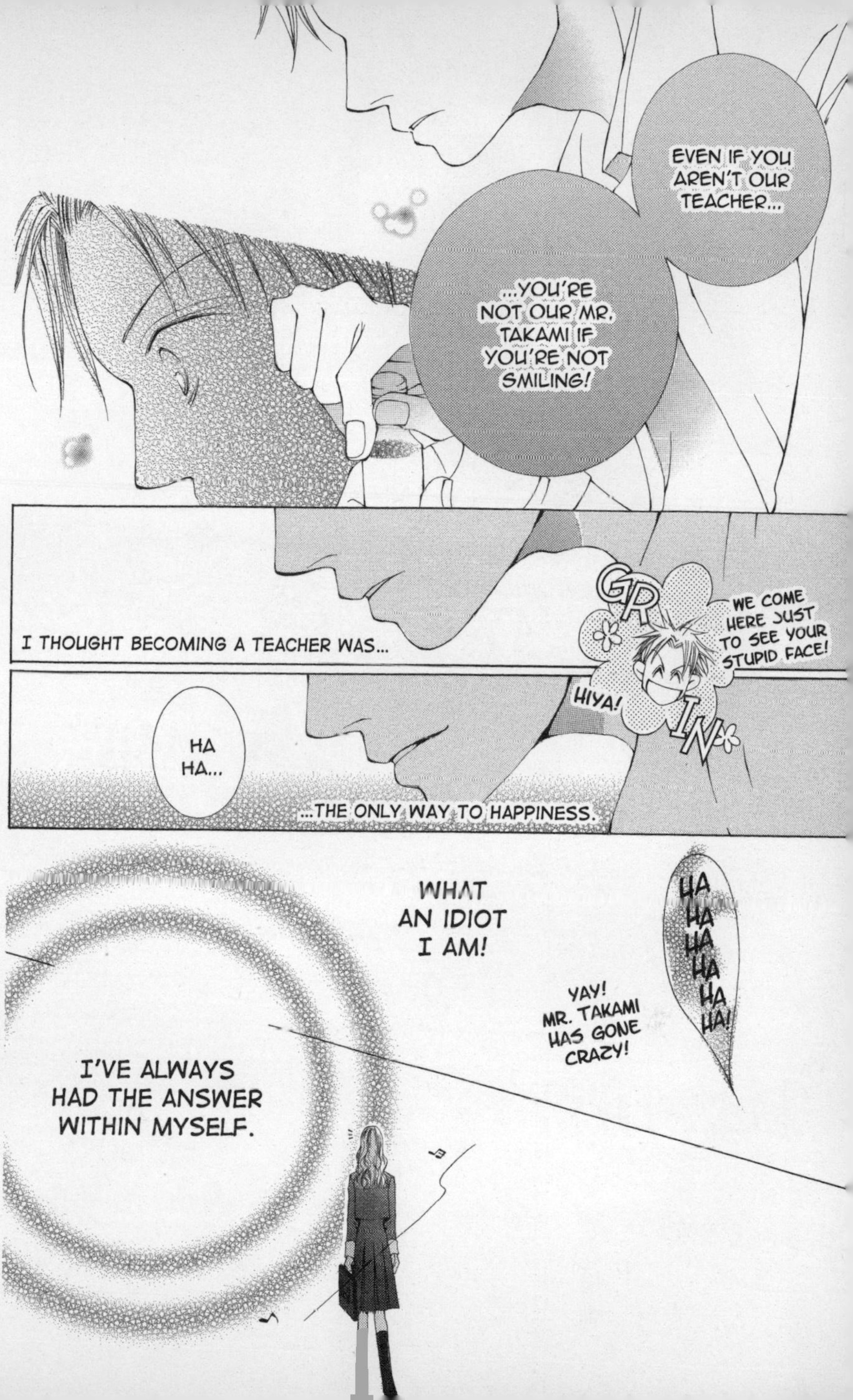
EVEN IF YOU AREN'T OUR TEACHER...
...YOU'RE NOT OUR MR. TAKAMI IF YOU'RE NOT SMILING!
GRIN
WE COME HERE JUST TO SEE YOUR STUPID FACE!
HIYA!
I THOUGHT BECOMING A TEACHER WAS...
HA HA...
...THE ONLY WAY TO HAPPINESS.
HA HA HA HA HA HA!
YAY! MR. TAKAMI HAS GONE CRAZY!
WHAT AN IDIOT I AM!
I'VE ALWAYS HAD THE ANSWER WITHIN MYSELF.

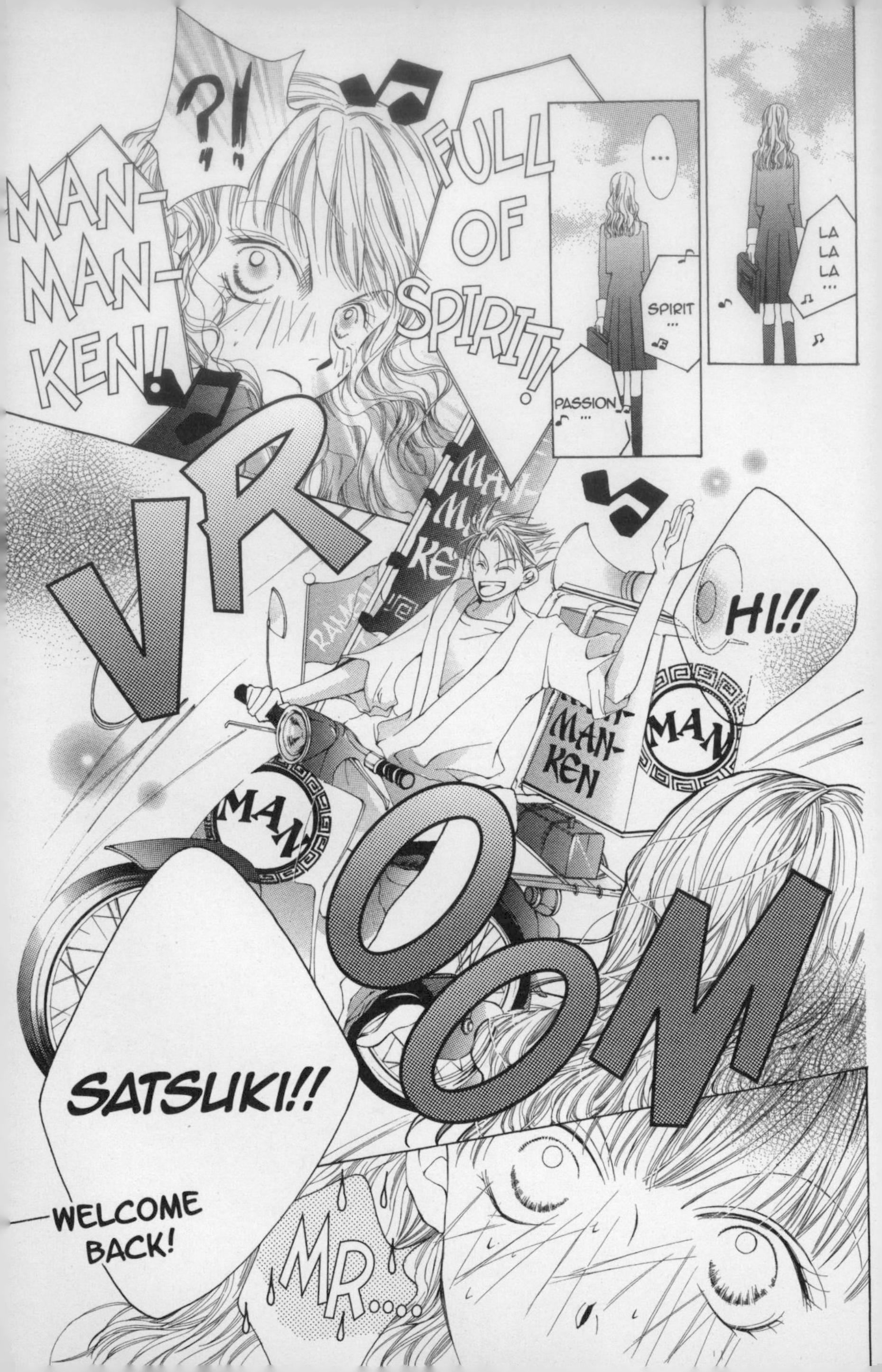

LA LA LA ...
...
SPIRIT ...
PASSION ...
FULL OF SPIRIT!
?!
MAN-MAN-KEN!
HI!!
MAN-MAN-KEN
MAN
VROOM
MAN
SATSUKI!!
MR....
—WELCOME BACK!

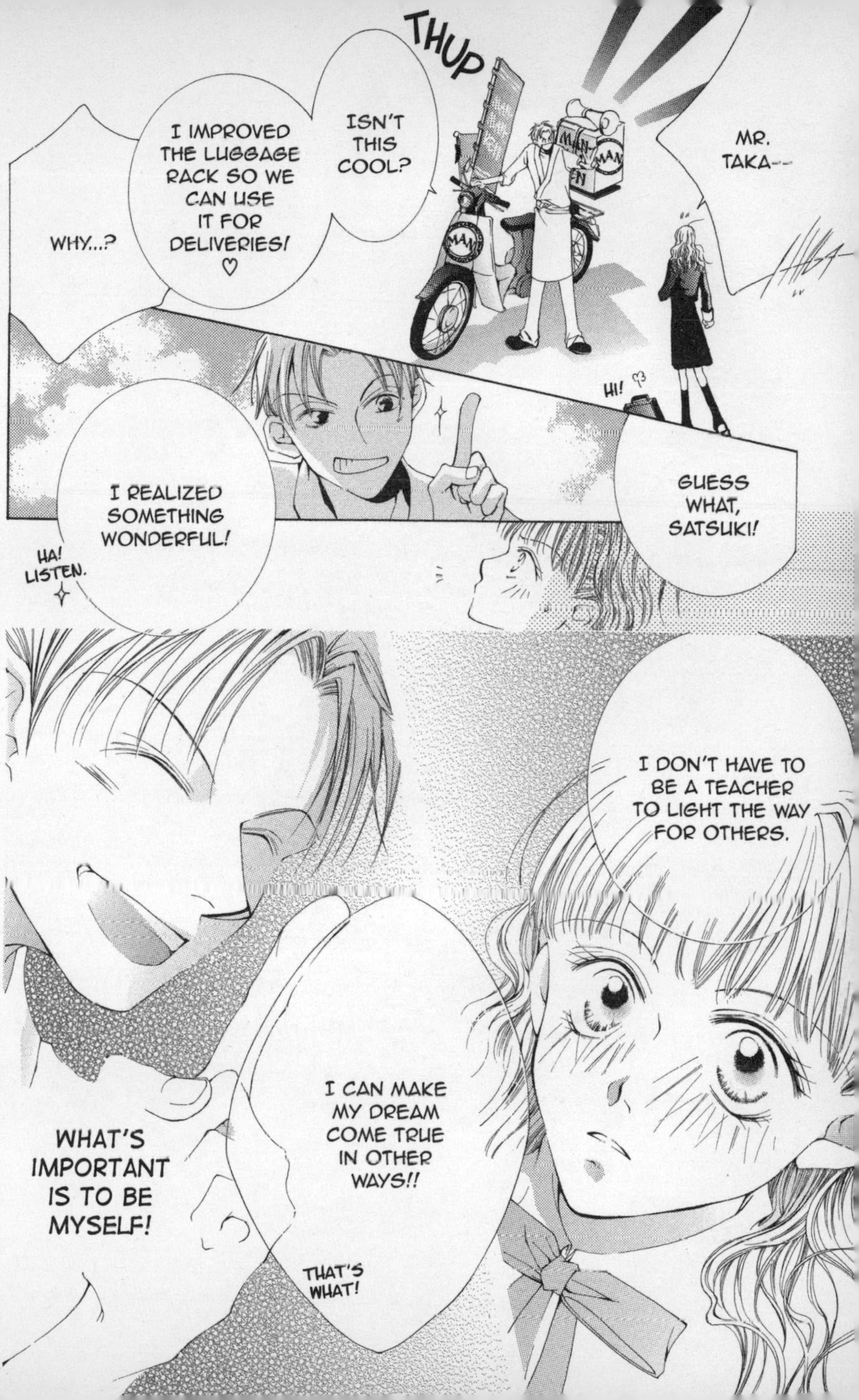
THUP
MR. TAKA--
HI!
ISN'T THIS COOL?
I IMPROVED THE LUGGAGE RACK SO WE CAN USE IT FOR DELIVERIES! ♡
WHY...?
GUESS WHAT, SATSUKI!
I REALIZED SOMETHING WONDERFUL!
HA! LISTEN.
I DON'T HAVE TO BE A TEACHER TO LIGHT THE WAY FOR OTHERS.
I CAN MAKE MY DREAM COME TRUE IN OTHER WAYS!!
THAT'S WHAT!
WHAT'S IMPORTANT IS TO BE MYSELF!

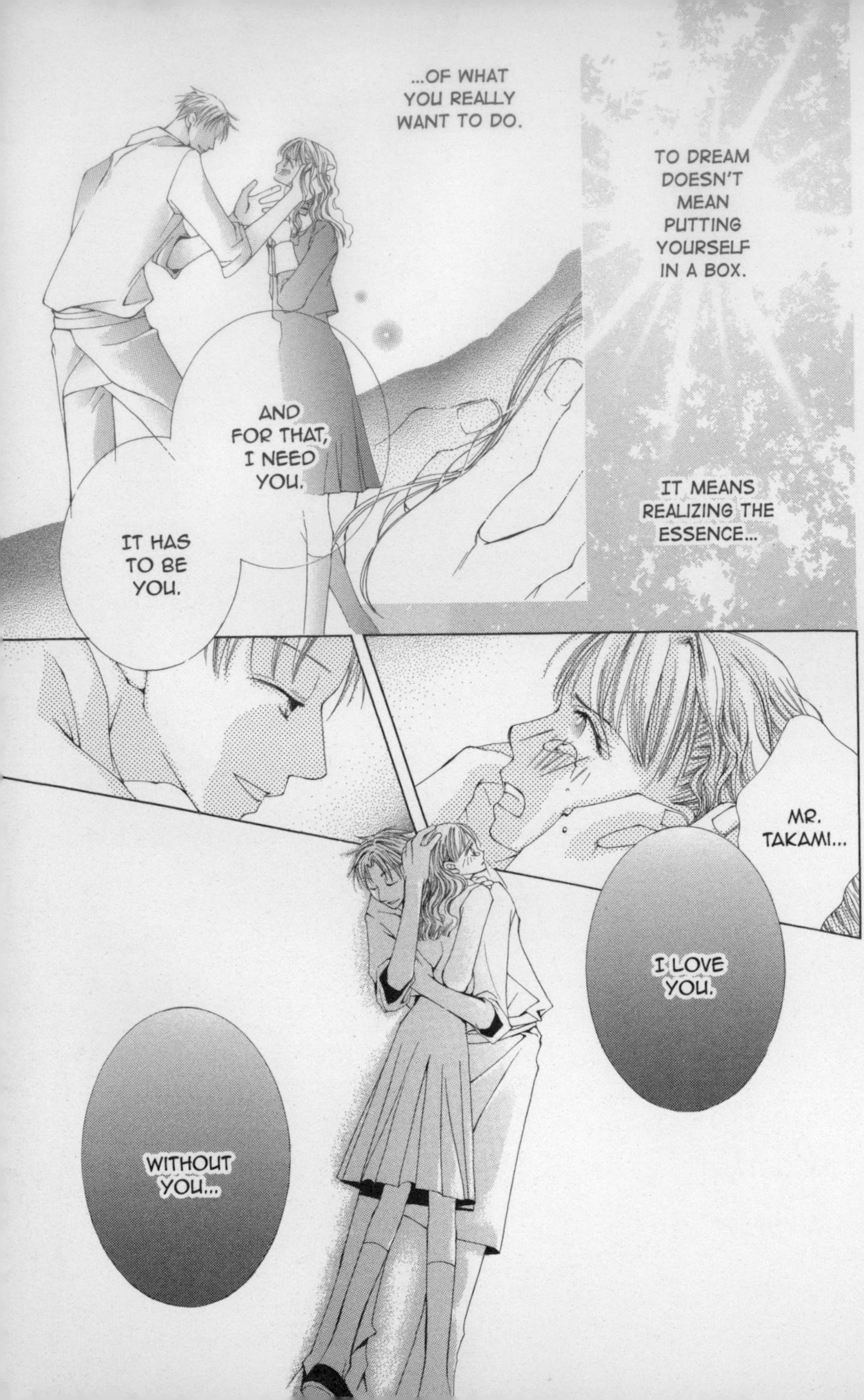
TO DREAM DOESN'T MEAN PUTTING YOURSELF IN A BOX.
IT MEANS REALIZING THE ESSENCE...
...OF WHAT YOU REALLY WANT TO DO.
AND FOR THAT, I NEED YOU.
IT HAS TO BE YOU.
MR. TAKAMI...
I LOVE YOU.
WITHOUT YOU...

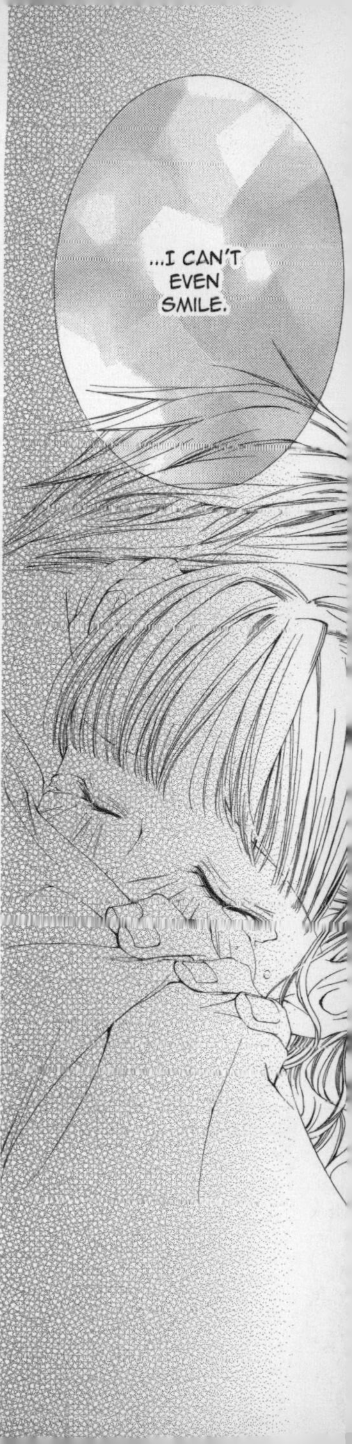
...I CAN'T EVEN SMILE.

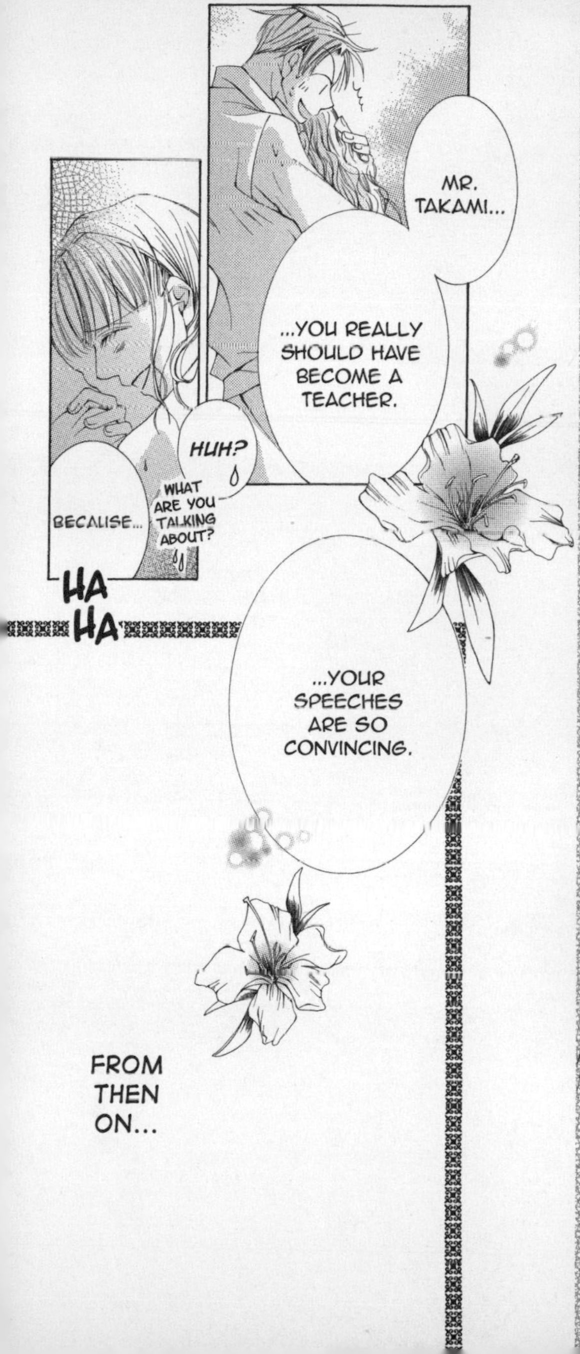
MR. TAKAMI...
...YOU REALLY SHOULD HAVE BECOME A TEACHER.
HUH?
WHAT ARE YOU TALKING ABOUT?
BECAUSE...
HA HA
...YOUR SPEECHES ARE SO CONVINCING.
FROM THEN ON...

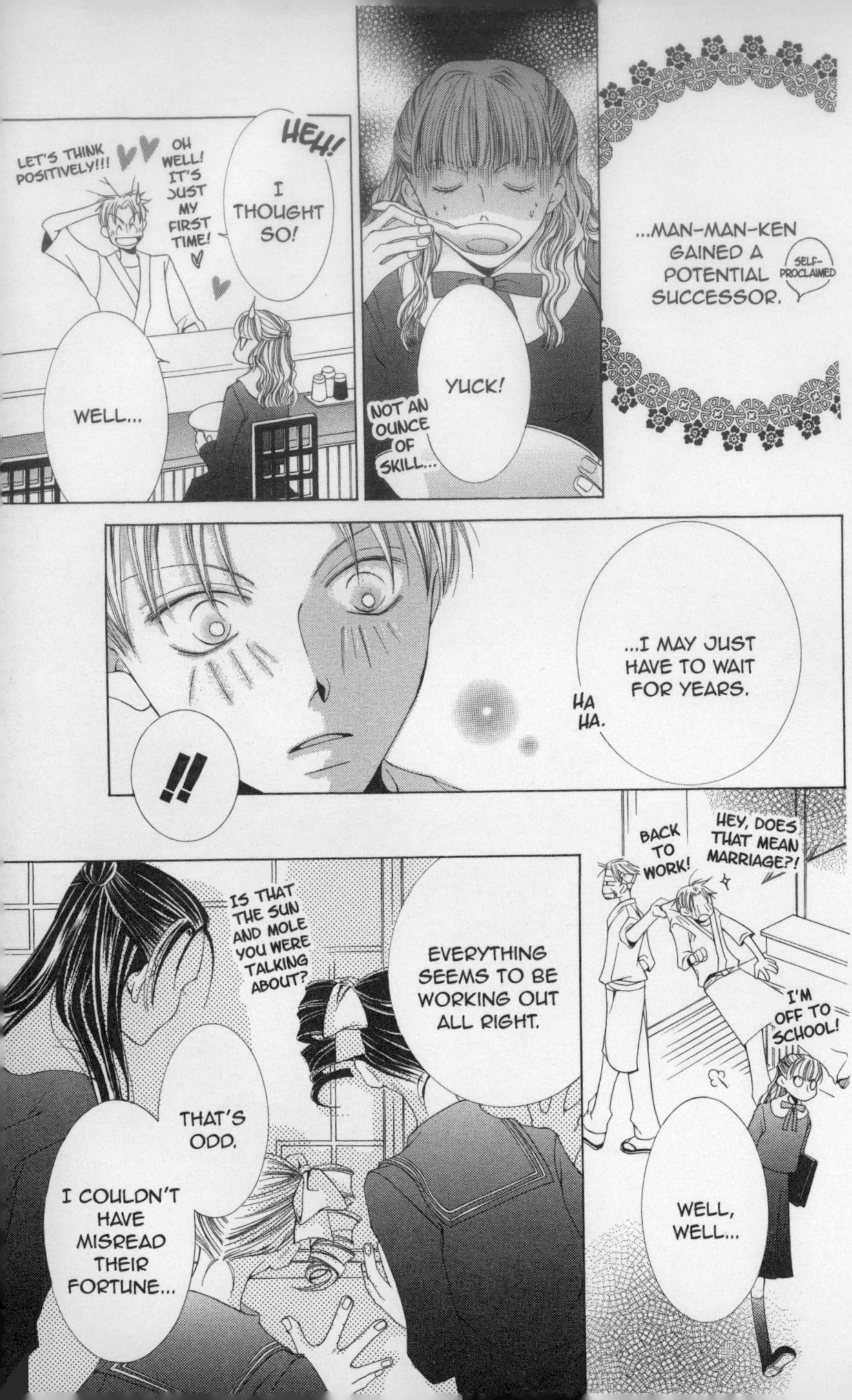
...MAN-MAN-KEN GAINED A POTENTIAL SUCCESSOR.
SELF-PROCLAIMED
YUCK!
NOT AN OUNCE OF SKILL...
HEH!
I THOUGHT SO!
OH WELL! IT'S JUST MY FIRST TIME!
LET'S THINK POSITIVELY!!!
WELL...
...I MAY JUST HAVE TO WAIT FOR YEARS.
HA HA.
!!
HEY, DOES THAT MEAN MARRIAGE?!
BACK TO WORK!
I'M OFF TO SCHOOL!
WELL, WELL...
EVERYTHING SEEMS TO BE WORKING OUT ALL RIGHT.
IS THAT THE SUN AND MOLE YOU WERE TALKING ABOUT?
THAT'S ODD.
I COULDN'T HAVE MISREAD THEIR FORTUNE...

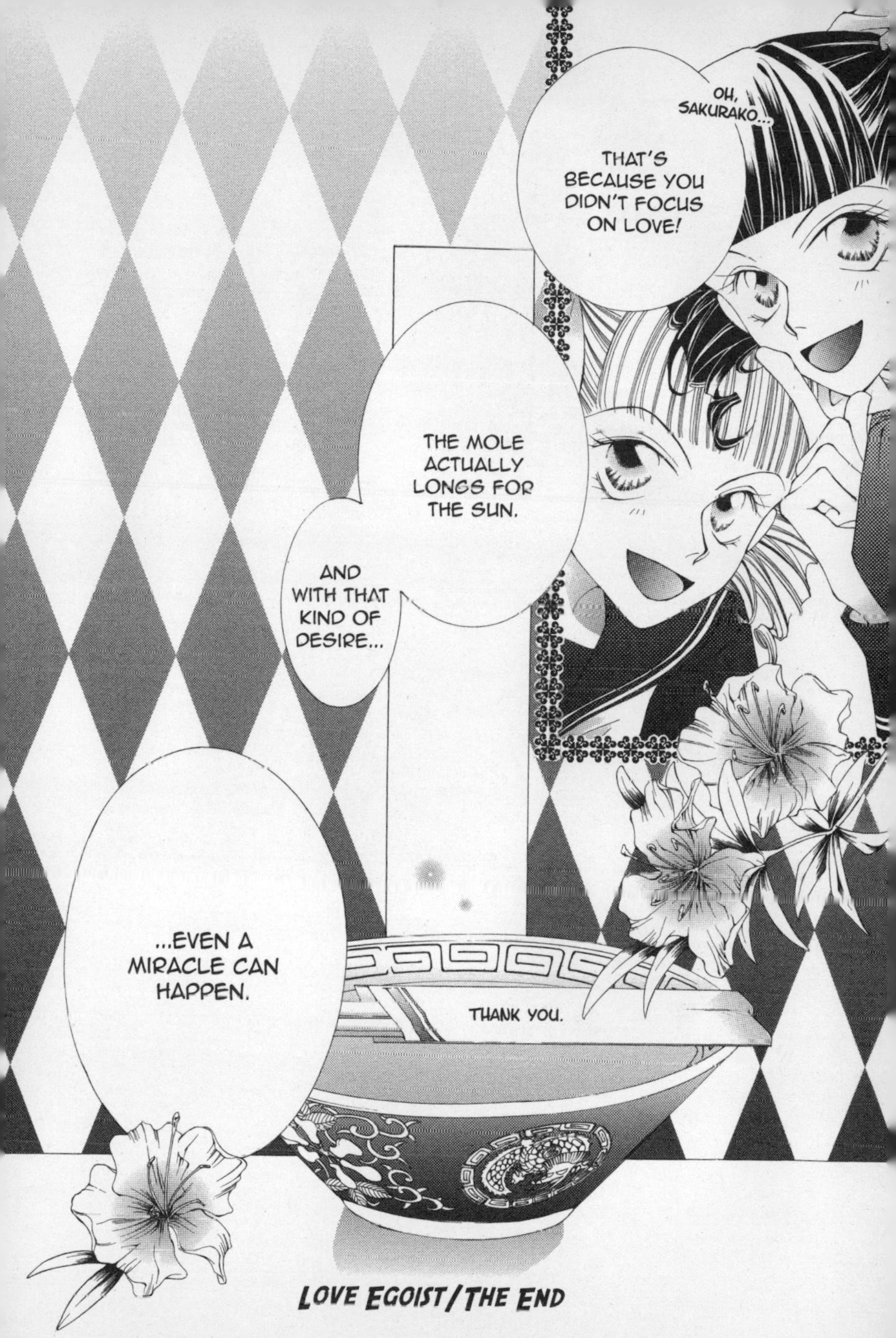
OH, SAKURAKO...
THAT'S BECAUSE YOU DIDN'T FOCUS ON LOVE!
THE MOLE ACTUALLY LONGS FOR THE SUN.
AND WITH THAT KIND OF DESIRE...
...EVEN A MIRACLE CAN HAPPEN.
THANK YOU.

LOVE EGOIST/THE END

EGOISTIC CLUB

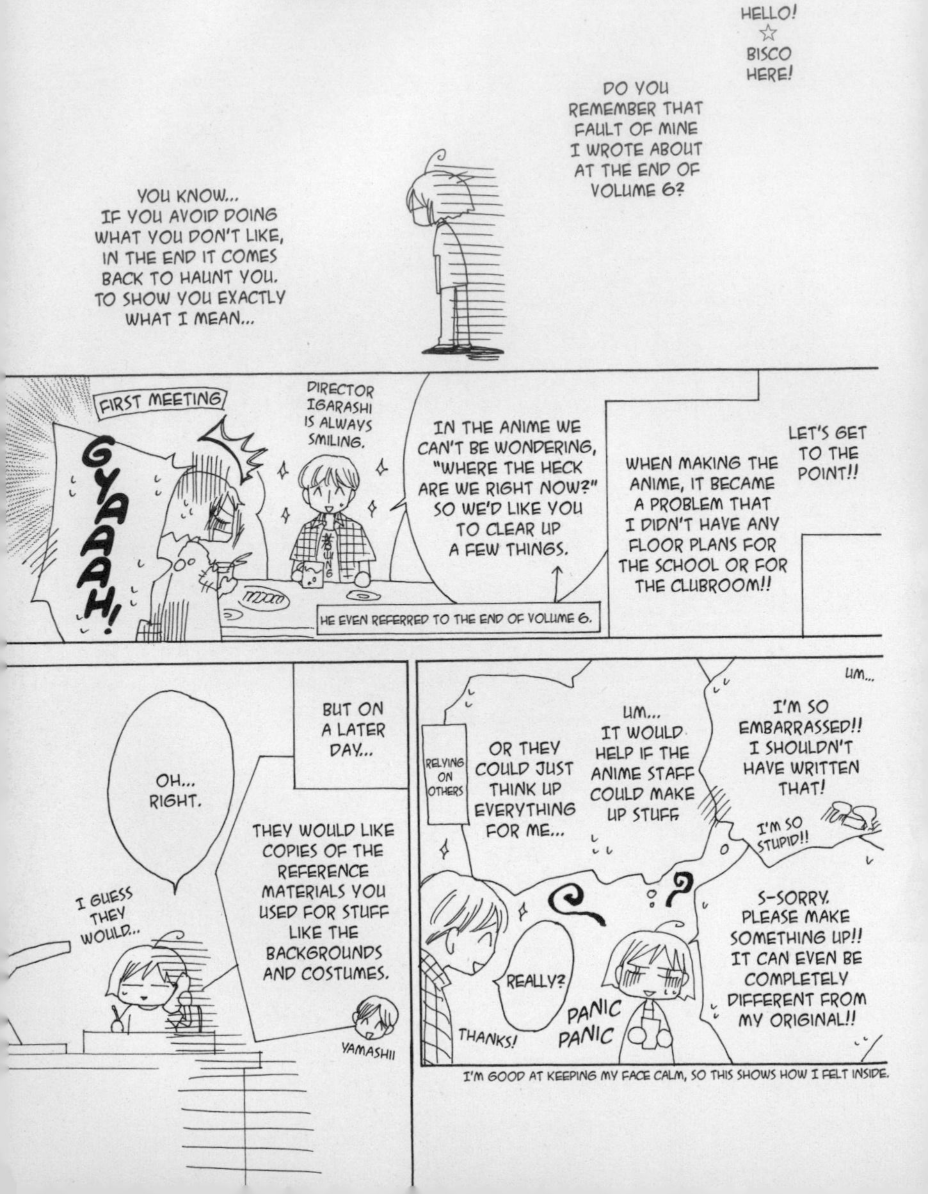
HELLO! ☆ BISCO HERE!
DO YOU REMEMBER THAT FAULT OF MINE I WROTE ABOUT AT THE END OF VOLUME 6?
YOU KNOW... IF YOU AVOID DOING WHAT YOU DON'T LIKE, IN THE END IT COMES BACK TO HAUNT YOU. TO SHOW YOU EXACTLY WHAT I MEAN...
LET'S GET TO THE POINT!!
WHEN MAKING THE ANIME, IT BECAME A PROBLEM THAT I DIDN'T HAVE ANY FLOOR PLANS FOR THE SCHOOL OR FOR THE CLUBROOM!!
DIRECTOR IGARASHI IS ALWAYS SMILING.
IN THE ANIME WE CAN'T BE WONDERING, "WHERE THE HECK ARE WE RIGHT NOW?" SO WE'D LIKE YOU TO CLEAR UP A FEW THINGS.
FIRST MEETING
GYAAAH!
HE EVEN REFERRED TO THE END OF VOLUME 6.
UM...
I'M SO EMBARRASSED!! I SHOULDN'T HAVE WRITTEN THAT!
UM... IT WOULD HELP IF THE ANIME STAFF COULD MAKE UP STUFF
OR THEY COULD JUST THINK UP EVERYTHING FOR ME...
RELYING ON OTHERS
I'M SO STUPID!!
S-SORRY. PLEASE MAKE SOMETHING UP!! IT CAN EVEN BE COMPLETELY DIFFERENT FROM MY ORIGINAL!!
REALLY?
PANIC PANIC
THANKS!
I'M GOOD AT KEEPING MY FACE CALM, SO THIS SHOWS HOW I FELT INSIDE.
BUT ON A LATER DAY...
OH... RIGHT.
THEY WOULD LIKE COPIES OF THE REFERENCE MATERIALS YOU USED FOR STUFF LIKE THE BACKGROUNDS AND COSTUMES.
I GUESS THEY WOULD...
YAMASHII

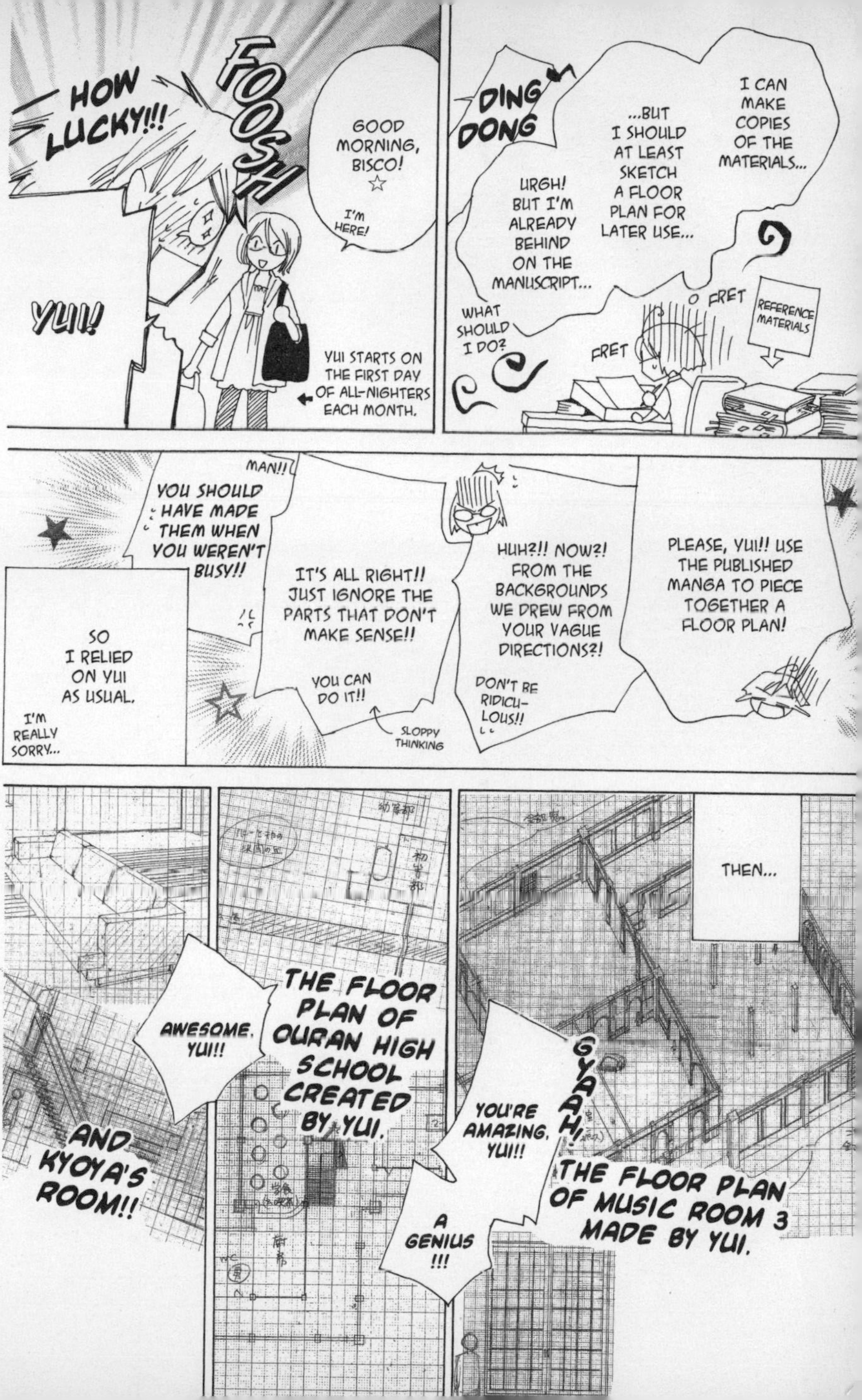
DING DONG
I CAN MAKE COPIES OF THE MATERIALS...
...BUT I SHOULD AT LEAST SKETCH A FLOOR PLAN FOR LATER USE...
URGH! BUT I'M ALREADY BEHIND ON THE MANUSCRIPT...
WHAT SHOULD I DO?
FRET
FRET
REFERENCE MATERIALS
FOOSH
GOOD MORNING, BISCO! ☆
I'M HERE!
HOW LUCKY!!!
YUI!
YUI STARTS ON THE FIRST DAY OF ALL-NIGHTERS EACH MONTH.
PLEASE, YUI!! USE THE PUBLISHED MANGA TO PIECE TOGETHER A FLOOR PLAN!
HUH?!! NOW?! FROM THE BACKGROUNDS WE DREW FROM YOUR VAGUE DIRECTIONS?!
DON'T BE RIDICULOUS!!
IT'S ALL RIGHT!! JUST IGNORE THE PARTS THAT DON'T MAKE SENSE!!
YOU CAN DO IT!!
SLOPPY THINKING
MAN!! YOU SHOULD HAVE MADE THEM WHEN YOU WEREN'T BUSY!!
SO I RELIED ON YUI AS USUAL.
I'M REALLY SORRY...
THEN...
GYAAH!
THE FLOOR PLAN OF MUSIC ROOM 3 MADE BY YUI.
YOU'RE AMAZING, YUI!!
A GENIUS !!!
THE FLOOR PLAN OF OURAN HIGH SCHOOL CREATED BY YUI.
AWESOME, YUI!!
AND KYOYA'S ROOM!!

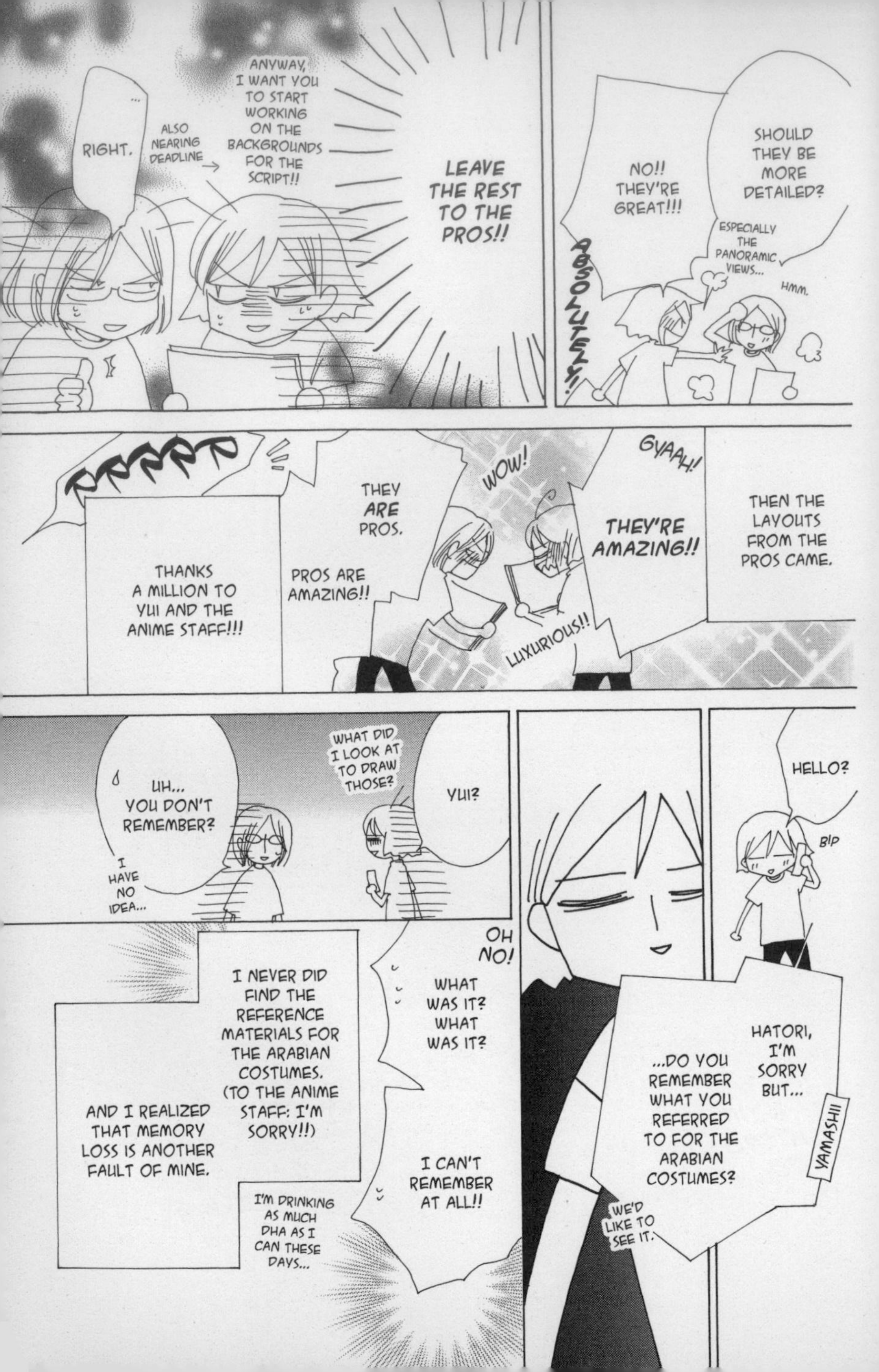
SHOULD THEY BE MORE DETAILED?
NO!! THEY'RE GREAT!!!
ESPECIALLY THE PANORAMIC VIEWS...
HMM.
ABSOLUTELY!!
LEAVE THE REST TO THE PROS!!
ANYWAY, I WANT YOU TO START WORKING ON THE BACKGROUNDS FOR THE SCRIPT!!
ALSO NEARING DEADLINE →
...
RIGHT.
THEN THE LAYOUTS FROM THE PROS CAME.
GYAAH!
THEY'RE AMAZING!!
WOW!
LUXURIOUS!!
THEY ARE PROS.
PROS ARE AMAZING!!
RRRRR
THANKS A MILLION TO YUI AND THE ANIME STAFF!!!
HELLO?
BIP
HATORI, I'M SORRY BUT...
YAMASHII
...DO YOU REMEMBER WHAT YOU REFERRED TO FOR THE ARABIAN COSTUMES?
WE'D LIKE TO SEE IT.
OH NO!
WHAT DID I LOOK AT TO DRAW THOSE?
YUI?
UH... YOU DON'T REMEMBER?
I HAVE NO IDEA...
WHAT WAS IT? WHAT WAS IT?
I CAN'T REMEMBER AT ALL!!
I'M DRINKING AS MUCH DHA AS I CAN THESE DAYS...
I NEVER DID FIND THE REFERENCE MATERIALS FOR THE ARABIAN COSTUMES. (TO THE ANIME STAFF: I'M SORRY!!)
AND I REALIZED THAT MEMORY LOSS IS ANOTHER FAULT OF MINE.

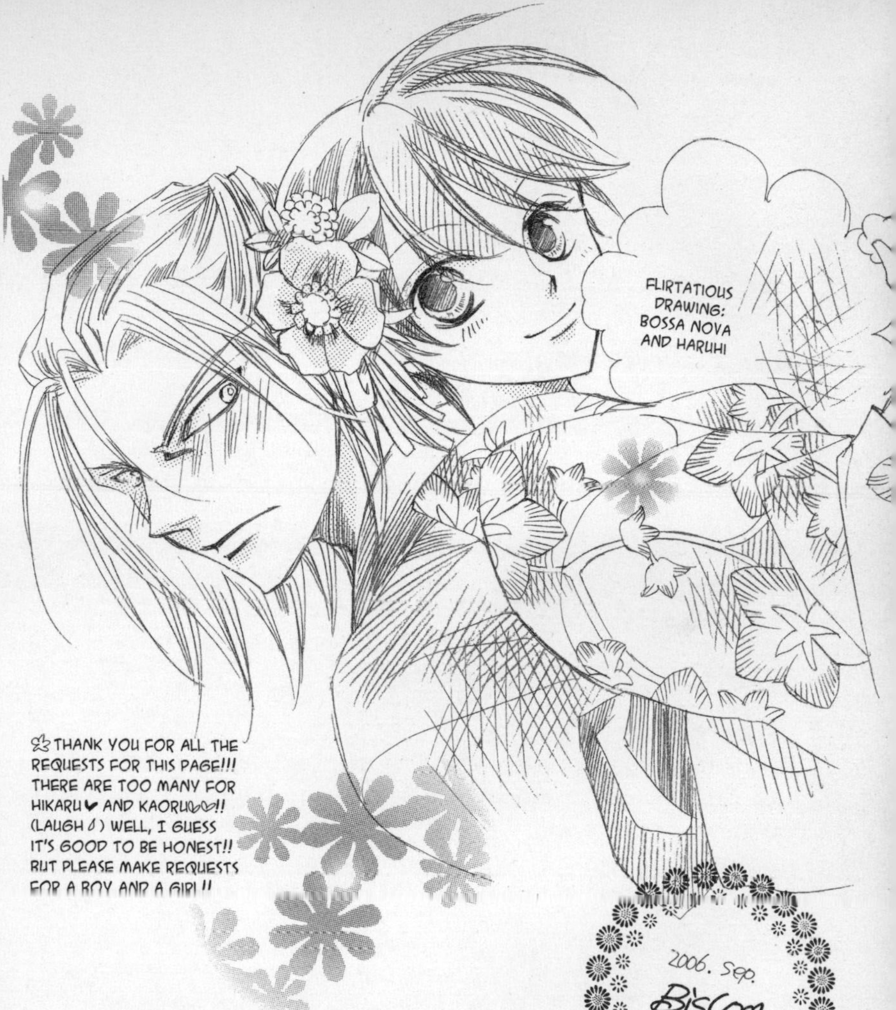
FLIRTATIOUS DRAWING: BOSSA NOVA AND HARUHI
2006. Sep.
Bisco

✿THANK YOU FOR ALL THE REQUESTS FOR THIS PAGE!!! THERE ARE TOO MANY FOR HIKARU♥ AND KAORU♥♥!! (LAUGH♪) WELL, I GUESS IT'S GOOD TO BE HONEST!! BUT PLEASE MAKE REQUESTS FOR A BOY AND A GIRL!!

✿Special Thanks✿

YAMASHITA✿, ALL THE EDITORS AND EVERYONE INVOLVED IN PUBLISHING THIS BOOK✿: AKANE OGURA✿, MIDORI SHIINO✿, ASUKA IZUMI✿, NATSUMI SATO✿, AND WATARU HIBIKI.
STAFF➪ YUI NATSUKI✿, RIKU✿, AYA AOMURA✿, YUTORI HIZAKURA✿, BISCO'S MOTHER, AND TO YOU, THE READERS OF THIS BOOK!!! THANK YOU VERY MUCH!♥♥

EGOISTIC CLUB/THE END

EDITOR'S NOTES

EPISODE 40

Page 106: *Shikishi* is a kind of mat paper with gold trim. It's used for writing poetry as well as for autographs. The *Vampire Knight* drawings Matsuri Hino did for *Shojo Beat* magazine readers were on autographed *shikishi*.

EXTRA EPISODE

Page 135: *Yami-nabe* literally means "dark pot." Guests bring different foods that aren't normally used in *nabe* dishes and add them to the pot. The guests must then eat whatever they've picked up with their chopsticks from the pot.

LOVE EGOIST

Page 162: Satsuki and Takami are playing the roles of the *tsukkomi* ("straight man") and the *boke* ("fool") in *manzai*, a type of comedy routine similar to Abbott and Costello. The *zubi* is the strident admonition given to the *boke*.

EGOISTIC CLUB

Page 188: In the Japanese version, Bisco Hatori referred to the all-nighters as *genko gasshuku*, or "manuscript camp." The *genko gasshuku* happens each month as the magazine deadline is nearing.

Author Bio

Bisco Hatori made her manga debut with *Isshun kan no Romance* (A Moment of Romance) in *LaLa DX* magazine. The comedy *Ouran High School Host Club* is her breakout hit. When she's stuck thinking up characters' names, she gets inspired by loud, upbeat music (her radio is set to MAGIC FM). She enjoys reading all kinds of manga, but she's especially fond of the sci-fi drama *Please Save My Earth* and *Slam Dunk*, a basketball classic.